CW00953076

Who's Who in
Horror and Fantasy Fiction

MIKE ASHLEY

Who's Who in
HORROR AND
FANTASY FICTION

ELM TREE BOOKS
LONDON

First published in Great Britain in 1977
by Elm Tree Books/Hamish Hamilton Ltd
90 Great Russell Street, London WC1B 3PT

SBN 241 89528 6

Printed in Great Britain by
Ebenezer Baylis and Son Ltd
The Trinity Press, Worcester, and London

Contents

Introduction

THERE can scarcely be a single author who has not at one time or other turned his hand to writing horror or fantasy. If not a story or two, then at least an episode in a novel will be contrived to create suspense and chill the reader. For fear is surely the most basic instinct of man, and a sure way for the writer to maintain reader involvement, an essential of all fiction, is to have the reader gripping the edges of the book, fearing to look beyond its pages in case that door handle is turning, that curtain is moving, or that shadow isn't his!

Within the entire literary sphere are a group of authors who have returned to the horror or fantasy fields time and again, some as a full-time occupation. It is these writers whose works and lives I have endeavoured to encapsulate here—400 of them.

Horror and fantasy fiction is itself a vast field. At its most extreme fantasy fiction covers any imaginative writing, since all stories are fabrications. In the strict sense however, fantasy relates to anything that happens contrary to accepted scientific laws and observations. A story in which a stone statue comes to life is fantasy. But if it is subsequently discovered that the statue works by a hidden mechanism, then the story ceases to be fantasy. For this reason the sub-genre of 'science fantasy' may seem a contradiction; in fact it is not. Writers can always be relied on to find loopholes in such confining nuisances as definitions. Consider: today people regard the so-called witches of the Middle Ages more as wise women who knew, though may not have understood, the medicinal properties of plants, and many basic laws of physics. The word 'wizard' is derived from the same source as the word 'wise'. Thus one need only imagine a world where magic works, but by scientifically controlled laws, and one has science fantasy. Several science fiction writers such as Henry Kuttner, Michael Moorcock and Lin Carter are noted exponents of this category.

Science fantasy apart, fantasy can be subdivided as follows: supernatural fantasy, heroic fantasy, and humorous fantasy, but with considerable overlapping. Supernatural fantasy covers the sub-genres of ghost fiction, tales of black magic, satanism, witchcraft, spiritualism and the occult, poltergeists and elementals, vampires, were-creatures, zombies, and all the undead. These rank among the most frequently used themes in all fiction, especially the ghost story. Today ghost fiction is no longer fully appreciated, but when it reached its height in the late

I

Victorian period, there could be no greater chill than a well-told ghost tale, and it requires the expertise of an artist to succeed in creating and maintaining a realistic atmosphere. Supreme among these artists are Sheridan Le Fanu and M. R. James, though Algernon Blackwood, Bulwer-Lytton and a brood of Victorian lady writers have equal skill. Blackwood popularised the idea of an occult detective, one who investigates and hopefully solves paranormal mysteries. Dion Fortune, Margery Lawrence, Jack Mann, Hesketh Prichard, Seabury Quinn and William Hope Hodgson invented their own similar psychic sleuths; real ghost-hunters include R. Thurston Hopkins, Shane Leslie and Elliott O'Donnell. Hope Hodgson was a master of the sea horror story, as were J. A. Barry and Clark Russell. Today's most popular writer of black magic fiction is Dennis Wheatley, and the current success of films like *The Exorcist* and *The Omen* shows a resurgence of interest in satanism. Many of the writers of weird fiction were members of occult orders—people like Blackwood, Sax Rohmer and Arthur Machen—not to forget the true exponents like Helena Blavatasky, Dion Fortune and Aleister Crowley. The best-known vampire story is undoubtedly Bram Stoker's *Dracula*, but earlier classics were Rymer's *Varney the Vampire* and Le Fanu's 'Carmilla'. The werewolf in fiction popularly started within Frederick Marryat's *The Phantom Ship*, but the definitive works are those by Clemence Housman and Guy Endore.

Heroic fantasy is certainly the oldest theme in literature. All early writings based on myths and legends like the Sagas and the Arabian Nights are heroic fantasies. The heroic human rights wrongs, is invariably on a quest, and fights all manner of supernatural foe, demons and wizards, aided by magical weapons and fantastic powers. This is the essence of heroic fantasy ranging from the Arthurian legends to *Lord of the Rings*. The modern revival of heroic fantasy is credited to William Morris and Lord Dunsany, but it is a fairly arbitrary line. A simplified form of heroic fantasy has been dubbed 'sword and sorcery', which covers the exploits of Conan and his brawny kith. Generalising on heroic fantasy, it encompasses historical fantasy (as best demonstrated by Thomas Burnett Swann) and adventure fantasy. The latter is dominated by the lost-race theme, of which the unchallenged king is H. Rider Haggard.

Humorous fantasy is best exemplified by the works of F. Anstey and Thorne Smith, and stories from the magazine *Unknown*, tales in which occur the most unlikely things, with uproarious results. A man might suddenly find he has a halo, or someone might find a lamp with a real genie which takes its orders too literally. Another example is the famous 'three wishes' plot.

Horror fiction, on the other hand, is quite different. There need be no supernatural or fantastic elements. The key is fear—being locked in a room with a psychotic murderer armed with an axe is much more frightening than being locked in a room with a mere ghost. These stories

2

fall neatly into two forms. Psychological horror—stories of fear and the macabre; and physical horror—the *conte cruel*, Grand Guignol and terror tale. The essential difference between horror and terror is that if you witness a man being murdered you are horrified. If the murderer than advances upon you, you are terrified. In the psychological horror story everything is implied and fear is totally in the mind. The physical horror story relies on descriptions, sometimes quite gruesome and nauseous, of bodily harm and pain. Such tales were once executed as an art, especially by writers like Villiers de l'Isle Adam and Maurice Level in France, and Charles Birkin in England; but more recently, especially in the pages of the American terror pulp magazines and the British *Pan Book of Horror Stories*, they have reached a nauseating low. It is often gore for gore's sake.

The main body of this *Who's Who* starts with the dawn of the eighteenth century, the earliest entries being Antoine Galland and Daniel Defoe. Fantasy and horror before that date is thus excepted, but it cannot be ignored. In order to give a quick, basic but comprehensive coverage of the growth and development of weird fiction, I have included a chronological chart at the end of this introduction. It merely presents dates, titles and authors with the occasional annotation, and is a brief listing intended to show what I feel are the most significant and/or influential works to appear in print. By referring to the A-Z which is abundantly cross-referenced, and also to Appendix I, you will be able to flesh the list out and it will take on an added meaning.

The 400 contributors treated here are by no means all the writers who have been actively involved in the genre. For every one I included, there were two or more I had to exclude. Space does not allow this work to be exhaustive—and I doubt that any volume could be definitive. No matter whom I include someone will always ask 'What about . . . ?' I have tried to be as thorough and varied in my selection as possible, choosing authors primarily for the originality and enjoyability of their fiction, as much as the quality or quantity of their work. An author with only a handful of stories may be included in preference to one who has written a score of novels, because the stories are first-rate essential reading, whereas the novels are potboilers and time-wasting. Another factor I had to consider was the extent to which the author's work spilled into other writing categories. For instance though a writer's output may be considered horror or fantasy, the basic theme of the work might be a detective thriller, or science fiction; or it might be written essentially for children. If I felt a writer belonged more in those categories than in this volume then I have excluded him or her. Hence Harlan Ellison, whose recent work is pure fantasy, and who now denies he writes science fiction, is nevertheless given ample coverage in Brian Ash's *Who's Who in Science Fiction* (Elm Tree Books) and need not be repeated here. Similarly C. S. Lewis and Alan Garner, both excellent fantasy writers, are sufficiently covered in Doyle's *Who's Who in Children's Literature* (Hugh

3

Evelyn). Whatever my choice, definitions are vague and nebulous, and there will always be overlapping. You will find included here many writers whose names are more closely associated with other fields of writing—Conan Doyle, Oscar Wilde, Margaret Irwin, Ivan Turgenev—but they have contributed important works to the horror genre and for this reason deserve a mention, albeit briefly. In the case of these authors I have avoided giving overmuch biographical information in favour of covering their fiction. However, writers who are associated primarily with weird fiction—Algernon Blackwood, M. R. James, H. P. Lovecraft—are given the full treatment.

It was my original desire to include several artists and illustrators in the volume, but I soon realised that space did not allow me to grant them the credit or coverage they deserve. Thus talents such as Sidney Sime, Arthur Rackham, Aubrey Beardsley and Virgil Finlay are sadly absent. Those artists who are included—Hannes Bok, Lee Brown Coye, Laurence Housman—appear because they have also fiction to their credit.

The final production of this *Who's Who* is entirely my own responsibility, including any errors or omissions. I will be extremely grateful to any reader who notifies me of any such mistakes or provides added information, which will help to make any further editions of this work that much more definitive. As it stands I hope it is more than a foundation and a guide to the realms of horror and fantasy fiction. It is the only work of its kind and I believe it fills a most necessary need for researchers, editors, publishers and above all readers who wish to find out more about their favourite writers.

Although it is my work, I cannot take sole credit for its final appearance. It has been a pooling of information from a diversity of sources. Many of the books I used are included in the bibliography listed at the end of this volume, but I must single out for special credit *The Encyclopedia of Science Fiction and Fantasy* compiled by Donald H. Tuck. In addition I found the catalogues of several second-hand book dealers most valuable especially Ferret Fantasy Ltd, run by Mr George Locke, G. Ken Chapman Ltd, Phantasmagoria Books, run by Mr John Eggeling (who also gave added assistance by dint of his excellent knowledge of the field), Fantast (Medway) Ltd, run by Mr Kenneth F. Slater, and Fantasy Centre run by Messrs Ted Ball and Dave Gibson.

But above all I must thank three people without whose help this book would have been a mere shadow of its present form: Mr Hugh Lamb who gave freely of his time, knowledge and patience in vetting the initial draft and providing many much-needed facts and figures; Mr Thomas G. L. Cockcroft of New Zealand who made available his formidable knowledge on *Weird Tales* and sister pulps, shrinking the 11,500 miles between us by uniting in a common cause; and Mr Richard Dalby, who similarly donated his time and knowledge in checking the final draft. I must also thank all those anonymous voices in libraries the length and

4

breadth of Britain who at the drop of a hat exhumed ancient facts from forgotten tomes, with a special thanks to Miss Riddell and her staff at Chatham Reference Library, who unstintingly coped with my erratic phone calls for obscure facts yet inevitably came up trumps.

Thanks must also go to all those authors who responded to my letters or questionnaires supplying invaluable data about themselves. Among those who gave additional information above and beyond the call of duty I must thank the following: Eddy C. Bertin, Sir Charles Birkin, Basil Copper, Mary E. Counselman, Mrs Doris Cowles, John Eggeling, Alex Hamilton, Philip Harbottle, Dom Sylvester Houédard, Robert K. Jones, David A. Kraft, Arthur H. Landis, Gordon Larkin, W. O. G. Lofts, Douglas Menville, Sam Moskowitz, Miss Alicia Muspratt, Frank Parnell, Michel Parry, Susan Payne, E. Hoffman Price, Jessica Amanda Salmonson, Dr Stuart Schiff, Milton Subotsky, David Sutton, Christine Campbell Thomson, Herbert van Thal, James Wade, Karl E. Wagner and Robert Weinberg. To all those and others I have omitted, my most grateful thanks.

MIKE ASHLEY
Sittingbourne, Kent
January 1977

Chronology

Note: Where the author's name is in bold print, that writer has an entry in the A–Z of contributors. For an indication of the scope of this chronology, see page 40.

B.C.
c 2000 The Sumerian epic poem *Gilgamesh*
c 1500 The Egyptian *Book of Thoth*
c 700 The *Iliad* and *Odyssey* of Homer
c 250 The *Argonautica* of Apollonius of Rhodes
c 19 *Aeniad* by Virgil

A.D.
60 The *Satyricon* of Petronius. Includes an early werewolf story
100 The *Epistles* of Pliny. Includes an early ghost story
c 120 *Philinnion and Machates* by Phlegon. The story of a corpse-bride
c 170 *Metamorphoses* or *The Golden Ass* by Lucius Apulius. Tells of a man transformed by witchcraft into an ass and his attempts to change back. A wonderful adventure, it is the first accredited novel of literature
c 750 *Beowulf*
c 800 Scheherazade tells her *Arabian Nights*
c 850 *The Voyage of Maelduin* by Aed Finn. A Gaelic Sinbad!
c 1000 The *Chanson de Roland*
1008 *Shah Namah,* the Persian epic by Firdausi
c 1050 The Elder *Edda* by Icelandic poet Sæmond Sigfusson
c 1140 *Historia Regum Britanniae* by Geoffrey of Monmouth. The real birth of the Arthurian legends
c 1210 The *Niebelungenlied* by Heinrich von Ofterdingen
c 1240 The Younger *Edda* by Snorri Sturlason
c 1270 The *Volsunga Saga*
c 1280 The *Grettir Saga* by Sturla Thórdarson
c 1290 The *Gesta Romanorum (Deeds of the Romans)*
c 1300 *Amadis of Gaul* by either Vasco de Lobeira or Joao de Lobeira
c 1300 The *Mabinogion* legends written down
1300 Dante's *Inferno*; followed by *Purgatory* (1308) and *Paradise* (1311)

7

c 1360   *The Voyages and Travels of Sir John Mandeville*. Presented as fact, these exploits were embellished tall-tales which took the travelogue to its fantastic extreme and formed the modern basis for most legends of 'Here There Be Dragons!'

1388   Chaucer's *Canterbury Tales*. Of special interest 'The Friar's Tale' and 'The Rime of Tropias'

1485   *Le Mort d'Arthur* by Sir Thomas Malory printed (completed in 1469)

1489   *Malleus Maleficarum* by Jakob Sprenger and Henricus Institor. A treatise on witchcraft used as a text-book at trials

1498   *Reynard the Fox* by Heinrich von Alkmaar. A noted early example of the use of fantasy as allegory to put forth a political viewpoint in this satire of the Church and Politics

1508   Montalvo translates *Amadis of Gaul* into Spanish, adds his own *Deeds of Esplandian* and thus starts a host of imitations eventually lampooned in *Don Quixote*

1516   *Orlando Furioso* by Ludovico Ariosto

1532   *Pantagruel* by François Rabelais; followed by *Gargantua* (1534)

1544   *Palmerin of England* by Francisco de Moraes

1590   *The Faerie Queen* by Edmund Spenser (first three books)

1595   *A Midsummer Night's Dream* by Shakespeare

1604   *Dr Faustus* by Christopher Marlowe

1612   *The White Devil* by John Webster

1613   *The Tempest* by Shakespeare

1623   *The Devil's Law Case* and *The Duchess of Malfi* by Webster. Charles Lamb said of Webster:

'To move a horror skilfully, to touch a soul to the quick, to lay upon fear as much as it can bear, to wean and weary a life till it is ready to drop, and then step in with mortal instruments to take its last forfeit, this only a Webster can do.' Unappreciated in his own day, Webster (*c* 1580–*c* 1625) was the first true writer of horror fiction.

1657   *Paradise Lost* by John Milton; followed by *Paradise Regained* (1671)

1678   *Pilgrim's Progress* by John Bunyan; part 2 followed, 1684

1704   *Les Mille et Une Nuit* by **Antoine Galland**

1706   *The True Relation of the Apparition of one Mrs Veal* by **Defoe**

1726   *Gulliver's Travels* by Jonathan Swift

1753   *Ferdinand, Count Fathom* by Tobias Smollett

1761   *The Poems of Ossian* by James Macpherson

1764   *The Castle of Otranto* by **Horace Walpole**. The match that lit the fuse to the Gothic explosion

1777   *The Champion of Virtue* by **Clara Reeve**

1785   *The Marvellous Travels of Baron Münchhausen* by R. E. Raspe

1786   *Vathek* by **William Beckford**

1794   *The Mysteries of Udolpho* by **Ann Radcliffe**. The fuse to the Gothic explosion

1795   *Tam o' Shanter* by Robert Burns

1796   *Ambrosio, or The Monk* by **Matthew Lewis**. The Gothic explosion begins

1798   *Wieland* by **Charles Brockden Brown**
       The *Rime of the Ancient Mariner* by Samuel Taylor Coleridge

1808   The first part of *Faust* by **Goethe**

1814   *Fantasiestücke*, first collection by **E. T. A. Hoffman**

1818   *Frankenstein* by **Mary Shelley**
       Northanger Abbey by Jane Austen. The Gothic influence spread into the higher echelons of nineteenth-century literature and Austen's novel marks its zenith

1819   'Rip van Winkle' legend immortalised by **Washington Irving**
       The Vampyre by **Dr. Polidori**. The first vampire story in English

1820   *Melmoth the Wanderer* by **Charles Maturin**. The enduring classic of the damned immortal

1822   *Traditional Tales of the English and Scottish Peasantry* by **Allan Cunningham**

1824   *Confessions of a Justified Sinner* by **James Hogg**. One of the earliest examples of a split personality in fiction

1826   *Gaston de Blondeville* by **Ann Radcliffe**

1832   'Metzengerstein' first story by **Edgar Allan Poe** (in *Saturday Courier* January 14th)

1837   *Ingoldsby Legends* by **R. H. Barham** began to appear

1838   *The Amber Witch* by **Wilhelm Meinhold**
       'Hugues, the Wer-Wolf' by Sutherland Menzies. The first werewolf story in English (in *Lady's Magazine*, September)

1839   *The Phantom Ship* by **Frederick Marryat**. Popularised the Flying Dutchman legend

1841   'String of Pearls' by **T. P. Prest**, popularised the Sweeney Todd legend

1842   *Zanoni* by **Bulwer-Lytton**

1843   *A Christmas Carol* by **Charles Dickens**

1844   *The Wandering Jew* by **Eugene Sue**

1845   *Varney the Vampire* by **J. M. Rymer**

1847   *Wuthering Heights* by Emily Brontë
       Wagner the Wehr-Wolf by **G. W. M. Reynolds**

1848   *The Lancashire Witches* by **W. Harrison Ainsworth**; witches have been typified as cackling crones ever since
       The Night Side of Nature by **Mrs Crowe**

1849   The *Kalevala* legends collected by Elias Lönnrot

1851   *Ghost Stories and Tales of Mystery* by **Sheridan Le Fanu**

1855   *The Shaving of Shagpat* by George Meredith
1857   *The Wolf-Leader* by **Alexandre Dumas**
1858   *Phantastes* by **George MacDonald**. Other-world fantasies enter a new phase with this profound, allegorical novel of perplexing yet bewitching imagery
1859   'What Was It?' by **Fitz-James O'Brien** (*Harper's* March)
      'The Haunters and the Haunted' by **Bulwer-Lytton** (*Blackwood's* August)
1861   *A Strange Story* by **Bulwer-Lytton**, serial in *All the Year Round*
1863   *The House by the Churchyard*, **Sheridan Le Fanu**
1864   *Uncle Silas* by **Sheridan Le Fanu**
1865   *Alice in Wonderland* by Lewis Carroll
1872   *In a Glass Darkly* by **Sheridan Le Fanu**
1880   *A Beleaguered City* by **Mrs Oliphant**
1882   *Vice-Versa* by **F. Anstey**
1885   *King Solomon's Mines* by **H. Rider Haggard**. So started the lost-race fantasy adventure
1886   *She* by **H. Rider Haggard**
1888   *The Strange Case of Dr Jekyll and Mr Hyde* by **R. L. Stevenson**
1890   *Phra the Phoenician* by **Edward Lester Arnold**. Took the damned immortal into a new dimension
      The Werewolf by **Clemence Housman**. The first classic werewolf story
      The Picture of Dorian Gray by **Oscar Wilde**
1891   *Tales of Soldiers and Civilians* by **Ambrose Bierce**
      The Witch of Prague by **F. Marion Crawford**
      Là-Bas by **Joris-Karl Huysman**. Took the lid off modern-day satanism
1892   *The Soul of Lilith* by **Marie Corelli**. Boosted the vogue for spiritualism
1893   *Can Such Things Be?* by **Ambrose Bierce**
1894   *The Great God Pan* by **Arthur Machen**
      The Wood Beyond the World by **William Morris**. The accepted date for the rebirth of the adult fairy-tale
1895   *A Bid For Fortune* by **Guy Boothby**
      The King in Yellow by **Robert W. Chambers**
      Black Spirits and White by **Ralph Adams Cram**
      The Lost Stradivarius by **J. Meade Falkner**
      Lilith by **George Macdonald**
      The Three Imposters by **Arthur Machen**
      A Deal With the Devil by Eden Phillpotts
1896   *A Houseboat on the Styx* by **John Kendrick Bangs**
      Shapes in the Fire by **M. P. Shiel**
1897   *The Beetle* by **Richard Marsh**

The *Ape, the Idiot and Other People* by **W. C. Morrow**
Dracula by **Bram Stoker**
1898 *The Turn of the Screw* by **Henry James**
1899 *The Lost Continent* by **Cutcliffe Hyne**
1900 'How Love Came to Professor Guildea' by **Robert S. Hichens**
1901 *The Hound of the Baskervilles* by **Conan Doyle**
1902 'The Monkey's Paw' by **W. W. Jacobs**
1903 *The Light Invisible* by **R. H. Benson**
1904 *Ghost Stories of an Antiquary* by **M. R. James**
Kwaidan by **Lafcadio Hearn**
1905 *The Gods of Pegana* by **Lord Dunsany**
1906 *The Empty House* by **Algernon Blackwood**
1907 *The Boats of the 'Glen Carrig'* by **William Hope Hodgson**
The Hill of Dreams by **Arthur Machen**
1908 *John Silence* by **Algernon Blackwood**
The House on the Borderland by **William Hope Hodgson**
1909 *The Necromancers* by **R. H. Benson**
Black Magic by **Marjorie Bowen**
The Ghost Pirates by **William Hope Hodgson**
1910 *The Return* by **Walter de la Mare**
1911 *Wandering Ghosts* by **F. Marion Crawford**
The Phantom of the Opera by **Gaston Leroux**
Widdershins by **Oliver Onions**
1912 *The Room in the Tower* by **E. F. Benson**
Tarzan of the Apes by **Edgar Rice Burroughs**
The Night Land by **William Hope Hodgson**
The Sorcery Club by **Elliott O'Donnell**
1913 *The Lodger* by **Mrs Belloc Lowndes**
Dr Fu-Manchu by **Sax Rohmer**
1914 'The Bowmen' by **Arthur Machen**. The story that created the legend of King Henry's archers at the Battle of Mons
1915 *The Golem* by **Gustav Meyrink**
1916 *Limehouse Nights* by **Thomas Burke**
1917/18 *Brood of the Witch-Queen* by **Sax Rohmer**
1919 *The Door of the Unreal* by **Gerald Biss**
Jurgen by **James Branch Cabell**
Conquest of the Moon Pool by **A. Merritt**
1920 *A Voyage to Arcturus* by **David Lindsay**
The Slayer of Souls by **Robert W. Chambers**
1921 *Adam and Eve and Pinch Me* by **A. E. Coppard**
Memoirs of a Midget by **Walter de la Mare**
1922 *The Worm Ouroboros* by **E. R. Eddison**
Lady Into Fox by **David Garnett**
The Undying Monster by **Jessie D. Kerruish**
The Haunted Woman by **David Lindsay**

1923   *Madam Crowl's Ghost*, stories by **Le Fanu** assembled by **M. R. James**

      March: first issue of *Weird Tales*

1924   *The Thief of Bagdad* by **Achmed Abdullah**

      'The Loved Dead' by **C. M. Eddy** in *Weird Tales* May

1925   *The Shining Pyramid* by **Arthur Machen**

      Not at Night anthology series begun by **C. Campbell Thomson**

      Lon Chaney's portrayal of *The Phantom of the Opera*

1926   *The Secrets of Dr Taverner* by **Dion Fortune**

      Topper by **Thorne Smith**. The ghost story given the 1920s' humorous treatment

1927   First of *The Ghost Books* edited by **Lady C. Asquith**

      Lukundoo by **Edward L. White**

1928   *The Beast With Five Fingers* by **W. F. Harvey**

      They Return at Evening by **H. R. Wakefield**

1929   *Medusa* by **E. H. Visiak**

1930   *His Monkey Wife* by **John Collier**

      War in Heaven by **Charles Williams**

1931   *Someone in the Room* by **Ex-Private X (A. M. Burrage)**

      Film versions of *Frankenstein* and *Dracula*

      The Supernatural Omnibus edited by **Montague Summers**

1932   'The Phoenix on the Sword' first Conan story by **Robert E. Howard** in *Weird Tales* December

1933   *The Hound of Death* by **Agatha Christie**

      The Werewolf of Paris by **Guy S. Endore**

      Lost Horizon by James Hilton. Shangri-La enters the English language

1935   *The Circus of Dr Lao* by **Charles G. Finney**

      The Devil Rides Out by **Dennis Wheatley**

1936   'The Devil and Daniel Webster' by **Stephen Vincent Benét**, in *Saturday Evening Post* October 24th

1937   *Winged Pharaoh* by **Joan Grant**

      The Hobbit by **J. R. R. Tolkien**

1938   *The Sword in the Stone* by **T. H. White**

1939   *The Outsider and Others* by **H. P. Lovecraft**

      March: first issue of *Unknown*

1940   *Miss Hargreaves* by **Frank Baker**

      Fear by **L. Ron Hubbard** in *Unknown* July

      Darker Than You Think by Jack Williamson in *Unknown* December. The werewolf story given the scientific treatment making it all shiveringly believable

1942   *The Uninvited* by **Dorothy Macardle**

      'The Candle' first weird story by **Ray Bradbury** in *Weird Tales* November

1943   *Conjure Wife* by **Fritz Leiber** in *Unknown* April

'Yours Truly, Jack the Ripper' by **Robert Bloch** in *Weird Tales* July

1944   *The Other Passenger* by **John Keir Cross**

1945   *Number Seven, Queer Street* by **Margery Lawrence**

1946   *Titus Groan* by **Mervyn Peake**

1947   *Dark Carnival* by **Ray Bradbury**
      Night's Black Agents by **Fritz Leiber**

1948   'The Lottery' by **Shirley Jackson**

1949   *Tomato Cain* by **Nigel Kneale**

1950   *Gormenghast* by **Mervyn Peake**
      The Dying Earth by **Jack Vance**

1951   *Fancies and Goodnight* by **John Collier**

1952   *The Sound of His Horn* by **Sarban (John Wall)**

1953   *The Brighton Monster* by **Gerald Kersh**

1954   *Atlantis* by **John Cowper Powys**
      I Am Legend by **Richard Matheson**

1954/5   *The Lord of the Rings* trilogy by **J. R. R. Tolkien**

1958   *A Scent of New-Mown Hay* by **John F. Blackburn**
      The Once and Future King by **T. H. White**

1959   *Psycho* by **Robert Bloch**
      The Haunting of Hill House by **Shirley Jackson**

1960   *A Fine and Private Place* by **Peter S. Beagle**

1961   'The Dreaming City' first Elric story by **Michael Moorcock** in *Science Fantasy* (June)

1962   *The Case Against Satan* by **Ray Russell**

1963   *Glory Road* by Robert A. Heinlein

1964   *The Kiss of Death* by **Charles Birkin**
      The Blue Monkeys by **Thomas Burnett Swann**, serial in *Science Fantasy*
      They Used Dark Forces by **Dennis Wheatley**

1965   *A Ring of Roses* by **John F. Blackburn**

1966   *Conan the Adventurer* by **Robert E. Howard**, first of the Conan adventures in paperback

1967   *Faust Aleph-Null* by James Blish serialised in *If*
      Rosemary's Baby by Ira Levin

1968   *The Last Unicorn* by **Peter S. Beagle**
      The Wizard of Earthsea by Ursula K. Le Guin

1969   *The Cell* by **David Case**

1970   *Deryni Rising* by **Katherine Kurtz**

1971   *Fengriffen* by **David Case**

1972   *Devil Daddy* by **John F. Blackburn**
      Watership Down by Richard Adams

1973   *From Evil's Pillow* by **Basil Copper**
      Legend of Hell House by **Richard Matheson**
      The Exorcist by William Peter Blatty

A–Z of contributors

Note on the entries

THERE is little that need be said about the A–Z of contributors except to clarify a few points.

Titles of books are printed in italic; short stories appear in single quotes. The date following a book or story indicates the first known publication of that work in the country where the writer is or was living at that time (unless otherwise noted). In the case of novels this may relate to a magazine serial which could be a year or more prior to first book publication. Other dates are given where book editions vary substantially. Title changes are also indicated with a note if American (US) or British (UK). In the case of collections an indication is given after the date as to the number of stories (s) or, for omnibus volumes, novels (n), included. I have taken the liberty of reducing titles of books to the main title and omitting any suffixes such as ' . . . and Other Stories' unless specially relevant. When a writer's name is in **bold type**, it indicates that he has a separate entry in the A–Z.

Following the entry is a summary of the author's relevant pen names for quick reference. When 'house' follows a name, it indicates that it is a pseudonym shared by the writer with other authors writing for the same book or magazine publisher. The lists of pen names are not necessarily exhaustive.

Abbreviations used:

b. born; d. died

n. novel; s. short story

rev. revised; trans. translated

F&SF. The Magazine of Fantasy and Science Fiction

PH. The Pan Book of Horror Stories (followed by the number)

WT. Weird Tales

Achmed Abdullah (b. Yalta, 12 May 1881; d. New York, 12 May 1945) Despite his full name of Achmed Abdullah Nadir Khan el-Durani el Iddrissyeh and his blood relation to the Russian Tsars, Abdullah was as British as they come: educated at Eton, he was an expert at polo and often sported a monocle. He served in the British Army in the Middle and Far East, and this supplied him with plenty of material when he later settled in America and became a prolific adventure writer for the pulp magazines. Many of his stories had elements of fantasy and mysticism as in the two series of connected stories *The God of the Invincibly Strong Arms* (1915–1916), novelised as *The Red Stain* (1915), and *The Blue-Eyed Manchu* (1916), dealing with a secret Oriental Society. His best weird stories appeared as *Wings: Tales of the Psychic* (1920; 12s); one UK selection was *Mysteries of Asia* (1934; 15s). Abdullah also wrote plays, and later had success in Hollywood, most notably with *The Thief of Bagdad* (1924).

Robert Aickman (b. London, date withheld by request) **Gahan Wilson** called him 'one of the very best ghost story writers ever to take pen in hand', but Robert Fordyce Aickman's talent has yet to receive true recognition in Britain. This is partly because of the diversity of his other interests in the fields of opera and ballet organisation, dramatic and film criticism, and (especially) as founder of the Inland Waterways Association, being the author of the popular book *Know Your Waterways* (1954). He also serves on many other boards and panels. On his mother's side Aickman is the grandson of writer **Richard Marsh**, but his father was an architect in which profession Aickman received some training.

His writings first appeared in *We Are For the Dark* (1951; 6s) which he wrote jointly (three stories each) with Elizabeth Jane Howard. It included Aickman's 'The Trains' about two girls holidaying on the bleak moors. They take refuge in a house only to find themselves in greater danger. The story showed not the signs of emerging talent, but of full-blown skill in the ability to create an intensely frightening atmosphere almost purely by implication. The pivotal point in Aickman's writing career came when **Cynthia Asquith** chose 'Ringing the Changes' for her *Third Ghost Book* (1955). This tale of the fatal consequences of a honeymoon rapidly became an acknowledged classic and has been adapted for television. It is included in his collection *Dark Entries* (1964; 6s). In 1964 Aickman became editor of *The Fontana Book of Great Ghost Stories* which he steered admirably through eight annual volumes until 1972 when **R. Chetwynd-Hayes** assumed control. Aickman likens ghost fiction to poetry and maintains it is not the ghost that is important but the human psychological reaction. He has written only some forty stories, but his output proves that it is quality not quantity that counts. 'Pages From a

Young Girl's Diary' (1973), told by a girl who gradually becomes a vampire, won the first World Fantasy Award for Best Short Fiction in 1975. Aickman's other collections are *Powers of Darkness* (1966; 6s), *Sub Rosa* (1968; 8s), *Cold Hand in Mine* (1976; 8s) and *Tales of Love and Death* (1977; 7s). His autobiography appeared as *The Attempted Rescue* (1966).

Joan Aiken (b. Rye, Sussex, 4 September 1924)

Noted for her thrillers and children's fiction, Joan Delano Aiken comes from a very literary family. Her father was the American writer Conrad Aiken, her sister is Jane Aiken Hodge, historical novelist, and brother John Aiken writes science fiction. Her mother, Jessie MacDonald, later married **Martin Armstrong**. Joan Aiken began by writing for BBC Radio in 1944, and her first books were for children. Several of these were fantasy collections, such as *All You've Ever Wanted* (1953), *A Small Pinch of Weather* (1969), *The Green Flash* (1971) and *A Bundle of Nerves* (1976). For adult readers, thrillers aside, her weird and bizarre tales have been collected as *The Windscreen Weepers* (1969; 24s). Though they have supernatural elements ('As Gay as Cheese' concerns a barber who has premonitions) many hinge predominantly on psychological horror and macabre humour.

Pseudonyms: Nicholas Dee, Rosie Lee

W. Harrison Ainsworth (b. Manchester, 4 February 1805; d. Reigate, Surrey, 3 January 1882)

A popular writer of historical melodrama, Ainsworth adapted the trappings of Gothic writing to English legends, and in so doing created myths of his own. His first novel, *Rookwood* (1834), created the legend of Dick Turpin's overnight ride from London to York, and the traditional image of witches stems from his *The Lancashire Witches* (1848) about the Yorkshire witch trials of the seventeenth century. Ainsworth started writing in his teens and his early stories will be found in the very rare book *December Tales* (1823). He moved to London in 1824, marrying a publisher's daughter in 1826. He set up in publishing and later edited his own magazine, but he preferred writing, by which he earned his main income. His novels are full of the accepted supernatural elements and include *Auriol; or, The Elixir of Life* (1844–46), the necromantic *Mervyn Clitheroe* (1851–52 and 1857–58) and *Chetwynd Calverley* (1876). His non-fantasy works such as *The Tower of London* (1840) and *Old St Pauls* (1841) also contain elements of horror.

Steffan B. Aletti
A young American who achieved much popularity in the *Magazine of Horror* in the 1960s with his **Lovecraft** imitation stories—'The Castle in the Window' (1968), 'The Eye of Horus' (1968), 'The Last Work of Pietro of Apono' (1969) and 'The Cellar Room' (1970). As a musician and composer by profession, Aletti was not reliant on fiction for income and when the magazines folded he disappeared from the genre.

Lloyd Alexander (b. Philadelphia, 30 January 1924)
Although Alexander is a writer of children's books, **Lin Carter** has likened his work to that of **Cabell**, and all his writing will be of interest to the fantasy fan. Set in the mythical world of Prydain is a series of six books that follows the life of a young boy who is tutored by a magician and who ultimately saves Prydain from the forces of evil. The series includes *The Book of Three* (1964), *The Black Cauldron* (1965), *The Castle of Llyr* (1966), *Taran Wanderer* (1967), *The High King* (1968) and a collection of earlier unconnected tales, *The Foundling* (1973). The first three novels are now receiving the Disney treatment as *The Cauldron*. Alexander used the *Mabinogion* Welsh legends as the basis for his stories, having first taught himself Welsh. For a different development of this theme see **Evangeline Walton**.

Grant Allen (b. Kingston, Canada, 24 February 1848; d. Haslemere, 28 October 1899)
Charles Grant Blairfindie Allen had a most cosmopolitan upbringing. Born in Canada of parents with Irish and French ancestry, raised in the United States, educated in France and England, he then taught in England and Jamaica before settling down to write in England in 1876. His early works were scientific essays under the alias J. Arbuthnot Wilson. He wrote fiction by accident when he cast the piece 'Our Scientific Observations on a Ghost', about the impossibility of knowing one had seen a phantom, in narrative form. It proved popular and the editor who bought it requested on the same day more fiction from Allen and fewer articles from 'Wilson', without knowing they were the same person. Over the next twenty years Allen wrote scores of books of all kinds. His weird fiction will be found in the collections *Strange Stories* (1884; 16s), *The Beckoning Hand* (1887; 13s) and *Ivan Greet's Masterpiece* (1893; 16s); *Twelve Tales* (1899; 12s) is a compendium of the best of these stories. His novels vary in quality but of interest is *Michael's Crag* (1893), a strange Cornish adventure, and fans of lost-race adventures will enjoy *The White Man's Foot* (1888) and *The Great Taboo* (1891) both set in the South Seas.

Edward Heron-Allen: *see* Heron-Allen

Poul Anderson (b. Bristol, Pa., 25 November 1926)
Primarily a science fiction writer, Poul William Anderson's Nordic ancestry inclines him to the fantasy field on occasions. Much of his space opera written for *Planet Stories* in the early 1950s ranks as fantasy on other worlds, such as 'Swordsman of Lost Terra' (1951). His pure fantasies rank as recognised classics, and include *Three Hearts and Three Lions* (1953) and *The Broken Sword* (1954), both set in 'faery-lands' with a battle between good and evil; and *Hrolf Kraki's Saga* (1973), a retelling of a Nordic legend. It won the August Derleth Fantasy Award the following year as best novel. He has also written a few shorter items such as 'The Merman's Children' in *Flashing Swords 1* (1973).

Pseudonyms: A. A. Craig, Michael Karageorge, Winston P. Sanders

Leonid Andreyev (b. Ovel, Russia, 18 June 1871; d. Finland, 12 September 1919)
The tragic life of Leonid Nikolaevich Andreyev is only too well reflected in his fiction. His father died early and he was reared in poverty. He attained a law degree, but failed as a lawyer. He had moderate success as a painter, but little money. Three times he tried to commit suicide. Eventually he became a police reporter and this started his writing career; his first story in 1898 was praised by Gorki. His success came with the novel *In The Fog* (1902) and in that year he married. But joy was short-lived. His wife died in 1906, and though he remarried, Andreyev became a wretched character, plagued with ill-health, always living on the edge of poverty, and obsessed with death. He died of a cerebral haemorrhage when only 48. All of Andreyev's suffering is contained in his famous short story 'Lazarus' (1906), which shows the burden borne by the man that Christ resurrected—that of life itself. The story embodies Andreyev's own wish for death. Likewise 'The Abyss' depicts his longing for the grave. Translations of his grim and macabre stories exist in the UK as *Silence* (1910: 16s), *When the King Loses His Head* (1919; 7s) and *Satan's Diary* (1920).

F. Anstey (b. London, 8 August 1856; d. London, 10 March 1934)
Thomas Anstey Guthrie signed his first writings T. Anstey, but a printer's error made it F. Anstey, and so it stayed, virtually supplanting his real name. The son of a military tailor, Anstey trained as a barrister but abandoned that career with the success of his hilarious novel *Vice-Versa* (1882), about a father and son who exchange bodies by means of an old

talisman. He cemented his reputation with *The Tinted Venus* (1885), in which a statue of the Greek goddess comes to life. Thereafter he worked on *Punch* and contributed many fantasies to the leading magazines. His other major success, *The Brass Bottle* (1900), told of the havoc created by jinn released from an old bottle. Some of his early short stories were collected as *The Black Poodle* (1884; 10s). Anstey ceased writing fiction after 1915 to concentrate on translating Molière's plays. When an omnibus of his work was issued as *Humour and Fantasy* (1931; 6n) it failed to sell well as by then his style was out of vogue. Nevertheless Anstey was an innovator of the humorous fantasy, establishing the trend that **John Collier** and **Thorne Smith** would follow.

Johann August Apel (b. Leipzig, 17 September 1771; d. Leipzig, 9 August 1816)
Apel lived most of his short life as a lawyer and later a librarian in Leipzig. He was an authority on old German folk tales, and these he recast with the help of Freidrich August Schulze (1770–1849) into a six-volume set of ghost stories, *Der Gespensterbuch* (1810–17), which proved highly popular. It includes the story 'Der Freischütz' ('The Free Shot') about a gamekeeper who makes a pact with the devil for an infallible gun. This was adapted by Friedrich Kind as the libretto for the famous opera by Weber in 1821.

Michael Arlen (b. Bulgaria, 16 November 1895; d. New York, 23 June 1956)
Although Bulgarian by birth, Arlen was educated in England and became a British citizen, changing his name from Dikran Kouyoumdjian. His first book appeared in 1913 and success came with his fashionable *The Green Hat* (1924). In many ways Arlen was the epitome of the 1920s, and time passed him by. He wrote no more after the Second World War, even though he went to Hollywood. Now his books are curios, and only his weird fiction keeps his name alive. These comprise two collections, *These Charming People* (1923; 15s) and *May Fair* (1925; 11s), from which a selection was made as *Ghost Stories* (1930; 7s). This includes his best-known story 'The Gentleman from America', about a man driven mad by a faked ghost in an old mansion. Arlen also wrote a vampire novel, *Hell! said the Duchess* (1934).

Martin Armstrong (b. nr Newcastle, 2 October 1882; d. 24 February 1974)
It is a sad loss that throughout his long writing career Martin Donisthorpe Armstrong only completed three collections of fantasy stories, for he was

a most original and versatile writer. The collections *The Bazaar* (1924; 19s), *The Fiery Dive* (1929; 6s) and *General Buntop's Miracle* (1934; 16s) contain some of the most fascinating stories ever written, and the two best examples of his versatility come from the last-named volume. His oft-reprinted 'The Pipe-Smoker' tells of a meeting with a man whose inner being murdered himself; 'Presence of Mind' is a delightfully humorous tale about a man with a far too creative imagination. A few more fantasies will be found in *A Case of Conscience* (1937; 21s).

T. I. Fytton Armstrong: *see* John Gawsworth

Edwin Lester Arnold (b. Swanscombe, Kent, 1857; d. London, 1 March 1935)
The creator of the immortal *Phra* was the son of the famous poet and philosopher Sir Edwin Arnold. He spent much of his early life in India, and returned there after his education and a period spent breeding cattle in Scotland, but caught malaria and finally settled in England and turned to writing. *The Wonderful Adventures of Phra the Phoenician* (1890), in which the hero is constantly reborn over the centuries, made Arnold's name, though he would never again write anything as popular. He re-used the theme in 'Rutherford the Twiceborn' (1892), where a ghost forces Rutherford back through earlier incarnations. This and other of Arnold's weird stories will be found in *The Story of Ulla* (1895; 10s). Later novels were *Lepidus the Centurion* (1901), a tedious tale about a revived Roman, and *Lieut. Gulliver Jones* (1905), a Martian adventure held by many to be the genesis of the Mars novels later written by **Edgar Rice Burroughs.**

Robert Arthur (b. 1 November 1909; d. 1969)
Noted as a master of chills and suspense on early American radio, the bulk of Robert Arthur Feder's fiction is overlooked. In 1929 he had taken a job as an oil operator while developing his writing abilities and one of his earliest sales was the science fiction horror story 'The Terror From the Sea' (1931). His reputation was first made as a skilful mystery writer and on this strength he joined MGM in 1937. Despite his distinguished film work he still wrote prodigiously for the pulp magazines. *Argosy* carried his amusing series narrated by Murchison Morks which included 'Obstinate Uncle Otis' (1941) for whom things existed only if he believed in them. Arthur also appeared in *Unknown* with both humorous and chilling stories. He wrote for the radio series *The Mysterious Traveller* and edited the spin-off magazine of the same name during 1951–52

(App. III). In many instances Arthur remained behind the scenes, ghost-writing and ghost-editing. He was responsible for many **Alfred Hitch-cock** anthologies such as *Stories My Mother Never Told Me* (1963: 26s). What few books carry his name are aimed at junior audiences, for instance his collection *Ghosts and More Ghosts* (1963; 10s) and the anthologies *Davy Jones' Haunted Locker* (1965; 15s) and *Monster Mix* (1968; 13s). A serious collection of his work is long overdue.

Cynthia Asquith (b. Wiltshire, 27 September 1887; d. Oxford, 31 March 1960)
One of the macabre field's most important early anthologists, Mary Evelyn Charteris married poet Herbert Asquith in 1910. When he returned from the war in 1918 too ill to take regular work she became private secretary to J. M. Barrie, creator of *Peter Pan*, a position she held until his death in 1937. An adept organiser, she was soon running Barrie's entire social and domestic life. For extra money she took to writing and earned a reputation for her biographies and children's books. She occasionally wrote ghost stories of her own, eventually collected as *This Mortal Coil* (1947; 9s: rev. *What Dreams May Come* (1951; 9s)). The best known is ' "God Grante That She Lye Stille" ' (1931), in which a young woman is gradually taken over by the spirit of her ancestor.

Cynthia Asquith had a vast circle of prominent literary friends, among them **L. P. Hartley, D. H. Lawrence, Hugh Walpole, Algernon Blackwood** and **Arthur Machen,** and from them she coaxed and bought many ghost and mystery stories. These she collected into some of the best weird fiction anthologies ever compiled starting with *The Ghost Book* (1927; 16s), then *The Black Cap* (1928; 14s), *Shudders* (1929; 15s), *When Churchyards Yawn* (1931; 15s) and *My Grimmest Nightmare* (1935; 22s). It was some years before she compiled *The Second Ghost Book* (1952; 20s) and finally *The Third Ghost Book* (1956; 27s). After her death the series was revived and continued by James Turner, **Rosemary Timperley** and Aidan Chambers (App. II).

Gertrude Atherton (b. San Francisco, 30 October 1857; d. 14 June 1948)
Born Gertrude Horn, and the great-grand niece of Benjamin Franklin, she was raised by her father after her parents separated when she was two. She married when just 18, but her husband died tragically a few years later, and she devoted the rest of her life to writing, starting in 1889. She wrote fifty-six books in all, right up to her ninetieth year. Her most noted collection of weird stories is *The Bell in the Fog* (1905; 9s) which includes her best story 'The Striding Place'. A later volume was *The Foghorn* (1934;

Her ghost stories have been likened to those by **Edith Wharton**. *Black Oxen* (1923), a novel about rejuvenation, formed the basis of a film.

Michael Avallone (b. New York, 27 October 1924)
Michael Angelo Avallone, Jr, is best known as American thriller writer Ed Noon. After rising to the rank of sergeant in the US Army during the Second World War, Avallone became a freelance writer. He can be honoured among the contributors to *Weird Tales*, having 'The Man Who Walked on Air' (1953) in one of the last issues. During the 1950s he edited over a score of men's magazines. His chief contribution to the terror field was the radio programme *Tales of the Frightened*, narrated by Boris Karloff. A record was issued of the series, and even a short-lived magazine (App. III) appeared, which Avallone edited and which published his impressive story 'The Man Who Thought He Was Poe' (1957). A subsequent collection appeared as *Tales of the Frightened* (1963; 26s).

More recently Avallone has been writing the macabre thriller series *The Satan Sleuth*, in which the hero, through terrible personal knowledge, becomes a lone fighter against satanism. So far published are *Fallen Angel* and *Devil Devil* (both 1974). He also edited *Edwina Noone's Gothic Sampler* (1967; 8s).

Pseudonyms: Priscilla Dalton, Mark Dane, Steve Michaels, Dorothea Nile, Ed Noon, Edwina Noone, Sidney Stuart

F. Baculard D'Arnaud (b. Paris, 18 September 1718; d. Paris, 8 November 1805)
As one of the earliest French writers in the Gothic medium, François-Thomas de Baculard D'Arnaud did much to popularise it in his country, chiefly through his plays. Most effective was *Le Comte de Comminges* (1764), a horrific drama set in a crypt among buried Trappist monks. Doom-laden abbeys and horror-haunted castles are the chilling settings of his plays. Later he wrote several short stories collected as *Les Epreuves du Sentiment* (1772–80) and *Nouvelles Historique* (1774–84), but not all are supernatural or horror. Many have an English setting, of which the best known have been translated as 'Anne Bell' (or 'The Cruel Father'), 'Warbeck' and 'The Witch of Eye'.

Denys Val Baker (b. Poppleton, Yorks., 24 October 1917)
Those acquainted with Val Baker's humorous reminiscences of his life in Cornwall might find it hard to imagine him a horror writer, but from his earliest sales his ouput has consisted of many weird and bizarre stories. After a stint as a reporter for several British daily and trade papers before

the Second World War, he sold his first novel in 1944 and followed it with the collection *Worlds Without End* (1945; 20s). Not all horror, many of the stories reflect his views of the war. It includes 'Passenger to Liverpool' about the bizarre episode in a railway carriage, and his best known 'A Strange Story', about a man pursued. Under the title 'The Face in the Mirror' the latter story was included in *The Fourth Ghost Book* (1965) and formed the title story to a US compilation of his best weird stories (1971; 12s). Seldom supernatural, his tales stress the psychological effects of the inexplicable upon people. Several bizarre stories appear in his other collection, *The Return of Uncle Walter* (1948; 17s). He has edited several anthologies of Cornish tales, and recently compiled *Stories of the Macabre* (1976; 15s) and *Stories of the Night* (1976; 15s).

Frank Baker (b. London, 22 May 1908)
Dissatisfied as an underwriter and an organist Frank Baker headed for Land's End where, sufficiently isolated, he devoted himself to writing. His first novel, *The Twisted Tree* (1935), was a Cornish tragedy, followed by *The Birds* (1936), not to be confused with **Daphne du Maurier's** story on which the **Hitchcock** film was based, although both share a common theme. Baker's success came with *Miss Hargreaves* (1940), about two men who invent an elderly poetess who then becomes real. Written as a joke, the novel was rejected by nine publishers; after it was published it was adapted as a play and the lead rôle was immortalised by Margaret Rutherford. Baker's best-known short story, 'In the Steam Room', tells of a man who finds he is sharing a Turkish Bath with a dead body. His other novels, both humorous and bizarre, include *Sweet Chariot* (1942), *Mr Allenby Loses the Way* (1945) a witty fantasy of wish-fulfilment, *Allanyr* (1941; US *Full Score*, 1942), *Before I Go Hence* (1946), *Embers* (1946), *The Downs So Free* (1948), a compelling novel of mysticism and poltergeists, and *Talk of the Devil* (1956).

John Kendrick Bangs (b. New York, 27 May 1862; d. New York, 21 January 1922)
Bangs was one of America's leading humorists at the turn of the century, for ever satirising well-known individuals. Although he had his serious side (in 1894 he campaigned unsuccessfully to be Mayor of Yonkers) it was his wit that earned his income. Hence when one approaches one of his supernatural stories one can never be sure if it is meant to be serious.

His most famous book, *A House-Boat on the Styx* (1896), is set in the hereafter where the male departed (Shakespeare, Napoleon, Mozart, Noah . . .) form a club. Females are banned and their rebellion under Cleopatra forms much of the plot, though the whole is merely a vehicle for lampooning the characters. A sequel, *The Pursuit of the House-Boat*

(1897), includes Sherlock Holmes as a character. *Olympian Nights* (1902) includes such episodes as the Greek gods using the planet Mars as a giant golf-course! Other examples of Bangs's humour will be found in his collections with such delightful titles as *Over the Plum Pudding* (1901; 11s), *Bikey the Skicycle and Other Tales of Jimmiboy* (1902; 13s) and *The Inventions of an Idiot* (1904; 12s). His more serious stories were collected as *The Water Ghost of Harrowby Hall* (1894; 8s) and *Ghosts I Have Met* (1898; 7s).

Richard H. Barham (b. Canterbury, Kent, 6 December 1788; d. London, 17 June 1845)
Richard Harris Barham had an intensely religious upbringing, becoming a minor canon of St Paul's, but he is remembered solely for the *Ingoldsby Legends*. His first novel, *Baldwin* (1819), had been a dismal failure, and this may have influenced his use of the Thomas Ingoldsby alias to recount his *Legends*, first published in *Bentley's Miscellany* from 1837 onwards, with a first book edition in 1840, a second in 1842, and a third in 1847 which revealed Barham's true identity. The contents are mostly narrative verse and frequently comic in nature, but it is the supernatural episodes that have become the best known, not least 'The Hand of Glory'—possibly inspired by a near fatal coach accident Barham had when 13 which partially crippled his right arm for life. Popular prose tales from the *Legends* include the humorous ghost story 'The Spectre of Tappington', 'The Leech of Folkestone', 'Jerry Jarvis's Wig' and 'Singular Passage in the Life of the Late Henry Harris'.

Maurice Baring (b. London, 27 April 1874; d. Inverness, 14 December 1945)
Baring led an extremely active early life, his flair for languages securing him a job in the Foreign Office, then later as a war correspondent in Manchuria, and news correspondent world-wide. He also served in the Royal Flying Corps, achieving the rank of Major. His writings began with the play *The Black Prince* (1902) and he became an expert on Russia and its literature. Many of his short stories are bizarre and off-trail and can be found in his collections *Orpheus in Mayfair* (1909; 25s), *The Glass Mender* (1910; 11s), an assemblage of legends, and *Half a Minute's Silence* (1925: 25s). **Vernon Lee**'s collection *For Maurice* was dedicated to him.

S. Baring-Gould (b. Exeter, Devon, 28 January 1834; d. Lew Trenchard, 2 January 1924)
An extremely prolific writer, Sabine Baring-Gould dabbled in almost

every field imaginable. His hundred or so books are equally divided between fact and fiction. The non-fiction books cover topics like theology, topography, mythology and history, and among them is *The Book of Were-Wolves* (1865). He also penned the stirring hymn 'Onward Christian Soldiers'. In 1881 he inherited the estate of Lew Trenchard, Devon, and he settled down as squire-parson, devoting more of his time to literary pursuits than to the running of his estate. He spent thirty years studying Icelandic and Danish languages in order to translate into prose the thirteenth-century *Grettir Saga* as *Grettir the Outlaw* (1889). Novels of fantasy interest include *The Crock of Gold* (1889) and the historical adventure set in North Wales, *Pabo the Priest* (1899). His few supernatural short stories were collected as *A Book of Ghosts* (1904; 21s) though some had been written as early as the 1850s.

Nugent Barker (b. London 1888; d. ?)
This writer has all but passed into oblivion although he was popular in the 1920s and 1930s, the volume *Best English Stories, 1929*, being dedicated to him. He is remembered today for his collection *Written With My Left Hand* (1951; 21s) from which comes 'Curious Adventure of Mr Bond' about the traveller who learns the bizarre truth behind the names of three inns.

Robert Barr (b. Glasgow, 16 September 1850; d. Surrey, 21 October 1912)
Today Barr is probably better remembered in the detective fiction genre, primarily for *The Triumphs of Eugene Valmont* (1906), said by some to have inspired **Agatha Christie**'s Hercule Poirot. Barr emigrated with his family to Canada when he was 4. Educated in Toronto, he became headmaster of a junior school while still in his teens. He later earned a reputation as a reporter on the Detroit *Free Press* with his dare-devil and often questionable means of gaining news. An Iroquois tribe even made him a chief. He was sent to London in 1881 as a correspondent for the paper and began a British edition. He soon established his own publishing business and became well acquainted with literary illuminati such as **Kipling** and **Doyle**. With Jerome K. Jerome he began the monthly magazine *Idler* which ran from 1892–1910, and included many fantasies in its pages.

Barr's most intriguing work is *From Whose Bourne* (1893), about the spirit of a dead man who enlists the aid of a ghost to help clear his widow of his murder. No single collection is composed entirely of his weird fiction, although the best will be found in *In a Steamer Chair* (1892: 13s), *The Face and the Mask* (1894: 24s) and *Revenge!* (1896; 20s). A later story, 'A Game of Chess' (1900), involves a man forced to play a human chess piece on a board where certain squares, he knows not which, are electrified.

J. A. Barry (b. Torquay, Devon, 1850; d. Sydney, 23 September 1911)
Like many adventurous lads in the nineteenth century, John Arthur Barry went to sea when 13 and spent twelve years voyaging round the world. He later settled in Australia and worked as a journalist. His first important book was *Steve Brown's Bunyip* (1893), about the mythical Australian monster. His short stories reflect his nautical life and, like **Hodgson** and **Russell**, he captures the alluring yet horrific mystery of the sea. They are collected as *In The Great Deep* (1896; 9s), *Red Lion and Blue Star* (1902; 15s) and *Sea Yarns* (1910).

Peter S. Beagle (b. Bronx, N.Y., 29 April 1939)
Peter Soyer Beagle has secured a large following with just two novels, *A Fine and Private Place* (1960), a neo-Gothic fantasy with bizarre characters set in a Bronx cemetery, and *The Last Unicorn* (1968), a touching, at times humorous story of the quest by the lonely unicorn for others of her kind. In between writing these two books Beagle had visited Europe and travelled across America by motor-cycle, a trip he recorded in *I See By My Outfit* (1965). 'Come Lady Death' (1963) was a short tale in the vein of **Poe**, though Beagle names his main influences as **T. H. White**, **Thurber** and **Dunsany**. Recent silence threatened that Beagle had abandoned the fantasy field, but 1974 saw the separate publication of a short story *Lila the Werewolf*. Beagle is currently adapting this for filming as well as working on a filmscript of *The Lord of the Rings*.

Charles Beaumont (b. Chicago, 2 January 1929; d. 21 February 1967)
Beaumont led a tough life, but never flagged from his ambition to write for Hollywood, which he achieved before fate struck its cruellest blow. When 12 Beaumont (then Charles Nutt) was incapacitated by spinal meningitis which curtailed his education. He spent his time devouring numerous fantasy books and became involved in sf fandom, editing his own fan magazine *Utopia* (1945). He did some radio work and tried acting without success, and at length turned to artwork, inking in cartoons for MGM's animation studios, and illustrating *Fantasy Book* in 1947. His first story sale was '"The Devil, You Say"' (1951), and although his sales increased thereafter Beaumont and his family lived on the edge of poverty until *Playboy* bought his controversial story of a homosexual future 'The Crooked Man' (1956). Thereafter his many grim tales found easy markets and were collected as *Hunger* (1957), *Yonder* (1958; 13s), *Shadow Play*

28

(1957; 16s), *Night Ride* (1960; 15s) and *The Magic Man* (1965; 18s), a compilation of the best. 'Miss Gentil-belle', telling of a young mother's cruelty, ranks as one of his most frightening stories.

He achieved his ambition by scripting *Queen of Outer Space* (1958) and thereafter worked on a number of films including *The Premature Burial* (1963) with **Ray Russell**, *Masque of the Red Death* (1964), *Burn, Witch, Burn* (1964) with **Richard Matheson** and *The Seven Faces of Dr Lao* (1964). He also edited *The Fiend in You* (1962; 16s), in which Beaumont summed up his views on horror fiction in the introduction: 'he is the most terrifying monster of them all. He's called The Mind.' Suddenly in 1964 Beaumont was struck with a strange and frightening disease from which he suffered terribly for three years as his body disintegrated and his mind became senile. When he died, aged 38, he looked over 100.

Pseudonyms: Keith Grantland, C. B. Lovehill, Charles McNutt, Michael Phillips

L. Adams Beck (b. ?; d. Kyoto, Japan, 3 January 1931)
Lily Moresby Adams Beck was a popular novelist and biographer during the 1920s, now all but forgotten. The daughter of Admiral John Moresby, she travelled widely and fell in love with the Orient. When she finally settled in Canada, she converted her grounds into an Oriental garden. She became well acquainted with the customs, beliefs and peoples of the East, and this knowledge gives an added depth to her fiction. Her short tales are all typically Oriental, as in the title story of *The Ninth Vibration* (1922; 8s) about a Rajah who builds a strange House of Beauty for his love of a great woman. Other collections are *The Perfume of the Rainbow* (1923; 16s), *Dreams and Delights* (1926; 11s) and *The Openers of the Gate* (1930; 10s). Her novels include *Key of Dreams* (1922), *The Treasure of Ho* (1924), *The Way of Stars* (1925), about an Egyptian queen reincarnated in modern India, and *The House of Fulfilment* (1927), plus *The Glory of Egypt* (1926) and *Captain Java* (1928) under the alias L. Moresby.

Pseudonyms: E. Barrington, Louis Moresby

William Beckford (b. Fonthill, Somerset, 29 September 1760; d. Bath, 2 May 1844)
Vathek (1786) is one of the classics of English literature although, true to the spirit of its eccentric creator, it was written in French. Clearly inspired by the *Arabian Nights*, it tells of the Caliph Vathek's quest to find the secret of the Universe, a quest that takes him through many terrifying adventures. He stops at nothing, making various pacts with evil entities which take their toll in his mental disintegration. Its author, William Beckford, had become the wealthiest commoner in England

when a combination of inheritances left him over £300,000 when he was 11. Because of his alleged evil practices Beckford was banned from England, and *Vathek*'s first English edition was unauthorised, due to some extent to Beckford's dithering with the final draft. Several chapters were omitted from the finished copy and they exist separately as *The Episodes of Vathek* (1912). They and several other short stories were only found in 1909. Returning to England in 1796 Beckford financed the construction of Fonthill Abbey, with a central tower three hundred feet high. This collapsed in 1800; Beckford was simply sorry he had not seen it fall.

H. Bedford-Jones (b. Ontario, 29 April 1887; d. Beverly Hills, Calif., 6 May 1949)

A prolific writer under a shower of pseudonyms, no complete listing has ever been made of his total output, and that may now prove impossible. Henry James O'Brien Bedford-Jones became an American citizen, and began writing in 1908.

The bulk of his one hundred books and numerous magazine contributions are swashbuckling historical adventures. Several have a tinge of fantasy, the most notable being his series set in a mythical fourteenth-century Middle East kingdom. The series began with *The Seal of John Solomon* (1915), and saw UK publication under the Allan Hawkwood alias as *The Seal of Solomon* (1925), *John Solomon, Incognito* (1925), *John Solomon, Supercargo* (1926), *Solomon's Carpet* (1926), *Solomon's Quest* (1926) and *The Wizard of the Atlas* (1926). A later series in *Blue Book* magazine was called *Trumpets From Oblivion*, and ran for thirteen monthly episodes during 1938–39. Several were fantasy such as 'Singing Sands of Prester John', 'Amazon Woman', 'The Lady and the Unicorn', 'Lady of the Evil Eye', 'The Wolf Woman', 'Woman of the Sea' and 'The Serpent People'. In 1940 he published a short series in *Weird Tales* whimsically entitled 'The Adventures of a Professional Corpse'. His stirring Eastern fantasy *The Temple of Ten* (1921), co-written with W. C. Robertson, had a US hardback edition in 1973. To further confuse bibliographers, Bedford-Jones wrote two entirely different stories called 'Mr Shen of Shensi' (1917 and 1919), so completists—watch out!

Pseudonyms: Donald Bedford, Montague Brissard, Cleveland B. Chase, Paul Ferval, Michael Gallister, Allan Hawkwood, Gordon Keyne, M. Lassez, George Souli de Mourant, Lucian Pemjean, Margaret Love Sangerson, Charles George Souli, Gordon Stuart, Elliott Whitney, John Wycliffe

Neil Bell: *see* Stephen Southwold

Stephen Vincent Benét (b. Pennsylvania, 22 July 1898; d. New York, 13 March 1943)

Benét was an extremely talented American poet and short story writer who received a Guggenheim fellowship in 1926 and went on to write the long narrative Civil War poem *John Brown's Body* (1928). He is best remembered today for his tale of a pact with the devil, 'The Devil and Daniel Webster' (1936), filmed in 1941 as *All That Money Can Buy*. The story's sequel, 'Daniel Webster and the Sea Serpent' (1937), was less popular, but that same year saw his warning tale of mankind's reversion to savagery, 'The Place of the Gods' (also titled 'By the Waters of Babylon'). An earlier story of note told of the feline peril, 'The King of the Cats' (1932). Several collections of Benét's work exist, but those with the most fantasy tales include *Thirteen O'Clock* (1937; 13s) and *Tales Before Midnight* (1939; 12s).

A. C. Benson (b. Wokingham, Berks., 24 April 1862; d. 17 June 1925)

Essayist Arthur Christopher Benson was the oldest surviving son of Edward White Benson (1829–96), who was then Headmaster of Wellington College and became Archbishop of Canterbury in 1877. In the supernatural fiction field Arthur Benson has been overshadowed by his two brothers (see below) and is now remembered mostly for his collection of essays *From a College Window* (1906) and for the words of 'Land of Hope and Glory', which he wrote for Elgar's famous *Pomp and Circumstance* march. Benson became housemaster at Eton in 1892 but disliked teaching there and removed to Cambridge in 1903. Becoming master of Magdalene College in 1915 he did much to rebuild and improve the College, aided financially by an anonymous admirer. He also edited Queen Victoria's letters.

He was a tall, heavy-set man, and a keen mountain climber, yet he was a nervous invalid and suffered frequently from bouts of melancholia, having an attack in 1917 that lasted for five years! This depressive mood pervades his fiction, where one feels the isolation and oppression. Two collections of his stories were published, *The Hill of Trouble* (1903; 12s) and *The Isles of Sunset* (1904; 7s), later combined and reissued as *Paul the Minstrel* (1911; 19s). He also wrote a weird novel of immortality, *The Child of the Dawn* (1911). After his death E. F. Benson found several unpublished ghost stories among his papers and he published two of them as *Basil Netherby* (1926; 2s). One wonders what happened to the others.

E. F. Benson (b. Wokingham, Berks., 24 July 1867; d. 29 February 1940)

By far the most active of the Benson brothers, Edward Frederic Benson showed an early interest in the classics and archaeology, before the success of his first society novel, *Dodo* (1893), led him to devote his time to writing. He produced a vast amount of material on numerous topics besides fiction, his most famous works being his biographies and his various social comedies. Benson's general works have, however, become dated, whereas his horror fiction retains its original flavour.

His first excursion into the genre was with the macabre novel *The Judgement Books* (1895), concerning an evil portrait. Subsequent novels include *The Image in the Sand* (1905), *The Angel of Pain* (1906), *Colin I* and *Colin II* (1926 and 1928), *The Inheritor* (1930) and *Raven's Brood* (1934). His true *métier*, however, was the short story, as evidenced in his collections *The Room in the Tower* (1912; 17s), *Visible and Invisible* (1923; 12s), *Spook Stories* (1928; 12s) and *More Spook Stories* (1934; 13s). Benson's penchant was for loathsome creatures rather than intangible ghosts, as in 'Caterpillars', where an Italian villa is overrun by crab-like caterpillars that foreordain death, and also in 'The Horror Horn' and 'Negotium Perambulans'. He also wrote several excellent vampire stories, among them 'The Room in the Tower', 'Mrs Amworth', 'The Thing in the Hall' and 'And No Bird Sings'.

Benson remained active all his life, even serving as Mayor of Rye from 1934–37, and he was awarded the MBE. He outlived both his brothers but similarly did not marry, and the Benson line stopped with his death. A representative selection of his best stories was edited by Alexis Lykiard as *The Horror Horn* (1974; 13s).

R. H. Benson (b. Wokingham, Berks., 18 November 1871; d. Salford, Manchester, 19 October 1914)
Educated first at Eton, Robert Hugh Benson studied theology at Cambridge and entered the Church of England in 1895. Over the ensuing decade his name appeared frequently in most literary magazines with fiction and essays. He later had doubts about his faith, and he converted to Roman Catholicism in 1903, becoming a priest and rising to be the private chamberlain to Pope Pius X. Pius died in August 1914 and Benson returned to England, contracted pneumonia and died soon after.

R. H. Benson's work reflects his religious background, especially *Come Rack! Come Rope!* (1912), a terrifying account of the persecution of Catholic martyrs in Elizabethan England, and *Lord of the World* (1908), an apocalyptic novel of the last days of the Catholic Church. *The Necromancers* (1909) is Benson's stand against spiritualism in the tale of a young man's desire for contact with his dead fiancée. Benson's short fiction is less often revived today, even though Montague Summers said of *The Mirror of Shalott* (1907; 14s) that 'there are few better stories of this kind'. It is a series of stories recounted by a group of priests, much in the *Canterbury Tales* vein, each telling of his supernatural experiences. An earlier collection, *The Light Invisible* (1903; 15s) includes the noted ghost story 'The Traveller'.

J. D. Beresford (b. Castor, Northants., 7 March 1873; d. Bath, 1 February 1947)
John Davys Beresford contracted infantile paralysis when he was 3 and remained lame throughout his life. This probably influenced his fiction, as his two best-known novels both deal with men with superhuman abilities: *The Hampdenshire Wonder* (1911) and *The Camberwell Miracle* (1933). His short fiction tends to underline the nastiness in people, as in his two oft-reprinted stories 'The Misanthrope' and 'Cut-Throat Farm', both in his collection *Nineteen Impressions* (1918; 17s). Other volumes include *Signs and Wonders* (1921; 17s) and *The Meeting Place* (1928; 26s), the latter including the fantasy 'The Summary', a tale of afterlife.

Eddy C. Bertin (b. Altona, Germany, 26 December 1944)
Born in Germany, his father Belgian, Eddy Charly Bertin moved to Belgium at a very early age and still lives there. His work has appeared in his native language plus German, Dutch, French, Spanish and English! It was the English market that first bought his fiction, starting with an experimental sf piece 'The City, Dying' (1968), although the first story in print was 'The Whispering Horror' (*PH9*, 1968). This told of the discovery of something nasty in an old cellar and showed the influence of H. P. Lovecraft, on whom Bertin is an authority, having recently completed a definitive *Chrono-Bibliography* of his work. In 1969 a Dutch magazine published thirteen of Bertin's stories as a special *Horror House* issue, for which he received no payment. His collection *De Achtjaarlijkse God* (*The Eight-Yearly God*, 1971; 15s) includes several stories that have subsequently seen English or American publication. 'I Wonder What He Wanted' (1970), 'Like Two White Spiders' (1971) and 'The Taste of Your Love' (1971) were selected by Richard Davis for his *Year's Best Horror* series. Further continental books include the collection *Something Small, Something Hungry* (1972; 15s), *Eye of the Vampire* (1973)—later expanded as *The Mark of the Vampire* (1974) in Germany—a large volume *Lonely Bloodbird* (1976; 1n, 9s) and a novel, *Dream Me to Death* (1977).
    Bertin also scripted and helped produce two psychological horror films and is currently working on several novels and story collections.

Pseudonyms: Edith Brendall, Doriac Greysun

Walter Besant (b. Portsea, Hants., 14 August 1836; d. London, 9 June 1901)
A prolific Victorian writer, Sir Walter Besant is best remembered today for the title story to the collection *The Case of Mr Lucraft* (1876; 12s) a strange variation on the pact-with-the-devil theme involving appetite rather than soul. It was written in collaboration with James Rice (1843-

1882), the editor of *Once a Week* with whom Besant wrote for all the Christmas issues of *All the Year Round* from 1872–82, when Besant continued alone till 1887. Besant showed an interest in the 'Jekyll & Hyde' theme, first in *The Doubts of Dives* (1889), a tale of identity exchange, and then in *The Ivory Gate* (1892). The former novel was included in his collection *Verbena Stephanotic Camellia* (1892; 2n, 2s) which also included the chilling novel of satanism, *The Demoniac*. Besant founded The Society of Authors in 1884.

Ambrose Bierce (b. Ohio, 24 June 1842; d. ?Mexico, *c* 1914)
A unique and gifted writer, Ambrose Gwinnett Bierce was born in a log cabin, the son of farmers. His overbearing father christened all his thirteen children with names beginning with A. After the Civil War, in which Bierce served in the Union Army and was severely wounded twice, he settled in San Francisco and took up journalism. He sold his first story, 'The Haunted Valley', in 1871. He married in Christmas that year and in 1872 visited England, where his fame grew. He became renowed for his misanthropic satire and caustic humour which earned him the nickname 'Bitter Bierce'. A few essays and stories saw limited edition publication, such as *The Fiend's Delight* (1872, as Dod Grile), and *The Dance of Death* (1877), written with Thomas Harcourt as William Herman. But Bierce failed to interest any editor in his many short stories until a San Francisco merchant financed a collection entitled *Tales of Soldiers and Civilians* (1891; 19s). It included his now famous Civil War dream story of a man facing inevitable death, 'An Occurrence at Owl Creek Bridge'. The success of the volume prompted *Can Such Things Be?* (1893; 37s) which cemented his fame.

Dreams, the workings of the mind and spiritual mastery over the physical fascinated Bierce more than the inexplicable supernatural. Stories like 'The Death of Halpin Frayser', 'The Realm of the Unreal' and 'John Bartine's Watch' look deeply into the mind and produce frightening results. Even when the supernatural enters his tales, as in 'The Middle Toe of the Right Foot', Bierce is more concerned with the mental anguish of the murderer than with the events. Bierce is thus the direct link between Poe and modern horror. He continued to write, often revising his collections. His first book saw official publication as *In The Midst of Life* (1898). He also compiled an amusing and thoroughly misanthropic *Devil's Dictionary* (1906).

By 1913 Bierce was weary of life, so settling his affairs he set off for Mexico where civil war was raging, on the trail of revolutionary Pancho Villa. He was never heard from again. Bierce's one-time collaborator Adolphe de Castro (1859–1959; *The Monk and the Hangman's Daughter*, 1892) later reported that Villa had shot Bierce, but it was never authenticated. The disappearance, which coincided with the vanishing of a certain

Ambrose Small, prompted Charles Fort to postulate that someone was collecting Ambroses. This later inspired Arthur J. Cox (b. 1929) to write 'A Collector of Ambroses' (1971).

Charles Birkin (b. Nottingham, 24 September 1907)
Sir Charles Lloyd Birkin, the son of Colonel Charles Birkin, succeeded his uncle as 5th Baronet Birkin in 1942. Earlier Birkin had been employed by the publisher Philip Allan for whom he edited the *Creeps* Library of anthologies (App. II), starting in 1932. Birkin had new stories of his own in most of the volumes and these were collected as *Devil's Spawn* (1936; 16s). They demonstrated his penchant for the *conte cruel*, emphasising the physical rather than supernatural side of horror. Birkin's writing was curtailed during the Second World War, and it was not until he took up residence in London in 1960 that he resumed. Then he experienced something of a revival. **Dennis Wheatley** heralded the return by specially including two new stories, 'A Right to Know', a grisly tale of a family curse, and 'A Lovely Bunch of Coconuts', in his paperback anthologies *Quiver of Horror* and *Shafts of Fear*; **van Thal** reprinted four early stories in *PH3*; and a new collection *The Kiss of Death* (1964; 15s) appeared. Since that year more collections have appeared: *The Smell of Evil* (1965; 13s), *Where Terror Stalked* (1966; 13s), *My Name is Death* (1966; 8s), *Dark Menace* (1968; 13s), *So Pale, So Cold* (1970; 9s), and *Spawn of Satan* (1971; 10s) the last-named published only in the US. To date his output just tops the 100-story mark.

All of Birkin's stories underline that evil is in man, not the spirit world, a philosophy admirably shown in his recent story 'A Low Profile' (1977), drawn from his experiences during the four years he lived in Cyprus until he was shelled out in 1974. Birkin also edited *The Tandem Book of Ghost Stories* (1965; 12s) and *The Tandem Book of Horror Stories* (1965; 11s), the latter being continued as a series by **Richard Davis**.

Pseudonym: Charles Lloyd

Gerald Biss
An early motor-car enthusiast, Biss (not Bliss as it is sometimes misspelt) is now solely remembered for his superlative werewolf novel *The Door of the Unreal* (1919). Among his earlier work is a weird novel of a macabre family curse, *The House of Terror* (1909), and an intriguing mystery, *The Fated Five* (1910). He was last heard of living in Hertfordshire in the early 1920s.

John F. Blackburn (b. Northumberland, 26 June 1923)
Described by the *Times Literary Supplement* as 'today's master of horror',
John Fenwick Blackburn was educated at Haileybury and Durham
University and served in the Merchant Navy during the Second World
War. Before taking up writing full-time he worked as a lorry driver, a
schoolmaster in London and Berlin, and for a time he and his wife ran an
antiquarian bookshop in Richmond.

His first novel, *A Scent of New-Mown Hay* (1958), concerned an un-
usually intelligent fungus and was a Literary Guild Choice in the US.
Since then, Blackburn has produced an average of more than one novel
per year, mainly devoted to horror and covering a wide field. They include *A Ring of Roses* (1965) with its revival of the Black Death, *Children
of the Night* (1966), in which murders are committed by a malignant
psychic force, *Nothing But the Night* (1968), where an occultist is called
in to solve some bizarre murders, *Bury Him Darkly* (1969), where evil
forces are released from an old tomb, *Blow the House Down* (1970), *For
Fear of Little Men* (1972), *Devil Daddy* (1972) and *Our Lady of Pain*
(1974), about the Evil Eye and a reincarnation of Elizabeth Bathori. His
most recent book *The Cyclops Goblet* (1977) is an attempt to merge horror
with humour.

Blackburn's work has seen many translations and has been filmed,
televised and serialised on radio. He has recently written a number of
short stories including a mild piece of erotica, 'Jenny Cut-Throat' (1976)
for the anthology *The Devil's Kisses*. His brother, the poet Thomas
Blackburn, has also written a novel of vampirism and possession, *The
Feast of the Wolf* (1971).

Algernon Blackwood (b. London, 14 March 1869; d. 10 December
1951)
Known familiarly to British audiences through his radio and television
appearances as 'the Ghost Man', Blackwood ranks as one of the top
horror writers in the world. The son of Sir Stevenson Blackwood, he
had a diverse education including Wellington College, the Moravian
Brotherhood and Edinburgh University. As if in rebellion to his strict
religious upbringing, young Algernon studied Oriental religions and the
occult, and became well versed in their lore. He was known later to have
joined certain occult societies. When Blackwood was 20 his father
despatched him to Canada on a meagre allowance, and there he spent
several bleak years before he entered the US and became a reporter on
the New York *Sun*. But his many experiences served as inspiration for
his stories.

Returning to Britain in the late 1890s he began to place his tales with
the popular magazines, starting with 'A Haunted Island' (1899), a narrative in first person set in the remote Canadian backwoods on an island

haunted by a murderous Indian. An acquaintance of Blackwood's sent these stories to a publisher, and the result was *The Empty House* (1906; 10s), followed by *The Listener* (1907; 9s) and *John Silence* (1908; 5s). The last was a series about an occult investigator. Blackwood had originally planned them as essays about his own psychic experiences, but fictionalised them at the publisher's behest. In essence John Silence is Blackwood, and it is Blackwood's intense involvement with his fiction that makes it all so real and thus more terrifying. He wrote over 150 stories during his long career, but the bulk appear in the ten collections up to *Tongues of Fire* (1924; 21s). The others are *The Lost Valley* (1910; 10s), *Pan's Garden* (1912; 15s), *Incredible Adventures* (1914; 5s), *Ten Minute Stories* (1914; 29s), *Day and Night Stories* (1917; 15s) and *The Wolves of God* (1921; 15s), written with Wilfred Wilson. All later collections were mostly reprints, a notable selection made by Blackwood himself being *Strange Stories* (1929; 26s).

He also wrote a few novels slanted more toward junior readers such as *Jimbo* (1909), *The Human Chord* (1910) and *The Wave* (1916)—about reincarnation—plus several humorous short fantasies and plays. These are now nearly forgotten while his short fiction is constantly reprinted. Among the best-known tales are 'The Wendigo', the monstrous forest demon, 'The Willows' and the frightening island in the Danube, the werewolf tale 'Running Wolf', the spirit that lingers on in 'The Listener', and his most reprinted story 'Ancient Sorceries', the John Silence adventure involving witches and cats. Nearly every one of his stories was inspired by some incident in his life. Remembering that makes one think twice before turning out the light.

Mrs Hubert (or E.) Bland: *see* Edith Nesbit

Wyatt Blassingame (b. Demopolis, Ala., 6 February 1909)
Today, Wyatt Rainey Blassingame is best remembered for his children's novels and standard reference works like *Great Trains of the World* (1953) and *The Navy's Frogmen in World War II* (1963). All but forgotten is the fact that during the 1930s he was one of the leading contributors to the terror pulps. He was also one of the few among them who worked supernatural elements into the tales of gore, as in 'The Horror at His Heels' (1936), in which an archaeologist is suddenly found dead, buried under stones that had been undisturbed for centuries. Most of his stories though, by convention, had natural solutions. They will be found chiefly in *Dime Mystery* and *Terror Tales*.

Pseudonym: W. B. Rainey

Helena P. Blavatsky (b. South Russia, 31 July 1831; d. 8 May 1891)
As the founder of Theosophy, Madame Helena Petrovna Blavatsky was at the forefront of the surge of interest in the occult during the mid-1800s. The daughter of novelist Helena von Hahn, she travelled widely in her youth with her father, and this wanderlust stayed with her even when she married in 1848—she soon left her husband to travel further. Her accounts of her travels are so unreliable that one can never be quite sure if she did enter forbidden Tibet, from whence came her inspiration! Her interest in the occult stemmed from meeting the medium Daniel Home (1833–86), and she began to create a sensation with her own séances. Failing to establish an occult society in Europe, India or Egypt she finally settled in the US in 1873, and in September 1875 formed the Theosophical Society. Based on Egyptian occultism it simply called for the brotherhood of man and the study of religion and the occult. Despite various scandals and exposés, she gathered a large following. She wrote a number of books on the subject including *Isis Unveiled* (1877), *The Secret Doctrine* (1888) and *Key to Theosophy* (1889). She became a naturalised American in 1878 but continued to travel, spending her last years in India, Italy and London. Her fiction was less common and was often intermingled with her other works. A set of stories written in London were published as *Nightmare Tales* (1892; 5s) and include her best-known 'The Ensouled Violin'. But they read more like texts and lack the spontaneity and involvement of good fiction. Her *Collected Works* was edited by A. Trevor Barker in three volumes (1933–36).

Christopher Blayre: *see* Edward Heron-Allen

Robert Bloch (b. Chicago, 5 April 1917)
Bloch has been immortalised by **Alfred Hitchcock** as 'the author of *Psycho*', one of the most popular shock films ever made. His interest in horror stemmed from being frightened by Lon Chaney's *Phantom of the Opera*. He later became a devoted reader of *Weird Tales* and a fan of **H. P. Lovecraft** with whom he corresponded. Lovecraft advised him on the craft of fiction and Bloch emulated his style. His first story in print, 'Lilies' (1934), told of an old woman who continues to deliver flowers after her death; his first professional sale was 'The Secret in the Tomb' (1935) about a man whose ancestor was a ghoul.
Most of Bloch's early sales were Lovecraftian, modelled on the Cthulhu Mythos, but during the 1940s he broadened his market. Besides sf and detective stories, he began to write humorous fantasies such as the adventures of layabout Lefty Feep, which began with 'Time Wounds All Heels' (1942). He also developed the psychological horror story, penning

the most crucial story of his early career—'Yours Truly, Jack the Ripper' (1943) in which the search for the Ripper continues in modern America. It was adapted for radio and led to Bloch scripting thirty-nine of his stories for the radio series *Stay Tuned For Terror* (1944). His first collection followed, *The Opener of the Way* (1945; 21s), but thereafter he concentrated on macabre mystery novels starting with *The Scarf* (1947) and including *The Kidnapper* (1954), *Spiderweb* (1954), *The Will to Kill* (1954) and the all-important *Psycho* (1959). Adapted for the screen by Joseph Stefano, it opened many doors for Bloch in the film industry and his name will often be seen among the credits for adapting his own or others' work. His own films include *Torture Garden* (1966), *The House That Dripped Blood* (1970) and *Asylum* (1972) and other writers have adapted some of Bloch's stories, such as *The Skull* (1965) scripted by **Milton Subotsky**. Other novels include *The Dead Beat* (1960), *Firebug* (1961), *The Couch* (1962), *Terror* (1962), about Kali worship, *Night Walker* (1964, effectively filmed that year), and most recently *American Gothic* (1974), a fictionalised account based on true events in the life of a mass murderer in Chicago in 1893.

He continued to write many stories and these have been collected as *Pleasant Dreams* (1960; 15s), *Blood Runs Cold* (1961; 17s), *Atoms and Evil* (1962; 13s), *More Nightmares* (1962; 10s), *Yours Truly, Jack the Ripper* (1962; 9s: UK *The House of the Hatchet*, 1965), *Bogey Men* (1963; 10s), *Horror-7* (1963; 7s), *The Skull of the Marquis de Sade* (1965; 7s), *Tales in a Jugular Vein* (1965; 10s), *Chamber of Horrors* (1966; 12s), *The Living Demons* (1967; 12s) and *Dragons and Nightmares* (1969; 4s) the last-named being a collection of his humorous fantasies. He achieved the paradoxical in 1959 by winning the *science fiction* Hugo award for his fantasy 'That Hell-Bound Train' (1958). In 1975 he was Guest of Honour at the First World Fantasy Convention where he received a Life Award for his contribution to the genre. One may even think he has turned full circle: a recent story, 'A Most Unusual Murder' (1976), centred on the Jack the Ripper murders, and Bloch is currently working on a new Cthulhu Mythos novel, *The Black Brotherhood*.

Pseudonyms: Tarleton Fiske, Will Folke, Nathan Hindin, Wilson Kane, John Sheldon

Hannes Bok (b. Minnesota, 2 July 1914; d. New York, 11 April 1964) It is as an artist more than a writer that Hannes Vajn Bok is remembered, although he was equally accomplished at both. An admirer and pupil of Maxfield Parrish he soon adopted a style of his own, the results looking much like woodcuts. He drew the covers for **Ray Bradbury**'s fan magazine *Futuria Fantasia* in 1939–40, and it was Bradbury who brought Bok's work to the notice of **Farnsworth Wright**, who commissioned

39

Bok to illustrate *Weird Tales*. His first cover illustrated **Keller's** 'Lords of the Ice' on the December 1939 issue.

Thereafter Bok's work appeared in many weird and sf magazines, but as the income was small he turned to writing, selling first to **R. A. W. Lowndes.** A fan of **A. Merritt,** and a friend of his widow, he emulated his style in novels like *Starstone World* (1942) where a man finds himself, after a car accident, in a world governed by the laws of magic, *The Sorcerer's Ship* (1942) and *The Blue Flamingo* (1948). The second saw book publication in 1969, and the full version of the third appeared as *Beyond the Golden Stair* (1970). He wrote as an artist, creating bizarre word-pictures. He also completed Merritt's two unfinished stories *The Fox Woman* (Bok's addition was called *The Blue Pagoda* (1946)), and *The Black Wheel* (1947).

Bok drifted away from the field in the 1950s to concentrate on astrology, and died of a heart attack when he was 50. His life-long friend **Emil Petaja** set up the Bokonalia Foundation to perpetuate the memory of Bok and his work, and he has published several portfolios and books about Bok, notably *And Flight of Angels* (1968).

Pseudonyms: Dolbokov (with Boris Dolgov), for artwork

Guy Boothby (b. Adelaide, 13 October 1867; d. Boscombe, Hants., 26 February 1905)
Boothby's grandfather had emigrated to Australia from England in 1853, and in 1874 Guy Newell Boothby was sent to England for his education. Returning to Australia in 1883 he held several jobs, including Private Secretary to the Mayor of Adelaide, and even crossed Australia north to south, out of which came his first book *On the Wallaby* (1894). That year he settled at Bournemouth in England where he married, bred cattle and horses, and wrote.

His success came with *A Bid For Fortune* (1895), the first of a series about occult adventurer Dr Nikola, and his search for immortality. It was followed by *Dr Nikola* (1896), *The Lust of Hate* (1898), *Dr Nikola's Experiment* (1899) and *'Farewell, Nikola'* (1901). The stories are straight adventure, precursors of **Sax Rohmer's** Fu Manchu. Boothby wrote some fifty books in all including other occult thrillers like *A Lost Endeavour* (1895), *Pharos the Egyptian* (1899) and *The Curse of the Snake* (1902), plus a collection of ghost stories *The Lady of the Island* (1904; 11s). He died unexpectedly of influenza at the age of 37.

Sydney J. Bounds (b. Brighton, 4 November 1920)
Although a frequent contributor to the Fontana *Ghost, Horror* and *Frighteners* series, Sydney James Bounds has had no collection of his

stories published. Yet for twenty years during the 1950s and '60s he was a full-time writer, mostly of science fiction and westerns. He sold his first horror story during the Second World War, but it never appeared and is probably now lost. His first in print was 'Strange Portrait' (1946) which follows the Dorian Grey theme. Bounds's horror stories are usually brief vignettes aimed at a clever plot twist as in 'The Relic' (1969), when a hunchback's hump comes alive, or 'The Mask' (1974) that takes control.

Pseudonyms: James Marshal and Wes Saunders (for westerns)

Elizabeth Bowen (b. Dublin, 7 June 1899; d. London, 22 February 1973) Primarily through her novel *The Death of the Heart* (1938), Elizabeth Bowen was regarded as one of the leading twentieth-century English novelists. She wrote a number of weird short stories, most of them using supernatural elements indirectly to explore human reactions to fear, as in her two best-known stories 'The Demon Lover' and 'The Cat Jumps' (1929) both set in houses where the dead return. Her stories have been collected as *Encounters* (1923; 14s), *Joining Charles* (1929; 11s), *The Cat Jumps* (1934; 12s) and *The Demon Lover* (1945; 12s). *Look At All Those Roses* (1941; 19s: 1967; 14s) and *A Day in the Dark* (1965; 20s) are mostly reprint volumes.

Marjorie Bowen (b. Hayling Island, Hants., 29 October 1886; d. London, 23 December 1952)
Mrs Gabrielle Margaret Vere Campbell Long used a variety of pen names to write historical, general and weird novels and short stories. Her best-known horror alias was Marjorie Bowen, which she used on her early success *Black Magic* (1909) concerning the rise of an Antichrist and involving satanism and witchcraft.

Born into a poor family she had to write prolifically to support her extravagant mother and sister. As George R. Preedy she wrote two short weird novels, *Dr Chaos, and The Devil Snar'd* (1933; 2n), while as Robert Paye she produced a most unusual novel *Julia Roseing Rave* (1933). *The Cheats* (1920), on the other hand, is a romantic fantasy. She had a talent for sustaining an atmosphere in her ghost stories even when, as was often the case, the ghosts were harmless as in 'The Crown Derby Plate'. Her collections include *Curious Happenings* (1917; 12s), *Sheep's Head and Babylon* (1929; 18s), *The Last Bouquet* (1932), and *The Bishop of Hell* (1949; 12s). She also edited two anthologies, *Great Tales of Horror* (1933; 29s) and *More Great Tales of Horror* (1935; 26s), translating some of the French stories herself.

Pseudonyms: Margaret Campbell, Robert Paye, George R. Preedy, Joseph Shearing, John Winch

41

Ray Bradbury (b. Waukegan, Ill., 22 August 1920)

Ironically Raymond Douglas Bradbury is one of the best-known and most highly-respected science fiction writers, but the truth is he writes fantasy. His renowned volume of connected tales about the colonisation of Mars, *The Martian Chronicles* (1950; UK, *The Silver Locusts*, 1951) is set on a fantasy Mars that was known not to exist even when he wrote them. Only a very small percentage of his output is pure science fiction, but a very large amount is weird, off-trail and horrific.

He began as an avid sf fan, editing his own fanzine *Futuria Fantasia* for four issues (1939–40), every one carrying stories of his own. 'The Pendulum' (1939), later rewritten by Henry Hasse, became his first professional sale (1941). But sales were elusive and he is reputed to have thrown away millions of words of fiction until **Dorothy McIlwraith** allowed him free rein in *Weird Tales*. He made twenty-five appearances there including 'The Candle' (1942), 'The Wind' (1943), 'The Crowd' (1943), 'The Jar' (1944) and 'Let's Play "Poison"' (1946), all macabre word pictures, many showing the inherent yet innocent evil in children. These stories composed his first collection, *Dark Carnival* (1947; 27s). By then he was selling to all the major magazines, developing his unique style, and his fiction—though always bizarre—was often non-fantastic. His later collections include *The Illustrated Man* (1951; 18s), *Golden Apples of the Sun* (1953; 22s), *Dandelion Wine* (1957; 17s), *A Medicine for Melancholy* (1959; 22s: UK *The Day it Rained Forever*, 1959; 23s) and *The Machineries of Joy* (1964; 21s). Most other collections are reworkings of these, such as *The October Country* (1955; 19s) and *The Small Assassin* (1962; 13s), though the recent *Long After Midnight* (1976; 22s) includes some new material.

Bradbury prefers the short story medium and has often adapted his stories to plays and occasionally film and television scripts. He wrote the screenplay for *Moby Dick* (1956). His novels are little more than long short stories and are generally aimed at young readers. His best is *Something Wicked This Way Comes* (1962), about eerie happenings at a carnival. Others are *Switch on the Night* (1955) and *The Hallowe'en Tree* (1972). He edited the anthologies *The Circus of Dr Lao and Other Improbable Stories* (1956; 12s) and *Timeless Stories For Today and Tomorrow* (1952; 26s).

Pseudonyms: D. R. Banat, Edward Banks, Leonard Douglas, William Elliott, Don Reynolds, Leonard Spaulding

Ernest Bramah (b. Manchester, 20 March 1868; d. Somerset, 27 June 1942)

Throughout his career Ernest Bramah Smith kept himself to himself. He was initially a farmer, writing a book about it in 1894, then a journalist and editor. His first fiction was a series of stories set in the traditional mythical China full of dragons and mandarins, loosely connected by the narrator Kai Lung. Like Scheherazade, he tells his tales to delay punishment for his alleged crimes. The tales have a charm that will sustain their delight for a handful of devotees for many years. Bramah wrote five books about Kai Lung, *The Wallet of Kai Lung* (1900), *Kai Lung's Golden Hours* (1922), *Kai Lung Unrolls His Mat* (1928), *The Moon of Much Gladness* (1932) and *Kai Lung Beneath the Mulberry Tree* (1940). A selection of the best appeared as *The Celestial Omnibus* (1963; 11s), and the remaining uncollected stories were assembled by a non-professional US publisher as *Kai Lung: Six* (1974). Apart from one sf novel about socialism, *What Might Have Been* (1907; retitled *The Secret of the League*), and further Chinese fantasies, *The Mirror of Kung Ho* (1905), Bramah wrote a series about a blind detective, Max Carrados. A few of these, such as 'The Ghost at Massingham Mansions', have mystical overtones but natural solutions.

Joseph Payne Brennan (b. Bridgeport, Conn., 20 December 1918)
An active writer and poet in the mystery and horror fields for a quarter of a century, Brennan has not received the recognition he deserves. He had submitted fiction to *Weird Tales* in his teens, with no success, and the lack of spare time after his father's death in 1938 caused him to concentrate more on poetry, selling his first piece in 1940. After the war, in which his unit received four battle stars, Brennan sold seventeen western stories before making *Weird Tales* with the brief ghost story 'The Green Parrot' (1952). Three more followed, including his famous 'Slime' (1953) about the horror in the swamp, before the magazine folded. In the gap left by its passing Brennan launched his own little magazine, *Macabre*, in 1957 (App. III). All this time he worked as a senior assistant at Yale University Library. Brennan's stories hinge predominantly on encounters with regions having a creepy and haunting atmosphere, often set around the village of Juniper Hill. His collections include *9 Horrors and a Dream* (1959; 10s), *The Dark Returners* (1959; 9s), *Scream at Midnight* (1963; 9s) and *Stories of Darkness and Dread* (1973; 18s). He has also written a series about psychic detective Lucius Leffing, not all with supernatural solutions, published as *The Casebook of Lucius Leffing* (1973; 17s) and *Chronicles of Lucius Leffing* (1977; 18s). He has several published volumes of verse to his name.

Leo Brett: *see* R. L. Fanthorpe

D. K. Broster (b. 1877; d. Battle, Sussex, 7 February 1950)
From her first book *Chantemerle* (1911) Dorothy Kathleen Broster was regarded as a leading British historical novelist. She is best remembered in the horror field for 'Couching at the Door', about a poet whose evil past haunts him in the tangible form of a malignant feather boa! Two collections exist, *A Fire of Driftwood* (1932; 13s) and *Couching at the Door* (1942; 5s), and with G. Forester she penned the fantastic adventure *World Under Snow* (1935).

Rhoda Broughton (b. Denbigh, Wales, 29 November 1840; d. Oxon, 5 June 1920)
A popular Victorian novelist who wrote about country life, she was the niece (by marriage) of **Sheridan Le Fanu**, who bought her first novel in 1867. He encouraged her writing, yet despite his influence she wrote few ghost stories. They were collected as *Tales For Christmas Eve* (1873), later reissued and enlarged as *Twilight Stories* (1879; 5s).

Charles Brockden Brown (b. Philadelphia, 17 January 1771; d. Phila., 22 February 1810)
Brown is regarded as America's first professional writer. He trained as a lawyer, but abandoned that with his first book *Alcuin* (1797), a dull dialogue on women's rights. It was followed by his Gothic masterpiece *Wieland* (1798), about a religious fanatic who hears voices that drive him mad. Later works were *Ormond*, *Arthur Mervyn* and *Edgar Huntly* (all 1799), a terrifying portrayal of a sleepwalker. His writing skill creates a frightening atmosphere, but the natural explanations are a disappointment. But here he foreshadowed **Poe** in his depiction of psychopathological horror rather than supernatural. Brown later entered politics, but contracted consumption in 1809 and died aged 39.

Valery Bryusov (b. Moscow, 13 December 1873; d. Moscow, 9 October 1924)
Valery Yakovlevich Bryusov (or Brussof) was a leading Russian symbolist writer and poet. His fiction is full of imagery, aimed primarily at highlighting the oppression of the workers. This is evident in the title story to his translated collection *The Republic of the Southern Cross* (US, 1919; 9s), about a community of millions of workers at the South Pole threatened by a mysterious epidemic. His novel, *The Fiery Angel* (Russia, 1907) is concerned with witchcraft in Germany at the time of Luther.

John Buchan (b. Perth, Scotland, 20 August 1875; d. Montreal, 11 February 1940)
Buchan's name is so indelibly connected with the spy thriller *The 39 Steps* (1915) that most of his other work, especially that in the weird field, is overlooked. Yet his interest in the supernatural is clear from his early stories, such as those collected in *Grey Weather* (1899; 15s). His standard weird volume is *The Watcher By The Threshold* (1902; 5s: rev. 1922; 8s), whose title story deals with a man oppressed by an evil presence. Buchan's legal and political career, which made him 1st Baron Tweedsmuir in 1935 and Governor-General of Canada for his last five years, did not stop his literary output. Other weird volumes are *The Moon Endureth* (1912), *The Runagates Club* (1928; 12s), which includes his popular 'The Green Wildebeest', *Witch Wood* (1922) and *The Gap in the Curtain* (1932; 6s); the adventurous *Prester John* (1910) is also of interest.

Gerald Bullett (b. London, 30 December 1893; d. 3 January 1958)
Gerald William Bullett worked as a bank clerk before devoting himself to writing, producing over forty books in all. His weird stories have a compelling aura of evil, and there is none better than 'Dearth's Farm', with the frightening implication of the horse with the malignant grin! This tale was in Bullett's first collection *The Street of the Eye* (1923; 10s). A later volume was *The Baker's Cart* (1925; 13s), and two novels of note are *Mr Godly Beside Himself* (1924) and *The Quick and the Dead* (1933). He also wrote a study of *The English Mystics* (1950).

Lord Bulwer-Lytton (b. London, 25 May 1803; d. Torquay, Devon, 18 January 1873)
Sir Edward Bulwer-Lytton's name grew longer through his life as he rose through the nobility, becoming Lord Lytton in 1866. His marriage in 1827 cut off most of his allowance and he was forced to write vigorously for a living. He produced a vast output and is best remembered today for his historical works like *The Last Days of Pompeii* (1834). But closest to his heart were his occult stories. The supernatural had fascinated him since his youth; one early ghost story was 'Glenallan' (1826). Other early pieces like 'The Tale of Kosem Kosamim the Magician' (1832) and *Zicci* (1838) served as partial drafts for *Zanoni* (1842), a huge novel dealing with a secret French occult society. He later wrote a long occult novel of a search for immortality, *A Strange Story* (1861), but his most effective piece is 'The Haunted and the Haunters' (1859) also known as 'The House and the Brain' which **Lovecraft** called 'one of the best short haunted-house tales ever written'. A later novel of interest is *The Coming Race* (1871), set in a bizarre society under the Earth.

John F. Burke (b. Rye, Sussex, 8 March 1922)
John Frederick Burke was an integral member of early British sf fandom, and a close friend of John Christopher and Charles Eric Maine. This proved his main market during the 1950s. In 1963 he became London story editor for Twentieth Century-Fox, and this has resulted in his name appearing on many books-of-the-films, including several horror film adaptations like *Dr Terror's House of Horrors* (1965) and also *The Hammer Horror Omnibus* (1966; 4s) and *The Second Hammer Horror Film Omnibus* (1967; 4s). He has also edited the anthology series of both new and reprint fiction *Tales of Unease* (1966; 21s), *More Tales of Unease* (1969; 22s) and *New Tales of Unease* (1976; 16s). His own short fiction may be found in several of the *Ghost Book* volumes.

Thomas Burke (b. London, November 1886; d. London, 22 September 1945)
This gifted writer was orphaned in infancy and many of his stories read like attempts to capture the lost youth that might have been. He is best remembered for the books that popularised the Chinatown area of London: *Limehouse Nights* (1916; 14s), *Whispering Windows* (1920; 18s), *East of Mansion House* (1926; 12s) and *The Pleasantries of Old Quong* (1931; 16s). They range from the macabre murder mystery 'The Hands of Mr Ottermole', to the charming fantasy of 'The Golden Gong' that summons a beautiful lady. Later collections were *Night Pieces* (1935; 18s) and *Dark Nights* (1944; 12s), the latter including his earlier short fantasy novel *The Bloomsbury Wonder* (1929). After his death **John Gawsworth** edited a volume of his *Best Short Stories* (1950; 20s).

Arthur J. Burks (b. 13 September 1898; d. 1974)
Dubbed 'Speed Merchant of the Pulps', Burks could sit and write instantly for almost any market. His first sales were in 1920 and by 1928 his income was sufficient for him to forsake the Army, in which he was a lieutenant, to write full-time. His early market was *Weird Tales*, to which he submitted a score of black magic stories starting with 'Thus Spake the Prophetess' (1924), but during the 1930s he wrote more for the better-paying terror pulps, though *Strange Tales* carried two of his best, 'The Place of the Pythons' and 'Guatemozin the Visitant' (both 1931).

Legends abound about Burks, such as the one about the editor who requested that Burks take his time and write a serial. Burks churned out the novel overnight but waited a few weeks before taking it to the editor who, after reading it, said 'See how much better you do when you take your time'. Burks never revised a story, so any rejections just piled up. It was known that writers suffering a dry spell would, with his permission, slightly rework a reject and sell it. Thus the full extent of Burks's output will probably never be known. Despite his near non-stop writing Burks had time to organise the American Fiction Guild. During the Second World War he supervised the training of Marines. He wrote less after the war, but lectured on psychic and supernatural topics. Two collections of his weird stories are *Look Behind You* (1954; 6s) and *Black Medicine* (1966; 16s).

Pseudonyms: Estil Critchie, Spencer Whitney

A. M. Burrage (b. Hillingdon, Middx., 1 July 1889; d. 18 December 1956)

Alfred McLelland Burrage was a well-known English novelist who wrote short weird stories as a regular part of his output. An early collection was *Some Ghost Stories* (1927; 13s) but his best are those masked by the alias 'Ex-Private X' in *Someone in the Room* (1931; 14s). They include 'The Sweeper', a ghost which annually creeps nearer a house, and the famous tale of the reporter who spends a night in the Chamber of Horrors, 'The Waxwork'. A recent selection of the best was *Between the Minute and the Hour* (1967; 14s). Burrage also wrote two weird novels, *Seeker to the Dead* (1942), about immortality and black magic, and *Don't Break the Seal* (1946).

Pseudonym: Ex-Private X

Edgar Rice Burroughs (b. Chicago, 1 September 1875; d. Tarzana, Calif., 19 March 1950)

Burroughs really belongs in the annals of science fiction with his adventures set on Mars, Venus, inside the Earth, in lost lands and elsewhere. But they are all essentially fantasy, and his development of larger-than-life humans like John Carter and especially Tarzan, is as much a basis of heroic fantasy as the works of **Morris** and **Dunsany**. **R. E. Howard** followed in the footsteps of Burroughs, and his influence is as strong today, particularly in the early inspiration of **Michael Moorcock**, and currently in the many emulative novels by **Lin Carter**.

James Branch Cabell (b. Richmond, Va., 14 April 1879; d. 5 May 1958)

There are writers who follow in the footsteps of others, and there are those who write as they wish and in so doing strike a rich vein that is entirely individual. Cabell belonged to the latter group. He owes his fame to having had his bawdy fantasy *Jurgen* (1919) banned, and thereby guaranteed sales! *Jurgen* is set in the fantasy world of Poictesme, roughly equatable with southern France, but populated with all the trappings of make-believe.

Cabell's first story sale was 'An Amateur Ghost' (1902), about a young man persuaded by the ghosts of his ancestors to haunt an old castle. Cabell enjoyed experimenting with genealogical charts and these evolved into the plan of the royal family that became the backbone of his Poictesme series. The first written was *The Line of Love* (1905), but first published was *The Eagle's Shadow* (1904). The novels were not written in strict chronological order of fictional events, and the reading order of the final published volumes runs: *Figures of Earth* (1921), *The Silver Stallion* (1926), *The Witch Woman* (1948; 3s), *The Soul of Melicent* (1913; rev. *Domnei*, 1920), *Chivalry* (1909), *Jurgen*, *The Line of Love*, *The High Place* (1923), *Gallantry* (1907), *Something About Eve* (1927), *The Certain Hour* (1916), *The Cords of Vanity* (1909), *From the Hidden Way* (1916), *The Jewel Merchants* (1921), *The Rivet in Grandfather's Neck* (1915), *The Eagle's Shadow*, *The Cream of the Jest* (1917), *The Lineage of Lichfield* (1922), plus several non-fiction books. Cabell also wrote a few straight weird novels such as *Smire* (1937) and *The Devil's Own Son* (1949).

Sir Andrew Caldecott (b. nr Maidstone, Kent, 26 October 1884; d. Sussex, 14 July 1951)
Caldecott was a civil servant who entered the Malay Service in 1907 and rose to the highest positions in the outposts of the Empire. A man of many talents—painter, poet, pianist—after his retirement in 1944 he turned to writing, composing several ghost stories much in the vein of M. R. James. Many reflected his colonial life, set in a fictional Kongea. They comprise two volumes, *Not Exactly Ghosts* (1946; 12s) and *Fires Burn Blue* (1948; 13s).

Ramsey Campbell (b. Liverpool, 4 January 1946)
When **August Derleth** bought and published 'The Church in High Street' in 1962, John Ramsey Campbell became one of the youngest recruits to horror fiction. Since then he has written several score stories, a novel, and is regarded as one of the leading British talents in the field.

He began as a disciple of **H. P. Lovecraft**, imitating the Cthulhu Mythos and under Derleth's direction establishing a milieu of his own in England. Those stories formed his first collection *The Inhabitant of the Lake* (1964; 10s) and several subsequent stories. His talent was soon recognised, and **Robert Lowndes** said that 'he makes the effort to be fresh and individual'. Leaving school in 1962 Campbell worked first for the Inland Revenue and then in a library until he became a full-time writer and film reviewer in 1973. During those years he developed, casting off the mantle of Lovecraft and using his own abilities to create frightening images in commonplace surroundings, as evidenced in his second volume *Demons By Daylight* (1973; 14s). His work now appears regularly in most leading UK and US anthologies and includes his stunning story 'Call First' (1975), in which a man is trapped by a guardian ghost.

Unlike many writers Campbell gives public readings of his own stories, very effectively. He has recently edited the anthology *Superhorror* (1976; 9s), published *The Doll Who Ate His Mother* (1976), a novel about a man driven to do inhuman things by an occult influence, and completed a new collection *The Height of the Scream* (1976; 18s). He is also compiling an original anthology, *New Tales of the Cthulhu Mythos*, and working on his new novel, a psychological thriller called *The Face That Must Die*. He has also completed several Solomon Kane stories by **Robert E. Howard** which should see publication in two volumes in 1978. Under the house pseudonym Carl Dreadstone he has written the novels of the films *The Wolfman*, *Bride of Frankenstein* and *Dracula's Daughter* (all 1977).

Pseudonyms: Montgomery Comfort (house), Carl Dreadstone (house), Errol Undercliffe

Robert S. Carr (b. Washington, D.C., 26 March 1909)
Robert Spencer Carr found overnight success with his novel of teenage life, *The Rampant Age* (1926). Prior to this he sold several stories to *Weird Tales*, the best known being the tale of an Egyptian tomb, 'Spiderbite' (1926). Carr owed much to **Farnsworth Wright** for his encouragement and advice with his first novel. After its success Carr left the pulps for Hollywood, later becoming a scriptwriter for Walt Disney. He sold several fantasy stories to mass circulation magazines and some were collected as *Beyond Infinity* (1951; 4s). A fantasy novel was *The Room Beyond* (1948).

Angela Carter (b. Eastbourne, Sussex, 7 May 1940)
If anyone has carved a special niche as a writer of what can only be termed Gothic science fiction, it is Angela Carter. She says of the genre that 'only horror fiction is a true reflection of the times we live in; only fantasy is true to life'. This philosophy she has proved in a handful of novels which also emphasise the growing loss of innocence by youth in a world both real and unreal.

Her books are *Shadow Dance* (1966), *The Magic Toyshop* (1967), which won the John Llewelyn Rhys Memorial Prize, *Several Perceptions* (1968), which won the Somerset Maugham Award, *Heroes and Villains* (1969), her purest science fiction work, set on a nuclear devastated Earth, *Love* (1971), *The Infernal Desire Machines of Dr Hoffman* (1972), and a fascinating collection *Fireworks* (1974; 9s), perhaps her most bizarre book. Her latest novel is *The Passion of New Eve* (1977). She is currently working on a study of the Marquis de Sade, a translation of Perrault's

Fairy Tales, plus new fairy tales of her own. She also wrote the radio play, *Vampirella* (1976).

Lin Carter (b. St Petersburg, Fla., 9 June 1930)
Linwood Vrooman Carter, to give him his full name and correct gender, is one of America's most prolific fantasy writers. An active member of sf fandom during the 1950s, Carter amassed an enviable collection of fantasy books that has made him an acknowledged expert in the field. He sold a few short stories at that time, but first came to prominence with his series of novels about the mighty swordsman Thongor, set at the dawn of civilisation. The series reflects Carter's love for the fiction of **Burroughs** and **Howard**. The titles include *The Wizard of Lemuria* (1965), *Thongor of Lemuria* (1966), *Thongor Against the Gods* (1968), *Thongor at the End of Time* (1968), *Thongor Fights the Pirates of Tarakus* (1970).

Carter's ability to emulate rather than simply copy a writer's work enabled him capably to assist **L. Sprague de Camp** in completing and writing new Howard-style Conan stories, as well as finalising the *King Kull* (1967; 13s) stories. He has also written further Burroughs-style novels in his *Jandar* and *Green Star* series, plus others in the mould of van Vogt and 'Doc Savage'. Another fantasy series is set on the last continent of Gondwaneland on a Dying Earth: *Giant of World's End* (1969), *The Warrior of World's End* (1974), *The Enchantress of World's End* (1975), *The Immortal of World's End* (1976) and *The Barbarian of World's End* (1977). Non-series novels of interest include *Tower at the Edge of Time* (1968), *Lost World of Time* (1969) and *The Quest of Kadji* (1971). He has also written many short stories in a variety of series, not least his imitation-Dunsany 'Simrana' stories, and the completion of several Clark Ashton Smith fragments. A selection appeared as *Beyond The Gates Of Dream* (1972; 7s).

In 1969 Carter became Editorial Consultant for the Ballantine Adult Fantasy series and under his guidance a wonderful array of lost work was 'resurrected'. He edited several anthologies for the series including *The Young Magicians* (1969; 18s), *Dragons, Elves, and Heroes* (1969; 14s) and *Golden Cities, Far* (1970; 13s), which traced the development of fantasy; plus several supporting anthologies—*New Worlds For Old* (1971; 15s), *The Spawn of Cthulhu* (1971; 12s), *Discoveries in Fantasy* (1972; 7s) and *Great Short Novels of Adult Fantasy, Vol. I* (1972; 4s) and *Vol. II* (1973; 4s). He also edited three reference books for the series, *Tolkien: A Look Behind the Lord of the Rings* (1969), *Lovecraft: A Look Behind the Cthulhu Mythos* (1972) and *Imaginary Worlds* (1973). Among his other anthologies are *The Magic of Atlantis* (1970; 7s), the series *Flashing Swords!* (1973–7), currently in four volumes, *Realms of Wizardry* (1976; 16s), and since 1975 the annual *Year's Best Fantasy Stories*.

David Case (b. New York, 22 December 1937)
David Francis Case arrived with a bang with his collection *The Cell* (1969; 3s). It caused **Gahan Wilson** to observe that he 'is an author who deserves to be closely watched'. The title story is a frightening psychopathic view of lycanthropy, and the other stories bear comparison with **Blackwood**. The three were promptly chosen by **van Thal** for *PH 11, 12* and *13*, by which time his second collection, *Fengriffen* (1971; 3s), had appeared. The lead story, a compelling tale of the enactment of a family curse, was subsequently filmed as —*And Now the Screaming Starts* (1972), and the other two appeared in *PH 14* and *15*. Thereafter Case mysteriously disappeared until the publication of *Plumb Drillin'* (1976), a Western! What is less known is that Case has been a full-time writer all his life. Under seventeen different pseudonyms he has written about three hundred 'porn' books. He settled in England in 1960 but lives partly in Greece, where he claims he once saw a werewolf!

Hugh B. Cave (b. Chester, Cheshire, 11 July 1910)
Hugh Barnett Cave is an Englishman by birth but grew up in America, emigrating with his family when he was five. After college he began editing trade journals and started a steady stream of sales to the pulps with 'Corpse on the Grating' (1930). Among his early output are three notable vampire stories, 'Stragella' (1932), 'The Brotherhood of Blood' (1932) and 'Murgunstruum' (1933). Although he wrote for *Weird Tales*, Cave's major market was the terror and detective pulps, primarily *Dime Mystery* where appeared 'The Corpse-Maker' (1933), a tale of an escaped criminal who gradually tortures to death the jury that convicted him. In later years his output turned more to adventure and western fiction. He lived for four years in Haiti and produced *Haiti: Highroad to Adventure* (1952), hailed as one of the best works about voodoo. He later settled in Jamaica, establishing a coffee plantation and pine forest. His experiences resulted in *The Witching Lands* (1962), an assembly of linked tales, many bordering on fantasy and voodoo.

Recent years have seen Cave's return to horror fiction, with stories appearing in *Whispers* and the completion of a weird novel. **Karl Wagner** has prepared a collection of his early stories called *Murgunstruum and Others* (1977; 26s).

Pseudonyms: Allen Beck, Justin Case, Geoffrey Vace

Robert W. Chambers (b. Brooklyn, N.Y., 26 May 1865; d. New York, 16 December 1933)
Robert William Chambers is revered in the horror field for his volume *The King in Yellow* (1895; 10s), a series of loosely connected stories

relating the hideous events consequent upon contact with the suppressed book of the title.

Chambers had set out to be an artist, studying and exhibiting in Paris in 1889. He returned to America, wrote a book of his life in Paris, and took to illustrating magazines until the success of *King* led him to concentrate on writing. Over the next ten years the bulk of his output was supernatural fiction. He often used the device of loosely connecting the stories by a narrator, but this sometimes weakened the effect, as in *The Maker of Moons* (1896; 8s) where the lead story about Oriental evil in America stands best on its own. Subsequent collections include *The Mystery of Choice* (1897; 7s), *In Search of the Unknown* (1904; 25s), connected stories about a big-game hunter after mythical creatures which had a kind of humorous sequel in *Police!!!* (1915; 6s), and *The Tree of Heaven* (1907; 10s).

Although he drifted away from the genre towards historical and biographical works (he wrote seventy-two books in all), he produced the occasional weird volume as in the novels *The Tracer of Lost Persons* (1906), about an Egyptian maiden revived after 2,000 years, and *The Slayer of Souls* (1920), about a young girl controlled by sorcery.

Alexandre Chatrian: *see* Erckmann-Chatrian

R. Chetwynd-Hayes (b. Isleworth, Middx, 30 May 1919)
Ronald Chetwynd-Hayes has only recently risen to some dominance in the horror field even though his first sale was in 1954. At that time he was a showroom manager and wrote only the occasional novel, mostly science fiction. Then, deciding most horror collections were awful, he thought he would try himself. The result was *The Unbidden* (1971; 16s), which includes the powerful tale of the spiritual return of Jack the Ripper, 'The Gatecrasher'. A second collection, *Cold Terror* (1973; 14s) included 'The Door', about a man who acquires an old door that exerts a psychic influence over him. These two stories, plus two others, including the title story from his third volume *The Elemental* (1974; 7s), were filmed as *From Beyond the Grave* (1973).

His fiction is variable. He has a sense of humour that can make but also spoils some stories, and his best are often those that follow traditional themes like haunted houses as in 'No One Lived There' (1971). Subsequent collections include *Terror By Night* (1974; 10s), *The Night Ghouls* (1975; 10s) and the clever *The Monster Club* (1975; 5s) where his humour succeeds. He invents offsprings from the consummation of two monsters, such as a werewolf and a ghoul producing a weregoo. A further volume is *Tales of Fear and Fantasy* (1977; 7s); a horror novel, *Kamtellar*, is scheduled.

Chetwynd-Hayes also works as an editor; he compiled *Cornish Tales of Terror* (1970; 12s) before he succeeded **Robert Aickman** with the *9th Fontana Book of Great Ghost Stories* (1973; 11s), and has now edited up to the *13th*. He contributes one story to each volume. Other anthologies include *Scottish Tales of Terror* (1972; 14s) as Angus Campbell, *Welsh Tales of Terror* (1973; 14s), *Tales of Terror From Outer Space* (1975; 14s) and *Gaslight Tales of Terror* (1976; 14s), as well as the *Armada Monster Books* for young readers.

Pseudonym: Angus Campbell (for anthologies)

Agatha Christie (b. Torquay, Devon, 15 September 1890; d. Wallingford, Oxon., 12 January 1976)
The inclusion of one of the world's foremost writers of detective fiction in a horror *Who's Who* might at first seem out of place. But apart from the frequent use of the macabre in her novels, Mrs Christie produced a superb collection of supernatural stories in *The Hound of Death* (1933; 12s), which includes such noted tales as 'The Last Séance' and 'The Witness For the Prosecution'. Although the ideas in her fiction might not be new, her treatment and style add an extra dimension. She also produced a strange detective volume, *The Mysterious Mr Quin* (1930; 12s), in which Mr Quin only ever seems to exist during the lifetime of a mystery and acts as a catalyst to another to help solve the problem. Here Mrs Christie invented a most enigmatic detective worthy of a wider reputation.

Brian Clemens (b. London, 1931)
One of the most prolific television and film scriptwriters and producers, Clemens is best known for his series *Thriller* and *The Avengers* (now *The New Avengers*). A breathtaking fountain of ideas, most of Clemens' scripts are trademarked by bizarre and complex mysteries with natural denouements. His film work has included scripts for *Dr Jeykll and Sister Hyde* (1970), *Blind Terror* (1971) and *The Golden Voyage of Sinbad* (1974). Several of the *Thriller* scripts were adapted to story form by Ted Hart as *Thriller* (1974; 5s) and *More Stories from Thriller* (1975).

Sir Hugh Clifford (b. London, 5 March 1866; d. London, 18 December 1941)
Like **Andrew Caldecott**, Hugh Charles Clifford spent his career in the Malay civil service, becoming High Commissioner in 1927. The life influenced him greatly, and he wrote several collections of weird stories telling of the beliefs and adventures of the natives. They appear in *In a*

Corner of Asia (1899; 8s), *The Further Side of Silence* (1916; 19s) and *In Days That Are Dead* (1926; 11s). He also wrote a novel, *The Downfall of the Gods* (1911).

Adrian Cole (b. Plymouth, Devon, 22 July 1949)
Adrian Christopher Synnot Cole is a talented new writer likely to make an impact on the field over the next few years. He has recently taken to writing full-time and has completed a number of novels. His first story was 'Love and a Time Machine' (1973), but only a few stories have appeared since. His novels are a blend of fantasy and science fiction and include the Dream Lords trilogy first published in the US: *Plague of Nightmares, Lord of Nightmares* (both 1975) and *Bane of Nightmares* (1977). Others include *Madness Emerging* (1976) and *Paths in Darkness* (1977). He has recently completed a fantasy novel, *Our Brother Elementals*, and is working on a black magic novel, *The Pact*.

Pseudonym: Adrian Bryant (in collaboration)

John Collier (b. London, 3 May 1901)
Collier's name has become synonymous in the fantasy field with the bizarre tale concocted in a light-hearted style but with serious undertones. He is best remembered for the story 'Thus I Refute Beelzy', which reveals the horrid results of not believing in a little boy's invisible playmate. His style and language caused quite a stir early in his career, especially with his novel *His Monkey Wife* (1930), and a few later books had private editions; the fantasy *No Traveller Returns* (1931) is now very rare.

Novels aside, Collier is noted for his clever short stories with surprise endings, and they range from 'Green Thoughts' with its more than cannibalistic plants, and the revelation of the canine identity in 'The Lady on the Grey', to the humorous genie in 'The Bottle Party' that gets its own way! Several collections exist, including an early rare *The Devil and All* (1934; 6s). His best known is *Fancies and Goodnight* (1951; 50s), which won the 1952 International Fantasy Award. Some of these tales were re-edited as *Of Demons and Darkness* (1965; 37s). His most recent compilation is *The John Collier Reader* (1976; 1n, 47s).

Wilkie Collins (b. London, 8 January 1824; d. London, 23 September 1889)
William Wilkie Collins, the friend and collaborator of **Dickens**, is noted for his two early detective mysteries *The Woman in White* (1859–60) and *The Moonstone* (1868), but he also wrote many macabre stories. His first remains his best known, 'A Terribly Strange Bed' (1852), though it has

lost its effect over the years. Dickens rejected Collins's next macabre piece, 'Mad Monkton' (1855) because it dealt with hereditary insanity. Collins appeared regularly in Dickens's Christmas annuals, which published 'The Ostler' and 'The Dream Woman' (both 1855). An early collection which included several weird tales was *After Dark* (1856; 5s). Later stories were 'The Dead Hand' (1857), 'John Jago's Ghost' (1874), 'The Devil's Spectacles' (1880) and 'The Ghost's Touch' (1880). His novel *The Two Destinies* (1875–76) is an early example involving a couple with telepathic affinity, while *The Haunted Hotel* (1877) is a noted ghost novel. *Jezebel's Daughter* (1880) is based on his earlier unsuccessful play 'The Red Vial' (1858) which included spooky scenes in a Frankfurt morgue where corpses are attached to bells which ring if the body retains life. His best stories have been collected by H. van Thal as *Tales of Terror and the Supernatural* (1972; 12s).

Oscar Cook: *see* Christine Campbell Thomson

Louise Cooper (b. Barnet, Mddx, 29 May 1952)
This promising young writer, who plunged straight into the medium after leaving school, produced a most impressive first novel, *The Book of Paradox* (1973), a compelling fantasy of another world with the hero in search of his dead beloved, aided by the book of the title. Finding fantasy harder to sell Cooper reverted to more traditional horror themes with a vampire novel *Blood Summer* (1976), which has a sequel *In Memory of Sarah Bailey* (1977) and the probability of a third *(The Sorcerer)*. A subsequent fantasy has been *Lord of No Time* (1977) and several more horror books are under way, plus an allegorical fantasy *The Angel of Vengeance*.

A. E. Coppard (b. Folkestone, Kent, 4 January 1878; d. 13 January 1957)
Alfred Edgar Coppard was recognised as a master of the short story. He left school when only nine and later worked in a variety of offices while he trained as an accountant. With the success of his first book he turned to writing full-time. The title story of *Adam and Eve and Pinch Me* (1921; 9s) tells of a man who finds himself in spirit form with the ability to see the future. A second collection, *Clorinda Walks in Heaven* (1922; 9s) was subsequently included in revised editions of the first book. The title story is a touching tale of a young virgin who dies and meets the husbands of her earlier incarnations in heaven.

Coppard's tales are trademarked by his adept feeling for character and his skilful prose. He has had over a dozen collections of stories published, each with a fair proportion of fantastic tales. **August Derleth** selected the best as *Fearful Pleasures* (1946; 22s); Coppard's own choice appeared as *The Collected Tales of A. E. Coppard* (1948; 38s).

Basil Copper (b. London, 5 February 1924)
Although much of his work is in the thriller field, it is as a writer of the macabre that Basil Copper is best known. For thirty years a journalist, he also edited a local newspaper before turning to full-time writing in 1970. He first appeared in the horror field with the tale of a man haunted by his dread phobia, 'The Spider' (*PH5*, 1964), followed by his most reprinted story of nightmarish justice 'Camera Obscura' (*PH6*, 1965), which has also been adapted for television. Both appeared in his collection *Not After Nightfall* (1967; 8s).

Copper has the ability to portray fear convincingly as in his story of mounting insanity, 'The Knocker at the Portico' (1971), and 'The House By The Tarn' (1971). His collection *From Evil's Pillow* (1973; 5s) was runner-up as the year's best book at the First World Fantasy Convention, and his novel *The Great White Space* (1974) earned him the accolade 'best writer in the genre since H. P. Lovecraft'. Subsequent collections have been *When Footsteps Echo* (1975; 10s) and *And Afterward, the Dark* (1977; 7s).

He has also written two Gothic novels, *The Curse of the Fleers* (1976) and *Necropolis* (1977), and two non-fiction studies *The Vampire: in Legend, Fact and Art* (1973) and *The Werewolf: in Legend, Fact and Art* (1977). He even wrote the sleeve-notes for the record album *Dracula* (1974)! Among his many projects in hand are a continuation of the Solar Pons stories of **Derleth** as *The Dossier of Solar Pons* and *The Further Adventures of Solar Pons*, a film script of M. R. James's 'Count Magnus', and radio work.

Marie Corelli (b. London, 1855; d. Stratford, Warwicks., 24 April 1924)
Born Mary Mackay, she was first destined for a musical career. Proficient on the harp, mandolin and piano she adopted Corelli as her stage-name. Then she had a psychic experience which turned her to research into that realm and resulted in *A Romance of Two Worlds* (1886), the first of her many books.

Her early work dealt with spirit power and universal love, and her fame came with *Barabbas* (1893). With *The Sorrows of Satan* (1895) she was called Britain's most popular novelist. Of her twenty-eight novels about half come within the sphere of weird or spiritual. These include *The Soul of Lilith* (1892); *Ziska, the Problem of a Wicked Soul* (1897), a brilliant novel of reincarnation; *Ardath, the Story of a Dead Self* (1889); *The Devil's Motor* (1910); and her famous psychological fantasy *The Life Everlasting* (1911). Her popularity waned considerably in her last years.

Her short stories were collected as *The Song of Miriam* (1898; 13s) and *The Love of Long Ago* (1921; 15s). A novel totally unlike her other work was *The Strange Visitation of Josh McNason* (1904), almost a straight imitation of Dickens's *A Christmas Carol*, but with goblins instead of ghosts.

Baron Corvo: *see* Frederick W. Rolfe

Juanita Coulson (b. Anderson, Ind., 12 February 1933)
Juanita Ruth Coulson was initially better known in the sf field. After her marriage to Robert Coulson in 1954, they co-edited the award-winning fanzine *Yandro* for many years. Her first story, 'Another Rib' (1963), was a fantasy about sex-change written with Marion Z. Bradley. Since then she has concentrated on novels, first in the sf genre, and then finding her forte in the gothic romance field. *The Secret of Seven Oaks* (1972) deals with the tarot and workings of fate; *Door Into Terror* (1972) tells of a satanist cult; *Stone of Blood* (1975) centres on the occult power of birth-stones; and *Fear Stalks the Bayou* (1976) involves astrology and Creole superstitions. In progress is a supernatural historical novel set in ancient Babylon, *Dark Priestess*; *Covenant Most Evil*, about elder religions; *Shadow Over Scorpio*, about pre-destination; and *Mountains of Dread*, involving the early Spanish legends in America. A completed long fantasy novel hangs in limbo, and Mrs Coulson has adapted two short stories from it, 'Wizard of Death' (1973) and 'The Dragon of Tor-Nali' (1975).

Pseudonym: John Jay Wells (with M. Z. Bradley)

Mary E. Counselman (b. Birmingham, Ala., 19 November 1911)
One of the most original writers for *Weird Tales*, Miss Counselman started by writing poetry, selling a poem when only six. Her first fantasy in *Weird Tales* was a straightforward ghost story 'The House of Shadows' (1933); in all thirty of her tales graced the pages of that pulp. Many are problem stories, such as 'The Accursed Isle' (1933), in which one of the persons shipwrecked on the island is a murderer, and 'The Three Marked Pennies' (1934), where townsfolk have to solve which of the three marks on the coins means fortune, travel or death. That story became one of the most popular the magazine ever published.

Mary Counselman (who married in 1941) has had several psychic experiences herself which have inspired stories. The ghost of a Confederate soldier who throws himself from the old shot-tower every dusk is immortalised in 'The Shot-Tower Ghost' (1949), and the sad girl's face at the window of a house she once investigated inspired 'The Green Window'

(1949). Although her stories are often anthologised and have been adapted to television, only one collection has been published, *Half in Shadow* (UK 1964; 14s), with an American revision scheduled.

Frederick I. Cowles (b. Cambridge, Cambs., 15 April 1900; d. 31 May 1949)

Frederick Ignatius Cowles was a bibliophile and antiquarian whose work in the horror field had been overlooked until recently revived by **Hugh Lamb**. By profession a librarian, serving for a while at Trinity College, Cambridge, Cowles produced a number of books, especially on folklore and travel. He and his wife travelled extensively in Britain collecting facts for these books, and many of the legends he transposed into fiction. He published two volumes of ghost stories, *The Horror of Abbot's Grange* (1936; 20s), and *The Night Wind Howls* (1938; 24s). A third collection, *Fear Walks the Night*, remained unpublished at his death, but several stories will be found in Hugh Lamb's recent anthologies. Cowles was a Fellow of the Royal Society of Literature, and was awarded the Silver Laureate Medal by the Institut Litteraire et Artistique de France in 1936.

Lee Brown Coye (b. Syracuse, N.Y., 24 July 1907)

Coye is not the most apt name for a man who can draw some of the nastiest, most hideous, bestial, repellent yet brilliant horror artwork. Coye was originally a medical illustrator, which is probably where he acquired his skill in portraying bodies in a state of decay, positively dripping flesh. But he also wrote, illustrating his own Gothic fantasy *The Seventh Ogre* (1932). He later came to the notice of **August Derleth** and illustrated his 1944 anthology *Sleep No More*. From July 1945 he provided covers for ten issues of *Weird Tales*. His interior artwork had started in the March 1945 issue, and from July 1947 to July 1951 he supplied a series of 'Weirdisms', illustrating vampires, wizards, witches and more. During the early 1960s he also did some of his best work for *Fantastic*. He is also a sculptor and has had several one-man exhibitions.

Ralph Adams Cram (b. 16 December 1863; d. 22 September 1942)

Cram was a leading exponent for the revival of Gothic architecture in America in the 1890s, writing several books on the subject. But foremost for horror fans is a small collection *Black Spirits and White* (1895; 6s), hailed as one of the most extraordinary volumes of terror tales published. It includes his best-known story of a frightening journey through 'The Dead Valley', which **Lovecraft** singled out for praise. He also wrote a long fantasy poem *Excalibur*.

58

F. Marion Crawford (b. Bagni di Lucca, Italy, 2 August 1854; d. Sorrento, 9 April 1909)
Although he spent much of his life in Italy, Crawford was an American writer, the son of a sculptor who had gone to Rome in 1835 to study sculpture. Young Francis was educated in America and became a Sanskrit scholar, spending many years in the Orient. The first of his forty-five books, *Mr Isaacs* (1882), was set in India. Mysticism fascinated him and it is evident in many of his works, but only a few are total fantasies. *With the Immortals* (1888) involves the resurrection of the spirits of famous men, *The Witch of Prague* (1891) centres on the evils of hypnotism, and the near forgotten *Khaled* (1891) is an Arabian fantasy. But Crawford's reputation rests mostly on his short horror fiction, collected posthumously as *Wandering Ghosts* (1911; 7s: UK *Uncanny Tales*), but written mostly in the 1890s. Paramount among them is the tale of the suicide-haunted stateroom, 'The Upper Berth', one of the most reprinted of all ghost stories. Others are the vampire story 'For the Blood is Life', and ghost tales 'The Screaming Skull' and 'The Dead Smile'. Crawford had a skill for raising his fiction to heights of terrifying power and he ranks almost unequalled among the masters of fear.

E. Crawshay-Williams (b. 4 September 1879; d. 11 May 1962)
Lieut.-Col. Eliot Crawshay-Williams was a prolific writer who began his career while in the Army. Having served in India he returned to England overland and wrote about it as *Across Persia* (1907). After a short political career he turned wholly to writing and his books include several fantasies. In *Night in No Time* (1946) the powers beyond grant a young man two trips through time, while in *Heaven Takes a Hand* (1950) heaven spies on Earth through special cameras to judge the worth of mankind. Two collections that include off-trail stories, many based on the mystery of time, are *Borderline* (1946; 17s) and *The Man Who Met Himself* (1947; 13s).

Richmal Crompton (b. Bury, Lancs., 15 November 1890; d. Chislehurst, Kent, 11 January 1969)
Richmal Crompton Lamburn is best remembered for her near-endless series of children's novels about the schoolboy rogue William that began with *Just William* (1922). Because of these her other works are overlooked, and it is worth recalling that she published a volume of weird stories, *Mists* (1928; 13s), and the fantasy novel *Dread Dwelling* (1926). Her brother John Lambourne (b. 1893) wrote a few adventure-fantasy novels such as *The Kingdom That Was* (1931), set in darkest Africa.

John Keir Cross (b. Scotland, 1911; d. 22 January 1967)
Among the annals of weird fiction one of the most sought after volumes is *The Other Passenger* (1944; 18s), not just for Cross's bizarre tales but also the eight surreal colour plates by Bruce Angrave in a style not unlike **Lee Coye**. The book includes the famous story 'The Glass Eye', involving the chilling confusion of ventriloquist and dummy. In most of Cross's stories the horror is usually right under your nose, but is only apparent when he underlines it. Alas most of Cross's other books were for children, but he did edit a series of horror anthologies, *Best Black Magic Stories* (1960; 13s), and two volumes of *Best Horror Stories* (1956; 16s and 1965; 15s). To followers of radio plays Cross's name would have been familiar as the adapter of many fine dramas.

Pseudonym: Stephen Macfarlane

Catherine Crowe (b. Borough Green, Kent, 1790; d. Folkestone, Kent, 14 June 1872)
Mrs Crowe was a renowned Victorian writer fascinated by the supernatural who spent many years researching the subject, publishing her findings in several books, most notably *The Night Side of Nature* (1848). Most of her volumes are non-fiction, though it is not clear just how much she embellished the facts. This is most evident in *Light and Darkness* (1850; 17s), a collection of sensational stories such as 'The Lycanthropist' on vampirism. The stories are related so that they read like fiction, and can be enjoyed either way. A further compilation was *Ghosts and Family Legends* (1858).

Aleister Crowley (b. Leamington, Warwicks., 12 October 1875; d. Hastings, Sussex, 1 December 1947)
Edward Aleister Crowley is remembered today purely as the black magician, dubbed 'The Wickedest Man in the World'. Reared by strictly religious parents he began to learn about the black arts while at Cambridge University, and he initially established two temples in London. He later moved to Scotland where the local populace feared his presence and suspected the worst of his activities. In later years he travelled Europe collecting facts for his definitive volume *Magick in Theory and Practice* (1929). He wrote his own fictional autobiography, *Diary of a Drug Fiend* (1922), and also wrote stories with strong echoes of actual events in his life. Best known is the novel of a young girl trapped in a war between good and evil, *Moonchild* (1929); one volume of occult stories is *The Stratagem* (1929; 3s). His biography was written by John Symonds as *The Great Beast* (1951).

Allan Cunningham (b. Keir, Scotland, 7 December 1784; d. London, 30 October 1842)
A noted Scottish writer and poet, and close friend of James Hogg and Walter Scott, he was fascinated by local legends and spent many years collecting information on folklore. He transposed them into readable stories as *Traditional Tales of the English and Scottish Peasantry* (1822) from which comes the oft-reprinted 'The Haunted Ships'.

Roald Dahl (b. Llandaff, Wales, 13 September 1916)
Although born in Wales of Norwegian parents, Dahl has spent many years in other countries, working in Tanganyika and Newfoundland before joining the RAF, with which he served in the Second World War until invalided out. He then worked in public service in the US where he began writing. He sold a script to Walt Disney Studios, and it later became the children's book *The Gremlins* (1943). Dahl's delight in children's fantasies has continued through several books and films—he wrote the screenplay for *Chitty, Chitty, Bang, Bang* (1968). It might seem hard to realise he also writes at the other extreme—very chilling and often gruesome tales of horror, mostly reflecting the evil in people. This was apparent from the collection *Someone Like You* (1953; 16s; rev. 1961; 18s) which won the Mystery Writers of America Edgar Award. It includes the story 'The Man From the South' about a boy who bets his car for fingers! Subsequent collections include *Kiss, Kiss* (1960; 11s) and *Switch, Bitch* (1974; 4s).

Madeleine Dahlgren (b. Gallipolis, Ohio, 13 July 1825; d. Washington D.C., 28 May 1898)
A life-long supporter of female suffrage, in later years Mrs Sarah Madeleine Vinton Dahlgren turned her thoughts more to fantasy, and she produced a charming novel, *South-Mountain Magic* (1882), and several ghost and weird short stories. These were collected as *The Woodley Lane Ghost* (1899; 24s).

Richard Dalby (b. London, 15 April 1949)
Dalby is a bookseller and horror enthusiast who produced a scoop in 1971 by unearthing a hitherto unreprinted story by M. R. James which he included in his anthology *The Sorceress in Stained Glass* (1971; 16s). A second anthology, *The Spectre Spiders*, was compiled but the publisher went bankrupt. It is scheduled to appear from a new publisher in 1977. Dalby does much research into the field and has been commissioned to write a biography of Arminius Vambery, the man who helped supply

much of the information to **Bram Stoker** for *Dracula*. He has also compiled *The Best Supernatural Stories of H. R. Wakefield*, to be published shortly.

Mary Danby (b. Dorking, Surrey, 26 May 1941)
With a pedigree that includes Charles Dickens as great-great-grandfather, Mary Danby has herself written several straight novels. In the horror field she is most noted as an anthologist, succeeding Christine Bernard with the *5th Fontana Book of Great Horror Stories* (1970; 15s), a series she has steered through to the tenth volume. A story of hers has appeared in every volume, starting with 'Quid Pro Quo' (1970), a tale of the malevolent transformation of a girl who kills her budgie. She also edits the original anthology series *Frighteners*, which began in 1974, and has compiled six volumes of the *Armada Ghost Book* for children.

Pseudonym: Mary Calvert (her married name), for children's stories

M. P. Dare (b. 1902; d. August 1962)
Marcus Paul Dare was the Ordnance Survey Archaeological Reviser for Nottinghamshire, and a prominent local historian. His researches brought many bizarre local legends to his notice and he used these as a basis for his short stories collected as *Unholy Relics* (1947; 13s). Although dedicated to **Montague Summers**, the stories are more in the vein of **M. R. James**.

Avram Davidson (b. New York, 23 April 1923)
Davidson has had considerable success as both a science fiction and mystery writer, winning top awards in both fields, but his fantasy output should not be overlooked. This consists mostly of imaginary world adventures, although his earliest in the vein, misleadingly titled *Clash of Star-Kings* (1966), tells of a series of supernatural mysteries among Aztec natives. He then focused on the Roman poet Virgil, but the sorcerous Virgil of legend, in *The Phoenix and the Mirror* (1966). His next fantasy was set in the frozen northern wastes, the story 'Arnten of Ultima Thule' (1971) followed by the novel *The Forges of Nainland are Cold* (1972; book *Ursus of Ultima Thule*). A further fantasy series began with *Peregrine: Primus* (1971), concerning the last pagan king in Europe, with a sequel, *Peregrine:Secundus* to be published. Most recently he has embarked upon a series about the occult investigator Dr Esterhazy, who inhabits a parallel, more magical world. The initial stories have been collected as *The Enquiries of Dr Esterhazy* (1975; 8s).

Davidson follows no patterns in his fantasy inventions, and can never be hailed to write in the **Burroughs** or **Tolkien** traditions. He writes in the Davidson tradition.

Richard Davis (b. London, 27 January 1945)

As writer, editor and scriptwriter, Davis is extremely active in the horror field. His first story was a clever murder mystery, 'Guy Fawkes Night' (*PH4*, 1963), and several new stories thereafter appeared in anthologies, including 'Female of the Species' (1963) which formed the basis of the film *Viola* (1969) which Davis helped produce. In 1966 he became assistant story editor of BBC's second *Out of the Unknown* sf series, and in 1968 he was story editor of BBC's *Late Night Horror* television series. Stories submitted for the series but not used formed the basis of a new anthology *Tandem Horror 2* (1968; 13s) followed by *No. 3* (1969; 9s). The stories emphasised the horror in the mind and this is most evident in Davis's 'The Lady By the Stream' (1968) which traces the fatal consequences of an elderly spinster's attachment to a young boy. His stories have also appeared in several *Ghost Book* volumes.

In 1971 he began an annual selection of *Year's Best Horror Stories* which has subsequently undergone various changes (see App. II). He also edits the *Space*, *Spectre* and *Armada Sci-Fi* anthologies for young readers. During 1974 he scripted part of the BBC World Service series *Price of Fear* starring Vincent Price, and subsequently published the volume *Price of Fear* (1976; 8s). Davis is currently working on further anthologies and radio programmes, plus an occult novel, *Lamb of Satan*.

Emma Frances Dawson (b. 1851; d. San Francisco, 6 February 1926)

Although praised generously by Ambrose Bierce as a writer 'head and shoulders' above her contemporaries, and although a gifted poet, writer and translator (with a knowledge of several languages), and a talented musician, Emma Dawson is today forgotten, even by her own countrymen. She wrote for most of the popular US periodicals in the 1880s and 1890s, and several of her ghost and horror stories were collected as *An Itinerant House* (1897; 10s). It includes the opium dream story 'The Dramatic in my Destiny', recently revived in the Winter 1973 *Weird Tales*. Much of her life was spent caring for an invalid mother, and it is believed she starved to death, unjustly forgotten.

D'Arnaud, François Baculard: *see* Baculard D'Arnaud

L. Sprague de Camp (b. New York, 27 November 1907)

As one of America's leading writers and scholars of fantasy and science fiction, Lyon Sprague de Camp has an enviable knowledge of fact and fiction in the occult, scientific and ancient worlds. Early employment as a patents engineer resulted in his first book, *Inventions and Their Management* (1937) with A. K. Berle. His first fiction, 'The Hairless Ones Come' (1939) was a tale of prehistory, but it only saw publication after the sale of several sf stories.

Science fiction formed the bulk of his output in the 1940s with the exception of his sales to *Unknown*. Firstly he collaborated with H. L. Gold (b. 1914) on 'None But Lucifer' (1939), the story of a man who so outdoes the devil that he replaces him. Then de Camp met **Fletcher Pratt** and found they had much in common, especially an interest in legends and languages. They collaborated on a series about Harold Shea who would find himself whisked off to various lands of legend—that of Norse mythology in 'The Roaring Trumpet' (1940), or the world of Spenser's *Faerie Queen* in 'Mathematics of Magic' (1940). These two adventures were combined as *The Incomplete Enchanter* (1941), and subsequent tales were *The Castle of Iron* (1941; book 1950) and *Wall of Serpents* (1960; 2s). A non-Shea collaboration but in the same vein was *Land of Unreason* (1941), set in the world of *A Midsummer Night's Dream*. De Camp also collaborated with Pratt on a series of tall tales as related by frequenters of a tavern, collected as *Tales From Gavagan's Bar* (1953; 23s). After the Second World War, more non-fiction books came from de Camp, including *Lands Beyond* (1952) with Willy Ley, *Lost Continents* (1954), and more recently a history of magic written with his wife Catherine, *Spirits, Stars and Spells* (1966).

In 1951 de Camp first encountered **Howard's** Conan stories, and learning of several unpublished manuscripts he set about revising them with help from **Lin Carter**. Thus began the posthumous collaboration that culminated in 1965 with the paperback publication of the entire Conan saga in twelve volumes, completely revised and chronologised by de Camp (see App. I). De Camp also wrote his own heroic fantasies, most being set in a mythical Atlantis called Poseidonis, beginning with *The Tritonian Ring* (1951; book, 1953; 1n, 3s). His heroic fantasies are enhanced by his superior knowledge of the ancient world and ancient mechanics, all of which combine to build a convincing world of fantasy. It has also led him to write several historical novels, all of which should be of interest to the fantasy fan. They include *An Elephant For Aristotle* (1958), *The Bronze God of Rhodes* (1960), *The Dragon of the Ishtar Gate* (1961) and *The Arrows of Herakles* (1965).

Returning to the fantasy field, de Camp was the first to edit a wholly sword and sorcery anthology called *Swords and Sorcery* (1963; 8s), and followed this with *The Spell of Seven* (1965; 7s), *The Fantastic Swordsmen* (1967; 8s) and *Warlocks and Warriors* (1971; 12s). He also returned to fiction with a splendid novel, *The Goblin Tower* (1968) and its sequel *The Clocks of Iraz* (1971). Another novel was *The Fallible Fiend* (1972).

He took up further research into fantasy writers, contributing a series to *Fantastic* now due in book form as *Literary Swordsmen* (1977), and producing the definitive biography of *Lovecraft* (1975). He is now writing short fantasy fiction again.

Daniel Defoe (b. London, 1660; d. London, 26 April 1731)
Daniel Foe, as he was born, is regarded by many as the founding father of supernatural fiction, primarily for his narrative *The True Relation of the Apparition of one Mrs Veal* (1706). For years believed to be fiction it was later established to be a true occurrence merely reported by Defoe, but as such it was the basis for the development of all future ghost stories. Defoe went on to greater things, notably *Robinson Crusoe* (1719–20) and *Moll Flanders* (1722), but he occasionally returned to the supernatural with stories like 'The Friendly Demon' (1726). His interest in the occult is further evidenced by his books *The Political History of the Devil* (1726), *System of Magic* (1726) and *Essay on the Reality of Apparitions* (1727).

Richard Dehan: *see* Clotilde Inez Mary Graves

Walter de la Mare (b. Charlton, Kent, 25 April 1873; d. Twickenham, Mddx. 22 June 1956)
Famous in his own right as a poet and a writer of children's books, Walter John de la Mare cemented his fame as a master of the English language by producing a wealth of excellent supernatural stories. His first in the vein, 'Kismet' (1895) was uncharacteristic in that it was a *conte cruel* underlining the ironies of fate. These early pieces were only recently collected by Edward Wagenknecht as *Eight Tales* (1971; 8s).
De la Mare's skill with the supernatural was first shown with *The Return* (1910), about a man possessed by an eighteenth-century suicide. The novel won the Polignac Prize. The following ten years de la Mare devoted to poetry, returning to prose with a novel about a two-foot high woman, *Memoirs of a Midget* (1921). This won the James Tait Black Memorial Prize. He also wrote a fairy play *Crossings* (1921), first performed in June 1919, and in 1925 it marked the last stage performance of Ellen Terry who took the silent part of the ghost. De la Mare now concentrated more on the short story form, producing his masterpiece, the ghostly 'Seaton's Aunt' (1921). His collections include *The Riddle* (1923; 15s), *Two Tales* (1925; 2s), *The Connoisseur* (1926; 9s), *On the Edge* (1930; 8s) and *The Wind Blows Over* (1936; 12s). Most later collections were reprints, such as *Ghost Stories* (1956; 7s), but his final volume, *A Beginning* (1955; 13s), consists of stories written earlier but not previously collected. His son, Colin de la Mare, edited a horror anthology *They Walk Again* (1931; 18s)

which was instrumental in reviving interest in the work of **William Hope Hodgson.**

De la Motte Fouque: *see* Fouque

De L'Isle Adam, Comte de: *see* Villiers de L'Isle Adam

Guy de Maupassant: *see* Maupassant, Guy de

August W. Derleth (b. Sauk City, Wis., 24 February 1909; d. Sauk City, 4 July 1971)
One of the world's most active authors, belonging to that select group of 100-plus book writers, it is sobering to realise that in literary eyes, August William Derleth's voluminous weird fiction output is regarded as a sideline! His major project consisted of a series of regional novels about Wisconsin's Sac Prairie, in addition to which he wrote considerable detective fiction. Add to that numerous short stories and time-consuming publishing and editorial duties, and there was the machine that was Derleth.

For many, Derleth was the backbone of most twentieth-century horror, holding a similar position to that of John W. Campbell in science fiction. He began writing at the age of 13 and his first horror story, 'Bat's Belfry' (1926), appeared when he was 17. While at the University of Wisconsin, Derleth chose as his B.A. thesis 'The Weird Tale in English since 1890' (1930), and briefly in 1931 he edited the occult magazine *Mind Magic*. Thereafter he wrote full-time.

Most of his early stories were straightforward supernatural tales, but he soon showed the influence of H. P. Lovecraft, and after the latter's death in 1937 Derleth assembled a collection of Lovecraft's best stories as a tangible memory of the man. Finding no publisher interested, Derleth and **Donald Wandrei** established their own publishing imprint, Arkham House, and published the collection as *The Outsider and Others* (1939; 36s). Derleth followed this with a volume of his own stories, *Someone in the Dark* (1941; 16s), and thereafter Arkham House continued as the only specialist weird fiction publisher. It continues to this day, and a full set of Arkham House volumes would be an excellent library of all that is good in horror fiction—not to say an invaluable financial asset! A second collection appeared as *Something Near* (1945; 21s). By then Derleth had started his series of stories continuing the Cthulhu Mythos of Lovecraft, and these eventually saw book publication as *The Mask of Cthulhu* (1958; 6s) and *The Trail of Cthulhu* (1962; 6s.)

Other Derleth collections include *Not Long For This World* (1948; 33s), *Lonesome Places* (1962; 18s), *Mr George and Other Odd Persons* (1963; 17s) as Stephen Grendon, *Colonel Markesan and Less Pleasant People* (1966; 17s) with Mark Schorer, and *Dwellers in Darkness* (1976). Derleth's wide knowledge of the field resulted in an excellent selection of anthologies that began with *Sleep No More* (1944; 20s) and include nearly a dozen weird anthologies (plus others of science fiction and verse). Initially reprint, his last four consisted of all new stories. They were *Dark Mind, Dark Heart* (1962; 17s), *Over the Edge* (1964; 18s), *Travellers By Night* (1967; 14s) and *Dark Things* (1971; 24s). Another, *Tales of the Cthulhu Mythos* (1969; 19s) was part new, part reprint. In these anthologies Derleth did much to encourage new writers like **Ramsey Campbell** and **Brian Lumley** as well as unearthing previously unpublished fiction by past masters like **Hodgson** and **Metcalfe**.

Derleth's own output of supernatural fiction decreased slightly after *Weird Tales* folded in 1954, and he concentrated on completing fragments of stories left by H. P. Lovecraft. Apart from a few, the bulk of these are entirely the work of Derleth inspired by some indirect reference in Lovecraft's notes. The results include the novel *The Lurker at the Threshold* (1945), and collections *The Survivor* (1957; 7s) and *The Watchers Out of Time* (1974; 16s). There is no denying that without Derleth, horror fiction in the twentieth century would have suffered immeasurably.

Pseudonyms: Stephen Grendon, Eldon Heath, Kenyon Holmes, Tally Mason, Michael West

Marquis de Sade: *see* Sade, Marquis de

Charles Dickens (b. nr Portsmouth, Hants., 7 February 1812; d. Gad's Hill, Kent, 9 June 1870)
The life of Charles John Huffam Dickens is too well known to repeat here. His contribution to the supernatural field is critical in that more than almost any other editor in the nineteenth century, Dickens encouraged spooky stories for the Christmas issues of his magazines (*Household Words* 1850–59; *All the Year Round* 1859–70). Here first appeared noted stories by **Wilkie Collins, Bulwer Lytton, Mrs Gaskell, Amelia Edwards,** and not least Dickens himself. His writing had started with the stories later collected as *Sketches by Boz* (1836) which included the macabre story 'The Black Veil'. There is an occult element in 'The Lamplighter's Story' (1841), but his supernatural mark was first made with the ghostly visitations to Ebenezer Scrooge in *A Christmas Carol* (1843). This began his tradition of Christmas stories, a later one being *The Haunted Man* (1848), when a man is visited by his own ghost!

Dickens could not only conjure up a terrifying atmosphere, but he could also be sympathetic in such fantasies as 'A Child's Dream of a Star' (1850), in which a dead child becomes an angel and awaits her brother, or 'The Haunted House' (1859), when the house turns out to be haunted by one's memories. His most reprinted ghost story is 'No. 1 Branch Line: The Signalman' (1866), but others will be found in *The Uncommercial Traveller* (1861) which includes the 'Nurse's Stories' (1860) recalling macabre tales told him when young like 'Captain Murderer' and 'The Rat Who Could Speak'. Another noted piece was 'The Trial for Murder' (1865) written with Wilkie Collins's brother Charles (1828–73). Other grim stories will be found within his novels, all of which reflect the greater horror of life in Victorian London. Dickens also wrote a fairy story, *Holiday Romance* (1868).

Dick Donovan (b. Southampton, Hants., 1842; d. 23 January 1934)
Under his real name of Joyce E. Preston-Muddock, he spent much of his early life working in India, then travelling extensively. He wrote nearly seventy books, mostly historical novels and travel guides. As Dick Donovan he wrote another seventy or so books, this time mostly spy and detective thrillers, and the bulk of this dual output was crammed into the period 1873–1910. His thrillers occasionally verge on the macabre, such as in *The Mystery of Jamaica Terrace* (1896) or *In The Queen's Service* (1907); *The Scarlet Seal* (1902) tells of witchcraft at the time of the Borgias. He wrote a number of short ghost pieces, collected as *Tales of Terror* (1899; 15s), and another selection under his real name appeared as *Stories Weird and Wonderful* (1889).

Arthur Conan Doyle (b. Edinburgh, 22 May 1859; d. Crowborough, Sussex, 7 July 1930)
Remembered as the creator of Sherlock Holmes, and a writer of several historical novels, Doyle's weird fiction output tends to be overlooked, even though it formed an equal third of his writings, and was his first and last love. His first sale, while training to be a doctor, was the terror tale 'The Mystery of Sasassa Valley' (1879). As early as 1886, when he was a practising doctor, he had a collection published, *Dreamland and Ghostland* (1886) which included most of his early efforts such as 'The Captain of the *Polestar*', whose hero pursues a spectre over the Arctic wastes, 'The Great Keinplatz Experiment', in which a professor and his student exchange bodies, and 'John Barrington Cowles', about a woman with a terrible secret that drives her suitors to suicide. With the later success of his Holmes stories, this volume saw several reprints under different titles, most notably *The Captain of the 'Polestar'* (1894; 10s), and it is fairly

certain Doyle would have written more had not other demands made it impossible. As it is he produced a fair number including a short novel of psychic vampirism, *The Parasite* (1894), and a variety of collections, *My Friend the Murderer* (1893; 5s), *Round the Red Lamp* (1894; 15s), *Round the Fire Stories* (1908; 17s) and *The Last Galley* (1911; 18s).

It should not be overlooked that when Doyle revived Holmes it was in that masterpiece of fear and the unknown *The Hound of the Baskervilles* (1901). Doyle's attention turned more to the bizarre, especially in the Professor Challenger series that began with *The Lost World* (1912). The crunch came when Doyle's brother-in-law was killed in the First World War. He had lost other friends and relatives and this drove him to spiritualism. He wrote many books on the subject and it also influenced his fiction in a new Challenger adventure, *The Land of the Mist* (1925), in which the Professor is converted to spiritualism. This was now Doyle's sole interest, and the last book to appear before his death, *The Edge of the Unknown* (1930), includes many of his own psychic experiences.

David A. Drake (b. Dubuque, Iowa, 24 September 1945)
1967 was an important year for David Allen Drake. He earned a B.A. in History, with Honours, he married, and his first story, 'Denkirch' was published. Since then he has become the assistant town attorney at Chapel Hill, and also acts as assistant editor on *Whispers*, and co-publisher at Carcosa House (see K. Wagner). He says his horror fiction is a good vehicle to reflect his black view of the world. This is clear in 'Arclight' (1973), which reflects the horrors of war as experienced by Drake in Vietnam. Several of his tales, such as 'The Song of the Bone' and 'The Shortest Way', will be found in *Whispers*.

Henry B. Drake (b. 1894)
An expert on modern literature, Henry Burgess Drake has been virtually forgotten by modern readers. At least four of his novels are worth investigations: *Cursed Be The Treasure* (1926), a thriller with a haunted pirate's hoard; *The Shadowy Thing* (1928), about a man with malignant psychic powers; *Hush-a-by Baby* (1954), about twin poltergeist children; and *The Woman and the Priest* (1955), in which the forces of good and evil clash on a small French island. Nothing has been heard of Drake since the mid-1960s.

Dryasdust: *see* M. Y. Halidom

Alexandre Dumas (b. Aisne, France, 24 July 1802; d. Dieppe, 5 December 1870)
An exceedingly prolific writer, Dumas has been immortalised by his historical novels *The Three Musketeers* (1844) and *The Count of Monte Cristo* (1844). But he also ventured into the supernatural, as in *The Wolf Leader* (1857), in which a man becomes a werewolf as a result of his pact with the devil. He wrote a volume of short stories first published as *The Thousand and One Plantoms* (1848) though doubt has been cast on his authorship of all the contents. The tales cover most traditional themes, especially vampirism, and saw a UK translation as *Tales of the Supernatural* (1907). Stories include 'The Castle of Eppstein', 'The Pale Lady' and 'The Convict's Son'.

Daphne du Maurier (b. London, 13 May 1907)
One of Britain's most popular novelists, several of her works enter the realms of the bizarre, such as *The Progress of Julius* (1933), *My Cousin Rachel* (1951) and *The House on the Strand* (1969). However it is her short fiction that shows her macabre talents to the full. Currently in vogue is her short story 'Don't Look Now' which was so successfully filmed and can be found in her collection *Not After Midnight* (1971; 5s). Other tales of note are 'The Blue Lens', which tells of a girl who finds her world penetrated by another; 'The Apple Tree', which relates how the tree begins to dominate the life of its owner; and her best-known story, 'The Birds', which was transformed into such a stunning film by **Hitchcock**. The bulk of her stories were originally collected as *The Apple Tree* (1952; 6s: UK *Kiss Me Again, Stranger*, 1953; 8s); a recent compilation containing both old and new stories is *Echoes From the Macabre* (1976; 9s).

Roger F. Dunkley (b. Coventry, Warwicks., 5 July 1943)
A new arrival on the scene is schoolteacher Roger Francis Dunkley. Since his first sale, 'A Problem Called Albert' (*PH15*, 1974), about a feline menace, he has appeared regularly in the *PH* and *Fontana* series. The majority of his work reflects his gift for black humour, especially 'The Man Who Sold Ghosts' (1975). 'Miss Brood's Speciality' (1975) and 'Cross Talk' (1976) are both exercises in fear, but his most chilling to date is 'Twisted Shadow' (1976). Dunkley is currently working on several radio and television scripts in the hope of cracking that market.

Lord Dunsany (b. London, 24 July 1878; d. Dublin, 25 October 1957)
The 18th Baron Dunsany, Edward John Moreton Drax Plunkett, was one of Britain's most important fantasists. A larger-than-life character, he went big-game hunting in Africa, fought in the Boer War and First World

War, received a bullet in his head in the Irish Easter Rebellion of 1916. He was chess champion of Ireland, one time drawing a game with the world champion Capablanca. He only narrowly escaped from Greece in the Second World War, characteristically wearing two hats since he saw no reason to leave one behind. This desire was strange for the man dubbed 'the worst dressed man in Ireland'! All that aside (and there is much more), Dunsany left behind over sixty volumes of stories, plays, verse and novels, the bulk of them fantasy—and most stubbornly written with a quill pen!

It is Dunsany who is credited with fathering the invented fantasy world in short story form. He began to write them in 1903, inspired after seeing the play *The Darling of the Gods* by David Belasco and John L. Long, set in a mythical Japan. Dunsany mused of distant gods and ancient days and the result was a series of connected vignettes published at his own expense as *The Gods of Pegana* (1905; 31s). Later he expanded his pantheon, broadened his scope and also lengthened the stories. Subsequent collections were *Time and the Gods* (1906; 20s), *The Sword of Welleran* (1908; 12s), *A Dreamer's Tales* (1910; 16s), *The Book of Wonder* (1912; 14s) and *The Last Book of Wonder* (1916; 19s). With *Fifty-One Tales* (1915; 51s) Dunsany began to drift from such dreams, the collection including many non-fantasies, some only one or two sentences long. His early plays also had fantasy settings, starting with *The Glittering Gate* (1909) (produced by W. B. Yeats at the Abbey Theatre) but making his mark with *King Argimenes* (1911) and *The Gods of the Mountain* (1911) which brought him to the London theatre.

The First World War soured Dunsany's outlook and no longer could he produce his light-hearted brand of imaginative fantasy. This is clear not only from the collections *Tales of War* (1918; 32s), *Unhappy Far-Off Things* (1919; 12s) and *Tales of Three Hemispheres* (1919; 14s), but from his novels, a new medium for him. His first attempts were also set in fantasy worlds, but all are overshadowed by evil. They were *The Chronicles of Rodriguez* (1922), *The King of Elfland's Daughter* (1924) and *The Charwoman's Shadow* (1926). He then faced the here and now with two straight macabre novels, *The Blessing of Pan* (1927) and *The Curse of the Wise Woman* (1933).

When Dunsany's humour returned he embarked on a fascinating series of tall tales as related by Jorkens to his cronies at the Billiard Club. With these, Jorkens often outdid Münchhausen at stretching credulity. They were collected as *The Travel Tales of Mr Joseph Jorkens* (1931; 13s), *Jorkens Remembers Africa* (1934; 21s), *Jorkens Has a Large Whiskey* (1940; 26s), *The Fourth Book of Jorkens* (1948; 33s) and *Jorkens Borrows Another Whiskey* (1954; 34s). Unconnected tales of charming and chilling fantasy also appeared in *The Man Who Ate the Phoenix* (1949; 41s) and *The Little Tales of Smethers* (1952; 26s). He also wrote the occasional novel, such as *My Talks With Dean Spanley* (1936) and *The Strange Journey of Colonel*

71

Polders (1950), both of which give an animal's-eye view of life. Recently, **Lin Carter** assembled three collections of Dunsany's fantasies for the Ballantine Adult Fantasy series.

James F. Dwyer (b. Camden, N.S.W., 22 April 1874; d. Pau, France, 11 November 1952)

James Francis Dwyer was an Australian writer of fantastic adventures much in the vein of **Haggard**. His father had been a gifted teller of fairy stories, which no doubt influenced the young Dwyer. While working in a post office he was convicted of forgery and imprisoned for seven years (but served only three) and it was in prison that he began writing. Released, he travelled widely throughout the Far and Middle East and Africa, and it was these experiences that were the basis of his fiction. Among his novels are *The White Waterfall* (1912), *The Spotted Panther* (1913), *O Splendid Sorcery* (1930) and *The City of Cobras* (1938); most of them focus on weird cults and lost races. Some of his short stories were collected as *Breath of the Jungle* (1915; 12s) which includes 'The Phantom Ship of Dirk von Tromp'. A later story was the highly original ghost tale 'The Cave of the Invisible One' (1937).

Nictzin Dyalhis (b. *c* 1879; d. Salisbury, Md., 8 May 1942)

Though the name might seem pseudonymous it was not. In answer to readers' queries in *Weird Tales*, fans learned that Dyalhis was an old English name derived from the same Roman word that produced Douglas. This gave rise to the belief that Dyalhis was a British writer, which he was not. His father was an English sea captain who married a Mexican Indian. Dyalhis travelled widely, living much in the Orient (where he joined a Chinese occult society). He even entered Tibet, and witnessed a voodoo ceremony in Haiti. His knowledge of the occult was shown in the story 'The Eternal Conflict' (1925), about a modern businessman who belongs to an occult order. Dyalhis began writing in the early 1920s with stories of Amerindian life, and only sold eight stories to *Weird Tales*, yet he remains immortal among its contributors. His first was 'When the Green Star Waned' (1925), about the Venusian invasion of Earth, which prompted a sequel. Later fantasies were 'The Dark Lore' (1927), 'The Red Witch' (1932), 'The Sapphire Goddess' (1934), 'The Sea-Witch' (1937) and 'Heart of Atlantan' (1940).

Arlton Eadie (b.?; d. Sussex, 20 March 1935)

Eadie was a regular and popular contributor to *Weird Tales*, with twenty-five stories to his credit. These include the serials *The World-Wrecker*

(1929), *The Carnival of Death* (1935) and, best-known, the tale of diabolism *The Trail of the Cloven Hoof* (1934), the only story later to see book publication. His short stories followed traditional themes, as in 'The White Vampire' (1928), 'The Ghost Ship' (1929) and 'The Wolf-Girl of Josselin' (1938).

E. R. Eddison (b. Adel, Yorks., 24 November 1882; d. 18 August 1945) Eric Rücker Eddison was a civil servant who, in his spare time, wrote one of the great fantasy classics, *The Worm Ouroboros* (1922). It has been compared to *The Lord of the Rings*, not in content, but scope. A massive work with a clumsy beginning, the adventure takes off as the reader is plunged into a parallel world of magic inhabited by humans misleadingly named Demons, Goblins, Imps, Ghouls and Witches, all involved in a mighty war.

By day, Eddison worked at the Board of Trade, and later held several leading posts, but one can imagine him returning home to escape into his world of Norse legends and fantastic adventures. *Styrbiorn the Strong* (1926) was a historical novel of interest, and *Egil's Saga* (1930) a translation of a Norse epic poem, but in later works he reverted to fantasy in a connected trilogy set in the heaven of his first world. Published in reverse chronological order of events they run *Mistress of Mistresses* (1935), *A Fish Dinner in Memison* (1941) and *The Mezentian Gate* (1958). The last title was unfinished at his death, but so complete were his notes that his widow was able to assemble the book for publication—but it does lack that final veneer.

Clifford M. Eddy (b. 1896; d. Providence, R.I., 21 November 1967) Clifford Martin Eddy and his wife Muriel were very close friends of **H. P. Lovecraft**, who would often revise Eddy's fiction. Eddy had been writing long before he met Lovecraft in 1923, chiefly detective stories but also songs. One of his first weird pieces was the ghost story 'Moonshine' (1922). He is best remembered for the Lovecraft-revised stories published in *Weird Tales* of which the best are 'The Ghost-Eater' (1924), 'Deaf, Dumb and Blind' (1925) and the notorious 'The Loved Dead' (1924) about a necrophiliac, which caused an uproar on its publication with shouts that the issue be banned. Legend has it that this controversy helped the finances of the magazine considerably, and the story certainly immortalised Eddy's name. After his death a volume of previously unpublished stories was collected as *Exit Into Eternity* (1973; 5s), and more stories and verse appeared as *Erased From Exile* (1976; 5s).

Amelia B. Edwards (b. London, 7 June 1831; d. Weston-super-Mare, Somerset, 15 April 1892)
A born writer, Amelia Ann Blanford Edwards had sold a poem when only 7, and the first of her eight novels appeared in 1855. Her career seemed assured when in 1873 she visited Egypt and thereafter devoted her life to studying its ancient history. In the intervening twenty years she had contributed to many periodicals and was noted for her regular ghost stories in **Dickens's** publications. They include 'My Brother's Ghost Story' (1860), 'The Phantom Coach' (1864) and 'The Engineer' (1866). None was ever collected but four appear in **Montague Summers's** *Supernatural Omnibus*.

H. M. Egbert: *see* Victor Rousseau

Guy S. Endore (b. New York, 4 July 1900; d. 12 February 1970)
Endore's name has been immortalised by virtue of his definitive lycan-thropy novel *The Werewolf of Paris* (1933). This was based on a real-life case of the French sergeant who claimed he had fits during which he turned into a wolf and dug up corpses to devour the rotting flesh! Endore transformed this into a story of pathological menace with strong sexual overtones. In fact Endore's work has often returned to historical charac-ters obsessed with sex. His first book was *Casanova: His Known and Unknown Life* (1929), and one of his last, *Satan's Saint* (1966), dealt with **de Sade.** In between he wrote several weird novels including *The Man From Limbo* (1930) and *Methinks the Lady* (1945), about a female Jekyll and Hyde. He also scripted several fantasy films including *Mad Love* (1935) starring Peter Lorre, and he collaborated on *The Devil Doll* (1936).

Erckmann-Chatrian
The combined pseudonym of two French writers, Emile Erckmann (b. Phalsbourg, 20 May 1822; d. 14 March 1899), Alexandre Chatrian (b. Soldatenthal, 18 December 1826; d. 3 September 1890). For many years these two collaborated on some of the best fiction published in France. They met as students in 1847, and began collaborating two years later, continuing after they parted company. Erckmann wrote the original in Alsace, Chatrian polished the draft and handled the business matters in Paris. They finally split in 1889 when Chatrian claimed sole honour for the works, which led to a law suit.
The two men wrote in most fields, their weird fiction consisting mostly of the short stories 'Histoires et Contes Fantastiques', which saw UK translation as four volumes: *The Polish Jew* (1872; 11s); *The Man-Wolf* (1876; 6s)—the title story a noted tale of lycanthropy and a hereditary

curse; *The Wild Huntsman* (1877; 3s); and *Strange Stories* (1880; 6s). H. W. Dulcken translated a twelve-volume set of their work in 1880 which included the first two collections. Strangely, no volume carried their most noted story 'The Crab Spider', about a giant spider in a cave by a French spa, but readers can find two different translations in **Sam Moskowitz's** *Ghostly By Gaslight* and **Hugh Lamb's** *The Taste of Fear*.

Paul Ernst (b. 1900)

Ernst now lives in seclusion in Florida, but in the 1930s he numbered among the million-words-a-year contributors to the US pulps. His stories were predominantly terror-slanted with few supernatural elements, which was why **Wright** chose Ernst to contribute a terror series to *Weird Tales* in rivalry to the terror pulps. This was the 'Dr Satan' series which ran for eight episodes during 1935–36 and concerned the enigmatic hero Ascott Keane who tried desperately to thwart the evil plans of the mysterious Doctor.

Ernst had travelled extensively in his youth and began writing during the 1920s, first appearing in *Weird Tales* with 'The Temple of Serpents' (1928). He turned full-time in the mid-1930s, and reached a writing peak in 1939 when he wrote the lead novels for the twenty-three issues of the pulp *The Avenger*, a super-hero companion to *Doc Savage*. Both series carried the by-line Kenneth Robeson, but the latter was the work of Lester Dent (1905–59). Ernst thought *The Avenger* novels his worst work, but they are currently having a popular revival in paperback. After the war Ernst wrote for better paying markets and his fantasy output rapidly dwindled.

Pseudonyms: George Alden Edson, Paul F. Stern

Dennis Etchison (b. Stockton, Calif., 30 March 1943)

An American short story and scriptwriter, Dennis William Etchison's horror fiction is alas all too rarely seen. He had started writing before his teens, winning $250 for an essay 'What America Means to Me' when twelve. At about this time he discovered the writings of **Ray Bradbury,** whom he regards as his greatest influence. His first professional sale was a science fiction story, 'Odd Boy Out' (1961), and several such sales followed intermingled with chilling mystery stories like 'A Nice, Shady Place' (1963) about something odd in the mountains. His fiction has appeared in a variety of magazines, with perhaps his most stable market being *F&SF*. He studied writing under, among others, **Charles Beaumont.** In 1969 Etchison was hired to write a feature-length screenplay based on Bradbury's 'The Fox and the Forest', but the film was never produced. Etchison has since worked on several more scripts. Recent horror stories include 'The Night of the Eye' (1970) and the atmospheric 'The Soft Wall' (1974). He is currently compiling a collection of these, tentatively entitled *Nightland*.

Mrs H. D. Everett

An obscure Victorian and Edwardian writer now remembered only for the title ghost story of her collection *The Death Mask* (1920; 14s). Under the Douglas alias she wrote many novels such as *Iras* (1896), *A Legacy of Hate* (1899) and *Nemo* (1900).

Pseudonym: Theo Douglas

Hans Heinz Ewers (b. Dusseldorf, 3 November 1871; d. Berlin, 12 June 1943)

One of the last of the great German weird fiction writers, Ewers began his career in 1901. He formed a literary vaudeville theatre and travelled extensively, mastering English and settling for a while in the US, where he was interned during the First World War. He wrote a powerful series of novels based on the exploits of Frank Braun. Published originally in Germany, Ewers translated some into English; others were the work of **Guy Endore** and Ludwig Lewisohn. *The Sorcerer's Apprentice* (1907) involves sorcery and satanism; *Alraune* (1911) tells of the artificial creation of a fatal soul-destroying female; and *Vampire* (1921) includes some terrifying vampire scenes at sea. His best weird short stories were collected as *Nachtmahr* (1922).

J. Meade Falkner (b. Wilts., 8 May 1858; d. Durham, 22 July 1932)

Falkner wrote little, earning his greatest fame from his county handbooks, but he has been immortalised in weird fiction for *The Lost Stradivarius* (1895), which links a young musician to the dominating ghost of a dead violinist. He also wrote *The Nebuly Coat* (1903) about the weird experiences of an architect sent to save a church.

Elizabeth Fancett (b. London)

Originally a freelance journalist and film critic, Miss Fancett entered the horror field when she submitted a story for Richard Davis's *Late Night Horror* series. Not included in the series, 'I'm Not Mad Yet' (1968) was anthologised in *Tandem Horror 2*. It tells of a man who fights loneliness and insanity as the sole survivor after 'the bomb'. Unlike most contributors to the genre, she often writes in the present tense, as in 'When

Morning Comes' (1969), chosen as one of that year's best ghost stories. She frequently appears in the two Fontana series and the *Ghost Books*. She has also had stories broadcast on Capital Radio's *Moment of Terror*. Apart from more short stories, she is planning four sf novels and a detective comedy, plus television and radio plays.

R. Lionel Fanthorpe (b. Dereham, Norfolk, 9 February 1935)
The day of the prolific horror writer was not limited to the American pulpsters of the 1930s; Britain had its paperback equivalent in the 1950s, and none so abundantly productive as Robert Lionel Fanthorpe. What makes his achievement so staggering (he also wrote sf and thrillers) is that it was accomplished in his spare time. He is a teacher by profession, and is now assistant headmaster of a school in Norfolk. He maintained his output by dictating on to tape, leaving the typing to his wife and his mother. In this manner he almost single-handedly filled all the issues of *Supernatural Stories* from 1954 to 1966. Naturally, at this rate quality suffered, but not as much as one might expect, for although there is repetition of theme, plot and character, Fanthorpe's knowledge of religions and his mastery of English shines through.

Of the complete novels, among the best are *The Immortals* (1962) as Leo Brett, and *The Unconfined* (1966). The alias Bron Fane was kept essentially for a series about occult investigator Val Stearman and his wife La Noire, and these often proved the best stories, especially the novels *Softly By Moonlight* (1963)—about a man who sees his own grave, *Unknown Destiny* (1964) and *The Macabre Ones* (1964).

Since 1966, Fanthorpe has concentrated on his teaching. He is also a member of the Society for Psychical Research, and is currently planning a mystery novel.

Pseudonyms: Neil Balfort, Othello Baron, Erle Barton, Lee Barton, Thornton Bell, Leo Brett, Bron Fane, Oben Lerteth, John E. Muller (house), Elton T. Neef, Phil Nobel, Peter O'Flinn, Lionel Roberts, Réné Rolant, Deutero Spartacus, Robin Tate, Neil Thanet, Trebor Thorpe, Pel Torro, Olaf Trent, Karl E. Zeigfried (house)

Frederick Faust (b. Seattle, Wash., 29 May 1892; d. Italy, 12 May 1945)
Frederick Schiller Faust was undoubtedly 'King of the Pulps'. In a writing career of less than thirty years he wrote over thirty million words. He was best known under the alias Max Brand, writing many western adventures and the *Dr Kildare* series. His contribution to the weird field is limited but important. Among his earliest sales was a story of reincarnation, 'John Ovington Returns' (1918), and 'Devil Ritter' (1918), which depicted the evil use of telepathy. 'That Receding Brow' (1919) deals

77

with the horrors of meddling with evolution. Faust later brought the fantastic into several of his westerns, such as the series about Dan Barry, a mysterious human with preternatural control over animals. The novels ran *The Untamed* (1918), *The Night Horseman* (1920), *The Seventh Man* (1921) and *Dan Barry's Daughter* (1923). *The Garden of Eden* (1922) involves a hidden valley with mutant horses. His *tour-de-force* of fantasy, however, was *The Smoking Land* (1937) under the Challis alias. It tells of a man's lone voyage to a hidden Arctic land. Unaccountably it never saw book form. Faust's prolific output ceased when he was killed while serving as war correspondent in Italy.

Pseudonyms: Frank Austin, George Owen Baxter, Lee Bolt, Max Brand, Walter C. Butler, George Challis, Peter Dawson, Martin Dexter, Evin Evan, Evan Evans, John Frederick, Frederick Frost, Dennis Lawton, David Manning, Peter Henry Morland, Hugh Owen, Nicholas Silver, Henry Uriel, Peter Ward

Charles G. Finney (b. Sedalia, Mo., 1 December 1905)
Charles Grandison Finney has carved himself a niche in fantasy's Hall of Fame with his bizarre novel *The Circus of Dr Lao* (1935), about the impact of Oriental culture and necromancy on a western town. It won the National Booksellers' Award for that year's most original novel, and was later adapted by **Beaumont** as the film *The Seven Faces of Dr Lao* (1963). Finney had served in China in the army from 1927 to 1930, and his knowledge of the Orient is also apparent in *The Unholy City* (1937), which concerns the ghoulish pleasures of Heilar-Way, and *The Magician Out of Manchuria* (1965). In 1930 Finney joined the Arizona *Daily Star* as proofreader and became its financial editor in 1965, retiring in 1970. In 1958 he began a series of short stories relating the strange happenings in a western town, collected as *The Ghosts of Manacle* (1964; 8s).

Violet Mary Firth: *see* Dion Fortune

Garrett Fort
Fort's name has been unforgivably forgotten, even by many fantasy devotees, chiefly because he wrote no books, and his name can easily be missed among the flickering credits at the beginning of a film. Yet Fort was responsible for scripting the best of the early horror films, including *Frankenstein* (1931) starring Boris Karloff, and *Dracula* (1931) with Bela Lugosi, and he collaborated on *The Devil Doll* (1936).

Dion Fortune (b. 1890; d. 1946)
When Violet Mary Firth joined the Order of the Golden Dawn she received the name 'Deo Non Fortuna' and the name stayed with her. Noted for her mediumistic powers, Dion Fortune acquired a substantial following when she split from the Order after the First World War and formed the Fraternity of the Inner Light. She wrote several treatises and essays on magic, notably *The Mystical Qabalah* (1935). Several of her own psychic experiences were fictionalised as *The Secrets of Dr Taverner* (1926; 11s) much in the same vein as **Blackwood's** John Silence. She also wrote a series of novels detailing the practice of magic and the occult: *The Demon Lover* (1927); *The Winged Bull* (1935); *The Goat-Foot God* (1936); *The Sea Priestess* (1938) and its sequel *Moon Magic* (1956).

Baron Fouqué (b. Brandenburg, 12 February 1777; d. Berlin, 23 January 1843)
Freidrich Heinrich Karl Fouqué, Baron de la Motte, was a noted German writer who served as a cavalry officer, writing in his spare time. He collected legends from the many villages he visited, reworking them into his own now classic stories. He devoted the years 1803 and 1813 to writing, but re-enlisted in 1813 to fight Napoleon, resigning again in 1815. He is best remembered for *Undine* (1811), about a water-spirit who marries a mortal and thereby gains a human soul. His trilogy of plays, *Der Held des Nordens* (1810) was based on the Icelandic *Edda*, and the most fantastic was the first part *Sigurd der Schlangentöter* with dragon-slaying and much magic. In the same vein was *Sintram* (1815), inspired by Dürer's woodcut *Knight, Death and the Devil*, and *Der Zauberring* (1813). His deal with the devil story 'The Bottle Imp' (1826) was the basis of a play that in turn inspired **R. L. Stevenson** to write his own 'Bottle Imp'.

Gardner F. Fox (b. Brooklyn, N.Y., 20 May 1911)
Gardner Francis Fox has made a name as a writer of swashbuckling historical romances such as *The Borgia Blade* (1953), and simply by changing the setting to space or magical lands one has Fox's contributions to sf and fantasy. He originally planned a career in law, but abandoned this for writing. His first fantasy was 'The Weirds of the Woodcarver' (1944), and he made regular sales of swashbuckling space opera to *Planet Stories*. He also writes for the comic-book field. Although his heroic fantasies suffer from lack of preparation and originality they do possess a certain zest and enthusiasm. His first series told of the mighty swordsman Kothar in *Kothar—Barbarian Swordsman* (1969), *Kothar of the Magic Sword* (1969), *Kothar and the Demon Queen* (1969) and *Kothar and the Wizard Slayer* (1970). His recent indistinguishable series runs *Kyrik, Warlock*

Warrior (1974), *Kyrik Fights the Demon World* (1975), *Kyrik and the Wizard's Sword* (1975) and *Kyrik and the Lost Queen* (1976).

Pseudonyms: Jefferson Cooper, Jeffrey Gardner, James Kendricks

Mary E. Wilkins Freeman: *see* Mary Wilkins-Freeman

Antoine Galland (b. Picardy, 4 April 1646; d. Paris, 14 February 1715) One of the greatest influences on fantasy fiction was the tales told by Scheherazade to Haroun Al-Raschid (763–809), *The Arabian Nights*. The man responsible for their introduction to Europe, in a French translation, was an Oriental scholar and extensive traveller. Galland's first volume, *Les Mille et Une Nuit* (1704) caused a sensation and other translations appeared throughout Europe over the next few years, although Galland's full translation was not complete until 1717 when the twelfth volume appeared posthumously. It started a vogue for Oriental fiction that echoed down the next few centuries and included books like James Ridley's *Tales of the Genii* (1765) and **Beckford's** *Vathek*.

David Garnett (b. Brighton, 9 March 1892) Over the last three generations, the Garnetts have supplied several worthy fantasies to literature. **Richard Garnett** (1835–1906), one-time Chief Keeper of printed books at the British Museum, wrote an enchanting volume of fables *Twilight of the Gods* (1888; 16s; rev. 1903; 28s). His son **Edward** (1868–1937) penned a weird collection *Papa's War* (1919; 22s), but it is his son, David, who provided the most famous weird story, *Lady Into Fox* (1922), about a beautiful woman transformed into a vixen. It won both the James Tait Black and the Hawthornden Prizes, and is a clever twist on the werewolf theme. Another bizarre book is *The Grasshoppers Come* (1931), which tells of the ordeal of an airman stranded alone and injured in a strange desert.

Elizabeth Gaskell (b. London, 29 September 1810; d. Alton, Hants., 12 November 1865) Mrs Elizabeth Cleghorn Gaskell was immortalised for her novels of Victorian life, *Cranford* (1853) and *North and South* (1854). But she is best remembered by ghost story enthusiasts for her contributions to **Dickens's** periodicals. Dickens had applauded Mrs Gaskell's *Mary Barton* (1848) which depicted the squalor in Manchester, and he requested she write for him, asking for a ghost story for his Christmas issue. The result was

'The Old Nurse's Story' (1852), a powerfully atmospheric tale of guilt that hangs over an old family. Her tale of a family curse, 'The Doom of the Griffiths' (1858) first saw print in the US. Surprisingly no single collection of her supernatural fiction exists even though the stories stand as the epitome of the Victorian ghost tale. Apart from unfinished fragments, her others are 'The Scholar's Story' (1853), 'The Squire's Story' (1853), 'Lois the Witch' (1859), 'The Ghost in the Garden' (1859; also called 'The Crooked Branch'), 'Curious if True' (1860), and a short Gothic novel, *The Grey Woman* (1861).

Jane Gaskell (b. Grange-over-Sands, Lancs., 7 July 1941)
The daughter of an artist, Jane Gaskell (now Jane Lynch) is the great-great-great-great niece of **Elizabeth Gaskell**. She began writing her first novel in a school exercise book, and it appeared as *Strange Evil* (1957). It deals with another world, whose people intrude on our own. Her second, *King's Daughter* (1958) was set among knights and magic on a moonless Atlantis, and forms an unconnected prelude to her subsequent fantasy trilogy *The Serpent* (1963), *Atlan* (1965) and *The City* (1966). By then her fiction had acquired that extra polish, but surprisingly her other novels are often overlooked. They include the vampirical *The Shiny Narrow Grin* (1964), and a bizarre and brutal portrayal of London, *A Sweet, Sweet Summer* (1969).

Théophile Gautier (b. Tarbes, 31 August 1811; d. Neuilly, 23 October 1872)
Gautier began as a painter, became a poet in his early twenties, and then turned to prose as well. Important and original, he often ventured into the realms of the mystical, an early memorable vision being 'One of Cleopatra's Nights' (1845), highlighted by **Lovecraft** as a masterpiece of horror. 'Clarimonde' is a poignant ghost story of a dead lover, but his best-known ghost tale is 'The Mummy's Foot' (1863). **Lafcadio Hearn** translated some of the best as *One of Cleopatra's Nights* (1882; 6s). Gautier's novels are equally exciting, and he reached the heights of originality in *Les Deux Etoiles* (1848), about an attempt to kidnap Napoleon from St Helena in 1821 by submarine! His best weird novels were *Avatar* (1857), which concerns a malevolent exchange of souls, and *Spirite* (1866), in which a young man falls in love with a ghost.

John Gawsworth (b. London, 29 June 1912; d. London, 23 September 1970)
Terence Ian Fytton Armstrong, who adopted the name Gawsworth for much of his writing, has been likened to **August Derleth**, not for any

prolific output, but because he encouraged new writers and endeavoured to publish their works in his anthologies. Gawsworth was first and foremost a poet, publishing his first collection *Confession* in 1931. Educated at the Merchant Taylor's School, he later became a Freeman of the City of London, but his greatest claim to nobility, albeit unrecognised, came when M. P. Shiel named him as heir to the kingdom of Redonda in 1947. For several years Gawsworth was a noted lecturer, and later an archivist. He received the Benson Medal of the Royal Society of Literature in 1939. Despite his large circle of friends, Gawsworth became something of an anachronism. He lived his last years in Italy, returning to London to exist on charity, sleeping on park benches and dying, forgotten and penniless, in a hospital.

Gawsworth's heyday was the 1930s. During that decade he assembled a number of huge anthologies containing the core of Britain's horror output between the wars. Here were new stories from Oswell Blakeston, **Edgar Jepson**, E. H. W. Meyerstein, M. P. Shiel and E. H. Visiak. Gawsworth wrote a few stories himself, best known being 'The Shifting Growth', a chilling tale of a malignant disease. The anthologies include *Strange Assembly* (1932; 14s), *Full Score* (1933; 26s), *New Tales of Horror* (1934; 30s), *Thrills* (*c* 1934, 20s), *Thrills, Crimes and Mysteries* (c 1935, 63s), *Crimes, Creeps and Thrills* (1936; 45s) and *Masterpiece of Thrills* (1936; 60s). He also edited collected stories by **Thomas Burke, Richard Middleton** and **M. P. Shiel**.

Vic Ghidalia (b. New York, 30 January 1926)
Recently Vic Ghidalia has proved himself a competent anthologist, either solo or in collaboration with Roger Elwood (b. 1943). Although all reprint selections, they reflect a good choice of material with items less known to US readers. They include *The Little Monsters* (1969; 8s), *More Little Monsters* (1973; 13s) and *The Devil's Generation* (1973; 9s) all of which deal with evil children; *Beware the Beasts* (1970;10s) and *Beware More Beasts* (1975; 7s) which, with *Satan's Pets* (1972; 10s), look at evil animals. *The Venus Factor* (1972; 8s) is tales by women; *Wizards and Warlocks* (1972; 9s) is a black magic assembly. Other compilations are *Horror Hunters* (1971; 8s), *Gooseflesh!* (1974; 7s) and *Nightmare Garden* (1976; 10s) with several more in the pipeline.

John U. Giesy (b. Ohio, 6 August 1877; d. Salt Lake City, 8 September 1947)
John Ulrich Giesy was a physician and physiotherapist who wrote as a sideline. He is best remembered for his Jason Croft trilogy, in which the hero's spirit travels to a far planet and undergoes adventures like **Burroughs's** John Carter. The novels were *Palos of the Dog Star Pack*

(1918), *The Mouthpiece of Zitu* (1919) and *Jason, Son of Jason* (1921). Earlier, Giesy had established a following for his series about Semi-Dual, a detective who used occult means to solve natural crimes. Usually written in collaboration with lawyer Junius B. Smith, the series began with 'The Occult Detector' (1911) and included *The House of the Ego* (1913), 'The Compass in the Sky' (1917) and *The Curse of Quetzal* (1914), all only seeing magazine publication. In his later years Giesy concentrated on writing westerns.

Theo Gift (b. Norfolk, 30 May 1847; d. London, 22 July 1923)
Under her real name of Dora Havers, she was a great friend and occasional collaborator with **E. Nesbit,** producing numerous children's stories. As Gift she penned a few weird stories collected as *Not for the Night-time* (1889).

R. Murray Gilchrist (b. Sheffield, Yorks., 6 January 1868; d. 4 April 1917)
Robert Murray Gilchrist was a Victorian novelist who specialised in novels set in his favourite part of England, Derbyshire and the Peak District. His ventures into the weird field were few, but none the less highly original. Most of his early stories were collected as *The Stone Dragon* (1894; 14s), but several more ghost stories were written thereafter, such as 'A Night on the Moor' (1900). A later novel of interest was *Weird Wedlock* (1913).

Johann W. von Goethe (b. Frankfurt, 28 August 1749; d. Weimar, 22 March 1832)
It is to be regretted that the author of the immortal *Faust* (finally published in two parts, 1808 and 1832) wrote so little else in the fantasy field. (See App. I for coverage of *Faust*.) Almost certainly Germany's greatest poet and dramatist, he was finally inspired to complete *Faust* during his friendship with **Schiller,** during which time Goethe was at his most fantastic. Another verse-play, *Pandora* (1808), recreates the Greek legend. His short story 'The New Melusina' (1817) deals with the love for a dwarf.

Nikolai Gogol (b. Ukraine, 31 March 1809; d. Moscow, 4 March 1852)
Nikolai Vasilievich Gogol led a rather unsuccessful life as teacher and lecturer, but his writings will not be forgotten. Influenced by **Hoffman,** a number of his stories are fantasies. His first collection, *Evenings on a*

Farm (1831) is a compilation of local folktales including 'The Terrible Vengeance'. The volume *Mirgorod* (1835) includes the humorous tale of the folk demon 'Vi'. 'The Portrait' (in *Arabesques*, 1835) tells of a picture which lives on as the evil of an old demonic merchant. 'The Nose' (1835) is the witty story of a nose that is shaved off and lives a life of its own. 'The Overcoat' (1842) is a supreme ghost story.

Golding, William (b. Cornwall, 17 September 1911)
William Gerald Golding's novel *The Lord of the Flies* (1954) has become a modern-day classic, often used for school examination studies. It tells of a party of schoolchildren stranded on a tropical island and of the society they form as the trappings of civilisation fall away. Like all Golding's subsequent work it explored the inherent evil in human nature and man's lack of free will. *The Inheritors* (1955), which followed, took a noble look at the last Neanderthal man. His later novels are less concerned with straight fantasy but nevertheless are superb studies of man's basic latent evil, as in *The Spire* (1964), about a man's compulsion to achieve the superhuman.

S. Baring-Gould: *see* Baring-Gould

Joan Grant (b. London, 12 April 1907)
Until ancestral memory can be proved or disproved, volumes about remembered previous lives can be equally well-labelled fact or fiction. Now Joan Marshall Kelsey, she began writing when Mrs Joan Grant, and had great success with *Winged Pharaoh* (1937), a first-person account by a co-ruler in ancient Egypt. It was noted for its astonishing insight into Egyptian life, its knowledge of the occult religion and its revelation of facts that have puzzled historians. The book has been highly recommended on all accounts. The bulk of her novels have been historical, not all with occult overtones, but all worthy of attention. They include *Life as Carola* (1939), about witchcraft, *Eyes of Horus* (1942), also set in Ancient Egypt, *Return to Elysium* (1947), about occult power in ancient Greece, and *So Moses Was Born* (1952). Her autobiography was *Time Out of Mind* (1956; US *Far Memory*).

Clotilde Inez Mary Graves (b. Co. Cork, 3 June 1863; d. Mddx., 2 April 1932)
Better known under her alías Richard Dehan, Clotilde Graves produced a number of non-fantastic humorous novels. Many of her short stories, however, deal with witchcraft and pagan religions, and these were

collected as *Off Sandy Hook* (1915; 24s), *Under the Hermes* (1917; 18s) and *The Eve of Pascua* (1920; 16s).

Davis Grubb (b. Moundsville, W. Va., 23 July 1919)
While learning the writing trade that would culminate in his successful novel *The Night of the Hunter* (1953), Davis Alexander Grubb wrote many short stories, a number of which were horror. 'The Horsehair Trunk' (1946) tells of a man who can leave his own body and sets out to commit the perfect murder; 'One Foot in the Grave' (1948), from *Weird Tales*, is about a severed foot with a life of its own. This story formed the title of the UK edition of his collection *Twelve Tales of Suspense and the Supernatural* (1964; 12s). He has recently returned to writing short horror fiction.

Neil M. Gunn (b. Caithness, 8 November 1891; d. Inverness, 15 January 1973)
Originally a civil servant, Neil Miller Gunn had a thorough knowledge of the wilds of Scotland that came to life in his fiction. Several of his novels have macabre overtones, like *Morning Tide* (1931), but five are of special interest to the fantasy devotee: *The Last Glen* (1932), *Second Sight* (1940), *The Green Isle of the Great Deep* (1944), perhaps his best-known novel set in a weird other world, *The Serpent* (1948), about an unexpected journey through time, and finally the quest for *The Well at World's End* (1951), not to be confused with **Morris's**.

Thomas A. Guthrie: *see* F. Anstey

H. Rider Haggard (b. Norfolk, 22 June 1856; d. London, 14 May 1925)
One of the greatest adventure writers who ever lived, Sir Henry Rider Haggard was educated at Ipswich Grammar School, but spent much of his early life in South Africa. He settled in England in 1881 to train as a barrister, but preferred writing.

His first book was political and was popular only in South Africa, so for his second he turned to native superstitions and produced *The Witch's Head* (1885) about the evil influence of a witchdoctor's severed head. It was followed by *King Solomon's Mines* (1885), the most famous and best-selling lost-race novel of all time, which started the vogue for adventures set in the Dark Continent, highlighting the pagan magic. The explorer hero dies in the sequel *Allan Quatermain* (1887), and thereafter Haggard related earlier adventures of the man, many of them fantastic. They include *Allan's Wife* (1889; 4s), *The Holy Flower* (1915), *The Ivory Child*

(1916), *The Ancient Allan* (1919), in which he experiences a previous incarnation in Babylon, *Heu-Heu, or, The Monster* (1923), *Treasure of the Lake* (1926) and *Allan and the Ice-Gods* (1927). In *She and Allan* (1920), he brought together Quatermain with the immortal heroine Ayesha who had sprung to fame in *She* (1886) with sequels *Ayesha* (1904–5) and *Wisdom's Daughter* (1923). These are the books for which he is remembered, yet it is less than half his output.

Many may feel that all his other work is stereotyped, but this is far from the truth. Even his African novels offer infinite variety. There are *Cleopatra* (1889), *The World's Desire* (1890), written with **Andrew Lang** and detailing the further wanderings of Odysseus with Helen of Troy in ancient Egypt, *Nada the Lily* (1891), which features the Wolf Brethren, *People of the Mist* (1894), about a lost city and its monster-god, *The Wizard* (1896), *The Yellow-God* (1908), *Morning Star* (1908), set in ancient Egypt, *Queen Sheba's Ring* (1909), *Moon of Israel* (1918), about the Exodus, and a rare collection *Smith and the Pharaohs* (1920; 6s). For other settings, there is the Viking fantasy *Eric Brighteyes* (1891), Aztec adventures in *Montezuma's Daughter* (1893), a Mayan city under a lake in *The Heart of the World* (1895), similar South American fantasy in *The Virgin of the Sun* (1922), and adventure in ancient Babylon in *Belshazzar* (1930). His other fantasies include *Stella Fregelius* (1903) with its aspects of fate, *The Lady of the Heavens* (originally *The Ghost Kings*, 1908), plotted with **Kipling**, a beautiful tale of a divine maiden who visits a magical land, *Red Eve* (1911), set at the time of the Black Death, *Love Eternal* (1918), about spiritualism, and *When the World Shook* (1919), in which the last king of Atlantis is revived. More than enough for all, and he wrote more!

Haggard was knighted in 1912, and awarded the KBE in 1919.

Peter Haining (b. Enfield, Mddx, 2 April 1940)

Peter Alexander Haining ranks as the most prolific anthologist of horror fiction in the world, having edited scores of collections in the last decade. He began his career as a journalist in Essex and was sent to investigate a case of grave desecration at a local churchyard which the rector thought was caused by satanists. This sparked an interest in black magic which he continued to research, resulting in his first book *Devil Worship in Britain* (1964), written with journalist A. V. Sellwood. Several similar books followed, and a by-product was the establishment of his anthologies, beginning with *The Hell of Mirrors* (1965; 14s; retitled *Everyman's Book of Classic Horror Stories*, 1976). Since then a regular flow has been maintained. He also ghost-edited six **Alfred Hitchcock** anthologies.

For his anthologies Haining strives to select lesser-known items, grouping them logically into cohesive themes that form a unit, like a novel. They are supported by comprehensive notes which add depth to the fiction. His most important anthologies are *The Craft of Terror* (1966; 15s), extracts from Gothic horror novels; *The Gentlewomen of Evil* (1967; 13s); *The Evil People* (1968; 13s), about witchcraft and voodoo; *The Midnight People* (1968; 18s), about vampires; *The Unspeakable People* (1969; 20s), stories either banned or which caused an uproar on publication; *The Hollywood Nightmare* (1970; 13s); *The Wild Night Company* (1970; 22s); *Clans of Darkness* (1971; 21s); *The Necromancers* (1971; 29s); *The Ghouls* (1971; 18s); *The Magicians* (1972; 12s); *The Lucifer Society* (1972; 24s: retitled *Detours Into the Macabre*, 1974), stories by writers not associated with horror; *Great British Tales of Terror* (1972; 30s) and *Great Tales of Terror from Europe and America* (1972; 30s); *The Nightmare Reader* (1973; 25s); *The Magic Valley Travellers* (1974; 23s); *The Ghost's Companion* (1975; 15s); *The Penny Dreadful* (1975; 23s); *The Fantastic Pulps* (1975; 21s); *The 1st Book of Unknown Tales of Horror* (1976; 12s); *Weird Tales* (1976; 22s); *The Ancient Mysteries Reader* (1976; 18s); and *The Black Magic Omnibus* (1976; 29s). He has also compiled *The Sherlock Holmes Scrapbook* (1974), *The Dracula Scrapbook* (1976), and in preparation are *The Edgar Allan Poe Scrapbook* and *The Shilling Shockers. Terror!* (1976) is a beautiful collection of horror artwork from books and magazines, followed by a similar compilation, *Mystery!* (1977).

Haining's other books are chiefly non-fiction and cover a host of topics from the Channel Tunnel to graveyard wit. He has written one straight novel, *The Hero*, currently being filmed.

M. Y. Halidom

This name was a pseudonym that superseded the alias 'Dryasdust', and probably hid the identities of more than one writer. Best known is the trilogy *Tales of the Wonder Club*, issued under the Dryasdust name in 1899 and 1900, and then under Halidom as *Volume I* (1903; 9s), *II* (1904; 6s) and *III* (1905; 2s). The two stories in the last volume probably also saw separate publication as *The Last of the Wonder Club* and *The Gipsy Queen*. The Dryasdust name had first appeared on *The Wizard's Mantle* (1890), a story of a cloak of invisibility during the Spanish Inquisition, reprinted as by Halidom in 1903. Halidom's by-line then continued on *The Weird Transformation* (1904), the vampire novel *The Woman in Black* (1906), *Zoe's Revenge* (1908), a rare novel about a life-size doll built up round the skeleton of a murdered girl which is haunted by her spirit, *The Poet's Curse* (1911), about the death that follows the desecration of Shakespeare's tomb, and finally *The Poison Ring* (1912).

Alex Hamilton (b. Bristol, 5 November 1930)

Though British, Alex Hamilton was raised mostly in South America and only returned to England after the war, taking his B.A. at Oxford. He has held a variety of jobs, but took to freelance writing in 1965. He now contributes columns to *The Times* and the *Guardian*.

His first horror story, 'The Attic Express' (*PH4*, 1963), came as a result of a serious attempt to write horror after his earlier efforts had turned to farce. It tells of a father who finds himself trapped as part of his son's train set. Hamilton has a talent for wresting horror from what might seem absurd situations, as in 'Kiss of Death' where a snowman dressed in a husband's clothes takes on his identity. In short Hamilton seeks nightmares in everyday situations. His collections are *Beam of Malice* (1966; 15s) and *Flies on the Wall* (1972; 14s). His novels are predominantly non-horror, though *The Dead Needle* (1969) is a psychological fantasy that builds up to a devastating climax. His anthologies include *The Cold Embrace* (1966; 18s), horror fiction by women, *My Blood Ran Cold* (1966; 15s) as Donald Speed, *Splinters* (1968; 14s), all new contents, and *Best Horror 3* (1972; 16s), which he took on when the series' editor, **John Keir Cross**, died.

Allison V. Harding
Sadly now forgotten, Allison Harding was one of the leading contributors to the latter-day *Weird Tales* with thirty-six stories from 'The Unfriendly World' (1943) to 'Scope' (1951). Her tales mostly reflect the inexplicable in the modern day, as in 'Death Went That Way' (1943), about a road that leads to death, and 'Guard in the Dark' (1944), in which a boy's toy soldiers come to life. 'The Murderous Steam Shovel' (1945) and 'The Frightened Engineer' (1948) reveal horrors inherent in modern gadgetry. She also wrote a chilling trilogy about a nasty corpse that began with 'The Damp Man' (1947).

L. P. Hartley (b. Whittlesea, Cambs., 30 December 1895; d. London, 13 December 1972)
Leslie Poles Hartley was a noted novelist of country life, as seen in *The Go-Between* (1953). But he also wrote a number of short stories in the horror vein. An early collection was *Night Fears* (1924) and he appeared regularly in **Cynthia Asquith**'s anthologies and the *Ghost Books*. His best-known stories tell of the dead man that returns in 'A Visitor From Down Under' (1927), and the fate of a man and the perfect coffin, 'The Travelling Grave' (1929) under which title **Derleth** assembled Hartley's best macabre fiction (1948; 12s). His *Collected Short Stories* (41s) appeared in 1968; *The White Wand* (1954; 14s) is also of interest.

W. F. Harvey (b. Yorkshire, 1885; d. Letchworth, Herts., 4 June 1937)

William Fryer Harvey trained as a doctor, but ill-health interrupted his course and after convalescence he became involved in adult education. He served as a doctor during the First World War, and received the Albert Medal for gallantry by saving a stoker petty officer trapped in a flooded engine room in imminent danger of breaking up. His lungs never recovered from the fumes and it exacerbated his ill-health. He spent the rest of his short life quietly, dying aged 52.

He remains an overlooked master of the psychological horror story, remembered chiefly for 'August Heat', a tale of a stone-cutter who cuts a gravestone for amusement and finds it comes true, and 'The Beast With Five Fingers', about the disembodied hand that seeks revenge, filmed in 1947 with Peter Lorre. Harvey's first book was a volume of ghost stories, *Midnight House* (1910; 16s), followed by *The Beast With Five Fingers* (1928; 20s) and *Moods and Tenses* (1933; 17s). After his death, Maurice Richardson compiled a collection of his best stories in *Midnight Tales* (1946; 20s). Here he highlights Harvey's predilection for stories where the central character is driven to hysteria by fear, as in 'Miss Avenal', 'Mrs Ormerod' and 'Miss Cornelius', Harvey's own favourite. A few more horror stories were published in *The Arm of Mrs Egan* (1951: 16s).

Wilhelm Hauff (b. Stuttgart, 29 November 1802; d. Stuttgart, 18 November 1827)
Hauff had a tragically short life, dying of typhoid when only 24. Yet in the short space of three years, while a private tutor, he established a reputation as a teller of fairy tales. Many can be enjoyed by adults, such as the ghost story 'The Story of the Haunted Ship'. A translation of some appeared as *Caravan Tales* (1912; 7s). A short novel was *The Wine-Ghosts of Bremen* (1827).

Dora Havers: *see* Theo Gift

Allan Hawkwood: *see* H. Bedford-Jones

Julian Hawthorne (b. Boston, 22 June 1846; d. 14 July 1934)
Although his father Nathaniel Hawthorne was more famous, Julian was more prolific and inventive. He trained as an engineer but preferred writing, which he did exclusively from 1871. With a career of some sixty years, it is no surprise that he covered a diversity of subjects, but he often returned to the supernormal, especially to the themes of possession and witchcraft. Most of these took the form of short stories and will be found in his collections *Ellice Quentin* (1885; 5s), *The Laughing Mill*

(1879; 4s), *David Poindexter's Disappearance* (1888; 5s) and *Six-Cent Sam's* (1893; 14s). His long novel *Garth* (1877) is a mystery with a Gothic atmosphere. *The Professor's Sister* (1888) is a bizarre romance later reprinted as *The Spectre of the Camera* (1915). Among his last writings was a series narrated by Martha Klemm, a reincarnation of a woman hanged for witchcraft. It included the novel *Sarah Was Judith* (1920), in which the spirit of a dead daughter possesses her mother.

Nathaniel Hawthorne (b. Salem, Mass., 4 July 1804; d. New Hampshire, 19 May 1864)

Salem is a New England town where in 1692 nineteen persons were hanged accused of witchcraft. Involved in the trials was Colonel John Hathorne, an ancestor of Nathaniel. Nathaniel's father was a sea captain who died in 1808, and his mother became a recluse. After college, Hawthorne was determined to make writing his career, and he too became a recluse striving at the art. He sold many stories to magazines and these were collected as *Twice-Told Tales* (1837; 18s); an expanded (35s) edition appeared in 1842, to ecstatic reviews from **Poe**. This and *Mosses From an Old Manse* (1846; 23s) include most of Hawthorne's weird fiction, not all supernatural, but all woven from a thread of evil. 'The White Old Maid' is a spectral, overly mystical tale, while 'Young Goodman Browne' is clearly influenced by his witch-haunted ancestry. 'My Kinsman, Major Molineux' has Satan directing a crucifixion, and in 'Roger Malvin's Burial' a supernatural monster is created out of guilt.

Hawthorne uses the macabre to symbolise the evil in man. This is true of his later novels such as the famous *The House of the Seven Gables* (1851) which involves a family curse, and *The Marble Faun* (1860; UK *Transformation*), set against a reputedly haunted Italian villa. What would have been his greatest fantasy was unfinished at his death. Dealing with an elixir of immortality and including ancient curses and a family who leave footprints of blood, the outline was taken up by both his daughter, Una, and his son **Julian**. Una completed the fragment as *Septimius Felton* (1873), a fairly conventional approach; Julian's *Dr Grimshaw's Secret* (1883) deals with an accursed house built near a burying ground and is a superlative result.

Brian Hayles (b. Portsmouth, Hants., 7 March 1931)

Primarily a television playwright, Hayles's name is most automatically linked with the *Dr Who* series for which he has written six serials. His first TV sale was *Legend of Death* (1965) and he has since contributed to *Out of the Unknown*, *Doomwatch* and *The Mind Beyond*, the last including his play on telepathy *Double Echo* (1976). He ghost-edited the anthology of the series *The Mind Beyond* (1976; 8s), credited to Irene Shubik. His radio play *Lord Dracula* (1974) is now being filmed as *Vlad the Impaler*; another of his film scripts was *Nothing But the Night* (1972), based on the novel by John Blackburn. He has written two children's plays, *The Hour of the Werewolf* (1975) and *The Curse of the Labyrinth* (1976).

Dorothy K. Haynes (b. Lanark, Scotland, 12 October 1918)
Although a frequent contributor to the Fontana ghost/horror series, Dorothy Kate Haynes has not been accorded the recognition she deserves. She sold her first story when 16, but her early work was not horror. Her weird stories first appeared in Jeremy Scott's anthologies. One of these tales told of the evil that befell a young girl thought to be a witch, and it formed the title story to her collection *Thou Shalt Not Suffer a Witch* (1949; 26s), enhanced by illustrations from Mervyn Peake. She is currently hoping to place a second collection of her stories that emphasise that evil is in the mind, *Peacocks and Pagodas*.

H. F. Heard (b. London, 6 October 1889; d. California, 14 August 1971)
Although born and educated in England, and a science commentator for the BBC from 1930 to 1934, Henry Fitzgerald Heard went to the US in 1937, and from then until his death was regarded more as an American. He wrote many books, several philosophical in nature, but was first noted as a writer of intriguing mystery novels as Jerald Heard, many bordering on horror, such as *A Taste For Honey* (1941) and *Murder By Reflection* (1942). Then his story 'The Great Fog' (1943) showed another facet. It deals with a mould that gives off a thick fog which brings civilisation to ruins. With other tales of terror it was collected as *The Great Fog* (1944; 9s). A second volume was *The Lost Cavern* (1948; 4s), the lead story of which dealt with a man captured by intelligent bats in a Mexican cave. Of his later novels, *Doppelgangers* (1947) is an anti-utopia not unlike *1984*, and *The Black Fox* (1950) is an outstanding supernatural adventure.

Heard was also a UFO enthusiast, reviewing the situation in *Riddle of the Flying Saucers* (1950; US *Is Another World Watching?*, 1951).

Lafcadio Hearn (b. Santa Maura, Ionia, 27 June 1850; d. Japan, 26 September 1904)
While Hearn is claimed as an American writer, one should remember that he was born on a Greek island of a Greek mother and Irish father, was raised in Ireland and England, went to the US when 20, but only found contentment when he settled in Japan in 1890. A childhood accident blinded him in one eye, and natural myopia meant he lived in fear

of total blindness. In America he became a journalist but remained poor and often slept on the streets. He soon became a star name with his newspaper because of his graphic descriptions of the more nauseating and horrific crimes. It earned him a reputation as a ghoulish writer, and Hearn enjoyed such notoriety, cultivating legends such as one that he often drank blood! In 1878 he settled in New Orleans where he wrote horror stories for the local newspapers. They were eventually collected by C. W. Hutson as *Fantastics* (1914; 33s), and they reflect his nauseous delight for blood, insects, ghosts and graveyards.

Hearn was fascinated by legends, retelling myths from Indian, Moslem and Nordic lands in *Stray Leaves from Strange Literature* (1884; 24s) and also compiling *Some Chinese Ghosts* (1887; 6s). Thus it is no surprise that when he was sent to Japan to write a series of studies he should fall in love with the country. He spent the rest of his life learning all he could of its history, legends and people. This was the basis of his later books, not all fantastic, but mostly strange and macabre. *Gleanings in Buddha Fields* (1897), *In Ghostly Japan* (1899; 14s), *A Japanese Miscellany* (1901; 14s), *Kotto* (1902; 20s) and *Kwaidan* (1904; 20s).

E. and H. Heron: *see* H. Hesketh Prichard

Edward Heron-Allen (b. London, 17 December 1861; d. Selsey, Sussex, 28 March 1943)
For many years the mystery man of weird fiction, masked behind the alias Christopher Blayre, Heron-Allen in turn created a fictional mystery. It began with *The Purple Sapphire* (1921; 8s), purported to be unofficial records from a mythical library. Listed on the book's contents page was 'The Cheetah Girl', but it was not included in the volume, nor in the revised and expanded edition *The Strange Papers of Dr Blayre* (1932; 12s), although this volume included all the other stories plus new ones like 'A House on the Way to Hell', about a library where unfinished classics are being completed by their dead authors. It finally became apparent that 'The Cheetah Girl' had been removed in case it contravened the obscenity laws of the time, since it dealt with the offspring of a prostitute and a cheetah. The story had been published privately in 1923, and only twenty copies exist. A later sequel, *Some Women at the University* (1934) is equally rare.

Heron-Allen was himself a noted scientist and scholar, with six sets of initials after his name. He was a marine biologist, a lecturer on protozoology, had been attached to Staff Intelligence in the First World War, had been admitted as a solicitor of the Supreme Court and spent several years in the US, and much more. His continuous output of books ranged in topics from violin-making to his own translation of the works of Omar

Khayyam. He was fascinated by fortune-telling, writing his own *Manual of Cheirosophy* (1885) and connected essays. He wrote a novel of psychic vampirism, *The Princess Daphne* (1888).

Pseudonyms: Christopher Blayre, 'Flavius'

Robert S. Hichens (b. Speldhurst, 14 November 1864; d. Zurich, 20 July 1950)
Having written his first novel when 17, Robert Smythe Hichens decided not to follow his career as musician, though he served as a music critic for some years. He wrote over fifty books, most of his weird fiction being concentrated in his early years. Hichens' weird fiction was never stereotyped: after a supernatural novel, *Flames* (1897) and a collection of his short pieces, *Bye-Ways* (1897; 9s), Hichens wrote his famous psychological ghost story 'How Love Came to Professor Guildea' (1900). Almost as popular is *The Black Spaniel* (1905), about a man aware of his reincarnation as a dog. Also of interest is the historical fantasy, *The Daughters of Babylon* (1899) written with Wilson Barrett, and *The Dweller on the Threshold* (1911) about psychic research. Later volumes include a collection *Snake-Bite* (1919; 6s) and a novel about rejuvenation, *Dr Artz* (1929).

Patricia Highsmith (b. Fort Worth, Tex., 19 January 1921)
Famous as a writer of realistic detective thrillers, her work should not be overlooked by horror fans. Her novels convey a frightening force of pure horror and two noted for their terrifying reality are *The Glass Cell* (1965) and *Those Who Walk Away* (1967). Her talent for the horrific short story was shown in 'The Snail Watcher' (1965), about a man whose hobby results in his nauseating death. It will be found in her collection of similar grotesquerie *Eleven* (1970; 11s).

Alfred Hitchcock (b. London, 13 August 1899)
As a director of suspense films Alfred Joseph Hitchcock ranks supreme, his ultimate in horror being *Psycho* (1960) and *The Birds* (1963), adapted from stories by **Robert Bloch** and **Daphne du Maurier**. Films aside, Hitchcock's name has adorned both a monthly mystery magazine (since 1955) and a series of anthologies. Hitchcock is not directly involved in either case, the anthologies often being the work of **Robert Arthur** or Harold Q. Masur. **Peter Haining** assembled several UK volumes. The anthologies take two forms, either macabre crime/mystery stories culled from the pages of his own and similar mystery magazines, or reprints of noted horror stories. The latter anthologies are more interesting and

rewarding, and they include the following: *Suspense* (1945; 14s), *Bar the Doors* (1946; 14s), *Hold Your Breath* (1947; 9s), *Fireside Book of Suspense* (1947; 27s), *Fear and Trembling* (1948; 13s), *Suspense Stories* (1949; 13s), *Stories They Wouldn't Let Me Do on TV* (1956; 25s), *My Favourites in Suspense* (1959; 22s), *Stories For Late at Night* (1961; 24s), *Haunted Houseful* (1961; 6s), *Stories My Mother Never Told Me* (1963; 26s), *Stories Not For the Nervous* (1965; 24s), *Stories That Scared Even Me* (1967; 19s) and *A Month of Mystery* (1969; 15s).

William Hope Hodgson (b. Blackmore End, 15 November 1877; d. Ypres, 19 April 1918)
The son of an Essex clergyman and the second of twelve children, Hodgson's youth was harsh and poor. One day he ran away to sea and, though caught, finally convinced his father of his wishes; in 1891 he embarked on a nautical life which lasted eight years. It was this that inspired the bulk of his later stories, most of which are unequalled in their ability to evoke the terrifying atmosphere of the unknown sea. Returning from sea, Hodgson became a muscle-building fanatic and he began to teach physical culture—his first sale was an article on that subject.

His first story, 'The Goddess of Kali' (1904), told of a series of odd murders apparently committed by a statue. His second story, 'A Tropical Horror' (1905), began his series of sea terror tales, epitomised by rotting wrecks haunted by fearful rats and terrifying denizens. His best atmosphere was created by utilising the legendary seaweed-bloated Sargasso Sea where ships and their crews are helplessly trapped. First used in 'From the Tideless Sea' (1906) and its sequel 'More News From the Homebird' (1907), it appeared again in 'The Mystery of the Derelict' (1907), 'The Thing in the Weeds' (1912), 'The Finding of the Graiken' (1913) and above all his first novel *The Boats of the 'Glen Carrig'* (1907). However his most reprinted story is 'The Voice in the Night' (1907), which concerns a ship hailed by something 'not quite right' out at sea. Hodgson's novels were all ahead of his time, particularly *The House on the Borderland* (1908) with its occupant menaced by frightful pig-things and undergoing strange cosmic experiences. *The Ghost Pirates* (1909) details the doom of a fated ship, and Hodgson shows his skill at maintaining a steadily rising pitch of suspense and fear. His strangest novel, *The Night Land* (1912) is set on a far future Earth inhabited by a terrifying array of hideous creations in a world of total night, and tells of the quest by a man across the land to rescue a girl.

During 1910 Hodgson wrote a series about the investigations of an occult detective collected as *Carnacki, the Ghost-Finder* (1913; 6s: US 1948; 9s). The volume can claim something of a record when in 1973 no less than three independent UK publishers had a paperback edition in print simultaneously. Hodgson's sea stories were collected as *Men of the*

Deep Waters (1914; 7s), *The Luck of the Strong* (1916; 8s), and a non-fantasy volume, *Captain Gault* (1917; 10s).

His output was terminated when he was killed in the First World War. For years he was forgotten, and it was in the US that his name was revived. **Derleth** published the four novels in an omnibus edition in 1946, and compiled the collection *Deep Waters* (1967; 13s). Since then much research has gone into Hodgson's life, and a magnificent biography has been written by **Sam Moskowitz**, included in a new collection of 'lost' stories *Out of the Storm* (1975; 7s).

E. T. A. Hoffman (b. Königsberg, 24 January 1776; d. Berlin, 25 June 1822)

Germany's master short story writer, Ernst Theodor Wilhelm (which he later changed to Amadeus because of his love of Mozart) Hoffman led a most precarious existence. His penchant for caricature often got him in trouble and he only obtained a secure job in 1816 as counsellor at the Berlin supreme court. His love of music had started him writing and the high spot in his career came with the performance of his opera *Undine* (see **Fouqué**) in 1816. Music also plays an important part in his early short stories—a spirit-haunted instrument figures in 'The Cremona Violin' and his earliest weird story, 'Ritter Glück' (1809), concerns the madness of a musician who believes himself to be Glück. 'Don Juan' (1813) is a haunting tale of a man who has an affinity with a dead singer.

Hoffman was also fascinated by the power of the mind, whether through hypnotic influence as in 'The Magnetiser' (1813) and 'The Sandman', or supernatural power as in 'The Sinister Ghost' (1819) and the devil-aided 'Ignaz Denner' (1816). Other tales are the ghost story 'The Legacy' (1817), the eerie 'The Lost Reflection' (1815) and the proto-detective story of a demented goldsmith with a dual personality, 'Fräulein von Scuderi' (1819). These and many more (not all supernatural) were collected as *Fantasiestücke* (1814–15), *Nachtstücke* (1816–17) and *Die Serapionsbrüder* (1818–21), but for those not proficient in nineteenth-century Prussian a recent US selection is *The Best Tales of Hoffman* (1967; 10s).

Predominantly a trendsetter, Hoffman came under the Gothic influence with his novel *Elixiere des Teufels* (1815–16; trans. *The Devil's Elixir*, UK 1824) about a monk who succumbs to the devil's temptations. Hoffman's name was immortalised by the composer Offenbach with his opera based on three *Tales of Hoffman*.

James Hogg (b. Ettrick, 24 November 1770; d. Altrive, 21 November 1835)

Hogg has been called the greatest peasant-poet in Scotland after Burns.

95

A rather eccentric protégé of **Scott**, he was raised a shepherd and turned to poetry in 1796. His early successes were tempered by farming losses and he only regained a recognised position in 1813. Many of his short stories dealing with the supernatural were inspired by local legends told to him by his mother. The bulk were collected as *Winter Evening Tales* (1820; 22s). Hogg also wrote a first-class Gothic novel, *The Private Memoirs and Confessions of a Justified Sinner* (1824; also titled *Confessions of a Fanatic*), which describes the gradual conquest by the devil of a righteous man who acquires a split-personality.

R. Thurston Hopkins (b. Bury St Edmunds, Suffolk, 1884; d. 23 May 1958)
A noted ghost-hunter, Robert Thurston Hopkins wrote a number of books about his experiences, such as *Adventures With Phantoms* (1947), *Ghosts Over England* (1953) and *The World's Strangest Ghost Stories* (1955). Like **Leslie** and **O'Donnell** he also invented his own ghost tales, and it is often difficult to distinguish the two. His first was *War and the Weird* (1916; 5s) with stories by Hopkins and an article by Forbes Phillips on psychic experiences in the trenches (then popular, see **Machen**). Other collections were *Uncanny Tales* (1941–45; 5s), *Weird and Uncanny Stories* (1945; 4s) and *Horror Parade* (1945; 5s) which includes vampires and other horrors. *Cavalcade of Ghosts* (1956; 22s) is a combination of true and fictional ghost stories by Hopkins and others.

Sydney Horler (b. London, 18 July 1888; d. 27 October 1954)
Although remembered mostly for detective thrillers, his weird fiction should not be overlooked. Several of his novels involve occult investigator Sebastian Quin (possibly inspired by **Christie**'s Harley Quin), as in the black magic based *The Evil Messenger* (1938). Quin features in some of the stories collected in *The Screaming Skull* (1935; 7s), but not in 'The Vampire' (1931) which had originally acted as a prelude to Horler's novel *The Vampire* (1931; book 1935). Other novels of interest, chiefly involving satanism, are *The Lady With The Lamp* (1944) and *The Devil Comes to Bolobyn* (1951).

Laurence Housman (b. Bromsgrove, Worcs., 18 July 1865; d. Glastonbury, Somerset, 20 February 1959)
Though his name is dwarfed by that of his brother, poet A. E. Housman, in the fantasy field Laurence was by far the greater, as both writer and artist, though he seldom illustrated his own work. His charming fairy tales and allegorical fantasies adorned many literary magazines of the 1890s, together with those beautiful idyllic illustrations, some by his

sister Clemence, or Sidney Sime. A rare fantasy novel was *Gods and Their Makers* (1897). His fables and fantasies were collected as *The Field of Clover* (1898; 10s), *Ironical Tales* (1926; 30s), *What Next?* (1938; 31s), *Strange Ends and Discoveries* (1948; 24s) and *The Kind and the Foolish* (1952).

Clemence Housman (1861–1955) wrote little. She and Laurence came to London in 1883 to study art, and during 1884 she wrote a novel to amuse the fellow students. It appeared as *The Were-Wolf* (1890) and has been hailed as the greatest story of lycanthropy ever written. Apart from *The Unknown Sea* (1898) her only other work was a psychological reconstruction of a story in *Morte d'Arthur, The Life of Sir Aglovale de Galis* (1905). Thereafter she became actively involved in the suffragette movement, after which she lived quietly with her brother.

Robert E. Howard (b. Peaster, Tex., 22 January 1906; d. Cross Plains, Tex., 12 June 1936)
Today his fiction is undergoing a phenomenal revival, to such an extent that it would be a full-time occupation to keep track of the various editions and reprintings of his stories. Howard was one of the old guard of the early days of *Weird Tales*. A puny, shy child, he took a body-building course that made him a muscle-bound youth, the image of the mighty heroes whose exploits he would later chronicle. Fixed on a writing career from the age of 15, rejections piled up until **Wright** bought a short tale about cavemen entitled 'Spear and Fang' (1925). His first impact, however, came with the creation of Solomon Kane, a six-teenth-century English puritan driven by an urge to seek out danger and right wrongs. Only seven stories saw print in Howard's lifetime, but subsequently discovered tales and fragments resulted in the volume *Red Shadows* (1968; 12s) with paperback selections as *The Moon of Skulls* (1969; 3s), *The Hand of Kane* (1969; 4s) and *Solomon Kane* (1971; 5s).

By 1929 Howard's output had expanded to westerns, boxing stories, straight adventure and other fields, but it was his inventions in *Weird Tales* that made him legendary. He was fascinated by primitive tribes, and an early sale called 'The Lost Race' (1927) told of a conflict between Celts and Picts. He then invented his own fictional Atlantis and detailed the adventures of the barbarian Kull. Only three appeared at the time, but further stories and fragments completed by **Lin Carter** form the book **King Kull** (1967; 12s). The original series metamorphosed into one about Bran Mak Morn (of which 'Worms of the Earth' (1932) is regarded by many as Howard's best weird tale), ultimately collected as *Bran Mak Morn* (1969; 8s: UK, *Worms of the Earth*, 1975), with sub-sequent adventures now being chronicled by **Karl Wagner**.

Howard's mightiest creation is Conan, who made his debut in 'The Phoenix on the Sword' (1932), and whose rise to kingship was elaborately detailed in numerous stories and serials first by Howard, and after his death steered to completion by **L. Sprague de Camp** (see App. I for full details). Conan was Howard's swan song. He was obsessed with his mother and knowing he could not live without her when she entered a terminal coma, he shot himself.

Howard was a surprisingly prolific writer, and long after his death a vast cache of unpublished manuscripts and unfinished drafts was discovered. The last few years have seen the publication of these in profusion, many in limited, deluxe, and very expensive editions. While of interest to the bibliophile and Howard specialist, they are not for recording here. His first posthumous collection was assembled by **Derleth** as *Skull-Face* (1946; 23s) and subsequent general collections have been *The Dark Man* (1963; 15s) and *Wolfshead* (1968; 7s); recent compilations like *Pigeons From Hell* (1976; 13s) are mostly repetitious. More specific collections include Oriental fantasies—*The Sowers of Thunder* (1973; 4s), *Swords of Shahrazar* (1975; 3s) and *The Lost Valley of Iskander* (1974; 3s), and tales of ancient Britain—*Tigers of the Sea* (1974; 4s), now being continued by Andrew Offutt starting with *Sword of the Gael* (1975). A novel set on a demon planet was *Almuric* (1939; book 1964). Real devotees can find plenty more.

Pseudonyms: Patrick Ervin, John Taverel, Sam Walser, Robert Ward

L. Ron Hubbard (b. Tilden, Neb., 1911)
Now the man behind the notorious Scientology sect, and one-time science fiction and adventure writer, many believe that Lafayette Ronald Hubbard was at his best when writing his fantasies for *Unknown*. His work for that magazine consisted of eight lead novels and six shorter pieces, most of which are out of print. Two of the earliest, *The Ultimate Adventure* (1939) and *Slaves of Sleep* (1939) are set in a parallel world of Arabian legend; *Death's Deputy* (1940) relates the fate of an accident-prone; *The Indigestible Triton* (1940; book *Triton*, 1949) is set in the god Neptune's domain; *Fear* (1940) is a psychological chiller about a man reconstructing four missing hours; *Typewriter in the Sky* (1940) is a rollicking farce of a man written into another's story; and *The Case of the Friendly Corpse* (1941) is set in the University of Unholy Names, which offers courses in the magical arts. Perhaps if Hubbard's name was not so blackened in Britain the public might get a chance to enjoy these and others of his imaginative gems.

Pseudonyms: Frederick Engelhardt, Rene Lafayette, Kurt von Rachen

Gilbert Hudlestone: *see* Roger Pater

Fergus Hume (b. England, 8 July 1859; d. nr Southend, Essex, 13 July 1932)

Fergusson Wright Hume never again achieved the phenomenal success accorded his detective novel *The Mystery of a Hansom Cab* (1886). Hume had sold the copyright for it in Australia for £50 and although the book sold nearly half a million copies he received no royalties. He returned to England in 1887 to capitalise on the success, but although he wrote some 150 books, he lived in near-poverty and died forgotten. Of fantasy interest are his lost-race novels *The Island of Fantasy* (1892), *The Harlequin Opal* (1893) and *The Mother of Emeralds* (1901), the last-named set in a giant South American cave system. *Aladdin in London* (1892) follows the results of using a magic ring; *The Golden Wang-Ho* (1898) is an Oriental fantasy. His best ghostly adventure is *The Yellow Hunchback* (1907), *The Spider* (1910) deals with witchcraft, and *A Son of Perdition* (1911) with the occult and Atlantis.

Other weird mysteries are *When I Lived in Bohemia* (1892), *The Mystery of the Shadow* (1906), *The Green Mummy* (1908), *The Solitary Farm* (1909) and *The Curse* (1910). A rare collection of fantastic tales 'for young and old' is *Chronicles of Faeryland* (1892; 9s); *The Dwarf's Chamber* (1896; 9s) is a volume of mystery stories—only the title tale is fantastic.

Violet Hunt (b. Durham, 1866; d. London, 16 January 1942)

The daughter of painter Alfred W. Hunt, Violet found her fame in journalism, writing regular columns for many leading Victorian periodicals. Her first novel appeared in 1894, but she later proved an excellent biographer. Her horror stories were collected as *Tales of the Uneasy* (1911; 9s) and *More Tales of the Uneasy* (1925; 4s), which includes her best-known 'The Corsican Sisters'. Miss Hunt had an ability for imbuing her stories with an original treatment, making even the hoariest old ghost chillingly refreshing.

Joris-Karl Huysman (b. Paris, 5 February 1848; d. Paris, 12 May 1907)

Huysman's life is much like an allegorical tale, with the moral 'don't dabble with the unknown'. In most eyes, Huysman was a respectable French civil servant writing in his spare time, his first novel appearing in 1874. But underneath he was fascinated by mysticism and the occult. The first signs of this were the weird dream sequences in *En Rade* (1887), but it exploded in *Là-Bas* (1891; trans. *Down There*, US 1902). In many ways autobiographical, it details his knowledge of the occult and portrays the depth and depravity of black magic. Huysman showed in a bad light two of the men who had taught him what he knew of occultism, and he was sure one, Guaita, was seeking revenge using spirit forces. Huysman took magical precautions himself and sought a devoutly religious outlet

99

as revealed in his later works. He finally found seclusion in a monastery.

Là-Bas remains a classic, responsible more than any other book for bringing the public's attention to the devil-worship that went on around them.

C. J. Cutcliffe Hyne (b. Bibury, Glos., 11 May 1865; d. Kettlewell, Yorks., 10 March 1944)
An active and widely travelled man, Charles John Cutcliffe Wright Hyne was able to draw on his experiences for his many volumes of fiction. He achieved fame for his series about the tough, ruthless Captain Kettle, a few stories of which enter the realms of the bizarre, as in 'Ice Age Woman' (1936) set among a lost Arctic race, and *Ivory Valley* (1938) with its elephants' graveyard in an extinct African volcano. Hyne's fantasy *tour-de-force*, however, is *The Lost Continent* (1899), a stirring adventure of the last days of Atlantis. Another novel, *Abbs—His Story Through the Ages* (1929) is not unlike **Arnold's** *Phra the Phoenician*. Most of Hyne's short weird fiction is scattered among his general collections, but the best will be found in *The Adventures of a Solicitor* (1898; 18s), a mixed-bag of sf and horror such as 'The Crimson Beast'—about an underground lake monster, a straight ghost story, 'The Seven Fluttering Hearts' and 'The Ghost of Farnley Abbey'—the tale of an invisible man. Several stories in *Man's Understanding* (1933), such as 'The Eeel', are worthy of investigation.

Pseudonym: Weatherby Chesney

Washington Irving (b. New York, 3 April 1783; d. Tarrytown, N.Y., 28 November 1859)
When today it is common for English writers to receive their first recognition in America, it might seem strange that Irving's fame first came in Europe. He spent many years travelling on the Continent, collecting legends, and also lived in England, becoming a close friend of **Walter Scott**. It was Scott who persuaded Irving to publish his *Sketch Book of Geoffrey Crayon, Gent.* (1819–20) from which come the immortal tales of 'Rip van Winkle' and 'The Legend of Sleepy Hollow'. Irving's only previous book had been a witty satire *A History of New York* (1809), pseudonymously published. Irving compiled three further collections of fictionalised legends, *Bracebridge Hall* (1822), *Tales of a Traveller* (1824), written after a few years in France and Germany, and *The Alhambra* (1832), inspired by Spain. The best-known supernatural tales from these volumes are 'The Spectre Bridegroom' (1819), 'The Adventure of the German Student' (1824; also titled 'The Lady of the Velvet Collar'),

'The Bold Dragoon' (1824), 'The Devil and Tom Walker' (1824) and 'Governor Manco and the Soldier' (1832).

Margaret Irwin (b. London, 1889; d. London, 11 December 1967)
Although she was primarily a historical novelist, Margaret Irwin wrote some very powerful supernatural stories. Her early book *Still She Wished For Company* (1924) was highly original. Narrated first by a girl who sees ghosts from the past, the viewpoint then switches to the dwellers in the past to whom the girl is a ghost from the future. Of her short fiction the most reprinted are 'The Book' (1930) which has a fatal influence over its owner, and 'The Earlier Service', about a haunted church. They will be found among non-fantasies and a play in *Madame Fears the Dark* (1935; 7s).

Shirley Jackson (b. San Francisco, 14 December 1919; d. Bennington, Vt., 8 August 1965)
The death of Shirley Jackson, aged 45, robbed the world of one of the most talented writers of psychological horror fiction. Wife of a literary critic, she claimed to be an amateur witch, specialising in small-scale magic! Certainly there was magic in her writing as seen from the torrent of response that followed her short story 'The Lottery' (1948), which told of a village and its annual cruel tradition. It resulted in the collection *The Lottery* (1949; 25s), which also carried her oft-reprinted 'The Demon Lover' and 'The Witch'. A variety of novels followed—a gothic thriller *Hangsaman* (1951), *The Bird's Nest* (1954), about split personality, and *The Sundial* (1958) with its bizarre people who await the end of the world (as revealed by a dead man) in an old mansion. Her crowning achievement was *The Haunting of Hill House* (1959), filmed as *The Haunting* (1963). The novel is not the traditional ghost story as the title implies. Instead it concentrates on the effects of fear upon the four people who risk staying in the house. By contrast, *We Have Always Lived in the Castle* (1962) is an amusing tale of three victims of poisoning whose spirits live on.

Jackson died before completing her next novel, but the existing portion was included with other stories in *Come Along With Me* (1968; 17s).

Carl Jacobi (b. Minneapolis, Minn., 10 July 1908)
Carl Richard Jacobi is one of those writers who methodically over the years produces above-average weird fiction yet is consistently overlooked. He has contributed to the genre for nearly fifty years. His first story, 'Mive', about a species of butterfly with an hallucinogenic wing-dust, won a competition, and one of the judges submitted it to *Weird Tales*

where it appeared in 1932. By then Jacobi had sold two other stories, and followed with his noted vampire story 'Revelations in Black' (1933). He appeared regularly in *Weird Tales* and *Thrilling Mystery* during the 1930s, but turned more to sf and other fields in the 1940s.

He has written about seventy weird stories and the best have been collected as *Revelations in Black* (1947; 21s), *Portraits in Moonlight* (1964; 14s) and *Disclosures in Scarlet* (1973; 17s).

W. W. Jacobs (b. London, 8 September 1863; d. London, 1 September 1943)

One of the most anthologised stories in the horror field is 'The Monkey's Paw' (1902), and deservedly so, since this tale of a paw that grants three wishes and the consequence of wishing that a dead son be alive ranks supreme among stories of implied horror. The story so overshadowed the other weird tales by William Wymark Jacobs that many people forgot his varied contribution to the genre and thought he only wrote sea stories. But he quite frequently returned to phantoms of an intangible or sometime more corporeal nature as in 'Jerry Bundler', 'The Interruption', 'My Brother's Keeper' and 'The Unknown'. Readers must rifle Jacobs's collections for these gems, but the volumes *The Lady of the Barge* (1902; 12s) and *Night Watches* (1914; 10s) will yield a good crop.

John W. Jakes (b. Chicago, 31 March 1932)

Always a prolific writer, mostly of detective thrillers and sf, of late John William Jakes has branched out into other fields, such as historical novels and children's books, plays, and even a musical adaptation of *The Wind in the Willows*.

Jakes first appeared in the fantasy field in 1950, and not long after was relieved of his duties as English teacher, apparently because he was writing science fiction! He has written several straight horror stories, but is best known for his Conan-like sword and sorcery series about Brak seeking his way home. He first appeared in 'The Devils in the Walls' (1963), and the stories have since been revised and expanded as the novel *Brak the Barbarian* (1968) with sequels *Brak vs The Sorceress* (1969; originally *Witch of the Four Winds*, 1963) and *Brak vs The Mark of the Demons* (1969). A serialised novel not in book form was *When the Idols Walked* (1964). As Agatha Christie did with Poirot, Jakes has already penned the final Brak story when he presumably reaches his homeland, but that is not yet for readers' eyes. Other novels of interest include *The Last Magicians* (1969), and a hilarious spoof on the whole heroic fantasy genre, *Mention My Name in Atlantis* (1972).

G. P. R. JAMES (b. London, 9 August 1799; d. Venice, 9 May 1860)
George Payne Rainsford James was one of those Victorian novelists
remembered for quantity rather than quality—but at his best, James was
good. His early Eastern fantasies, collected as *The String of Pearls* (1832)
were praised by Irving. His prodigious output of seventy-seven books,
mostly historical and biographical, was maintained by dictating to a
secretary. In his later years he ceased writing and became the British
consul to America and later Italy. A further fantasy was *The Last of the
Fairies* (1845) but his masterpiece of terror was *The Castle of Ehrenstein*
(1854), a superb portrayal of a ghost-riddled castle spoiled only at the
close by its natural solution.

Henry James (b. New York, 15 April 1843; d. London, 28 February
1916)
An American by birth, James emigrated to Europe in 1875 and became a
naturalised Englishman in 1915. His famous novels involve Americans
in Europe, and his works remain controversial for their style and pro-
lixity. Yet in *The Turn of the Screw* (1898) he produced a classic of the
supernatural about the evil spirits of two dead servants that possess the
bodies of two young children. It was admirably filmed as *The Innocents*
(1961). James's first ghost story, with a similar theme, had been 'The
Romance of Certain Old Clothes' (1868), and he continued to write them
for most of his life, the last being 'The Jolly Corner' (1908). Leon Edel
collected all of them as *The Ghostly Tales of Henry James* (1948; 18s), a
volume that reflects James's preoccupation with possession.

M. R. James (b. Goodnestone, Kent, 1 August 1862; d. Eton, Beds.,
12 June 1936)
The name of Montague Rhodes James at once signifies the very best in
ghost fiction, yet he wrote only a little over thirty such stories. His father,
a Fellow of King's College, Cambridge, had been a Curate in Kent from
1854, moving to Suffolk in 1865 where Montague was raised. The youth
showed an early interest in antiquarian studies and during his education
he won several prizes for his Latin prose and verse. He went on an archaeological expedition to Cyprus in 1887, and though adept in that sphere his
leanings were more to old manuscripts and buildings. He became a
Fellow of King's in 1887, and later became its Provost, finally becoming
Provost of Eton from 1918 to his death.
   He began his ghost stories for amusement, reading them to his friends
at King's at Christmas time. The first was 'Canon Alberic's Scrap-book'
(1894) which shows his specialist knowledge of old books, followed by
'Lost Hearts' (1895). They were collected as *Ghost Stories of an Antiquary*
(1904; 8s) which included the horror-in-the-tomb tale 'Count Magnus'

and the equally famous '"Oh, Whistle and I'll Come to You, My Lad"'.
It was followed by *More Ghost Stories of an Antiquary* (1911; 7s) including the tale of the accursed piece of paper, 'Casting the Runes', later
filmed as *Night of the Demon* (1957). Later volumes are *A Thin Ghost*
(1919; 5s) and *A Warning to the Curious* (1925; 6s) which includes 'The
Haunted Doll's House', written specially as one of a library of two hundred doll-size books for the doll's house presented to Queen Mary in
1924. The *Collected Ghost Stories* (1931; 31s) omits two he wrote subsequently: 'The Experiment' (1931) and 'A Vignette' (1936), reprinted in
Hugh Lamb's *The Thrill of Horror* and **Richard Dalby's** *The Sorceress in Stained Glass* respectively.

James maintained three rules for writing ghost stories: that there be no
verbose occult pedantry, that the stories be set in common-place surroundings, and above all that the ghost be malevolent. This, combined
with his unquestionable knowledge of old churches and ancient tomes,
resulted in some of the most powerful ghost stories one could hope to
read. James named as his original inspiration **Sheridan Le Fanu**, and
spent much time searching out more of Le Fanu's stories and collected
them as *Madame Crowl's Ghost* (1923; 12s). In turn M. R. James was an
inspiration to others, and among his best imitators are **F. I. Cowles,
M. P. Dare, R. H. Malden, A. N. L. Munby** and **E. G. Swain**. James
also wrote a children's novel, *The Five Jars* (1922). The jars successively
enhance the senses and awareness of the young boy who finds them to
the animals and little people around him.

Edgar Jepson (b. London, 28 November 1863; d. 11 April 1938)
A popular writer of detective fiction, Jepson ventured into fantasy more
than most people realise. In his last years he was associated with **John
Gawsworth**, often appearing in his anthologies, and collaborating
with him on stories such as the 'The Shifting Growth' (1936). Earlier
he had been a close friend of **E. Nesbit**, who encouraged his writing. His
first book appeared in 1895. His novel *The Horned Shepherd* (1904), based
on the Pan legend and dealing with sorcery, was originally privately published, and in that edition is extremely rare. His best novel was *The Moon
Gods* (1930), concerning a lost colony of Carthaginians in the Sahara.
Another novel is *The Garden at Number 19* (1910) and an unusual short
story, 'A Successful Experiment' (1921) tells how a cat's life-force is
transferred to a young girl.

Jasper John: *see* Rosalie Muspratt

Robert Barbour Johnson
Though his name only appeared in *Weird Tales* six times, between 1935 and 1941, every time it was with a memorable story. 'Far Below' (1939), chosen by Dorothy McIlwraith as one of the best stories ever published in the magazine, told of hideous things that appear in a New York subway. The war and other commitments kept Johnson from writing for a while, and then a new story, 'The Life-After-Death of Mr Thaddeus Warde', was accepted by *Weird Tales*, but the magazine folded before the story was published, and it finally saw light in 1963. A few other stories exist, enough for some enterprising publisher to assemble a superb collection.

Henry Bedford-Jones: *see* H. Bedford-Jones

Franz Kafka (b. Prague, 3 July 1883; d. nr Vienna, 3 June 1924)
As a seminal writer of experimental and allegorical fantasy there is no better example than Kafka. It is generally believed he was overlooked during his miserable life, but this is not so. Many writers appreciated his work, and he received the Fontane Prize in 1915. It is only because his most impressive work appeared after his death that it is thought his fame was posthumous. Three novels are of particular interest to the fantasy devotee: *The Castle* (1930), about a traveller in a village dominated by a symbolic castle; *The Trial* (1937), about a man's loneliness against incomprehensible and uncontrollable authority; and *Metamorphosis* (1937), which tells of a salesman who transforms into a cockroach, and reflects much of Kafka's own domination by his father. Of his short stories, 'In the Penal Colony' is the most striking. Kafka's effect on later writers is immeasurable; it is clearly evident in the weird fiction of Italian Dino Buzzati (1906–72) and Argentinian Julio Cortázar (b. 1914). Kafka's life was cut short after he contracted tuberculosis, but this may have been for the best, as his three younger sisters were all later murdered in Nazi concentration camps.

David H. Keller (b. Philadelphia, 23 December 1880; d. 13 July 1966)
During the years 1928 to 1935 Keller ranked as one of the leading science fiction writers, but he was also a gifted writer of horror stories, and ideally qualified in this respect—he was a psychiatrist in a mental hospital. Keller had started to write at age 14 but sent stories only to amateur magazines, not selling professionally till 1928. He married in 1903 and set up practice as a country doctor. In 1915 he became a junior physician at Illinois mental institution. During the First World War he made a name for himself helping shell-shock victims, a subject about which little

was then known. After the war he became a prominent psychiatrist until his retirement in 1945.

His knowledge of the workings of the mind was invaluable for his fiction, as seen in 'The Thing in the Cellar' (1932), the story of a young boy who fears something lurks in the cellar, and the results of a psychiatrist's attempts to cure him. The story goes that in 1932 Harry Bates (editor of *Strange Tales*) challenged Keller to write a truly horrific story. The result was 'The Dead Woman', about a man who, convinced his wife is dead although she seems alive to everyone else, decides he must bury her himself. *Strange Tales* folded before using it, and **Farnsworth Wright** rejected it as too shocking. Ironically its first professional publication was in the UK anthology *Nightmare By Daylight* (1936) edited by **C. C. Thomson**. Keller's weird fiction books include *The Eternal Conflict* (France, 1939 (incomplete): book, US 1949), about schizophrenia; *The Sign of the Burning Hart* (France, 1938 (private): US, 1948); *The Devil and the Doctor* (1940), a twist on the deal with the devil theme; and two short novels published together—*The Solitary Hunters* (originally 1934), about criminals secretly fed to a giant insect, and *The Abyss* (1948), in which a drug impregnated into chewing gum makes New Yorkers lose their inhibitions and a month of madness follows. Both weird and sf will be found in *Life Everlasting* (1949; 1n, 10s), *Tales From Underwood* (1952; 23s) and *The Folsom Flint* (1969; 17s).

At the time of his death Keller had completed a fantasy series tracing the chronology of the Hubelaire family from 200 B.C. through the ages. Entitled 'Tales From Cornwall', a few had first appeared in *Weird Tales* in 1929–30, and more appeared in *Magazine of Horror* in the late 1960s, but the full sequence has yet to be published.

Jessie Douglas Kerruish (b. nr Hartlepool, ?; d. Hove, Sussex, 1949) Born in County Durham of Manx descent, Jessie Kerruish was keen on archaeology, so it is little wonder that she should write historical fantasies. After a few story sales to magazines, including 'The Gold of Hermodyke' (1914) about a family curse, and some Arabian fantasies, she entered a publisher's first novel competition and won £1,000 with *Miss Haroun-al-Raschid* (1917). A second novel, *The Girl From Kurdistan* (1918), sold easily, but her third was rejected nearly everywhere. Yet it was this, *The Undying Monster* (1922), that was her masterpiece, and was subsequently filmed. It concerns a curse that manifests itself horribly in successive generations, and a psychic detective who discovers it is the result of hereditary lycanthropy. Her next book was a comedy, and for a fifth her early Arabian tales were collected as *Babylonian Nights Entertainment* (1934). But thereafter failing health and near blindness made writing impossible, and Jessie Kerruish slipped into oblivion.

Gerald Kersh (b. Teddington, Mddx, 6 August 1911; d. Middletown, US, 5 November 1968)
Kersh was so much larger-than-life. A huge, burly man who delighted in bending sixpences with his teeth as souvenirs, he loved telling wildly fantastic tales in his roaring deep bass voice. His jobs were many and varied, from baker to nightclub bouncer, fish-and-chip cook to wrestler. He was a Coldstream Guardsman in the Second World War, and later settled in the US, becoming an American citizen in 1959. He had married in 1938, but that was dissolved in 1943 when he remarried, again dissolved in 1955 when he married a third time. This fiery nature translated itself into his fiction, his first novel *Jews Without Jehovah* (1935) being withdrawn to save libel suits! Kersh wrote over twenty novels, but it is his short fiction that engraves his name in the horror roll of honour. His early collection, *The Horrible Dummy* (1944; 23s), includes his views on war in 'Comrade Death'. *The Brighton Monster* (1953; 12s) includes his best work, contrasting the delicate charm of 'Frozen Beauty' with the harsh poignant reality of 'Queen of Pig Island'. The title story of *Men Without Bones* (1955; 22s) reveals the shocking origins of humanity.

A selection of some of his stories appeared as *On an Odd Note* (1958; 13s); Harlan Ellison edited his own choice as *Nightshade and Damnations* (1968; 11s). Of Kersh's novels, most of the later ones fall into the weird category, such as *A Long Cool Day in Hell* (1965), *The Angel and the Cuckoo* (1967) and *Brock* (1969), with its bizarre array of exotic characters.

Stephen King (b. Portland, Maine, 21 September 1946)
The success of *Carrie* (1974) as a book and a film has rocketed Stephen Edwin King to the forefront of horror fiction writers. The novel tells of an innocent teenager who possesses terrifying telekinetic powers. King followed the book with a novel about a small town where the population vanishes overnight, *Salem's Lot* (1975). He sold his first two stories to *Startling Mystery Stories*, 'The Glass Floor' (1967) and 'The Reaper's Image' (1969), both cleverly reflecting the terror held by mirrors. His latest novel, *The Shining* (1977), tells of an evil entity in a Colorado luxury hotel closed for the winter, and King is currently adapting it for the screen. *Night Shift* (1977; 15s) is a collection of his stories. Future projects include an epic fantasy *The Stand*.

Rudyard Kipling (b. Bombay, 30 December 1865; d. London, 18 January 1936)
The creator of Mowgli and Gunga Din was born in India, but sent to England for his education. He started to write at college, and while he was still at Westward Ho, his parents privately published his first book, *Schoolboy Lyrics* (1881), in India. In 1883 Kipling returned to India, became a journalist, and later sub-edited a local newspaper which carried

several of his stories such as 'The Strange Ride of Morrowbie Jukes' and 'The Phantom 'Rickshaw' (both 1885). They were both included in his first weird collection *The Phantom 'Rickshaw* (1888; 4s), though the earlier *Plain Tales From the Hills* (1887; 40s) had carried some fantasy, all inspired by his Indian background. His most noted weird story is 'The Mark of the Beast' (1890), in which a man cursed by a priest begins to transform into a leopard. Later stories of note are the ghost story 'The House Surgeon' (1909) and the psychological horror tale 'In the Same Boat' (1911). Kipling's fame rests securely on his charming *Jungle Books* (1894–95), and successive volumes like *Kim* (1901) and the *Just So Stories* (1902). A subsequent children's fantasy telling of Britain's distant past was *Puck of Pook's Hill* (1906), with a sequel *Rewards and Fairies* (1910).

Russell Kirk (b. Plymouth, Mich., 19 October 1918)
Since the publication of *The Conservative Mind* (1953), Russell Amos Kirk has been regarded as one of the leading philosophers of the new American conservatism. In 1946 he had been appointed as Assistant Professor of the History of Civilisation at Michigan State College but left in 1953 because he was dissatisfied with the job. Since then he has concentrated on writing philosophical and educational books. Occasionally he has ventured into weird fiction, mostly ghost stories that owe much inspiration to the time he spent in remote parts of Scotland in the 1950s. They were collected as *The Surly Sullen Bell* (1962; 10s; retitled *Lost Lake*, 1966). He also wrote a weird novel, *Old House of Fear* (1961). Subsequent short stories will be found in *F&SF*.

Otis Adelbert Kline (b. Chicago, 1891; d. New York, 24 October 1946)
Kline was a prolific adventure writer for the pulp magazines, before the success of his literary agency consumed most of his time. Initially a song writer and publisher, his first fiction sale, 'The Thing of a Thousand Shapes' (1923) had the honour of being the first serial in *Weird Tales*. He appeared regularly in the magazine over the next decade, his contributions including an occult novel *The Bride of Osiris* (1927), a jungle adventure *Tam, Son of the Tiger* (1931), and a swashbuckling space opera, *Buccaneers of Venus* (1932). The last two were written much in the style of E. R. Burroughs and a myth grew up that a feud existed between the two writers over stealing locales. It's a legend that has never been entirely put to rest, but suffice it to say both writers were adept at the same thing. Kline also wrote a series of Oriental fantasies about a dragoman, which began with 'The Man who Limped' (1930), and he was a great friend and collaborator with E. H. Price.

Nigel Kneale (b. Lancaster, 1922)
To British audiences Kneale's name is instantly linked to that of Professor Quatermass as a result of the three successful television serials *The Quatermass Experiment* (1953), *Quatermass II* (1955) and *Quatermass and the Pit* (1958), a thorough blend of sf and horror. All were subsequently filmed.

Kneale had trained as a lawyer, but received his diploma as a playwright after studying at RADA, and for a while he acted. Then came his collection *Tomato Cain* (1949; 29s) which won the Somerset Maugham Award. Its contents are frequently reprinted and include 'The Photograph' and 'Oh, Mirror, Mirror' which reflect man's insanity, 'The Pond', about the batrachian revenge upon a man who kills frogs, and the haunting 'Minuke'. Kneale's work is best known on television, and subsequent off-trail plays include *The Road* (1963) and *The Stone Tape* (1972), both showing scientific investigations of haunted places with frightening results. The scripts received book publication with a third as *The Year of the Sex Olympics* (1976). Kneale also scripted a series of six plays, *The Beasts* (1976), which reflect the horrific interaction between humans and animals, and he is currently planning a fourth Quatermass serial.

Vernon Knowles (b. Adelaide, 1899)
Knowles came to England in the 1920s when he began his many novels and poems. He struck special originality with his collection *The Street of Queer Houses* (1925; 15s), about a street built by an eccentric architect with houses that reflect the peculiarities of its occupants: in 'The House of Yesterdays' each door opens into the past and costs you ten years of life; 'The House That Took Revenge' creeps gradually nearer the cliffs. Later collections are *Silver Nutmegs* (1927; 7s), which shows the influence of **Dunsany**, and *Here and Otherwhere* (1926; 9s). A selection from these three appeared as *Two and Two Make Five* (1935; 12s). *Eternity in an Hour* (1932) is a charming fantasy about childhood.

Katherine Kurtz (b. Coral Gables, Fla., 18 October 1944)
One of the most promising of the new generation of fantasy writers, Miss Kurtz has worked in a variety of fields such as oceanography, anthropology, cancer research, television and with the Los Angeles Police Department. She had also, by her mid-20s, studied many topics. She burst into prominence with her trilogy about the deryni, an alternate medieval world name for witches and warlocks—certain gifted humans who find themselves hunted by the church. Their fight for survival and freedom is brilliantly chronicled in *Deryni Rising* (1970), *Deryni Checkmate* (1972) and *High Deryni* (1973). She is currently working on a trilogy set a few centuries earlier, starting with *Camber of Culdi* (1976).

Henry Kuttner (b. Los Angeles, 7 April 1915; d. California, 3 February 1958)
Kuttner has been called one of the most versatile imitators in fantasy fiction, yet this is an understatement, since beyond merely copying style he embellished and sculptured it to obtain the best. Once he mastered a writer's style, he invariably improved on it.

Kuttner's early sales to *Weird Tales*, starting with 'The Graveyard Rats' (1936)—regarded by some as one of the most horrifying stories ever written— showed the influence of **Lovecraft**, but with the sympathetic 'I, the Vampire' (1937) he moved on. His Elak series, beginning with 'Thunder in the Dawn' (1938) was in imitation of **Howard**'s Conan. Thereafter he drifted more into the sf field, encouraged by his marriage in 1940 to **C. L. Moore**, but he also produced some stunning fantasies for *Unknown* (now in the style of **Thorne Smith**), epitomised by 'The Misguided Halo' (1939) about a man who acquires one! During the 1940s he combined certain fantasy styles, predominantly that of **Merritt**, in a series of action-packed fantasy novels such as *The Dark World* (1946), set in a sorcery-dominated alternate world, *Valley of the Flame* (1946), set among the lost race of jaguar people, and his best *The Mask of Circe* (1948), in which a man finds himself enacting the part of Jason on his quest for the Golden Fleece. Unaccountably most of his weird fantasies have been forgotten, although his sf is nearly all in book form. During the 1950s the Kuttners took to writing film screenplays, and all but left the fantasy field. He died from an acute coronary, aged 42.

Pseudonyms: Paul Edmonds, Noel Gardner, Keith Hammond, Hudson Hastings, Peter Horn, Kelvin Kent, Robert O. Kenyon, C. H. Liddell, K. H. Maepenn, Scott Morgan, Lawrence O'Donnell, Lewis Padgett, Woodrow Wilson Smith, Charles Stoddard (Many joint with C. L. Moore.)

Hugh Lamb (b. Sutton, Surrey, 4 February 1946)
An accomplished and thorough anthologist, Hugh Charles Lamb specialises in unearthing long-forgotten authors and stories from musty old books. By profession a journalist, in his spare time he has thoroughly researched many of the abandoned by-ways of horror.

His first anthology, *A Tide of Terror* (1972; 17s), was assembled in an attempt to rectify the general anthology situation of the same standard stories being reprinted endlessly. He can claim credit for having recently revived the names of A. C. Benson, V. Bryusov, F. Cowles, Erckmann-Chatrian, R. M. Gilchrist, L. A. Lewis, L. T. C. Rolt, Eleanor Scott and E. H. Visiak. He was also the first to commission short fiction from John Blackburn and Robert Haining, and achieved a scoop by unearthing a lost M. R. James story in his anthology *The Thrill of Horror*

(1975; 22s). His other anthologies (further details in App. II) run: *A Wave of Fear* (1973; 17s), *Victorian Tales of Terror* (1974; 15s), *Terror By Gaslight* (1975; 14s), *The Taste of Fear* (1976; 13s), *Return from the Grave* (1976; 20s), *Victorian Nightmares* (1977; 21s) and *Cold Fear: New Tales of Terror* (1977; 15s). He has also edited *Star Book of Horror No. 1* (1975; 13s) and *No. 2* (1976; 15s). A forthcoming anthology is *The Man-Wolf* (1978; 12s), featuring the short novel by Erckmann-Chatrian.

Andrew Lang (b. Selkirk, Scotland, 31 March 1844; d. Banchory, 20 July 1912)
A popular Victorian literary figure, Lang specialised in researching into fantastic literature, mythology and the occult. After obtaining a first-class degree in Classics at Oxford he became a busy journalist. His first books were mostly verse, but he soon branched into reference works on philosophy and mysticism. So respected was he in this field that he was commissioned to write many entries on ghosts and the occult for the ninth edition (1875) of the *Encyclopædia Brittanica*.

As an editor he is best remembered for his charming series of fairy tale anthologies for children that ran to eight volumes from *The Blue Fairy Book* (1889) to *The Lilac Fairy Book* (1910) every one identified by a different colour. But he also edited *Poems of E. A. Poe* (1881), and a collection of French horror stories, *The Dead Leman* (1889; 7s).

By and large his own fiction is largely forgotten. An early volume was the collection *In the Wrong Paradise* (1886; 9s). A great friend of Haggard, Lang wrote a parody of *She* called *He* (1887), and they later collaborated on the further exploits of Odysseus in *The World's Desire* (1890). Other novels are a macabre mystery *The Mark of Cain* (1886), and a grim historical fantasy *A Monk of Fife* (1896).

Noel Langley (b. Durban, 25 December 1911)
Langley's best claim to fantasy fame rests on his film scripts, as most of his books are straight fiction. Only the collection *Tales of Mystery and Revenge* (1950; 7s) ranks within the field. It includes the noted tales of African black magic 'Serenade for Baboons' and 'The Bone Bead Necklace', plus a charming fantasy of a dead soldier's return to be with his dying sweetheart, 'Saint Wilbur'. Langley began writing in 1935 and co-wrote the screenplay to the Judy Garland version of *The Wizard of Oz* (1938), still one of the best fantasy films ever made. Later ventures into the field include *Scrooge* (1951), *Trilby and Svengali* (1954) and *The Search for Bridey Murphy* (1957).

Sterling Lanier (b. New York, 18 December 1927)
Because Sterling Edmund Lanier's work is predominantly marketed as science fiction, fantasy and horror fans may easily pass it by, but it fits neatly into both fields. By profession a sculptor (of miniature metal figures) and a writer, he is distantly related to Tennessee Williams. His fiction has been appearing in the sf magazines since 1961, and of strict interest to the fantasy fan will be the recollections of Brigadier Ffellowes as related at the club that began with 'Soldier Key' (1968), in which he stumbles over the native worship of a massive hermit crab. These were collected as *The Peculiar Exploits of Brigadier Ffellowes* (1972; 7s), and subsequent tales have appeared in *F&SF* together with unconnected horror stories like '. . . No Traveller Returns' (1974). He has also written the grand post-nuclear quest novel *Hiero's Journey* (1973) and is working on the sequel *Prince Hiero*.

Greye La Spina (b. Wakefield, Mass., 10 July 1880; d. 17 September 1969)
A name that evokes fond memories among devotees of *Weird Tales*, to which she contributed some of her best stories—such as the menace of the feline guardian in 'The Tortoise-Shell Cat' (1924), 'The Gargoyle' (1925), about devil-worship, and the vampire novel *Fettered* (1926). She gave several original treatments to the werewolf theme, as in 'The Devil's Pool' (1932), *Invaders from the Dark* (1925; book 1960; also titled *Shadow of Evil*, 1966) and her first published story, 'Wolf of the Steppes' (1919), in the first issue of the rare *Thrill Book*.
　　Born Fanny Greye Bragg, the daughter of a methodist clergyman, she had married in 1898, but her husband died in 1900. She married again in 1910, this time to Robert La Spina, Barone di Savuto, descended from Russian nobility. She wrote stories for a variety of pulp magazines, but primarily for *Weird Tales*. At one time a newspaper photographer, and a typist for writers, she was also a self-made Master Weaver and won prizes for her rugs and tapestries. She lived for many years on a Pennsylvania farm, and when she moved to New York found she could not sleep unless she played a tape of the sound of crickets! Her personal experience with the bold and menacing rats near her farm inspired the story 'The Rat Master' (1942). A recent limited edition booklet of her stories was *The Gargoyle* (1975; 2s).

Pseudonym: Isra Putnam

Francis Lathom (b. Norwich, Norfolk, 1777; d. Scotland, 19 May 1832)
One of the lesser-known though one-time popular Gothic writers, Lathom wrote a lively and successful play while still in his teens. He followed it

with *The Castle of Ollada* (1794), a striking haunted castle novel with natural explanations. More important was *The Midnight Bell* (1798) about another gloomy, haunted castle with its midnight spectre. It was listed as one of the library of Gothic novels in *Northanger Abbey* (1818). Despite this success, Lathom spent most of his time writing comedies for the theatre and, apart from *Mysteries* (1800), seldom returned to the field until his last work *Mystic Events* (1830), which centred on witchcraft and other evils in Anne Boleyn's day. Lathom fell in love with Scotland and its legends which he adapted into several short stories like 'The Water Spectre' (1809).

Harold Lawlor

Lawlor was an Irish American who contributed twenty-nine stories to *Weird Tales* from 'Spectre in the Steel' (1943) to 'The Dream Merchant' (1953). His chosen career had been as a concert pianist and composer, but deafness precluded this, and he turned to writing while working as a clerk in Chicago. Most of his tales, like 'What Beckoning Ghost?' (1948) and 'The Cinnabar Redhead' (1946), are ghost stories, and others show his scholarly interest in music, as in 'The Terror in Teakwood' (1947), when a pianist's severed hand stays alive.

Margery Lawrence (b. Wolverhampton, Staffs., c 1896; d. London, 13 November 1969)

A prolific novelist, mostly in the adventure-romance field, Miss Lawrence also maintained a healthy contribution to the horror field. This began with an excellent volume of tales narrated by members of the Club of the Round Table, called *Nights of the Round Table* (1926; 12s); a further selection was *The Terraces of Night* (1932; 12s). Her most important collection is *Number Seven, Queer Street* (1945; 7s), which recounts the investigations of occult detective Miles Pennoyer. Highly recommended, the book displays Miss Lawrence's not inconsiderable knowledge of the supernatural. A further series appeared as *Master of Shadows* (1959; 4s). A few weird stories also appear in *Strange Caravan* (1941; 9s) and *Cardboard Castle* (1951; 7s).

In her later years her novels touched more on the occult, though two earlier examples were *Madame Holle* (1934) and *The Bridge of Wonder* (1939). *The Rent in the Veil* (1951) tells of a woman who finds she is living in both Roman and modern Britain. *The Yellow Triangle* (1965) used faked spiritualists as its theme. *Bride of Darkness* (1967) is about a man married to a modern witch, and *A Residence Afresh* (1969) is an adventure of life after death. Bordering on sf, *The Tomorrow of Yesterday* (1966) tells of the founding of Atlantis by exiles from Mars.

Errol Lecale: *see* Peter Saxon

Vernon Lee (b. nr Boulogne, 14 October 1856; d. San Gervasio, 13 February 1935)

Violet Paget, who wrote the majority of her books as Vernon Lee, lived most of her life in Italy and her works, over forty volumes, deal chiefly with the life, art and literature of that country. She occasionally turned to weird fiction, and earned the praise of **Montague Summers** who equalled her talent to that of **M. R. James**. Her first work in the genre was *Hauntings* (1890; 4s), in which the haunted villa in 'Amour Dure' shows her knowledge of Italy, and 'Oke of Okehurst' is a traditional haunted English manor. Two of these stories were included in *Pope Jacynth* (1904; 7s: retitled, *Ravenna and Her Ghosts*, 1962; 6s) and a further compilation was *For Maurice* (1927; 5s). This included some of her earliest and most unusual stories, such as 'The Doll' (1899), an object made by a Count, in the likeness of his dead wife, which lives on after his death, and 'Marsyas in Flanders' (1900), about the sudden appearance of a supposed statue of Christ that possesses a will of its own. A representative compilation of her stories appeared as *The Snake Lady* (1954; 8s) in the US; it has had UK editions as *Supernatural Tales* (1955; 6s; retitled *The Virgin of the Seven Daggers*, 1962; 6s).

J. Sheridan Le Fanu (b. Dublin, 28 August 1814; d. Dublin, 7 February 1873)

Acclaimed by many as the greatest writer of the supernatural who ever lived, Joseph Sheridan Le Fanu must rank as the British **Poe** as the link between the Gothic horror school and modern psychological fear. The grand-nephew of playwright Richard Brinsley Sheridan, Le Fanu was born into an upper-class family and had a solid education. This did not stop him becoming acquainted with the Irish peasantry and their folk-tales, which were an early inspiration to him. From 1839 he devoted himself to journalism, acquiring several Dublin journals and amalgamating them as the *Evening Mail*. He would later (1869–72) edit the *Dublin University Magazine* (not connected with the University), and it was in this that he published most of his weird fiction.

Probably the earliest was 'The Ghost and the Bone-Setter' (1838), the first of a series of supposed discoveries among the papers of a parish priest, Francis Purcell. Most of these tales recounted the local legends, and were later published as *The Purcell Papers* (1880; 13s). At the same time appeared 'Schalken the Painter' and 'Passage in the Secret History of an Irish Countess', which was the basis of *Uncle Silas*. Le Fanu often rewrote his stories two or three times after publication, and with title changes it gives the impression that he wrote more than he did.

He married in 1844 and turned to writing novels, initially historical. He collected his early tales as *Ghost Stories and Tales of Mystery* (1851; 4s).

In 1858 his wife died; Le Fanu became a recluse and took to writing most of his weird fiction, starting with *Uncle Silas* (1864)—which E. F. Benson called 'a masterpiece of alarm'. There followed *The House by the Churchyard* (1863), *Wylder's Hand* (1864), *Guy Deverell* (1865), and a stunning collection of short stories *In a Glass Darkly* (1872; 5s). Among them is 'Green Tea', the psychological classic of a man haunted by a monkey-like creature, 'Carmilla', about a female vampire and recently filmed as *The Vampire Lovers* (1970), and 'Mr Justice Harbottle', in which a tyrannical judge is haunted by a man he sentenced to death.

Le Fanu's ability to build an atmosphere of suspense by implied horror and maintain it at a frightening level has been an inspiration to many later writers, not least M. R. James, who unearthed many of Le Fanu's lost stories and published them as *Madame Crowl's Ghost* (1923; 12s). A variety of different compilations have appeared since, including *The Vampire Lovers* (1970; 7s). In 1976 a US publisher released the complete *Collected Works* in fifty-two volumes for $1,000. David Sutton has compiled *Masters of Terror: J. Sheridan Le Fanu* (1978).

Fritz Leiber (b. Chicago, 24 December 1910)
Fritz Reuter Leiber, Jr is a paradox. Highly regarded as a writer of science fiction, for which he has won awards, he is predominantly a fantasy writer, and much of his sf falls within that category.

The son of a noted Shakespearean actor who had starred in a few silent films, Fritz Jr joined his father's road company in 1934 for two years, and even made a few film appearances himself. He married in 1936 and settled for a steady job, also starting his writing. Correspondence with a friend, Harry Fischer, had inspired the idea of two fantasy characters, the spritely Grey Mouser and his tall friend from the northern climes, Fafhrd. Leiber turned the concept into a brilliant story, 'Adept's Gambit', set in an imaginary world full of inspired creations. Sword and sorcery at its best, it owed no allegiance to the Conan school of barbarism. By contrast Fafhrd and the Mouser are civilised, but there is no end of clashing swords and mystic magic. Yet the story was rejected. Leiber wrote another, 'Two Sought Adventure' (1939), which he sold to *Unknown* and thereafter he added to the saga of these two lovable rogues, producing what many consider the most literate and important sword and sorcery series available. Initially collected as *Two Sought Adventure* (1957; 7s), Leiber has since reworked them into a chronology and they saw paperback publication as *Swords and Deviltry* (1970; 3s), *Swords Against Death* (1970; 10s), *Swords in the Mist* (1968; 6s), *Swords Against Wizardry* (1968; 4s), *Swords of Lankhmar* (1968) and *Swords and Ice Magic* (1977), the order in which they should be read. One of the series, 'Ill Met in

Lankhmar' (1970), won the Hugo *science fiction* award! Leiber deservedly wins awards, and other fantasies so acclaimed are 'Gonna Roll the Bones' (1967) and 'Ship of Shadows' (1969), and at the Second World Fantasy Convention he received a Life Award for his contribution to the genre.

Fantasy aside, Leiber has carved a special niche in the horror field by concentrating on the modern horror of city life. Such stories include 'The Automatic Pistol' (1940), about a gun that did its own killing and 'Smoke Ghost' (1941), with its grimy modern-day phantom, but he developed the theme completely in his recent novel *Our Lady of Darkness* (1977). Concentrating on San Francisco, he weaves an occult thriller around the reasons why so many of that city's coterie of writers (**Bierce, London,** Sterling) met such tragic deaths, with a special emphasis on the life of **Clark Ashton Smith.** Leiber's early novel, *Conjure Wife* (1943) dealt with witchcraft in a modern university, and was filmed as *Night of the Eagle* (1962). He again used witchcraft in *Gather, Darkness!* (1943), where he foresaw it returning as a dominant political force in the future. Most of his early stories were collected as *Night's Black Agents* (1947; 11s) which included the first publication of 'Adept's Gambit'. Since then his many collections are mergings of fantasy and sf, such as *Shadows With Eyes* (1962; 6s) and *The Secret Songs* (1968; 11s).

Gaston Leroux (b. 1868; d. 16 April 1927)
One of France's major mystery writers, Leroux's name has been eclipsed by the popularity of his novel *The Phantom of the Opera* (1911) which supplied film parts for Lon Chaney Sr, Claude Rains and Herbert Lom in 1925, 1943 and 1962.

Leroux was a lawyer and a reporter, travelling widely and often risking his life. This supplied endless ideas for his novels, which began with a classic early locked-room thriller, *The Mystery of the Yellow Room* (1907), and its sequel *The Perfume of the Lady in Black* (1911). His weird novels include *Balaoo* (1912), about the discovery of the Missing Link, *The Man With the Black Feather* (1912), about a man cursed by an earlier, evil incarnation, and *The Man Who Came Back From the Dead* (1916). After his death several stories appeared in translation in *Weird Tales*, including the novel *The Haunted Chair* (1931) and a series related by a circle of friends including 'The Inn of Terror', 'The Woman With the Velvet Collar' and the powerful 'In Letters of Fire', most having been written in the early 1900s.

Shane Leslie (b. London, 29 September 1885; d. Hove, 13 August 1971)
John Randolph Shane Leslie, who became 3rd Baronet Leslie in 1944, was something of a phenomenon. After taking his degree in 1907, he went to Russia where he became a friend of Tolstoy. He became noted

as a biographer, but for a while lived as a tramp. He spent most of his life painstakingly investigating unexplained phenomena, and collated the most fascinating in his *Ghost Book* (1955). He wrote several fictional ghost stories, which read just like his factual accounts. An early collection was *Masquerades* (1924; 21s), followed by *Fifteen Odd Stories* (1935; 15s).

Maurice Level (b. 1875; d. 1926)
Like his countryman, **Villiers de L'Isle Adam,** Level was a master of the *conte cruel,* yet today he is almost forgotten. By profession a doctor and surgeon, Level knew much about the tortures of the human body as witnessed in hospitals and later during the First World War. He began writing in the early 1900s, his stories seeing frequent UK translation in magazines. They were eventually collected as *Crises* (1920; 26s: also titled *Tales of Mystery and Horror,* US 1920; *Grand Guignol Stories,* UK 1922). His best story, 'Night and Silence', is a very effective piece about two brothers, one blind, the other a deaf-mute, and what happens when they find their sister, believed dead, is still alive in her coffin! Level also wrote the macabre novels *The Grip of Fear* (1909) and *The Shadow* (1923; US *Those Who Return*).

Philip Levene (b. London, 1928; d. London, March 1973)
Levene was a radio and television scriptwriter of mystery stories, many of them in the horror/fantasy realm. He had originally trained as an actor, but turned to writing after selling a play to BBC Radio in 1956. His ability to create tension and suspense fitted admirably a series of fifteen-minute radio plays, *Just Before Midnight* (1964), to which Levene contributed twenty scripts such as 'The Watchman' who is discovered boiled alive, and 'Death Sentence', about a man who becomes a murderer when told he has only a month to live. For television he contributed to the *Invisible Man* series in 1958, and wrote many of the bizarre episodes for *The Avengers,* such as *Man-Eater of Surrey Green* (1966)—about carnivorous plants and the Cybernaut adventures. He only wrote three books, two thrillers and a collaboration about a race of troglodytes that threaten the world, *City of the Hidden Eyes* (1960). His death after a series of operations for cancer robbed TV and radio of a major talent.

L. A. Lewis
Research has yet to uncover any facts about L. A. Lewis, but suffice it to say he produced some of the most original tales of terror published as *Tales of the Grotesque* (1934; 10s), several of which have been reprinted in Hugh Lamb's anthologies. His story 'The Author's Tale' was included in **C. C. Thomson's** *Terror by Night* (1935).

Matthew Gregory Lewis (b. London, 9 July 1775; d. at sea, 10 May 1818)

If any novel marks the pinnacle of Gothic horror, it is *The Monk*, and if any writer is synonymous with the style it is M. G. Lewis. He had visited Weimar in Germany in 1792 and met **Goethe**. Fascinated by the supernatural he read several important works while in Germany. Then in 1794 he read **Radcliffe's** *Udolpho* and, his imagination fired, he launched into *Ambrosio, or The Monk* (1796). It tells of a young monk who succumbs to the devil's temptations and sinks to the depths of depravity. Lewis threw in as much licentious and erotic material as he could, and there was naturally an uproar when it appeared that guaranteed it a best-seller. It was classed obscene, and Lewis had to tone down a few passages, but the book was in its fourth edition before his amendments appeared. He wrote several other horror works, such as his plays *The Castle Spectre* (1798) and *Adelgitha* (1828), the demonic verse *The Isle of Devils*, and he edited a collection of specially written stories, *Tales of Wonder* (1801; 23s), which included contributions from **Scott**. But his other most important volume is *Romantic Tales* (1808; 5s) which includes his other stories of witchcraft, devilry and pure horror—'The Anaconda', 'My Uncle's Garret Window', 'The Spirit of the Frozen Ocean', 'The Fair Facardins' and 'Mistrust'.

In 1812 Lewis inherited two large estates in Jamaica, and it was while returning from there that he died of yellow fever. Buried at sea, the story goes that his coffin did not sink at first, as air trapped under the sheet kept it afloat, and it drifted away eerily into the morning mist.

Jonas Lie (b. Eker, 6 November 1833; d. 5 July 1908)

Jonas Lauritz Idemil Lie set out in life as a lawyer, but fatal speculation in timber made him bankrupt. He took to writing and became one of Norway's leading novelists, and was so successful that he rapidly repaid his debts. He was renowned for his realistic accounts of the sea and fishermen, but in later years he brought in mystical elements. His final works reveal a belief that weird forces are at work in the mind to bring about evil. Recommended novels are *Evil Powers* (1890), *Niobe* (1893) and *The Reindeer* (1896). His collection *Trolls* (1891; 11s: UK *Weird Tales from Northern Seas*, 1893) blends the superstitions and magic of the Lapp races. The UK edition was illustrated by **Laurence Housman**.

David Lindsay (b. London, 3 March 1878; d. Brighton, 6 June 1945)

Lindsay is a tragic example of a writer who strives to produce a masterpiece which goes unrecognised until after his death. *A Voyage to Arcturus* (1920) is today acclaimed a classic. Telling of a spiritual journey to the planet Tormance, it is by no means science fiction, but as bizarre, absorbing and bewildering a fantasy as one could wish for. The first edition sold under 600 copies, and Lindsay found it increasingly difficult to sell subsequent work. *The Haunted Woman* (1922) is a beautiful story of a peculiar house with a phantom staircase leading to an other-worldly room. Other metaphysical tales of fantasy were *Sphinx* (1923) and *Devil's Tor* (1932). Two other novels remain unpublished, though he did sell a historical novel *The Adventures of M. de Mailly* (1926: US *A Blade For Sale*, 1927). A worthy memorial to him is *The Strange Genius of David Lindsay* (1970) with critical articles by **Colin Wilson, E. H. Visiak** and **J. B. Pick**.

Charles Lloyd: *see* Charles Birkin

Jack London (b. San Francisco, 12 January 1876; d. 22 November 1916)
At the turn of the century Jack London was one of America's leading adventure writers. Yet it might not have been. His early life had been a string of unsuccessful ventures, and though determined to write, rejections piled up. By 1899 he was on the verge of suicide when *Black Cat* magazine bought his short horror story 'A Thousand Deaths'. With a new lease of life, London launched into a profusion of writing that reached its pinnacle with *The Call of the Wild* (1903).
    His fantasy-orientated work includes *Before Adam* (1906), in which by racial memory a man recalls a previous existence as one of a paleolithic tribe. It caused a fracas with Stanley Waterloo who accused London of plagiarism of his own novel *The Story of Ab* (1897), which had ostensibly founded the prehistory theme in fiction. *The Star Rover* (1914) tells of the experiences of a convict's mind as it drifts through space. *The Iron Heel* (1908) was sf set in a dictator-dominated future. London's short fantasies are often grouped with his general fiction, but worth investigation are *Children of the Frost* (1902; 10s), *Moon-Face* (1906; 8s), *When God Laughs* (1911; 12s), *The Strength of the Strong* (1914; 7s) and *The Red One* (1918; 5s). Despite his success, London still suffered from fits of depression, and he committed suicide by morphine sulphate.

Frank Belknap Long (b. New York, 27 April 1903)
Long is descended from one of the crew of *The Mayflower* who became the first man to fight a duel on American soil. His grandfather was the builder who erected the pedestal for the Statue of Liberty in 1883. Long was first recognised as a poet, and his first books to appear (in limited editions and now very rare), *The Man from Genoa* (1926) and *The Goblin Tower* (1935), were collections of verse. Long's weird fiction had started with 'The Desert Lich' (1924), followed by the popular 'The Ocean Leech' (1925), in which a ship is menaced by a sea-monster.

As one of the closest friends of **Lovecraft,** Long's stories betrayed not a little influence. 'The Hounds of Tindalos' (1929) was the first non-Lovecraft Cthulhu story to appear. The character of Lovecraft can be seen in stories like 'The Man With a Thousand Legs' (1927) and 'The Brain-Eaters' (1932). Long appeared regularly in *Weird Tales,* but he later branched out to *Thrilling Mystery, Unknown,* and the sf and detective markets. Most of his early weird stories were collected as *The Hounds of Tindalos* (1946; 21s; paperback split, half-titled *The Dark Beasts,* 1963; 9s). Subsequent collections have been *The Rim of the Unknown* (1972; 23s) and *The Early Long* (1976; 17s). His short Cthulhu novel, *The Horror from the Hills* (1931), was given casebound publication in 1963 and paperbound as *Odd Science Fiction* (1964; 3s). Most of Long's novels have been outside the weird field, but he recently wrote a few 'Gothic' romances starting with *So Dark a Heritage* (1966). He has also written a personalised biography of Lovecraft, *Dreamer on the Night Side* (1975).

Mrs Gabrielle Long: *see* Marjorie Bowen

Julius Long
Long was a lawyer from Washington who specialised in detective stories. His delight for weird fiction was attested to by the frequent letters he wrote to *Weird Tales,* but he only had nine stories in its pages from 'The Dead Man's Story' (1933) to 'The Defense Rests' (1938). All however were highly original, such as the unusual ghost story 'He Walked By Day' (1934).

Robert Lory (?b. 1937)
Despite research it has not been possible to ascertain the identity of Lory, which may be a house pseudonym masking two or more writers. For the by-line Robert Lory has appeared on numerous fantasy and sf novels in the past few years and while he may be exceedingly prolific, it seems more feasible that other writers are at work. Lory's identity seemed real enough at first with a few short sf stories in *F&SF* and *If* in 1963–64, and he was described as 'a 26-year-old public relations writer from upstate New York'. A period of silence was then followed by a steady increase in novels such as *The Eyes of Bolsk* (1969), and the recommended heroic fantasy *Master of the Etrax* (1970). The name has been most prominent of late on two successive series: firstly the vampirical exploits of the revived Dracula in *Dracula Returns!, Hand of Dracula, Dracula's Brother, Dracula's Gold, Drums of Dracula, Witching of Dracula, Dracula's Lost*

World, Dracula's Disciple and *Challenge to Dracula*; and secondly, the astrological Horrorscope series that began in 1974 and so far includes *The Green Flames of Aries, Revenge of Taurus, The Curse of Leo,* and *Gemini Smile, Gemini Kill.* It also adorns the collection *More Tales of the Frightened* (1975; 26s—see **Avallone**).

H. P. Lovecraft (b. Providence, R.I., 20 August 1890; d. Providence, 15 March 1937)
No deceased horror writer in recent years has received as much attention and criticism as Howard Phillips Lovecraft. Feelings for his work range from fanatical praise to abhorrent dislike. It is up to the reader, and it is sufficient to say that while his work can claim no literary excellence (and Lovecraft never pretended it did), it is readable and above all original. Many of his stories are built around the basic concept that the Earth was once the abode of another race which, through dabbling in evil, was expelled from Earth by the benign Elder Gods, who hold these Ancient Ones in restraint. But ignorant mortals, tampering with unknown lore such as that detailed in the fictitious *Necronomicon* and kindred tomes, allow the Ancient Ones access to Earth. This was later dubbed the Cthulhu Mythos, to which other writers have contributed more than Lovecraft! (see App. I) Lovecraft owed much of his fictional inspiration to **Arthur Machen**, and there is a similarity of approach and theme in their work, but Lovecraft was extremely widely read, especially in the weird field as evident in his long essay *Supernatural Horror in Literature* (1927).

Lovecraft's early life was dominated by women, his mother following her husband into a mental home leaving Lovecraft (then 29) with his two aunts. He had started writing even before his teens, producing his own hand-written scientific journals. His earliest story to survive, 'The Beast in the Cave', a quite readable tale of bestial man, was written in 1905 and saw print in 1918, but apart from a few other efforts, Lovecraft ceased writing for nearly a decade. Then he became active in amateur publishing circles, and his first story to see print was 'The Alchemist' (1916) written in 1908. Most of his stories which were professionally published in *Weird Tales* had first been printed in these little magazines.

His first fiction sale was the series 'Grewsome Tales' (1922; retitled 'Herbert West—Reanimator'), but the key date was the October 1923 issue of *Weird Tales* which carried 'Dagon' (1919). This introduced him to his widest and most adoring audience, and most of his fiction appeared there. Before encountering *Weird Tales* Lovecraft had passed through a Dunsanian period when he produced a number of other-world fantasies such as 'The Cats of Ulthar' (1920; *WT* 1926) and 'Celephais' (1922; *WT* 1939), but during the 1920s he began writing (in longhand, he hated typing) longer, more involved stories, and these include his best. 'The

Outsider' (1926) has the narrator discover horrifically that he is a monstrosity, 'The Colour Out of Space' (1927), which was Lovecraft's own favourite, 'The Horror at Red Hook' (1927), which reflects Lovecraft's racist feelings and hatred of city life (he was a devout anglophile with pretensions of an eighteenth-century gentleman), and 'Cool Air' (1928), which reflects his dread of draughts (he was only happy at tropical temperatures yet paradoxically he usually went out only at night and once, caught unawares by a drop in temperature, he collapsed). 'The Call of the Cthulhu' (1928) ostensibly started the Mythos, and this was the bulk of his output over the next decade. However, Lovecraft regarded the sale of fiction as ungentlemanly. He wrote because he enjoyed it. He regarded his real job as the revision of other's manuscripts which he did for minimal fees. Without Lovecraft it is doubtful if the names of Adolphe de Castro, C. M. Eddy, Hazel Heald or others would be remembered at all.

Only one of his own books appeared during Lovecraft's lifetime, *The Shadow over Innsmouth* (1936), and only 150 copies were ever bound. An earlier attempt, *The Shunned House* (1928), was printed but not bound for many years. After his death of nephritis when only 46, **Derleth** and **Wandrei** formed the publishing company Arkham House in order to perpetuate Lovecraft's name in the shape of a collection, *The Outsider and Others* (1936; 36s), now one of the most sought-after fantasy items. Since then a quantity of variant volumes has appeared, each deftly pioneered and ultimately controlled by Derleth. These include several editions of Lovecraft's published letters. He was an inexhaustible correspondent and one estimate places his number of letters at 100,000. The other major original collections were *Beyond the Wall of Sleep* (1943; 23s) which included revisions and poetry, and *Something About Cats* (1949; 6s) mostly revisions, essays and verse. There was also *Collected Poems* (1963). The more generally available collections are *The Haunter of the Dark* (1951; 10s), *The Dunwich Horror* (1963; 6s). *At the Mountains of Madness* (1964; 8s: UK, 1967; 6s), *The Lurking Fear* (1964; 13s), *Dagon* (1965; 37s: UK, 1969; 14s split with *The Tomb*, 1969; 17s), and a US specialist fantasy volume *The Dream-Quest of Unknown Kadath* (1970; 6s). His revisions are available as *The Horror in the Museum* (1970; 19s: UK split, 1975; 9s with *The Horror in the Burying Ground*, 1975; 11s). Other fragments were completed by Derleth. Many articles have been written about Lovecraft, but the best recent books about him are those by L. S. de Camp and F. B. Long.

Marie Belloc Lowndes (b. 1868; d. Hampshire, 14 November 1947)
Initially a writer of historical and general fiction, Mrs Lowndes (the sister of Hilaire Belloc), scored with *The Lodger* (1913), a fictionalised version of Jack the Ripper's murders. This established her as a mystery writer, but she only occasionally ventured into the horror field, as with

her novel of psychic detection *From the Vasty Deep* (1920). An earlier weird mystery had been *The Uttermost Farthing* (1908). A collection of her early weird fiction was *Studies in Love and in Terror* (1913; 5s), and she later contributed to **Cynthia Asquith**'s anthologies.

Robert A. W. Lowndes (b. Bridgeport, Conn., 4 September 1916)
While he has written weird fiction, Robert Augustine Ward Lowndes's greatest service to readers has been as an editor of a host of magazines. His enthusiasm fired by *Ghost Stories*, the sf magazines and *Weird Tales*, Lowndes was active in sf fandom during the 1930s and in 1941 became editor of two sf magazines. His delight for weird fiction soon intruded into the sf stalwart *Future* which became the hybrid *Future Fantasy* in 1942, though the experiment was not a success. At this time Lowndes was the first editor to buy fiction from **Hannes Bok**.

Lowndes also wrote prolifically, much of it sf, but some weird tales such as 'The Abyss' (1941) which borrowed from the Cthulhu Mythos. During the 1950s he edited a chain of sf, detective, western and romance magazines and when they folded in 1960 he became editor of an occult non-fiction magazine *Exploring the Unknown*. He was soon able to add to this the fiction titles *Magazine of Horror*, *Startling Mystery Stories*, *Weird Terror Tales* and *Bizarre Fantasy Tales* (see App. III). Besides reprinting many long unavailable stories from the great days, he also revised much of his own fiction such as 'Clarissa' (1963; orig. 1946), the ultimate in gourmetism, 'Lilies' (1967; orig. 1942), about witchcraft, and the Lovecraftian 'Leapers' (1967; orig. 1942). Since these magazines ceased in 1971 he has become the senior assistant editor with *Sexology*.

Brian Lumley (b. Horden, Durham, 2 December 1937)
One of the more recent writers to follow in **Lovecraft**'s footsteps and rapidly becoming one of the most accomplished, ingeniously updating the Cthulhu Mythos to the 1970s. Nearly all his longer work comes within this framework. Trained as a sawyer, he joined the Army when 21 and has spent time in Germany and Cyprus, where he started to write. His first sale was 'The Cyprus Shell' (1968), since when nearly fifty stories have appeared. Some will be found in the collections *The Caller of the Black* (1971; 14s) and *The Horror at Oakdene* (1977; 8s). His novels are *The Burrowers Beneath* (1974), *Beneath the Moors* (1974), *The Transition of Titus Crow* (1975) and the forthcoming *De Marigny's Dream-Quest* and *Spawn of the Winds*.

Lord Lytton: *see* Lord Bulwer-Lytton

Dorothy Macardle (b. Dundalk, 1889; d. Drogheda, December 1958)
Dorothea Marguerita Callan Macardle was a noted Irish author and historian. A staunch nationalist, she took part in the Irish National Movement and spent some time in gaol. She would eventually vividly record the state of affairs in Ireland in *The Irish Republic* (1951). Widely travelled, after the Second World War she gathered facts on war refugees, published as *Children of Europe* (1949). It might be hard to imagine therefore that she should also write ghost fiction, but such is the case. At least three of her novels are worthy of attention, the most popular being *The Uninvited* (US 1942: UK *Uneasy Freehold*) about a young couple who find the house they have bought is haunted. The book sold over half a million copies and was filmed in 1944. The other novels are *The Unforeseen* (US 1946: UK *Fantastic Summer*), about extra-sensory perception, and *Dark Enchantment* (1953), about sorcery in France.

George Macdonald (b. Huntly, Scotland, 10 December 1824; d. Ashtead, 18 September 1905)
Though born and raised on a remote Scottish farm, MacDonald received a good education and became a minister. Ill-health encumbered him, so in 1851 he relinquished his ministry and spent the rest of his long life writing. Much of his work is straight fiction, and a sizable portion—for which he is best remembered—is children's fiction like *The Princess and the Goblin* (1872). His two most fascinating books are both allegorical fantasies set in bizarre dream/mirror worlds, and they span his writing career: *Phantastes* (1858) and *Lilith* (1895). Both need more than a little thought and can be read as forerunners to the work of **David Lindsay**. They were much praised by C. S. Lewis. He also wrote a number of short stories, often overlooked as children's tales, but most containing an extra depth of meaning. Roger Lancelyn Green collected the complete fairy tales as *The Light Princess* (1961; 8s) and **Lin Carter** assembled another choice as *Evenor* (1972; 3s).

Arthur Machen (b. Caerleon, Wales, 3 March 1863; d. nr Amersham, Bucks., 15 December 1947)
Recognised as one of the top writers of horror fiction, in the last analysis it is apparent that his general fame rests almost solely on his short story 'The Bowmen' (1914) about the appearance of King Henry's ghostly archers at the Battle of Mons. When published in *The Evening News*, for which Machen worked, it was accepted as fact and was followed by a storm of similar reports. Machen never did convince everyone it had all come from his imagination.

Born Arthur Llewellyn Jones, he was fascinated by the Welsh legends and beliefs and these all pervade his later work. Although he worked periodically as a clerk, teacher, actor and journalist he regarded himself a writer by vocation. Moving to London, he spent his early years translating books from the French, including the now standard *Memoirs of Casanova*. He studied the occult, and later joined several mystical societies becoming quite an adept himself. An early fantasy was a privately published volume of medieval tales, *The Chronicle of Clemendy* (1888), but his first noted supernatural works were the two short novels *The Great God Pan & The Inmost Light* (1894). The latter tale of a man's evil endeavours for wealth at the expense of his wife's soul was meant as a warning against dabbling in the occult. The former is a powerful story about the evil Helen, the offspring of a young girl and Pan, who has no soul. Next came *The Three Impostors* (1895; 8s; retitled *Black Crusade*, 1966), structured as a novel but essentially stories including 'The Novel of the Black Seal' and 'The Novel of the White Powder', both hinting at man's non-human origin, a theme later taken further by Lovecraft. The book was poorly received and this, combined with his failure to sell *The Hill of Dreams*, turned him to acting.

A decade later his earlier works were reprinted as *The House of Souls* (1906; 12s) and he finally sold *The Hill of Dreams* (1907) which, in its depiction of a man vainly attempting to break free of his dream world and live normally, was partly autobiographical. After the success of 'The Bowmen' and the subsequent volume *The Angel of Mons* (1915; 5s) Machen was able to exist more comfortably, though he never made much money from writing. Later novels include *The Great Return* (1915), about the return of the Holy Grail to modern Wales, *The Terror* (1917) in which animals and insects infected by the hatred of war turn against mankind, *The Secret Glory* (1922) and *The Green Round* (1933), a mystical display of alchemy, dream psychology and the supernatural. He produced more short fiction during these inter-war years and some of the best are in *The Shining Pyramid* (1925; 8s) relating the continued existence of the evil Little People. Later volumes were *The Cosy Room* (1936; 19s) and *Children of the Pool* (1936; 6s); of the many reprint collections the best are *Holy Terrors* (1946; 14s) and the standard if incomplete *Tales of Horror and the Supernatural* (1949; 14s).

In his last years Machen received a pension and lived quietly on the south coast of England. His fiction ranks supreme because of its depth of feeling, since, no matter what Machen might have said to the contrary, inwardly he believed in what he wrote.

Dorothy McIlwraith

Little has been recorded of the life of Miss McIlwraith, who for years was the gifted editor of *Short Stories*, and in 1940, when an elderly spinster, succeeded Wright as editor of *Weird Tales* and stayed until the magazine folded in 1954. The magazine took on an entirely different outlook, and because it lacked some of the verve of Wright's day, Miss McIlwraith is often maligned as being a poor editor. That was not the case. She kept the magazine alive against considerable odds, acquiring fiction from many of the old favourites like **Derleth, Wellman, Quinn** and Edmond Hamilton. She acquired the first weird fiction from **Ray Bradbury,** encouraged **Robert Bloch** to broaden his style, and introduced new writers like **Allison Harding, Brennan,** David Eynon and Manly Banister. She bought early artwork from **Lee Coye,** Boris Dolgov and Matt Fox. She instituted the Weird Tales Club, and on the whole kept the publication eminently readable. Its demise was not through any fault on her part; the magazine was a victim of circumstance.

R. H. Malden (b. 19 October 1879; d. 19 August 1951)
There is much of **M. R. James** in the fiction of the Reverend Richard Henry Malden. Malden became acquainted with James while studying at King's College, Cambridge, and from 1909 onwards wrote his own ghost stories in the James tradition. Malden went on to be Canon of Ripon, and from 1933 to 1950 was Dean of Wells. Like James, Malden was interested in archaeology, and was President of the Somerset Archaeological Society in 1943–44. Of his eighteen books all but one are religious, and they include a noted volume about Wells Cathedral. The one exception was the collection of his stories in *Nine Ghosts* (1943; 9s).

Jack Mann: *see* E. Charles Vivian

Frederick Marryat (b. London, 10 July 1792; d. Langham, 9 August 1848)
The undisputed master of the sea story, noted for such classics as *Mr Midshipman Easy* (1834). Marryat was also enchanted with the Gothic horror field and produced two chilling excursions into the supernatural, first with *Snarleyyow, or The Dog Fiend* (1836), then *The Phantom Ship* (1839), a stirring and lusty retelling of the Flying Dutchman legend. Both novels are much overlooked today, except for the werewolf episode from the second book, often reprinted separately as 'The White Wolf of the Hartz Mountains'.

Richard Marsh (b. *c* 1857; d. Hayward's Heath, Sussex, 9 August 1915)
Marsh's name has been unjustly overlooked in the horror field, with the exception of his weird novel of sorcery and the Egyptian cult of Isis, *The Beetle* (1897). Marsh was educated at Eton and Oxford, and had been writing for boys' magazines since he was twelve. Of his seventy

books the majority are thrillers and mysteries, but a few border on the fantastic. One of the earliest was *The Mahatma's Pupil* (1893), and after *The Beetle* came *The Goddess* (1900)—replete with spectral visitations in the London smog, albeit rationally explained, *The Joss* (1901), *A Metamorphosis* (1903), *The Death Whistle* (1905), and *A Spoiler of Men* (1911), which involved hypnotism and magic. An early collection of mysteries, though not all weird, was *Curios* (1898; 7s), but his best volumes were *The Seen and the Unseen* (1900; 12s), *Marvels and Mysteries* (1900; 9s) and *Both Sides of the Veil* (1901; 11s).

Edison Marshall (b. Indiana, 28 August 1894; d. Augusta, Ga., 29 October 1967)
Edison Tesla Marshall ranked as one of America's leading writers of historical fiction with novels like *The Vikings* (1951), filmed in 1958. He began writing in 1915 and his second sale, 'Who is Charles Avison?' (1916) is regarded as a science fiction classic about a duplicate Earth orbiting on the other side of the sun. His early life was spent hunting and exploring in Africa and Asia, and this knowledge is clear in his books.

Five of his novels rank as fantasy: *Ogden's Strange Story* (1928; book, 1934) is about a man who loses his memory after a plane crash which revives his racial memory of a caveman existence; *Dian of the Lost Land* (1935) is a lost race adventure in an Antarctic valley; *The Infinite Woman* (1950) tells of a woman who defied the all-powerful goddess Kali; *Earth Giant* (1960), based on the twelve labours of Hercules; and *The Jewel of Mahabar* (1938). Marshall also wrote a series 'From a Frontiersman's Diary' (1919) which includes several fantasies like 'The Flying Lion' and 'The Serpent City'.

Felix Marti-Ibanez (b. Spain, 25 December 1911; d. 24 May 1972)
By profession a doctor, for a while after the Spanish Civil War he was the Under-Secretary for Public Health and Social Service, then moved to the US in 1939 and worked as a lecturer. He was noted as founder and editor of the cultural medical magazine *MD*. He had a fondness for bizarre stories, selling two to *Weird Tales* in 1953, and later to *F&SF*. His best was 'A Tomb in Malacor' (1954), about a man who finds his grave in a Guatemalan village where he seems to have lived a dual life. His tales were collected as *All the Wonders We Seek* (1963; 13s).

Kirk Mashburn (b. 1900; d. 13 February 1968)
Although he sold more stories to the western and crime pulp magazines, W. Kirk Mashburn, Jr is fondest in the memories of readers of *Weird Tales*, to which he contributed just twelve stories from 'The Garret of

Madame Lemoyne' (1928) to 'The Toad Idol' (1935). Undoubtedly his most popular was the werewolf tale 'Placide's Wife' (1931) and its sequel 'The Last of Placide's Wife' (1932).

Richard Matheson (b. New Jersey, February 1926)

A leading scriptwriter of horror films, and a major novelist both in and out of the field, Matheson started by contributing to the sf magazines, though all his tales were tinged with the macabre right from his first sale about a mutant, 'Born of Man and Woman' (1950). It lent its title to his first collection (1954; 17s) which was chiefly science fiction. His essentially weird collections are *Shock!* (1961; 13s), *Shock 2* (1964; 13s) and *Shock 3* (1966; 13s). He has a most original way of treating old themes, as can be seen in 'No Such Thing as a Vampire' (1959). His modern treatment of vampires was used to great effect in *I Am Legend* (1954) when the whole future population, bar one, turn into vampires. *A Stir of Echoes* (1958) tells how hypnotism frees a man's mind of its restrictions but leaves it open to psychic attack.

Matheson made the transition to scriptwriter by adapting his own sf novel *The Incredible Shrinking Man* (1956; film 1957). Since then he has adapted several of Poe's works including *The Pit and the Pendulum* (1961) and *The Raven* (1963), the latter starring Karloff, Price and Lorre. The height of hilarious horror was reached in *The Comedy of Terrors* (1964). Matheson has also scripted several television series such as *The Twilight Zone* and *Circle of Fear* for which he was script editor. Among his recent film work is the adaptation of his novel *Hell House* (1971), about the investigation of a haunted house with terror piling upon terror, as *Legend of Hell House* (1973). It has been compared with Shirley Jackson's *Haunting of Hill House*. His time fantasy *Bid Time Return* (1975) won the Howard Award for the year's best fantasy novel at the Second World Fantasy Convention.

Norman H. Matson (b. 1893)

Norman Haghelm Matson was born in America of Norwegian descent. He started his career as a journalist, and travelled widely. Among his novels are several fantasies, such as *Flecker's Magic* (1926; retitled *Enchanted Beggar*) about the friendship between a student and an old witch, and *Doctor Fagg* (1929), in which a professor finds a beautiful girl buried in a cylinder in his garden. But Matson's fame rests chiefly on his completion of Thorne Smith's *The Passionate Witch* (1941) on which both the film *I Married a Witch* (1942) and the television series *Bewitched* were based. Matson wrote a sequel, *Bats in the Belfry* (1943).

Charles R. Maturin (b. Dublin, 1782; d. Dublin, 30 October 1824)
In Gothic fiction, Maturin's name has become as immortal as that of his fictional creation Melmoth. His parents were exiled French Protestants, and Charles Robert Maturin was raised in poverty, educated for the Church and became a curate. Most of his writings first appeared anonymously or pseudonymously. His fiction began with the terrifying melodrama *The Fatal Revenge* (1807), and progressed through *The Wild Irish Boy* (1808), *The Milesian Chief* (1812) and several plays, to his masterpiece *Melmoth the Wanderer* (1820). This tells of a necromancer who sells his soul to the devil for near immortal life, but as the years pass the burden grows heavier, and Melmoth tries to find another to assume his rôle, and thus grant him salvation. The work was acclaimed by writers all over Europe, not least Honoré de Balzac, who wrote his own sequel *Melmoth Reconciled* (1835).

Maturin's final novel was *The Albigenses* (1824), but it is alleged that after his death his son William (1803–87) destroyed much correspondence and many unpublished manuscripts. His only known short story, 'Leixlip Castle' (1825) was reprinted in Haining's *Great British Tales of Terror*.

Pseudonym: Dennis Jasper Murphy

Guy de Maupassant (b. Normandy, 5 August 1850; d. Paris, 6 July 1893)
It is doubtful that any other writer, with the possible exception of **Poe**, put so much of himself into his horror fiction. Guy Henri Rene Albert de Maupassant ranks as one of the formulative masters of the short story, and is one of the geniuses of literature. Yet always over his head hung the fear of madness, and this phobia is reflected in much of his fiction. Maupassant reluctantly found himself in the Army in 1870, serving in the Franco-Prussian War, and it was only by writing that he found any pleasure in life. Apart that is from his frequent promiscuity which ultimately led to his contracting syphilis. This induced hallucinations which further contributed to his fear of madness! He carried a revolver with him which he fired at imaginary enemies. Thus his story 'He?', where a man imagines there is another person in his empty room, is not entirely fabricated.

Later stories portray characters on the borders of madness, such as his famous 'The Horla', and 'Was He Mad?' which opens with the prophetic comment that a friend had died in an asylum. One of his last stories, 'Who Knows?' is narrated in first person by a man in a mental hospital. The consequences make one shiver. Shortly afterwards Maupassant died in a private mental hospital, aged only 42. His fear of madness had driven him mad, and one feels his stories were in some way a plea for help. Alas, it went unrecognised. Of his many collected volumes of stories only a few are devoted to horror. An early one was *Allouma* (1895; 11s), but the best recent selections, translated by Arnold Kellett, are *Tales of Supernatural Terror* (1972; 16s) and *Diary of a Madman* (1976; 16s).

André Maurois (b. Elbeuf, France, 26 July 1885; d. Paris, 9 October 1967)
An exceedingly prolific writer on a bewildering variety of subjects (his biographies being the most noted), Maurois—born Emile Herzog—delved into the fantasy field only rarely. Best is *The Weigher of Souls* (1931) about a London doctor who bottles souls! Others include the satirical fantasies *A Voyage to the Island of the Articoles* (1928), *Fattypuffs and Thinifers* (1930) and *The Thought-Reading Machine* (1937). The last is more science fiction, in which field Maurois also wrote *The Next Chapter* (1927), a future history from 1970 to 1992, hinging on the war with the moon.

Vivian Meik (b. 1895; d. ?)
He led a most active life, travelling widely in Asia and Africa. He was wounded in both wars, being a noted war correspondent in the Second. He was also a railway engineer in India and Africa, and witnessed many inexplicable events that inspired his fiction. This consists of a collection, *Devil's Drums* (1933; 10s) with the emphasis on African magic; *Veils of Fear* (1934), a series of connected weird episodes; and an Oriental fantasy *The Curse of Red Shiva* (1936), about a curse that strikes every five generations.

J. Wilhelm Meinhold (b. Usedom, 1797; d. Charlottenburg, 30 November 1851)
Johann Meinhold was a Lutheran pastor in Prussia where he earned some repute as a poet and playwright. His fame came with *Mary Schweidler*, *The Amber Witch* (1838; UK 1844) expanded from his earlier story 'The Priest's Daughter' (1826), which tells of a virtuous young girl condemned as a witch. Praised by **Lovecraft** for its 'convincing realism and freedom from Gothic stock devices' it ranks as one of the leading novels about witchcraft. Meinhold failed to repeat his success with *Sidonia the Sorceress* (1847).

A. Merritt (b. Beverly, N.J., 20 January 1884; d. Florida, 30 August 1943)
Abraham Merritt has been hailed as one of the patron saints of science fiction, but his works are essentially fantasy. He studied to be a lawyer,

but insufficient finances precluded his completing his training. He became a reporter, and is rumoured to have witnessed something so devastating that he was sent away for a while till things cleared over. He rapidly rose in the ranks and became editor of *American Weekly* in 1937, a position he held till his death.

Lack of time eclipsed his writing, yet on the strength of little more than eight novels, he has become a legend. His first sale was 'Through the Dragon Glass' (1917) about an adventurer who passes through a stolen jewel into a fantasy world. Merritt rapidly rose to fame with his story 'The Moon Pool' (1918) and its sequel *The Conquest of the Moon Pool* (1919), about the discovery of a bizarre world entered via a pool of force. Subsequent novels were *The Metal Monster* (1920); *The Face in the Abyss* (1923) and its sequel *The Snake Mother* (1930), about the last remaining member of a human/reptilian race; *The Ship of Ishtar* (1924); *Seven Footprints to Satan* (1927), about a super-criminal; *The Dwellers in the Mirage* (1932), probably his best lost-race work; *Burn, Witch, Burn!* (1932), later filmed as *The Devil Doll* (1933), and its sequel *Creep, Shadow!* (1934; UK *Creep, Shadow, Creep*, 1935), about ancient witchcraft.

His two unfinished novels were completed by **Hannes Bok**. The first was entitled *The Fox Woman and the Blue Pagoda* (1946) and should not be confused with the collection of Merritt's short stories and fragments collected by **Wollheim** as *The Fox Woman* (1949; 9s). Though Merritt's work is not suited to all tastes, his fantastic and beautiful imagery and depth of wonder is unique in the field.

John Metcalfe (b. Heacham, Norfolk, 1891; d. London, 31 July 1965) Primarily a writer of straight fiction, Metcalfe has carved himself a special niche in the horror field for his skilful and bizarre short stories, comparable to the work of **L. P. Hartley**. After a variety of jobs and serving many years in the RAF, Metcalfe spent most of his last years teaching in New York. His best-known story is 'The Smoking Leg', though it is a rather uninspired piece about an unscrupulous doctor who smuggles a cursed gem to a colleague, sewn into a negro's leg! It was the title story of his first collection (1925; 18s), followed by *Judas* (1931; 10s) which includes the story of the too life-like guy 'The Funeral March of a Marionette' (which was the title of the music that introduced **Hitchcock**'s television series).

Metcalfe's short fiction underlines the evil in man, but occasionally alludes to supernatural machinations. This can be seen in 'Brenner's Boy' (1932), first published in a private edition of only 125 copies and now extremely rare. His novels similarly develop evil in an outwardly normal world, as in the grisly *The Feasting Dead* (1954) and especially *My Cousin Geoffrey* (1956), where the normal world is revealed to be a hunting ground for the dark forces of the spirit.

Gustave Meyrink (b. Vienna, 19 January 1868; d. Starnberg, 4 December 1932)

The illegitimate son of an actress and an aristocrat, Gustav Meyer (who later changed his name) took a banking job in Prague when he was 20. A series of business failures led him to believe that the spiritual world was opposing civilisation and he took to investigating the occult. A volume of collected bizarre facts appeared as *The German Philistine's Horn* (1909). Meyrink's first story, 'The Hot Soldier' (1903), tells of a legionnaire who takes a magic draught and finds his body temperature continues to rise until he bursts into flames! His most famous novel was *The Golem* (1915), about the Hebrew man of clay brought to life by an ancient spell. Others, all reflecting his grim view of life (more so after the First World War), include *Orchids* (1904), *The Waxworks* (1907), *The Clock* (1914), *The Green Face* (1916), *Walpergisnacht* (1917) and *At The Threshold of the Beyond* (1923); story collections are *The Violet Death* (1922) and *The Malicious Mushrooms* (1925).

Richard B. Middleton (b. Staines, Mddx, 28 October 1882; d. Brussels, 1 December 1911)

It is tragic irony that the man who wrote one of the most successful *humorous* ghost stories, 'The Ghost Ship', should himself be dreadfully unhappy to the point that he killed himself when only 29. Richard Barham Middleton earned a living as a clerk, trying to make a name at writing, but he was born out of his time. Success came, but too late. His collection *The Ghost Ship* (1912; 20s) includes his other popular tongue-in-cheek story 'On the Brighton Road'. A later volume was published posthumously, *The Day Before Yesterday* (1913). In the 1930s **Gawsworth** championed his cause, editing a miscellaneous collection *The Pantomime Man* (1932), and including no less than six stories in the anthology *New Tales of Horror*.

Mrs Mary Molesworth (b. Rotterdam, 29 May 1839; d. London, 20 July 1921)

Mary Louisa Molesworth wrote many much-acclaimed children's stories, but in the tradition of most Victorian female writers she also produced a few ghost stories. In her case they rank among the best and will be found in *Four Ghost Stories* (1888; 4s) and *Uncanny Tales* (1896; 6s), the latter including the wonderfully atmospheric 'The Shadow in the Moonlight'.

Michael Moorcock (b. London, 18 December 1939)

Moorcock's writing career has two seemingly incomparable and divergent paths which he nevertheless frequently intertwines. Among the vanguard of the sf New Wave, Moorcock served for ten years as editor of *New*

Worlds and has written several off-trail sf novels. In his youth Moorcock, then a Burroughs fan, had edited *Tarzan Adventures*. Shortly after he made an arrangement with a US magazine to write a series of Conan-imitation stories, but the magazine folded. Moorcock reworked the stories with the lead character Elric who first appeared in 'The Dreaming City' (1961). Elric is the opposite of Conan. He is a weakling albino whose survival depends upon his symbiosis with his sword Stormbringer, which sucks the souls from its victims and thereby revitalises Elric.

Moorcock later expanded the series to create a whole cycle of novels centred upon an Eternal Champion who exists in all planes and realities and whose fate it is to help those who summon him. Moorcock has interwoven the novels so that one must read them all for a complete understanding. The Elric books run as follows: *Elric of Melniboné* (1972), *The Stealer of Souls* (1963; 5s), *The Sleeping Sorceress* (1971; 3s), *The Jade Man's Eyes* (1973), *The Sailor on the Seas of Fate* (1976) and *Stormbringer* (1965; 4s). The collection *The Singing Citadel* (1970; 4s) includes certain connected stories. The Dorian Hawkmoon books: *The Jewel in the Skull* (1968), *The Mad God's Amulet* (1968), *The Sword in the Dawn* (1968), *The Secret of the Runestaff* (1969) and the subsequent trilogy *Count Brass* (1973), *The Champion of Garathorm* (1973) and *The Quest for Tanelorn* (1975). This last title includes all the characters. The Erekosë books: *The Eternal Champion* (story, 1962; book, 1970) and *Phoenix in Obsidian* (1970; US *The Silver Warriors*, 1973). The Corum books: *The Knight of the Swords* (1970), *The Queen of the Swords* (1971), *The King of the Swords* (1971), followed by *The Bull and the Spear* (1973), *The Oak and the Ram* (1973) and *The Sword and the Stallion* (1974).

In addition Moorcock wrote a deliberately Burroughsian Martian trilogy originally under the alias Edward P. Bradbury. It runs: *Warriors of Mars* (1965; retitled *City of the Beast*, 1970), *Blades of Mars* (1965; retitled *Lord of the Spiders*, 1970) and *Barbarians of Mars* (1965; retitled *Masters of the Pit*, 1970). Moorcock's latest fantasy work is the massive *Glomana* (1977), based on Edmund Spenser's *Faery Queen*.

Pseudonyms: Edward P. Bradbury, James Colvin

C. L. Moore (b. Indianapolis, Ind., 24 January 1911)

Catherine Lucille Moore was given a standing ovation when she intimated at the Second World Fantasy Convention in 1976 that she would be returning to the fantasy field from which she has been woefully absent since the death of her husband, **Henry Kuttner**, in 1958. In fact she really deserted the field when they married in 1940, since their creative talents were tuned more to the sf and mystery fields than fantasy. Yet in the 1930s she produced some of the most original weird fiction available.

Most of her tales fit into two series. The first is about Northwest Smith, a planetary adventurer—though the planets are far more fantastic than factual. Her first sale was one of this series, 'Shambleau' (1933), in which Smith saves a young Martian girl only to fall hypnotically victim to her loathsome charms. The best of this series were published as *Shambleau* (1953; 7s) and *Northwest of Earth* (1954; 7s). These also included stories from the second series, straight fantasy, about Jirel of Joiry, set in a medieval world of magic. The first, 'The Black God's Kiss' (1934) appeared in *Weird Tales* when Conan was at his height, yet these tales with their female hero have far more depth and fascination. They were collected as *Jirel of Joiry* (1969; 5s).

Bassett Morgan

A popular contributor to *Weird Tales* with thirteen stories from 'Laocoon' (1926) to 'Midas' (1936), and others in *Strange Tales*. Over half the stories dealt with brain transplants between humans and an array of creatures, especially apes, tigers, or sea-creatures. It is believed the name hid the identity of a female writer.

William Morris (b. London, 24 March 1834; d. London, 3 October 1896)

Regarded as the modern founder of other-world fantasies, William Morris was one of the founders of the Pre-Raphaelites, the art movement advocating a return to realism. The bulk of his fantasy output was in his last years, but it was a return to his first love since while at Exeter College, Oxford, he and his colleagues had founded *The Oxford and Cambridge Magazine* (1856) to which he contributed several fantasies, most notably 'The Hollow Land', set in a mythical world. These were later collected, and a recent US edition is *Golden Wings* (1976; 8s).

Morris's delight in the world of the Middle Ages, when he believed there was true craftsmanship and freedom from civilisation and industrialisation, was evident from the start. It later made him a confirmed socialist. It took further shape in his verse, *The Defence of Guenevere* (1858), *The Life and Death of Jason* (1867) and *The Earthly Paradise* (1868–71), Morris's tribute to Chaucer. A prose version of this was made by Madalen Edgar as *Stories from the Earthly Paradise* (1919; 14s). Morris translated many classics such as the *Aeneid* (1875) and the *Odyssey* (1887) and several Icelandic tales and sagas.

In 1861 he established a company for the manufacture of artistic household decorations, notably wallpaper, with many of the designs still popular today. In his last days, realising he would be a long time dying, Morris lost himself in the fantasy worlds of his desires and thus came his novels. They were printed by his Kelmscott Press, established in 1891 to produce especially beautiful editions. (In 1969 the Kelmscott edition of *The Wood Beyond the World* was auctioned for £600.) After a few straight historical novels he began to create his magical worlds, starting with *The Story of the Glittering Plain* (1891). Less noticeable in this novel, but progressively more pronounced, was Morris's adoption of archaic English which though it creates an atmosphere does make heavy reading for the unprepared. His subsequent fantasies were *The Wood Beyond the World* (1894), *Child Christopher and Goldilind the Fair* (1895), *The Well at the World's End* (1896), *The Water of the Wondrous Isles* (1897) and *The Story of the Sundering Flood* (1898).

W. C. Morrow (b. Alabama, 1853; d. San Francisco, 3 April 1923)
William Chambers Morrow was an American writer whose fame rests on a volume of short stories *The Ape, the Idiot & Other People* (1897; 14s), but such a collection of tales of revenge, terror and the supernatural is unique. Stories like 'His Unconquerable Enemy' and 'Over an Absinthe Bottle' attain powerful heights of story-telling. Morrow's only other works are a short horror novel *A Man: His Mark* (1900) and a lost-race fantasy *Lentala of the South-Seas* (1908), though uncollected stories in magazines exist.

Sam Moskowitz (b. Newark, N.J., 30 June 1920)
Renowned as science fiction's historian, in recent years Moskowitz has provided more of a service to horror fans in his editorial and archaeological duties. He has one of the largest collections of sf and fantasy in the world and his detailed knowledge of the field is almost incomparable. Often criticised for the errors that occur in his books, he is seldom credited for the tremendous job he has done in establishing a pedigree for the fantasy genre. He is often the power behind the throne. For instance he edited the anthologies *Weird Tales* (1964; 8s) and *Worlds of Weird* (1965; 7s) credited to Leo Margulies, and similarly all the anthologies credited solely or jointly to Alden H. Norton. The last-named concentrate on lost stories from forgotten magazines and he has unearthed many worthy gems. They run, *Horror Times Ten* (1967; 10s), *Masters of Horror* (1968; 9s), *Hauntings and Horrors* (1969; 10s), *Great Untold Stories of Fantasy and Horror* (1969; 11s), *Horrors Unknown* (1971; 11s), *Ghostly By Gaslight* (1971; 11s), *Horrors in Hiding* (1973; 9s), and *Horrors Unseen* (1974; 9s). He also edited the ingenious *A Man Called Poe* (1969; 11s) (see App. II). In 1973 Moskowitz had the honour of being the editor of the revived *Weird Tales*, but alas distribution problems caused the magazine to fold again. Moskowitz also compiled a collection of lost **Hodgson** stories as *Out of the Storm* (1975), to which he added a definitive biography.

J. E. Preston Muddock: *see* Dick Donovan

A. N. L. Munby (b. London, 25 December 1913; d. Cambridge, Cambs., 26 December 1974)
The man who came closest to inheriting the mantle of M. R. James was Alan Noel Latimer Munby. The son of an architect, and himself an antiquarian, he had been educated at King's College, Cambridge and later became its librarian. He had established himself in the book trade in 1935 and wrote several studies and biographies. His ghost stories were written in a totally different surrounding however, the prisoner-of-war camp at Eichstatt between 1943 and 1945. They were published as *The Alabaster Hand* (1949; 14s).

Talbot Mundy (b. Surrey, 23 April 1879; d. Florida, 5 August 1940)
Although he was born in England, educated at Rugby, and served as a government official in Africa and India from 1900–10 (when he gleaned most of his occult knowledge), Mundy went to the US in 1911 and in 1917 became a naturalised citizen. He earned a reputation as one of the leading writers of adventure novels such as *King of the Khyber Rifles* (1916) and *Jimgrim* (1931). The bulk are non-fantasy, but they frequently contain elements of mysticism and a few have more than a hint of the supernatural. Of special interest are *Om: the Secret of Abhor Valley* (1924) and *Full Moon* (1935; UK *There Was a Door*), set in secret valleys in Tibet and India respectively. These reveal Mundy's interest in the occult as propounded by Madame Blavatsky, and during the 1920s he joined the Theosophical Society.

Perhaps his most lasting contribution to the genre is his series of historical fantasies about Tros of Samothrace and his exploits at the time of Caesar. The early tales appeared in the pulp *Adventure* during 1925, and they finally saw book form as *Tros of Samothrace* (1934; 7s) after the success of the sequel *Queen Cleopatra* (1929). A third book was *Purple Pirate* (1935; 4s). The early adventures were paperbound as *Tros, Helma, Liafail* and *Helene* (all 1971). It was recently discovered that Mundy's real name was William Lancaster Gribbon.

H. Warner Munn (b. Athol, Mass., 5 November 1903)
Harold Warner Munn remained for many years a shadowy figure, one of the old guard of *Weird Tales* who has recently returned to the field with deserved success. His first sales to the magazine came about when H. P. Lovecraft, with whom Munn corresponded, bemoaned the werewolf tale and suggested a story be told from the wolf's viewpoint. Thus Munn wrote 'The Werewolf of Ponkert' (1925) and several sequels in-

cluding the serial *The Werewolf's Daughter* (1928). Thirty years later the initial stories saw a limited edition book publication as *The Werewolf of Ponkert* (1958; 3s) and most recently all have been issued as *Tales of the Werewolf Clan* (1976; 10s). Among his other stories was 'The Wheel' (1933), a classic tale of torture and revenge.

His last appearance at that time was with *King of the World's Edge* (1939; book 1966) set after the death of King Arthur. It tells of the voyage of Merlin, the Roman centurion Varro and others to a distant land (America) and their fight for survival. Thereafter Munn had to devote his time to raising a family, but he never abandoned the weird scene. His hobbies included collecting books on witchcraft and demonology and he even declined an invitation to join a witch coven. He also became a noted poet. Then Munn returned to writing with a sequel to that last novel, *The Ship from Atlantis* (1967; the two have since been reissued as *Merlin's Godson*, 1976). They serve as a prelude to *Merlin's Ring* (1974), which relates the fantastic voyage across the ancient world. Munn is now busier than ever. He has completed an epic poem about Joan of Arc, *The Banner of Joan* (1975) and a historical novel *The Lost Legion* (1977), and is working on four new novels including *Sword of Merlin*. There are plans for a complete collection of his short fiction as *The Melldrum Box*.

H. H. Munro (b. Akyob, Burma, 18 December 1870; d. France, 13 November 1916)
As Saki, Hector Hugh Munro rated as one of the best-known and most skilled of all British short story writers. Widely travelled, he first served in the Burma Police, and later became a foreign correspondent for the *Morning Post*. He refused a commission during the First World War, and was killed in action. Just before the war he had completed a novel about a German invasion, *When William Came* (1914).

Of his horror tales his best known is the werewolf story 'Gabriel-Ernest'. He made special use of legends and tales he had heard on his travels and adapted them in his deft style, never overplaying the horror, but creating fear by subtle insinuation with a deliberate punch at the end. Stories like 'Sredni Vashtar', 'The Open Window', 'Laura', 'Louis' and 'The Music on the Hill', are sprinkled all through his collections which ran *Reginald* (1904; 15s), *Reginald in Russia* (1910; 15s), *The Chronicles of Clovis* (1911; 28s), *Beasts and Super-Beasts* (1914; 36s) and posthumously *The Toys of Peace* (1923; 33s) and *The Square Egg* (1924; 8s), with his *Complete Short Stories* (1930; 136s).

Pseudonym: Saki

Rosalie Muspratt (b. Freshfields, Lancs., December 1906; d. London, 7 September 1976)
Rosalie Helen Muspratt wrote two books of supernatural stories, *Sinister Stories* (1930; 20s) as Jasper John, and *Tales of Terror* (1931; 12s). All but forgotten today, two of her tales reflecting the ill-use of magic will be found in **Montague Summers**'s *Supernatural Omnibus*. Although she was a freelance journalist for several years, she never returned to the horror field.

Pseudonym: Jasper John

E. Nesbit (b. London, 15 August 1858; d. Dymchurch, Kent, 4 May 1924)
Today Edith Nesbit's name lives on for her children's books, notably *The Railway Children* (1904). Many were fairy tale fantasies like *The Phoenix and the Carpet* (1904) and *The Enchanted Castle* (1908). But she also wrote numerous short horror stories, often masking her sex under the by-line E. Nesbit or after her marriage in 1880, E. Bland or Mrs Hubert Bland. The stories were also frequently narrated in first person by a man, thus fooling many literary admirers. She had three collections, *Something Wrong* (1893; 8s), *Grim Tales* (1893; 7s) and *Fear* (1910; 14s). Best known is the story 'Man-Size in Marble' (1886) where a husband learns to his horror not to disbelieve local legends. Another is 'The Head' (1907), an early venture into waxwork horrors, and it shows much the same inspiration as her novel *Salome and the Head* (1909; retitled *The House With No Address*) about a dancer tricked into dancing with a real severed head, and later isolated with it in a fearful house. A fantasy was *The Story of the Amulet* (1907) set in ancient Atlantis, Egypt and Babylon.

Pseudonyms: E. Bland, Mrs Hubert Bland

Hume Nisbet (b. Stirling, Scotland, 8 August 1849; d. Australia, c 1921)
Another overlooked Victorian writer, although **Michel Parry** recently revived his story linking spiritualism and Jack the Ripper, 'The Demon Spell', in *Jack the Knife*. Nisbet had gone to Australia in 1865 and returned to England in 1872 to teach art but with little success. Turning to writing he produced many adventure romances and several occult mysteries. First was *Ashes* (1890), followed by *The Jolly Roger* (1891) with its pirate city, mass hypnotism and witchcraft. *Valdemar the Viking* (1893) and *The Empire Makers* (1900) are both lost-race fantasies. Other works include *The Great Secret* (1895), *The Revenge of Valerie* (1900), *The Divers* (1900), plus two ghostly collections *The Haunted Station* (1894; 12s) and *Stories Weird and Wonderful* (1900).

Frank Norris (b. Chicago, 5 March 1870; d. San Francisco, 25 October 1902)
Benjamin Franklin Norris, Jr is not normally linked with the horror field, but is championed as one of America's early masters of realism. His early psychological thriller *McTeague* (1894) presaged *Vandover and the Brute* (1914) which details a man's mental disintegration till he lives and acts like a wolf. Recently **Moskowitz** unearthed several short horror stories, paramount among them 'The Ship that Saw a Ghost' (1902). A selection of such stories will be found in *A Deal in Wheat* (1903; 10s). Alas, Norris did not fully enjoy his fame, as he died from a burst appendix when only 32.

Amyas Northcote
Montague Summers listed Northcote among the writers of superior ghost fiction in the introduction to *The Supernatural Omnibus*, in which he included the story 'Brickett Bottom'. This came from Northcote's collection *In Ghostly Company* (1922; 13s). Since then Northcote has sunk into oblivion.

Andre Norton (b. *c* 1912)
By virtue of book sales, Alice Mary (Andre) Norton ranks unrivalled as the most popular female sf writer. In some cases though her sf and fantasy are almost indistinguishable, and each is aimed at both adult and junior readers.

For many years the children's librarian in Cleveland, she began writing historical novels in the 1930s and during the 1940s added adventure and espionage. Her most fantasy-orientated historical novel has been *Shadow Hawk* (1960) set in ancient Egypt. She had placed some short sf and fantasies with a semi-professional publisher in 1935 and some saw light in *Fantasy Book* in 1947. That same year her junior fantasy *Rogue Reynard* appeared, based on the French folktale, and she followed it with *Huon of the Horn* (1951), similarly inspired. A subsequent sequel was *Steel Magic* (1965; retitled *Gray Magic*, 1967) followed by *Octagon Magic* (1967), *Fur Magic* (1968), *Dragon Magic* (1972) and *Lavender Green Magic* (1974). Other junior fantasies of interest are *Here Abide Monsters* (1973) and *Merlin's Mirror* (1975).

Her major contribution however has been the adult series set on an alternate Earth where sorcery and enchantment hold sway. They are *Witch World* (1963), *Web of the Witch World* (1964), *Year of the Unicorn* (1965), *Three Against the Witch World* (1965), *Warlock of the Witch World* (1967), *Sorceress of the Witch World* (1968), *Spell of the Witch World* (1972; 3s), *The Crystal Gryphon* (1972) and *The Jargoon Pard*

(1974). A recent Gothic-style fantasy was *White Jade Fox* (1975); other short fantasies will be found in *High Sorcery* (1970; 4s).

Alfred Noyes (b. Wolverhampton, Staffs., 16 September 1880; d. Isle of Wight, 28 June 1958)
Noyes the poet is best remembered for such school-memorised classics as 'The Highwayman' and 'Forty Singing Seamen'. Noyes the story-teller is less well recalled to mind, yet he wrote several weird tales, the bulk collected as *Walking Shadows* (1918; 11s) and *The Hidden Player* (1924; 11s), although neither includes his best-known doppelgänger story 'Midnight Express'. Two novels of interest are *The Last Man* (1940), about survivors of a future war, and *The Devil Takes a Holiday* (1955), a satire about the devil taking a holiday on Earth to find man doing his work for him.

Fitz-James O'Brien (b. Limerick, 31 December 1828; d. Maryland, 6 April 1862)
The son of a lawyer, O'Brien inherited over £8,000 which he squandered in under three years. That combined with an unsuccessful affair with a married woman led him to leave for America in 1852. Living a Bohemian life he became a noted poet, but it is his fiction for which he is now remembered. First collected in 1881, the bulk of his weird stories were reissued as *The Diamond Lens* (1885; 13s). O'Brien never saw either book. Having enlisted in the Union Army in the Civil War he was fatally wounded, dying when only 33.

'The Diamond Lens' (1858) remains his best-known story, telling of the discovery of life on a microscopic world in a drop of water. It is marred by O'Brien's lengthy arguments about spiritualism. His best story is 'What Was It?' (1859), about a malevolent invisible creature. Other stories of interest are the touching ghost tale 'The Pot of Tulips' (1855), an Oriental fantasy, 'The Dragon Fang' (1856), the surreal fantasies 'The Lost Room' and 'From Hand to Mouth' (both 1858) and the exploits of the evil mannikins created by 'The Wondersmith' (1859).

Elliott O'Donnell (b. nr Bristol, 27 February 1872; d. 8 May 1965)
Like **Leslie** and Hopkins, O'Donnell was a hunter after supernatural phenomena and he published many volumes of non-fiction about his findings, such as *Some Haunted Houses of England and Wales* (1908), *Haunted Houses of London* (1909), *Animal Ghosts* (1913), *Werwolves* (1912), *20 Years' Experience as a Ghost Hunter* (1917), *Strange Sea Mysteries* (1926) and many more. Among all these spectral titles it is easy to overlook his fiction. His experiences had inspired an early autobiographi-

cal novel *For Satan's Sake* (1904), and he had several stories in **Birkin's** *Creeps* series such as 'The Haunted Spinney'. His novels began with the Middle East adventure *Dinevah the Beautiful* (1907) followed by his masterpiece *The Sorcery Club* (1912), about three men who learn the occult secrets of Atlantis and put them to evil use. He continued his ghostly detection throughout his life, and a later novel of interest about black magic was *The Dead Riders* (1952).

Mrs Margaret Oliphant (b. Wallyford, UK, 4 April 1828; d. Windsor, Berks., 25 June 1897)
Popular in her day as a historical novelist, Mrs Oliphant is another of that bevy of Victorian ladies remembered today for their excursions into the supernatural. She had initially wanted to be an artist, but was forced to write to maintain hers and her brother's families. Her weird fiction began with *A Beleaguered City* (1880), about demonic happenings in a French village, and subsequent novels include *A Little Pilgrim* (1882), *The Wizard's Son* (1883) and *The Land of Darkness* (1888). Her short tales were collected as *Stories of the Seen and Unseen* (1889; 4s).

Oliver Onions (b. Bradford, Yorks., 1873; d. 9 April 1961)
Though he later changed his name to George Oliver, he always wrote as Oliver Onions, and as such is regarded as one of the great writers of ghost fiction. Most highly praised is the long story 'The Beckoning Fair One', a subtle tale of a room haunted by impressions of a young girl with whom the lodger becomes enamoured. It was included in his collection *Widdershins* (1911; 9s). None of Onions' phantoms moan, wail or rattle chains. They impinge on the mind and intangibly haunt the senses. Other collections are *Back o' The Moon* (1906; 5s), *Ghosts in Daylight* (1924; 5s) and *The Painted Face* (1929; 3s), all available as *The Collected Ghost Stories* (1935; 19s).
    Of his novels, *The Power of Oblivion* (1921) is about immortality and his last, *A Shilling to Spend* (1965), is an amusing fantasy about a man with a pocket that cannot be emptied.

Frank Owen (b. 1893; d. 13 October 1968)
Although one of the major contributors to *Weird Tales*, Owen's name is seldom linked with the greats of that magazine. This is because he struck out in a vein all his own and never became involved with **Lovecraft's** eldritch horrors, **Howard's** barbarians, **Smith's** sorceries or **Quinn's** fear fighters. From his first, 'The Man Who Owned the World' (1923) to his last, 'The Unicorn' (1952), Owen related a beautiful and exotic series of Oriental fantasies. These were not set in the real China, like

those of **Beck**, but like **Bramah**, it was a China of the imagination, the one we all think exists. Owen was obsessed with colour and this is clear in the many brilliant descriptive passages that embroider his tales. Many were collected as follows: *The Wind That Tramps the World* (1929; 7s), *The Purple Sea* (1930; 11s), *Della Wu, Chinese Courtesan* (1931; 11s), *A Husband for Kutani* (1938; 4s) and *The Porcelain Magician* (1948; 14s), a reprint volume.

His novels are less well known but include *Rare Earth* (1931), about a man who regains his sight by a miracle; under his Williams alias an Oriental love story, *Loves of Lo Foh* (1936), with a most chilling sequence involving spiders; and, untypically, a straight horror novel, *Madonna of the Damned* (1935). *The Scarlet Hill* (1941) is a historical Chinese novel.

Pseudonyms: Richard Kent, Hung Long Tom (poetry), Roswell Williams

Gerald W. Page (b. Chattanooga, Tenn., 12 August 1939)
Gerald Page is better known as an editor in the fantasy field, though he has sold both sf and horror to the magazines since 'The Happy Man' (1963). Among his best is 'Thirst' (1972), an updated vampire story, around which he is compiling a horror collection. He advocates that horror writers should look to the present rather than the past for their plots and cites **Fritz Leiber** as the most important writer of ghost fiction since **M. R. James** and **Oliver Onions**.

Currently an editor on the world's largest-selling weekly magazine, *TV Guide*, Page was first noted in the fan domain as editor of *Lore*, an amateur journal that acted as a forum for those with puzzling questions about sf and fantasy. In 1970 he became editor of *Witchcraft & Sorcery* (see App. III). He edited the original anthology *Nameless Places* (1975; 27s) for Arkham House, and recently succeeded **Richard Davis** in the US as editor of *The Year's Best Horror Stories* starting with Volume 4 (1976; 14s). He is currently completing a fantasy novel.

Pseudonyms: Carleton Grindle, Kenneth Pembrooke

Norvell W. Page (b. Richmond, Va., 1904; d. 1961)
A prolific writer for the pulps, Page was more noted in the detective fiction field writing the lead novels for *The Spider* (1933 to 1943) and many terror tales for *Dime Mystery*. In the fantasy field he produced two most memorable lead novels for *Unknown*, based on the legend of Prester John, set in the Far East and peopled with evil magicians—*Flame Winds* (1939) and *Sons of the Bear God* (1939). Both saw paperback publication in 1969.

Violet Paget: *see* Vernon Lee

Barry Pain (b. Cambridge, Cambs., 28 September 1864; d. Watford, Herts., 5 May 1928)
Pain ranks as the English **John Kendrick Bangs:** a journalist and humorist noted for his satire, it is difficult to know when to take him seriously. His satire is clear in *Robinson Crusoe's Return* (1907) with the 300-year-old Crusoe coming back to Edwardian Britain. He continued the treatment in *The New Gulliver* (1913). Of his serious weird novels, the best is *The Shadow of the Unseen* (1907) with James Blyth, about witchcraft. Others include *An Exchange of Souls* (1911) and *Going Home* (1921), about a man with wings and a girl with angel-eyes. His supernatural short fiction is sprinkled throughout his collections but is concentrated most in *Stories and Interludes* (1892; 16s), *Three Fantasies* (1904; 3s) and *Stories in the Dark* (1901; 10s) from which comes the oft-reprinted 'The Moon Slave'.

Michel Parry (b. Brussels, 7 October 1947)
A British writer and anthologist, Michel Patrick Parry was born in Belgium of a Welsh father. His interest in the horror field first manifested itself in the cinema, and he began to sell reviews and news items to magazines like *Castle of Frankenstein* from 1961 onwards. He is still closely involved with the industry, having produced his own short surreal black magic film, *Hex* (1969), and written the book of the film *Countess Dracula* (1971). He has also written many screenplays, with *The Uncanny* (1977) the first to be filmed. His first story sale, 'The Last Bus' (1968), dealt with a man's obsession. A later fantasy was *Chariots of Fire* (1974), but most of his fiction is westerns under the pen name Steve Lee.

His main contribution to the horror field lies in many anthologies, all of which reflect his deep knowledge of the genre. First was *Beware of the Cat* (1972; 13s) followed by *The Hounds of Hell* (1974; 16s); his drug trilogy *Strange Ecstasies* (1973; 10s), *Dream Trips* (1974; 10s) and *Spaced Out* (1977; 8s); *Christopher Lee's X Certificate* (1975; 10s: US *From the Archives of Evil*); *The Devil's Children* (1974; 12s); *Jack the Knife* (1975; 10s); *The Supernatural Solution* (1976; 9s); *Roots of Evil* (1976; 12s); *The Devil's Kisses* (1976; 11s); *The Great Villains* (1978; 11s) with Christopher Lee; *Waves of Terror* (1976; 14s); and *Savage Heroes* (1977; 9s). He also edits the *Mayflower Book of Black Magic Stories* (1974, 6 volumes to date), and the *Reign of Terror series. Rivals of Dracula* (1977; 12s) has been followed by *Rivals of Frankenstein* (1977; 11s), *Rivals of King Kong* (1977; 11s), and *More Devil's Kisses* (1977; 13s), with *Rivals of the Wolfman*, *Rivals of Superman* and *Devil's Kisses 3* in preparation.

Parry has recently completed a non-fiction book about mercenaries, *Fire Power*.

Pseudonyms: Carlos Cassaba, Nick Fury, Linda Lovecraft, Eric Pendragon

Roger Pater (b. nr Penrith, Cumberland, 27 December 1874; d. Downside Abbey, 5 August 1936)
The 1920s saw the publication of two intriguing and now very rare books, *Mystic Voices* (1923) and *My Cousin Philip* (1924). Both were a connected series of stories related by a fictional Philip Roger Pater, squire and priest, who is supposed to have lived from 1834 to 1913. The former title is of special interest as it concentrates on various supernatural experiences of Pater, who is haunted not by ghostly visions, but ghostly voices. Stories frequently reprinted include 'A Porta Inferi' and 'De Profundis'. The man behind Pater was Dom Gilbert Roger Hudlestone, a Benedictine priest who wrote numerous books, mostly religious, the proceeds from which he gave to his parish, then at Little Malvern. He was noted for his highly active brain (*The Times* crossword in half an hour), his excellent memory and the ability to speak fluent Latin with an Italian accent!

Mervyn Peake (b. Kuling, China, 9 July 1911; d. 17 November 1968)
Of all the writers in fantasy literature Mervyn Lawrence Peake must rank as one of the most gifted. Educated in China and later at Eltham College, his early days were spent designing stage sets and illustrating books. He married in 1937, and during the war served in the Army—at one time he managed to burn down his barracks.

In 1941 his first book of poems, *Shapes and Sounds*, was published. Thereafter he produced further volumes of verse, a play, and children's books. He was commissioned to illustrate children's books such as *Treasure Island* and *Alice in Wonderland*. But his life-work was his *Gormenghast* trilogy. It began with *Titus Groan* (1946), then *Gormenghast* (1950) and finally *Titus Alone* (1959); the last-named is set apart from the other two and many consider it a lesser work. One must remember though that at this stage Peake was working under the strain and stress of his increasing illness which produced a gradual physical and mental decline over his last ten years. After his death his admirer Langdon Jones worked from Peake's original documents and managed to a great extent to produce a revised *Titus Alone* (1970) reflecting much of Peake's intended style. Peake had also planned a further volume, *Titus 4*. The first two volumes are set in the massive Gormenghast Castle, which is peopled by an exotic and bizarre array of characters, and essentially they trace the rise to fame and subsequent fall of a kitchen boy, Steerpike.

Titus Alone chronicles his exploration of the bizarre world beyond the castle. The delight of these books is Peake's mastery of language. He ranks with **Dickens** for his ability to capture all that is human and all that is alien in one frame. The novels steer from the heights of absurdity to the depths of tragedy in moments and one is emotionally torn between laughing at one episode and shivering in anticipation of the next.

Peake's other output includes an amusing fantasy, *Mr Pye* (1953), about a man who is so good he sprouts wings and so becomes evil and sprouts horns!, and a handful of short stories. Devotees will also like *A Book of Nonsense* (1972), and *Letters from a Lost Uncle* (1948).

G. G. Pendarves (b. *c* 1885; d. Wirral, Cheshire, 1938)
Born Gladys Gordon Trenery, she was a British writer who sold a few stories to British magazines, but is best remembered for her nineteen stories in *Weird Tales* from 'The Devil's Graveyard' (1926) to 'The Withered Heart' (1939), her most popular being 'The Eighth Green Man' (1928). Her stories reflect her knowledge of the occult, but she also wrote a few traditional ghost stories like 'Thing of Darkness' (1937) and several Oriental fantasies.

Emil Petaja (b. Montana, 12 April 1915)
The last decade has seen a variety of books from Petaja, some science fiction, others science fantasy such as those based on the Kalevala—*Saga of Lost Earths* (1966), *The Star Mill* (1966), *The Stolen Sun* (1967) and *Tramontane* (1967). But Petaja has been around a long time, his first story 'The Two Doors' appearing in 1935. At that time he was holding various office jobs, but his chief hobby was photography and he became a film technician for Technicolor from 1940 to 1945 and later a professional photographer. He published several stories in *Weird Tales* during the 1940s and still appears occasionally today. A representative selection, many reflecting the **Lovecraft** influence, was published as *Stardrift* (1971; 14s). Petaja was a life-long friend of **Hannes Bok**, after whose death he began the Bokanalia Foundation.

Pseudonym: Theodore Pine

Eden Phillpotts (b. Mt Aboo, India, 4 November 1862; d. Exeter, Devon, 29 December 1960)
When Phillpotts died at the age of 98 it brought to a close one of the longest writing careers in English literature, lasting over sixty years. He wrote over 250 books on a variety of subjects including regional novels about Devon, boys' books, detective and historical fiction, plays and a

healthy proportion of fantasy. He might possibly have written more had not his first ambition been acting, followed by a period in an insurance company.

He began to write in the 1880s and several of his early tales, not all weird, were collected as *Loup-Garou* (1899; 10s). An early weird novel was *A Deal with the Devil* (1895) which has the protagonist growing younger by the day. Subsequent novels include *Number 87* (1922, as Hext) about an apparition known as 'The Bat', *The Thing at Their Heels* (1923, as Hext), *A Voice from the Dark* (1925), *The Monster* (1925), and the noted werewolf tale *Lycanthrope* (1937: US *The Mystery of Sir William Wolf*).

For his fantasy novels Phillpotts delighted in reworking the Greek and Roman myths as in *The Girl and the Faun* (1916), *Evander* (1919), *The Treasures of Typhon* (1924), *Arachne* (1927), *The Miniature* (1927; reprinted in **Carter**'s *Discoveries in Fantasy*), and *The Owl of Athene* (1936). *The Lavender Dragon* (1923) is a delightful medieval fantasy of knights and dragons; the later *Table Top* (1939) an adventure fantasy in a land with huge spiders and 'nameless things'. There are many more besides but all are now out of print.

Pseudonym: Harrington Hext

Edgar Allan Poe (b. Boston, 19 January 1809; d. Baltimore, 7 October 1849)

Could any other name be more synonymous with horror fiction? Few will deny that Poe ranks as one of the best known, and possibly the greatest of all horror writers, and the father of modern horror. Yet so versatile was this tragic genius that he has equally valid claims to being the father of scientific and detective fiction. His horror fiction is effective and authentic because it was written out of fear, it represents his own phobias. There is little of the supernatural in his writing, short of inclusion for symbolical or satirical reasons. His horror is that of the mind, of dread and the depressive absence of hope.

Poe led a tragic life. Orphaned before he was 3, he was raised by a Richmond, Va., merchant, John Allan, who later disowned him. He spent two years in the Army, and was later at the West Point military academy until dismissed for deliberate neglect of duty. In 1836 he married his 13-year-old cousin, Virginia, who burst a blood vessel in 1842 while singing, and remained in poor health till she died of tuberculosis in 1847 when still only 23. Poe attempted suicide in 1848 while suffering from frequent bouts of depression and madness. In September 1849 he went to Baltimore, vanished for some three days, and was found dying, soon after.

Poe had set out as a poet, publishing a volume *Tamerlane* in 1827, but

146

he only reached fame with the appearance of *The Raven* (1845) and for his last few years he was known as 'Mr Poe the poet'. His short stories, though admired, never gained him much wealth or recognition until after his death. The bulk of his income came from his employment as an editor on various periodicals which generally prospered under him, and for which he wrote much copy. Many of these journals offered prizes for fiction and Poe received his first boost when his sea horror story 'MS Found in a Bottle' (1833) won a fifty-dollar first prize. This was one of a series called *Tales of the Folio Club* which Poe collected into a special handwritten volume. Initially eleven stories, he added a further five. All saw newspaper publication. Poe's first story, 'Metzengerstein' (1832), set in an old castle with its insane occupants, had all the trappings of Gothic horror, but from then on he carved out his own style, and later condemned the Gothic tale by saying, 'I maintain that terror is not of Germany, but of the soul'. This he portrayed with stunning effect in such classics as 'The Fall of the House of Usher' (1839), 'William Wilson' (1839), 'The Black Cat' (1843), 'The Tell-Tale Heart' (1843), 'The Pit and the Pendulum' (1842), 'The Premature Burial' (1844) and, finally, 'The Facts in the Case of M. Valdemar' (1845), in which a man's mind is kept alive under hypnosis after his body has died.

He had a versatile and active mind. An expert on cryptograms (see 'The Gold Bug' (1843)) and solving problems, Poe is noted for having predicted the conclusion of **Dickens**'s *Barnaby Rudge* from its opening chapters. He brought this talent to bear in several detective stories and in the solution of real-life crimes, one of which is also a noted horror story, 'The Murders in the Rue Morgue' (1841). Poe assembled a collection as *Tales of the Grotesque and Arabesque* (1840; 25s) and a New York publisher assembled *Tales* (1845; 12s) to cash in on the success of *The Raven*. A *Complete Tales and Poems* (1938; 73s) has appeared, but most standard editions are titled *Tales of Mystery and Imagination*. Poe's only novel, *The Narrative of A. Gordon Pym* (1837), a frightening sea voyage, was incomplete; attempted conclusions and continuations were made by Jules Verne in *The Sphinx of the Ice-Fields* (1897) and **Lovecraft** in *At The Mountains of Madness* (1936).

John Polidori (b. London, 7 September 1795; d. London, August 1821) Polidori's name survives since, as Byron's physician, he was one of the select group of four who gathered at Lake Geneva in June 1816 and challenged each other to write a convincing horror story. The major outcome was **Mary Shelley**'s *Frankenstein*. Percy Shelley never completed his, and neither did Byron, though the latter was published as 'A Fragment' (1817; also titled 'The Burial'). Polidori completed his tale which has much in common with Byron's, and when it first appeared as *The Vampyre; a Tale* (1819) it was thought to be the poet's work, though

Byron promptly denied authorship. It is important as the first vampire story written in English.

As a doctor, Polidori had a good knowledge of the workings of the mind and had written a thesis on nightmares in 1815. He now had the writing bug, but separated from Byron he lacked inspiration, and heavily in debt he poisoned himself, aged 26. Seven years later his sister became the mother of Dante Gabriel Rossetti.

Arthur Porges (b. Chicago, 20 August 1915)

While Porges has received deserved recognition in the detective field, credited with having invented the first wheelchair detective, his output of sf and horror is unjustly overlooked. For many years a college mathematics teacher, he retired in 1975. He sold his first story in 1950 and soon began to make regular appearances in the sf/fantasy fields, his best stories being published in *F&SF* and *Fantastic*. Probably best known is 'Solomon's Demon' (1961), about something evil released from an old box, but equally entertaining are 'The Mirror' (1966), about the horror lurking beyond a looking-glass, 'Nightquake' (1960), showing the terror of a mute child who realises something nasty is in his room, and 'Third Sister' (1963), detailing the workings of Fate. There is more than enough for a bumper collection. His brother, Irwin, has written the definitive biographies of **Edgar Rice Burroughs** and **Edgar Allan Poe**.

Pseudonyms: Peter Arthur, Pat Rogers

Count Jan Potocki (b. Ukraine, 8 March 1761; d. 2 December 1815)

A Polish nobleman, historian, archaeologist, ethnologist and balloonist, Jan Nrabia Potocki wrote a wonderful collection of stories in the style of the *Arabian Nights* with stories-within-stories dealing with haunted inns and castles, forest chapels, execution grounds, lust, revenge, cabalism and much else. It first appeared as *The Saragossa Manuscript* (1804), but other portions appeared over the ensuing years with a complete Polish edition in 1847, running the full sixty-seven days. A US volume appeared in 1960 and it was filmed in 1966. The original served as source material for the writings of N. **Hawthorne** and **Irving**.

John Cowper Powys (b. Shirley, Derby, 8 October 1872; d. Blaenau, 17 June 1963)

During a staggering writing career of nearly 65 years, Powys wrote only fifteen novels, but nearly all of them are woven with a mystic strangeness, and about half relate directly to the fantasy medium. These appeared mostly in his latter years, though an early interest in fantasy as a means to convey mood or message is evident in *Ducdame* (1925) with a scene in which a father meets the ghost of his unborn son. A rare short story, 'The Owl, the Duck, and—Miss Rowe!' (1930), concerns two old people in a small room along with a ghost and phantoms of their own creation.

Mystical elements enter his novels *A Glastonbury Romance* (1932), *Maiden Castle* (1936) and his historical fantasies *Owen Glendower* (1940) and *Porius* (1951). The last-named is set in fifth-century Wales and includes an unrivalled portrayal of Merlin. But his major fantasies begin with *Morwyn: or, The Vengeance of God* (1937), almost a combination of Dante and Verne, in that it describes a descent through Earth to Hell. *Atlantis* (1954) is a stunning rendition of Greek mythology relating the further voyage of Odysseus to the lost continent and beyond. Powys's interest in that period is also apparent in *Homer and the Aether* (1959) a free rendition of the *Iliad*. Other fantasies are *The Inmates* (1952), set in a mental home, and *The Brazen Head* (1956), set in a mythical Middle Ages.

His last novels, *Up and Out* (1957: 2n) and *All or Nothing* (1960) can only be described as bizarre space opera, but will be abhorrent to the sf purist and hold no interest for the fantasy fan.

T. F. Powys (b. Shirley, Derby, 20 December 1875; d. Mappowder, Wales, 27 November 1953)
Unlike his elder brother, Theodore Francis Powys concentrated more on short fiction, most notably *Fables* (1929; 19s), amusing and pointed allegories. His work is predominantly symbolic, especially the novel *Mr Weston's Good Wine* (1927) in which God, in the shape of Mr Weston, stops time in a small village and then offers the villagers the choice of his wine—dark or light. Several collections of his short stories exist, no single one containing all his horror tales, of which the best are 'The Two Thieves', 'The House of the Echo' and 'The Hunted Beast'.

Mrs Campbell Praed (b. Queensland, 27 March 1851; d. Torquay, Devon, 10 April 1935)
Born Rosa Caroline Murray-Prior, Mrs Praed came to England in the 1880s and wrote a number of novels about Australian life. Nearly forgotten are her weird works, starting with *The Brother of the Shadow* (1886) which shows a deep knowledge of the occult. It was followed by *The Soul of Countess Adrian* (1891), a tale of psychic vampirism, *The Insane Root* (1902), about the magic of the mandrake, *Fugitive Anne* (1903), about a lost race of Tortoise Worshippers in the Australian Bush, and *Nyria* (1904). This was later revised as *The Soul of Nyria* (1931), and is based on her companion Nancy who was believed to be the reincarnation of a Roman slave, Nyria.

Fletcher Pratt (b. nr Buffalo, N.Y., 25 April 1897; d. 10 June 1956)
Murray Fletcher Pratt became renowned as a naval and American historian, noted for his history of the American Civil War *Ordeal By Fire*. Initially torn between being a boxer or librarian, Pratt chose the latter and devoted himself to considerable study. He mastered many languages and during the 1930s translated several foreign novels for Hugo Gernsback's sf magazines. He also sold a few sf stories of his own. Later he became friends with **L. Sprague de Camp**, collaborating with him on the Shea and Gavagan's Bar series. But his fame in the fantasy field rests on two novels set in magical versions of Europe, *The Well of the Unicorn* (1948) and *The Blue Star* (1952). Both show his detailed knowledge of history, legends and politics. He died of cancer of the liver when he was 59.

Pseudonym: George U. Fletcher

Thomas Pecket Prest (b. 1810; d. London, 5 June 1859)
Prest's fame in the annals of weird literature has slightly diminished of late with the consensus of opinion that the most famous work attributed to him, *Varney the Vampire*, was the work of **J. M. Rymer**. Nevertheless, Prest was so prolific that robbed of even that dubious honour, there is much to his credit. He was one of that breed who churned out an endless stream of 'penny dreadful' fiction, and became noted for his clever imitation of **Dickens** as Bos. It was as much about Prest's work as any other's that the term 'blood and thunder' was coined. He wrote pure melodrama, adapting the Gothic novel from distant European castles to England, especially London. The most legendary by Prest was 'The String of Pearls' (1841) which gave birth to the story of Sweeney Todd, the Demon Barber. He also compiled a volume *The Calendar of Horrors* (1835) but it is not clear how much of the content was his. Prest poured his life into writing and made his publisher prosperous, but he himself died of phlebitis when only 49.

E. Hoffman Price (b. Fowler, Calif., 3 July 1898)
Edgar Hoffman Price was one of the major writers of adventure fiction for the pulps in the 1930s and '40s. Having served in the 15th US Cavalry between 1917 and 1919 in the Philippines, Mexico and France he had many experiences to inspire his fiction. Also proficient in military tactics, horsemanship, gun, sabre and duelling épée, he knew what he was writing about. He did not stay in the Army but took a civilian job while learning to write. A non-fantasy sale was followed by 'Rajah's Gift' (1925), the first of nearly forty stories he would sell to *Weird Tales* and its companion. He specialised in Oriental fantasies, and although he had

never visited China, he became a Buddhist, joined the Theosophists, and became an honorary citizen of San Francisco's Chinatown.

A great friend of **Otis Kline**, with whom he frequently collaborated, Price was also the only writer to have a story published as a joint collaboration with **Lovecraft** during that man's lifetime—'Through the Gates of the Silver Key' (1934). Price wrote a series about a tough old aristocratic Frenchman, Pierre d'Artois, who often became involved with a cult of devil-worshippers. Two collections of his work have appeared, *Strange Gateways* (1967; 12s) and *Far Lands, Other Days* (1975; 31s). He still writes the occasional story and is working on a fantasy novel plus his memoirs, since as an inveterate traveller he met more of the *Weird Tales* coterie than anyone else.

Pseudonym: Hamlin Daly

H. Hesketh Prichard (b. Jhansi, India, 17 November 1876; d. Gorehambury, Herts., 14 June 1922)
Hesketh Vernon Hesketh Prichard was born six weeks after his father had died of typhoid and the infant returned with his mother, Kate Ryall, to England four months later. The two travelled widely, and Prichard became a noted big-game hunter throughout the Americas and Europe, led an expedition to Patagonia in 1900, and for relaxation played cricket for Hampshire. He collaborated with his mother on many occasions, and these included a series about the exploits of psychic investigator Flaxman Low. Twelve of these appeared as two separate series in *Pearson's* in 1898 and 1899, where they were presented as 'Real Ghost Stories' accompanied by photographs of the stricken houses. Published in the magazine under the by-line E. & H. Heron, they were first collected as *Ghosts* (1899; 12s) under the name K. & H. Prichard, with a cheaper edition as *Ghost Stories* (1916; 6s) again under the Heron name.

Prichard continued to write after his mother's death, and fought in the First World War, becoming a Major. He died when only 45 after fourteen operations for disorders caused by an obscure blood disease.

Pseudonym: E. & H. Heron

Dorothy Quick (b. New York, 1900; d. 15 March 1962)
A popular contributor to *Weird Tales* and *Unknown* in the 1930s and '40s, she first appeared in *Oriental Stories* with 'Scented Gardens' (1932). Her trilogy in *Unknown* which began with 'Blue and Silver Brocade' (1939) tells of a Scots girl who experiences earlier lives. Her *Weird Tales* contributions, like 'The Woman on the Balcony' (1949), were noted for their tender treatment of spirits. She also wrote several thrillers, and her last book was *Enchantment* (1961).

Arthur Quiller-Couch (b. Fowey, Cornwall, 21 November 1863; d. Fowey, 12 May 1944)
A noted scholar and lecturer, Sir Arthur Quiller-Couch spent most of his life in literary pursuits, and his fiction was compressed into his early years. A staunch Cornishman, as is evident from his fiction, he relies heavily on legends. His ghost stories, of which the best known are 'A Pair of Hands' and 'The Seventh Man', are found in several collections, predominantly *Wandering Heath* (1895; 14s) and *Old Fires and Profitable Ghosts* (1900; 15s). An early novel, *Dead Man's Rock* (1887), tells of the search for a giant ruby and the consequences of its discovery.

Seabury Quinn (b. Washington D.C., 1 January 1889; d. 24 December 1969)
Despite all the legendary names that contributed to *Weird Tales*, Seabury Grandin Quinn was *the* most popular writer. He was also the most regular and consistent contributor with 145 stories plus articles in its pages between 1923 and 1952. He also wrote for other markets, but it is his *Weird Tales* stories that remain his monument, and within that his series about the French occult investigator, Jules de Grandin.

Quinn was educated in law and medicine and after the First World War he taught both medical jurisprudence and mortuary law at different times, and edited several trade journals including the morticians' *Casket and Sunnyside*! He began his fiction around 1917 with stories in *Young's Magazine* and *Thrill Book*. One early tale was 'The Cloth of Madness' (1920). The first de Grandin exploit was 'The Horror on the Links' (1925) and in all 93 appeared up to 'The Ring of Bâstet' (1951), including the serial *The Devil's Bride* (1932; book 1976). All were modelled on the Watson/Holmes format, with Dr Trowbridge as the narrator. Not all the solutions were supernatural, but all were bizarre and evil, and de Grandin was never squeamish in handing out a villain's just deserts. A handful were revised for book publication as *The Phantom Fighter* (1966; 10s) and belatedly they are now all in paperback as the series *The Adventures of Jules de Grandin* (1976; 7s), *The Casebook of . . .* (1976; 7s), *The Skeleton Closet of . . .* (1976; 6s), *The Hellfire Files of . . .* (1976; 6s), and *The Horror Chambers of . . .* 1977; 6s) with more planned.

Paradoxically, despite the popularity of the series, Quinn's two best stories are not connected. They were his werewolf story 'The Phantom Farmhouse' (1923) and the touching fantasy rendition of the Santa Claus myth, 'Roads' (1938; book, 1948). A limited edition volume of other stories appeared as *Is the Devil a Gentleman?* (1970; 9s).

Mrs Ann Radcliffe (b. London, 9 July 1764; d. 7 February 1823)
After **Walpole** and **Reeve**, Gothic horror fiction really developed with

Mrs Radcliffe, whose work was possibly more influential. The daughter of respectable tradespeople, she married a law student in 1787 who later became a newspaper editor. Her first novel was a Scottish historical romance, *The Castles of Athlin and Dunbayne* (1789), followed in quick succession by *A Sicilian Romance* (1790), *The Romance of the Forest* (1791), her classic *The Mysteries of Udolpho* (1794) and *The Italian* (1797). All these carried natural solutions to the eerie and terrifying events, and only in her last novel, *Gaston de Blondeville* (completed 1802 but published 1826), did she allow any hint of the supernatural.

Jean Ray (b. Ghent, 8 July 1887; d. Ghent, 17 September 1964)
Jean-Raymond De Kremer was a Belgian journalist who wrote prolifically in both French (as Ray) and Flemish (as John Flanders). He maintained a façade as a sailor, smuggler and adventurer, but in life was none of those. *Terra D'Aventures* (1910) was the first of over twenty novels and collections, of which his masterpiece is *Malpertuis* (1943), about the dying Greek gods imprisoned in an accursed house. *Weird Tales* printed several of his stories (as Flanders) in the 1930s, but his only translated collection is *Ghouls in My Grave* (1965; 8s), mostly examples of the *conte cruel*.

Clara Reeve (b. Ipswich, Suffolk, 1729; d. Ipswich, 3 December 1807)
She led a quiet, retiring life, wrote five novels, a history of fiction and translated *Argenis*, and would most likely be long forgotten had not one of those novels been *The Champion of Virtue* (1777). Inspired by Walpole's *Otranto*, she rationalised some of its more random elements and put the Gothic novel firmly on the road. Walpole didn't like it. With its second edition its title became *The Old English Baron* (1778). She also wrote a short ghost story, 'Castle Connor' but it was lost in the post in 1787!

G. W. M. Reynolds (b. Sandwich, Kent, 23 July 1814; d. London, 17 June 1879)
In 1828 George William Macarthur Reynolds inherited £120,000 and he promptly abandoned his Army career, travelled Europe and settled in Paris where he established, albeit unsuccessfully, a newspaper. Returning to London in 1837 he devoted himself to writing, achieving fame for his Dickens imitations. He later established his own *Miscellany* (1846) and *Weekly* (1850). A prolific writer for the cheap press he wrote a few supernatural adventures, paramount among them *Wagner, the Wehr-Wolf* (1847), the tale of a young man given the gift of eternal youth in return for becoming a wolf once a month. Reynolds's most popular work was *The*

Mysteries of London (1845) and several successive *Mysteries* which lifted the lid on the vice and squalor in the capital. A later novel was *The Necromancer* (1857), another pact-with-the-devil thriller.

Mrs L. Baillie Reynolds (b. Teddington, Mddx, *c* 1875; d. 22 November 1939)
Though now near forgotten, Mrs Louis Reynolds wrote a fair selection of weird fiction, notably the novels *A Castle to Let* (1917), about a lady who finds herself in a dragon-haunted castle, and *The Spell of Sarnia* (1925), an occult adventure in Guernsey. Her short stories were collected as *The Terrible Baron* (1933) with the long title story about lycanthropy, and *The Relations and What They Related* (1902; 10s).

Flavia Richardson: *see* Christine Campbell Thomson

Mrs J. H. Riddell (b. Antrim, 30 September 1832; d. Hounslow, Mddx, 24 September 1906)
Born Charlotte Eliza Lawson Cowan she was another of the eminent Victorian female novelists. She began writing in 1856 when her husband lost his money. She wrote prodigiously, often under male pen names, and a number of her tales were ghost stories. She was a noted contributor to Christmas annuals starting with 'Fairy Water' (1873), and these formed the basis for her collections *Weird Stories* (1884; 6s), *Idle Tales* (1887; 8s) and *The Banshee's Warning* (1894; 6s).

Pseudonyms: Rainey Hawthorne, F. G. Trafford

Tod Robbins (b. 1888; d. 1949)
Seldom supernatural, the writings of Clarence Aaron Robbins are often macabre and grotesque. This was clear from his first novel *Mysterious Martin* (US 1912), which concerned an author who murders so that he can accurately describe the sensation. His fame came with *The Terrible Three* (1917), in which three circus freaks—a dwarf, a giant and a ventriloquist—combine forces in an evil alliance. It was filmed in 1925 and saw UK book publication as *The Unholy Three* (1917) and *The Three Freaks* (1934). Robbins re-used the theme for his short story 'Spurs', which was the basis of the film *Freaks* (1932). A US collection of his stories appeared as *Silent, White and Beautiful* (1920; 4s); a UK compilation was *Who Wants a Green Bottle?* (1926; 8s). A later volume of stories about death was *In the Shadow* (US 1929; 8s).

Morley Roberts (b. London, 29 December 1857; d. London, 8 June 1942)
Roberts spent his early life travelling extensively, helping to build railways in Australia in 1876. He is chiefly remembered for the clever story 'The Anticipator' (from *The Keeper of the Waters*, 1898) about a writer who finds his fiction is always written first by another. Less known are some of his other stories, such as those in *Midsummer Madness* (1909; 9s). This includes 'The Fog', 'A Thing of Wax' and 'The Blood Fetish', the last-named about a disembodied hand that can absorb blood and briefly make itself into a whole body.

Morgan Robertson (b. Oswego, N.Y., 30 September 1861; d. Atlantic City, 24 March 1915)
Fame comes to writers in odd ways, but perhaps none so bizarre as with Robertson. In 1898 he wrote a long story 'Futility', which told of the maiden voyage of an 'unsinkable' luxury liner that struck an iceberg and sank. It was called the *Titan*. Fourteen years later the *Titanic* suffered the same fate! Robertson wrote a number of sea stories. Many deal with telepathy, hypnotism and dual personality. He was a firm believer in reincarnation. His best tales are in the volumes *The Grain Ship* (1914; 10s), *Over the Border* (1914; 13s) and *Where Angels Fear to Tread* (1899; 11s). Robertson's death was equally bizarre. He was found standing half upright in his hotel room, stone dead!

Sax Rohmer (b. Birmingham, 15 February 1883; d. London, 1 June 1959)
Simply mention the description 'insidious Oriental' and it conjures up the name Dr Fu-Manchu, one of literature's most immortal creations. The evil doctor with his designs on world domination at any cost and the attempts by Nayland Smith to thwart his plans appear in the internationally famous series of thirteen novels from *Dr Fu-Manchu* (1913) to *Emperor Fu-Manchu* (1959) (see App. I).

Rohmer, born Arthur Henry Ward (becoming A. Sarsfield Ward in 1901), set out as a journalist with little success and turned to writing clever mystery stories. On the whole all his novels fall into the occult mystery category. Another example of his creation was the detective Morris Klaw, who solved his mysteries by sleeping at the scene of the crime. These stories were collected as *The Dream Detective* (1920). Paul Harley solves further weird problems in *Bat-Wing* (1921) and its sequel *Fire-Tongue* (1921). Rohmer was fascinated by the occult, and he became a Member of the Order of the Golden Dawn. He also wrote a study of it in *The Romance of Sorcery* (1914). His chief love was the mysticism of Egypt and this is clearly apparent in his best novel *Brood of the Witch-Queen* (1917) and his collections *Tales of Secret Egypt* (1918; 9s) and *The*

Haunting of Low Fennel (1920; 7s). His short fiction is often overlooked, and other volumes of interest are *Tales of Chinatown* (1922; 10s) and *Tales of East and West* (1932; 10s: US 1933; 13s).

Of his many novels, others of note include *The Sins of Severac Bablon* (1914), *The Orchard of Tears* (1918), *The Quest of the Sacred Slipper* (1919), *The Golden Scorpion* (1919) and its sequel *Dope* (1919), *The Green Eyes of Bâst* (1920), *Grey Face* (1924), *Yellow Shadows* (1925), *Moon of Madness* (1927), *She Who Sleeps* (1928), *The Day the World Ended* (1930), *Yu'an Hee See Laughs* (1932), *The Bat Flies Low* (1935), *White Velvet* (1937), *Egyptian Nights* (1944; US *Bimbashi Baruk of Egypt*), *Seven Sins* (1943), *Wulfheim* (1950, as Furey), *Hangover House* (1950), *The Moon is Red* (1954), and a series about *Sumuru*, a female Fu-Manchu; *The Sins of Sumuru* (1950; US *Nude in Mink*), *Sumuru* (1951; UK edition different *The Slaves of Sumuru*, 1952), *The Fire Goddess* (1952; UK *Virgin in Flames*, 1953), *The Return of Sumuru* (1954; UK *Sand and Satin*, 1955) and *Sinister Madonna* (1956).

Pseudonym: Michael Furey

Frederick Rolfe (b. London, 22 July 1860; d. Venice, 26 October 1913) Frederick William Rolfe was one of those more unsavoury characters in English literature whom we could well do without. Eternally ungrateful, he lived most of his life in poverty relying on the compassion of gullible friends. He trained as a priest but was a failure at schooling and though transferred to Rome he merely ran up debts. Intruding upon the hospitality of a rich Italian family, by whom Rolfe claimed he was conferred the title of Baron Corvo, he turned to writing. He made an enemy of anyone who befriended him, yet still people helped. A final friend obtained advances on books that Rolfe had no intention of writing—but he still squandered the money. Of his works, the most readable are those that poke fun at Catholicism as in his series *Stories Toto Told Me* (1895) and *In His Own Image* (1901), in which he retold legends like St George and the Dragon. A later novel, *The Weird of the Wanderer* (1912), dealt with reincarnation, and *Hubert's Arthur* (1934) is set in an alternate world where Prince Arthur had not been killed by order of King John.

Pseudonyms: Baron Corvo, Prospero and Caliban

L. T. C. Rolt (b. Chester, Cheshire, 11 February 1910; d. 9 May 1974) Lionel Thomas Caswell Rolt had a life-long interest in modes of travel. Acquiring a garage in 1934 he specialised in veteran, vintage and racing cars. In 1940 he bought a canal boat as a home and began writing. His forty-three books cover topics like inland waterways (he helped set up the Inland Waterways Association with **R. Aickman**), railways, ballooning, engineering, plus biography, topography and even philosophy—his volume *The Clouded Mirror* (1955) contains four essays about spiritual death. But of major interest here is his volume of ghost stories, *Sleep No More* (1948; 12s), which reflect his interests in engineering by setting ghosts in some unusual places. Shortly before his death he completed two new stories which can be found in **Hugh Lamb's** anthologies.

Victor Rousseau (b. London, 1879; d. New York, 5 April 1960)
Half-Jewish by birth, Victor Rousseau Emanuel converted to Catholicism and after training in journalism in South Africa he secured an editorial post in New York. He started to write and soon was appearing in many of the pulp magazines. An early story, 'The Seal Maiden' (1913), was based on the Canadian legend that seals were once human, and if a seal woman can win a mortal's love she gains a soul. Other early works include *The Sea Demons* (1916), about transparent sea-creatures invading England, and his classic if short-sighted *The Messiah of the Cylinder* (1917), a variation on Wells's *When the Sleeper Wakes*. *Fruit of the Lamp* (1918; UK *Mrs Aladdin* 1925, as Egbert) tells of a bachelor who acquires an old lamp with its beautiful female genie.

Rousseau's later stories show his perceptive knowledge of the occult, especially in the series about Dr Martinus, Occultist, that ran in *Ghost Stories* (including the serial *The House of the Living Dead*, 1927) and the psychic adventures of Dr Ivan Brodsky 'The Surgeon of Souls' in *Weird Tales* (1926–27). His best stories appeared in *Strange Tales* and include the vampire tale 'A Cry From Beyond' (1931) and the Egyptian curse in 'The Curse of Amen-Ra' (1932).

Pseudonym: H. M. Egbert (on UK books)

Anthony M. Rud (b. Chicago, 1893; d. 1942)
Rud had the honour of having the best story in the very first issue of *Weird Tales*, 'Ooze' (1923), a now cliché-ridden yarn of a menacing blob! His story of madness, 'A Square of Canvas', was the best story in the second issue. Rud went on to become editor of *Adventure* and *Detective Story Magazine*, and a later novel was *The Stuffed Men* (1935), about a Chinese Secret Society who wreak dreadful revenge on their victims with a fungus that grows in the lungs, stomach and brain.

Ray Russell (b. Chicago, 4 September 1924)
When Ray Robert Russell became executive editor of *Playboy* in its formative years he created one of the major adult markets for sf and horror writers in the 1950s. It was Russell who really launched **Beaumont.**

Russell is no mean writer himself, and specialises in giving modern treatment to the old Gothic thrillers. His classic is 'Sardonicus', which he adapted to the screen as *Mr Sardonicus* (1961). It led his collection *Sardonicus* (1961; 17s), and the other stories with a few additions form his UK collection *Prince of Darkness* (1971; 17s). His best work is the novel *The Case Against Satan* (1962), a striking description of a priest's fight against the devil for possession of a young girl—this years before Blatty's *The Exorcist*. Another Gothic volume is *Unholy Trinity* (1964; 3s). His latest novel of demonic possession is *Incubus* (1976).

W. Clark Russell (b. New York, 24 February 1844; d. Bath, Somerset, 8 November 1911)

The lure and mystery of the sea has supplied many plots for horror stories. Almost all of Clark Russell's work deals with the sea and naturally not a few are bizarre. *The Frozen Pirate* (1887) tells of an eighteenth-century rogue who survives frozen in thick ice. *The Death Ship* (1888) is a chilling recount of the Flying Dutchman legend. His weird short fiction was collected as *The Phantom Death* (1895).

James Malcolm Rymer (b. 1814; d. 1884)

The works of Rymer were among the most popular of the 'penny dreadful' melodramas. His name was first thought to have been an alias of **Prest**, to whom his two greatest works were first ascribed. *Varney the Vampire* (1845) ranks as the most noted vampire novel before *Dracula* and runs to three-quarters of a million words. *The Black Monk* (1844) is a historical fantasy set during the reign of Richard I. Rymer was a Scottish engineer who forsook that in the 1840s to write, and at his death left an estate of £8,000.

Marquis de Sade (b. Paris, 2 June 1740; d. Charenton, 1 December 1814)

Few writers' names have passed into the English language, and one we could well do without is de Sade, from whence came 'sadism'. There were of course sadistic people before the Marquis, but his gross and immoral practices were carried to such a degree that he was viewed as the epitome of cruelty.

A *bona fide* nobleman and soldier, de Sade was frequently imprisoned for his activities, and it was while incarcerated at Vincennes in 1778 that he began writing his nauseous novels and short stories which revel in horrific descriptions of appalling practices. His most noted books include *Justine* (1791), *La Philosophie dans le Boudoir* (1793) and *Juliette* (1798).

A few of his short stories show an ability to write, and the best of these were translated by Margaret Crosland as *Eugenie de Franval* (1965; 8s). Released and again imprisoned, de Sade spent his last years in an asylum where he died of gangrenous fever and a pulmonary obstruction. Many say he died mad, but the question is, was he ever sane?

Saki: *see* H. H. Munro

Jimmy Sangster (b. N. Wales, 2 December 1927)
Ever since he left school at 15, Sangster has been involved with the film industry, as freelance director, production manager, and since 1957 scriptwriter and producer—chiefly with Hammer Films. His first film was *The Curse of Frankenstein* (1957) followed by *Dracula* (1958) and *The Mummy* (1959). Among his original scripts are *Taste of Fear* (1961), about a girl investigating her father's death, and *Maniac* (1963), about a young artist whose life is imperilled by an escaped lunatic. Sangster's highpoint was the film that sustained Bette Davis's comeback in the macabre field, *The Nanny* (1965). A later Davis film was *The Anniversary* (1968).

William Sansom (b. London, 18 January 1912; d. 20 April 1976)
One of Britain's most noted short story writers, his career began in a bank. Then, after a stint in an advertising agency, he became a fireman, and this provided ample terrifying inspiration for the stories that formed his first book, *Fireman Flower* (1944; 12s). A later collection, *Something Terrible, Something Lovely* (1948; 21s) includes his story of the lady too perfect to be true—'A Woman Seldom Found'. Most of his best uncanny stories will be found in *Collected Stories* (1963).

Sarban: *see* John W. Wall

Peter Saxon (b. Scotland, 8 March 1921)
Under a profusion of pseudonyms, Wilfred McNeilly has been a prolific writer since 1950. He spent several years in India where his interest in the occult grew from conversations with various 'saddhus'. Later he learned much from West Indians with an interest in voodoo and obeah.
  During the 1950s he wrote mostly for the detective field, contributing to the *Sexton Blake Library*, and his occult output, inspired by **Wheatley**, began with *The Darkest Night* (1966), about the horrors of the festival of Kali. *The Torturer* (1967) is a twist on the vampire theme with an evil

that lives on down the ages; *The Disorientated Man* (1967) was a variant on the Frankenstein theme, and was filmed as *Scream and Scream Again* (1969). These appeared under the Saxon alias as did his series about The Guardians who rage a war in London against black magic. The novels in this series were *The Killing Bone* (1968), *Dark Ways to Death* (1969) and *The Haunting of Alan Mais* (1969). Other Saxon books include *Through the Dark Curtain* (1968), *Black Honey* (1968) and *The Vampires of Finisterre* (1970). Then McNeilly adopted the alias Error Lecale for a series about the Specialist in all things occult. These include *Tigerman of Terrahpur* (1973), *Castledoom* (1974), *The Severed Hand* (1974), *The Death Box* (1974), *Zombie* (1975) and *Blood of My Blood* (1975).

Pseudonyms: W. A. Ballinger, Desmond Reid (house), Martin Gregg, Joe Hunter, Errol Lecale

Dorothy L. Sayers (b. Oxford, 13 June 1893; d. Witham, Essex, 17 December 1957)
The popularity of Dorothy Leigh Sayers as a writer of detective fiction is such that it is unnecessary to say more here. Her major contribution to the horror field was with her gargantuan anthology series *Great Short Stories of Detection, Mystery and Horror* (1929, 1931 and 1934—see App. II). These bumper selections of some of the best weird fiction had an incalculable effect in converting new recruits to the field. She wrote a few horror stories herself, such as some of the short Wimsey stories in *Lord Peter Views the Body* (1928), and especially 'The Cyprian Cat' and 'Scrawns'.

Dorothy Scarborough (b. Mt Carmel, Texas, 1877; d. Colombia, 7 November 1935)
Of the several noted research works in the horror field, one of the best and most praised is *The Supernatural in Modern English Fiction* (1917) with which Dorothy Scarborough obtained her Ph.D. It remains a most authoritative work marred only by the perplexing omissions of **M. R. James** and **Hope Hodgson**. She also edited the anthologies *Famous Modern Ghost Stories* (1921; 15s) and *Humorous Ghost Stories* (1921; 19s).

Johann von Schiller (b. Marbach, 10 November 1759; d. Weimar, 9 May 1805)
Schiller's contribution to the horror genre was more as a catalyst. One of Germany's greatest poets and dramatists, his only weird fiction is 'Der Geisterseher' (1787–89), involving the summoning of the dead—and he never even completed that. But the bizarre fascinated him and he often

inspired others to look further into unknown realms. He was a great friend of **Goethe** and it is more than possible that without Schiller, *Faust* may never have been completed.

Sir Walter Scott (b. Edinburgh, 15 August 1771; d. Abbotsford, Scotland, 21 September 1832)
Without a doubt Britain's, if not the world's, greatest historical novelist, Scott had more than a passing interest in the supernatural. He encouraged many writers who were dabbling in the field such as Hogg and Irving, and had a reciprocal professional relationship with M. G. Lewis. Lewis influenced Scott's historical novels, and he acquired some of Scott's earliest supernatural stories, such as 'Glenfinlas' (1801), for his *Tales of Wonder*. There is much of Lewis in Scott's later stories 'Wandering Willie's Tale' (from *Redgauntlet*, 1824; rev. as 'A Night in the Grave', 1826) and 'The Tapestried Chamber' (1829). Less well known is 'My Aunt Margaret's Mirror' (1828), which is about magic.

William B. Seabrook (b. Westminster, Md., 22 February 1886; d. Rhinebeck, N.Y., 20 September 1945)
Seabrook led a wild, active life which ultimately proved too much for him. At first a journalist and foreign correspondent, he became an author and explorer in 1934, venturing into Arabia, Kurdistan, Africa and Haiti. He is alleged to have participated in voodoo rites, and eaten human flesh in Africa! He wrote many travel books and an *An Analysis of Magic and Witchcraft* (1940). *Asylum* (1935) is about his seven months in hospital as an alcoholic. His stories like 'Toussel's Pale Bride' and 'The Witch's Vengeance' show his knowledge of native magic, but 'The Salamander' (1944) is a stunning study of madness. Seabrook burned himself out before he was 60 and committed suicide with an overdose of pills.

Claude Seignolle (b. Perigueux, France, 25 June 1917)
It is unfortunate that Seignolle's writings have seen so little English translation. He has had a lifetime's interest in local legends, his first book being *Le folklore du Hurepoix* (1937). He spent much of the war in a prison camp which made him aware of new horrors, and his subsequent books have a solid theme of diabolism. They include *Le rond des Sorciers* (1945; rev. 1959), *La Malvenue Roman Fantastiques* (1952), *Le Bahut Noir* (1958), *Le Diable en Sabots* (1959), *Les Maledictions* (1963), *Les Evangiles du Diable selon la Croyance Populaire* (1964), *La Valvennue* (1965) and *La Nuit des Halles* (1965). *Les maledictions* was translated by Bernard Wall as *The Accursed* (1967; 2s), an excellent novel about a girl possessed by the evil from a strange statue.

Mary W. Shelley (b. London, 30 August 1797; d. London, 21 February 1851)

There can scarcely be anyone who has not heard of the name Frankenstein, but there is a fair number of people who believe it was the name of the monster rather than its creator. This confusion really stemmed from the title of the sequel to the famous film *Frankenstein* (1931)—called *The Bride of Frankenstein*, (1935) it was about the creation of a mate for the monster. The original novel, *Frankenstein, or a Modern Prometheus* (1818), was the work of a teenager, Mary Shelley, only child of William Godwin and the early female emancipator Mary Wollstonecraft. She eloped with the poet Shelley in 1814 and married him in 1816. That year they spent at Lake Geneva, and it was there that they met with Byron and **Polidori** and challenged one another to write a horror story. Mary's idea came as the result of a nightmare five months later, and then she worked on it furiously. She never repeated the success of that book, but a later novel of note was *The Last Man* (1826), in which a plague in the future destroys most life.

She wrote several short stories, with fantasies among them. One, 'The Heir of Mondolfo', did not see print until 1877. Most were assembled by **Richard Garnett** as *Tales and Stories* (1891; 17s).

M. P. Shiel (b. Montserrat, 21 July 1865; d. Chichester, Sussex, 17 February 1947)

Matthew Phipps Shiel is one of the overlooked masters of the horror story. Born in the West Indies, his father conferred on him the title of King of Redonda—an uninhabited islet near Antigua—in 1880. Britain never recognised this and a legal wrangle continued for years. Shiel regarded it as binding, since he later made his friend and biographer, **John Gawsworth**, his successor.

Shiel came to England to complete his education, and became adept in several languages. He took to teaching mathematics; tiring of that he chose medicine, but then abandoned that for writing. He found success with *Prince Zaleski* (1895; 3s), a detective recluse who lives in a grotesquely decorated 'vast palace of the older world' and solves baffling crimes by deduction, never leaving his abode. An early striking story was 'Huguenin's Wife' (1895), about a monstrous reincarnation on a Greek island. His first collection was *Shapes in the Fire* (1896; 6s), which includes two of his best stories, 'Vaila' (later rev. as 'The House of Sounds'), set on a Norwegian island battered by the unremitting din of demonic elements, and 'Xelucha'. 'Xelucha', along with later stories 'The Bride' and 'The Tale of Henry and Rowena', show Shiel's penchant for detailing revenge wreaked by once-dead females. This theme recurs in *This Above All* (1933; UK *Above All Else* 1943), in which an immortal woman spends the centuries searching for Lazarus. Other volumes were *The Pale Ape* (1911) and

Invisible Voices (1935). After his death Gawsworth assembled *Best Short Stories* (1948; 12s), and recently the stories Shiel had specially revised for US publication finally appeared as *Xelucha and Others* (1975; 12s).

Most of his novels were non-fantasy but of interest are *The Yellow Danger* (1898; originally *The Empress of the Earth*), in which the Chinese nearly conquer the world, and *The Purple Cloud* (1901), in which a gas nearly destroys all life on Earth. This was effectively filmed as *The World, the Flesh and the Devil* (1959).

May Sinclair (b. Rock Ferry, Cheshire, 1865; d. nr Aylesbury, Bucks., 14 November 1946)
A noted novelist who began writing in 1895, she became a convinced spiritualist and this is reflected in her weird fiction, collected as *Uncanny Stories* (1923; 7s) and *The Intercessor* (1931; 5s). Her best-known story is 'Where Their Fire is Not Quenched', a modern look at eternal hell. 'The Villa Desiree' is a noted ghost story.

Kurt Singer (b. Vienna, 10 August 1911)
Today known for his horror anthologies, Singer has led a varied life. His underground newspaper caused trouble with the authorities in Germany in 1933 and he escaped to Sweden, where he wrote *The Coming War* (1934). When it came he went to America and became naturalised in 1941. He has written many books about the Second World War, and both fiction and non-fiction about spies. His horror editing began with *Kurt Singer's Horror Omnibus* (1965; 15s), of which most of the contents had then just appeared in *Magazine of Horror*. While his many subsequent anthologies contain good stories they are by and large well known and easily available. Subsequent volumes include *Ghost Omnibus* (1965; 16s), *Weird Tales of the Supernatural* (1966; 19s), *Tales of Horror* (1967; 14s), *I Can't Sleep at Night* (1966; 13s), *Tales of the Uncanny* (1967; 15s), *Tales of the Macabre* (1969; 9s) and many more. *The Unearthly* (1965; UK *World's Greatest Stories of the Occult*) is a compilation of twenty-four 'true' tales.

Curt Siodmak (b. Germany, 1902)
Predominantly a science fiction writer, Siodmak moved to America when his novel *FP1 Does Not Reply* (1930) was filmed in 1933. He became a writer/director in Hollywood and scripted many of the well-known 1940s horror films including *Black Friday* (1940), *The Invisible Man Returns* (1940), *The Wolf Man* (1941), *Frankenstein Meets the Wolf Man* (1943), *I Walked With a Zombie* (1943, a noted masterpiece), *The Climax* (1944), and adapted W. F. Harvey's *The Beast with Five Fingers* (1947). His own

novel *Donovan's Brain* (1942), about a criminal's brain which is kept alive and controls men, has been filmed several times, first as *The Lady and the Monster* (1944). He scripted mostly sf films in the 1950s, and has recently returned to writing sf short stories.

Clark Ashton Smith (b. Long Valley, Calif., 13 January 1893; d. Pacific Grove, Calif., 14 August 1961)
Generally linked with Lovecraft and Howard as the 'Three Musketeers' of *Weird Tales* in the 1930s, Smith's work showed more imagination.

His first desire had been to be a poet. Leaving school when 14 he continued his education by studying the *Encyclopædia Britannica* and reading an entire dictionary. This gave him a phenomenal vocabulary which he used extravagantly, often leading to consternation among readers faced with archaic words. There is no denying, however, that they created an atmosphere appropriate to the thaumaturgical mysticism with which much of his work dealt. His early poetry was modelled on Poe and George Sterling (1869–1926), a friend of Bierce. Bierce thought highly of Smith's verse. His early and now very rare volumes of poetry were *The Star-Treader* (1912), *Odes and Sonnets* (1918) and *Ebony and Crystal* (1922). He had several poems published in *Weird Tales* from 1923 on, and also translated verse by Baudelaire for the magazine. A lady-friend suggested Smith try fiction. He had sold a few non-fantasy adventure stories in 1911–12 and, later, a vignette of a nightmare confrontation, 'The Ninth Skeleton' (1928). But his fiction really began with 'The Last Incantation' (1930), a clever tale of a mage who has his childhood sweetheart conjured up only to find memory plays him false!

Smith wrote prodigiously for the next six years for a variety of magazines, chiefly *Weird Tales*. Of his 110 stories, 41 are set in one of four special mileux—Zothique, the last continent on a dying Earth; medieval Averoigne; the polar continent of Hyperborea; and ancient Atlantis. It is these fantasy worlds for which he is chiefly remembered. Lin Carter recently assembled the relevant tales into chronological sequence as *Zothique* (1970; 16s), *Hyperborea* (1971; 15s), *Xiccarph* (1972; 10s) and *Poseidonis* (1973; 21s)—the *Averoigne* volume was not published. Since Smith lived much of his life as a virtual recluse it is not surprising to find him writing about solitary wizards ensconced in their demon-haunted towers summoning diverse malevolent entities. Not all his fiction is fantasy. He wrote some science fiction, though of the most bizarre form. No Mars could ever be as frightening as that portrayed in 'The Vaults of Yoh-Vombis' (1932) or 'Dweller in Martian Depths' (1933). Two confusing titles are 'The Monster of the Prophecy' (1932), in which the narrator is saved from suicide to be transported to another world, and 'A Prophecy of Monsters' (1954), a short werewolf tale.

By and large his writing ceased in 1936, perhaps because he grew tired of the form, perhaps because his parents had died and he no longer needed the money. He finally married in 1954. At his death he left behind many story fragments which **Lin Carter** is attempting to complete. All of Smith's stories are now in book form as follows: *Out of Space and Time* (1943; 20s), *Lost Worlds* (1944; 23s), *Genius Loci* (1948; 15s), *The Abominations of Yondo* (1960; 17s), *Tales of Science and Sorcery* (1964; 14s), and *Other Dimensions* (1970; 26s). There is also *Poems in Prose* (1964; 46s). Smith had published his own private collection *The Double Shadow* (1933; 6s), which is now a much sought-after item.

Lady Eleanor Smith (b. Birkenhead, Cheshire, 1902; d. London, 20 October 1945)
Eleanor Furneaux Smith was extremely proud of her gypsy background inherited through her paternal great-grandmother, and most of her work reflects this and her circus interests. She had once performed in the ring, so it is not surprising that her horror stories, such as 'Satan's Circus', centre on the theme. They were collected as *Satan's Circus* (1932; 11s).

Guy N. Smith (b. Tamworth, Staffs., 21 November 1939)
Guy Newman Smith has been writing since he was 12, selling to a variety of fields from stories of country life to detective fiction. He entered the horror domain with *Werewolf By Moonlight* (1974), followed by *The Sucking Pit* (1975), *The Slime Beast* (1976), and *Night of the Crabs* (1976), which is to be filmed. He also wrote the book of the film *The Ghoul* (1976). In 1975 he gave up his job in banking to write full-time.

Thorne Smith (b. Annapolis, Md., 1893; d. Sarasota, Fla., 21 June 1934)
One of the most accomplished writers of humorous fantasies, he underwent years of near-poverty until he struck success with *Topper* (1926), about a meek little man haunted by the ghost of a mischievous girl. The sequel was *Topper Takes a Trip* (1932), and these were made into the successful films of those titles (1937 and 1939) with a third, *Topper Returns* (1939). Topper aside, Smith's other clever fantasies were *The Stray Lamb* (1929), in which Mr Lamb is transformed into various domestic animals, *Night Life of the Gods* (1931), with Greek and Roman statues coming to life, *Skin and Bones* (1933), in which an X-Ray accident causes the hero to appear unpredictably as a skeleton, *Turnabout* (1933) about a husband and wife who exchange bodies, and *The Glorious Pool* (1934) which rejuvenates those who enter. His last novel, *The Passionate Witch*, was completed by **Norman Matson** when Smith died suddenly of a heart attack at the age of 40.

Jack Snow (b. 1907)
Snow's career has been mostly in radio and his fiction is often over-looked. He had sold two stories to *Weird Tales* in 1927 and two more in the mid-1940s. These and others were collected as *Dark Music* (1947; 18s), effective ghost and weird stories. Snow also had a life-long fascination with the *Oz* books by L. Frank Baum, and contributed to the series starting with *The Magical Mimics of Oz* (1946) and writing the final book *Who's Who in Oz* (1954).

Fedor Sologub (b. St Petersburg, 1863; d. Petrograd, 5 December 1927)
Fedor Kuz'mich Teternikov, who wrote as Sologub, was not a typical Russian writer, his work spearheading the Russian symbolist movement as a reaction against the revolutionary works of others. Initially a teacher, he turned to writing with the success of *The Little Demon* (1907), an excellent portrayal of a totally evil man. His most ambitious work was the trilogy *The Created Legend* (1908–12), with its satanist enchanter hero. Only the title volume saw UK translation, the other two being *Queen Otruda* and *Drops of Blood*. Interested in Russian folklore, he adapted many of the legends into short stories, most of which were collected as *The Sweet-Scented Name* (UK trans. 1915), which includes 'The Herald of the Beast' and 'The White Dog'. Another compilation was *The Old House* (1915; 11s) translated by John Cournos.

Stephen Southwold (b. Southwold, Suffolk, 1887; d. 5 June 1964)
Although Southwold was his generally accepted name, there is evidence to presume it was really Stephen H. Critten. During his career he kept his Southwold and Bell identities clearly separate. Southwold was used chiefly for children's stories such as *The Tales of Joe Egg* (1936), fantasies related by a robot.

Southwold began as a freelance journalist, but after the First World War turned more to fiction. *The Seventh Bowl* (1930, as Miles) is a future world catastrophe, a theme he again mined in *The Gas War of 1940* (1931, as Miles; retitled *Valiant Clay* 1934, as Bell), in hindsight quite prophetic. *Precious Porcelain* (1931, as Bell) tells of a man who can create projections of himself, while the ability of a man to fly in *The Facts About Benjamin Srede* (1932, as Bell) enables him to become a prophet. *Death Rocks the Cradle* (1933, as Martens) is a fantasy about mass vivisection; *Who Was James Carey?* (1949) tells of a man leading a peculiar double-life. Other novels of interest are *Lord of Life* (1933) and *The Dark Page* (1951). Of his few short fantasies, all as Bell, the bulk will be found in *Alpha and Omega* (1946; 53s) and *Who Walks in Fear* (1953; 3s); *The House at the Crossroads* (1966; 21s) appeared after his suicide.

Pseudonyms: Neil Bell, 'Miles', Paul Martens

Count Eric Stenbock (b. Cheltenham, Glos., 12 March 1860; d. nr Brighton, 26 April 1895)
Stanislaus Eric Stenbock was one of those bizarre Victorian eccentrics whose life was more fantasy than reality. Of Swedish nobility, he was wont to dine seated in a coffin with a pet toad on his shoulder or coiled within a mighty snake! Obsessed with death and addicted to drugs, he finally sank into madness, although Arthur Symons's description of him as 'one of the most inhuman beings I have ever met' might be an exaggeration. Apart from a noted werewolf story, 'The Other Side' (1893), he wrote a volume of poems called *The Shadow of Death* (1893) and a few short stories on demonism and vampirism, *Studies of Death* (1894; 6s).

Robert Louis Stevenson (b. Edinburgh, 13 November 1850; d. Samoa, 3 December 1894)
Stevenson's career as one of the world's greatest adventure writers began in 1878, but rocketed after he wrote *Treasure Island* (1883) to amuse his stepson Lloyd Osbourne. He had earlier written a series of fantasies, *The New Arabian Nights*, but his masterpiece of horror was *The Strange Case of Dr Jekyll and Mr Hyde* (1888), written at an astonishing rate after a series of nightmares. Stevenson wrote several short horror stories, the most noted being 'The Body Snatchers'—inspired by the murderous Burke and Hare—the devil-tempted 'Markheim' and the ghost tale 'Thrawn Janet'. He also strove to perfect the fable and 'The Song of the Morrow' with 'The Sinking Ship' show him a master of that medium.

Suffering from tuberculosis, he finally settled in Samoa in 1890 where he wrote further fantasies based on local legends, as in his *Island Nights' Entertainment* (1893; 3s) from which comes 'The Bottle Imp' (see **Fouqué**). Another macabre novel, *The Wrong Box* (1889), was completed by Lloyd Osbourne.

Bram Stoker (b. Dublin, 24 November 1847; d. London, 20 April 1912)
The author of the immortal *Dracula* was a weak child, but he grew to be a strong youth, versatile in sports. Stoker had a love for the theatre, and was bored by his civil service job. When the chance came in 1877 to be Henry Irving's manager, he accepted instantly. Over the years Stoker had written the occasional story, 'The Crystal Cup' (1872) being possibly his first. A mixture of grim and fabulous tales appeared as *Under the Sunset* (1882; 8s). A few more adventure stories followed while Stoker was collecting the facts and obtaining the information (from an enigmatic Hungarian professor, Arminius Vambery) that resulted in his vampire masterpiece *Dracula* (1897). Thereafter he never achieved the same success, although *The Lair of the White Worm* (1911), about an evil entity in an old English castle, is his best remaining novel. Others are

The Mystery of the Sea (1902), *The Jewel of the Seven Stars* (1903) and the inferior *The Lady of the Shroud* (1909).

Stoker's short stories are far better, and a posthumous collection was *Dracula's Guest* (1914; 9s). The title story had been a chapter in the original novel removed before publication. Other contents include the feline revenge of 'The Squaw', and a sinister haunted room in 'The Judge's House'. A recent compilation by Charles Osborne is *The Bram Stoker Bedside Companion* (1973; 10s). Stoker also wrote a non-fiction volume, *Famous Imposters* (1910), which includes chapters on magicians, witches and immortal men.

Theodore Sturgeon (b. New York, 26 February 1918)

Born Edward Hamilton Waldo (which he changed after his mother's remarriage), Sturgeon is one of those science fiction writers whose work is essentially fantasy.

An early desire for a gymnastic career was smashed when an illness weakened his heart. He later went to sea and began selling straight fiction in 1937. His fantasy career began when he encountered *Unknown*, to which he contributed such stories as 'A God in the Garden' (1939), in which an ancient god endows a man with the sinister gift that every word he speaks comes true. Another was the classic 'It' (1940), about a loathsome, slimy life-form that reactivates an old corpse. 'Bianca's Hands' (1947) won the $1,000 first prize in a competition offered by the British *Argosy* since no US magazine would buy it. It tells of a man with the morbid desire to be strangled by the hands of an idiot woman. He also sold to *Weird Tales* and *Beyond* and stories like 'The Professor's Teddy Bear' (1948) and 'Talent' (1953) show the sinister side of children.

Most of his fantasy is mingled with sf in his collections but the majority will be found in *E Pluribus Unicorn* (1953; 13s), *Caviar* (1955; 8s) and *Beyond* (1960; 6s). A novel of note is *Some of Your Blood* (1961), a chilling updating of the vampire theme.

Pseudonyms: E. Waldo Hunter, E. Hunter Waldo, Billy Watson

Milton Subotsky (b. New York, 27 September 1921)

Currently one of the most active film producers and writers in the horror and fantasy field. After studying chemical engineering, he came to Britain in the 1950s, and later formed Amicus Productions Ltd to specialize in horror films. These started with *City of the Dead* (1959), based on a story by Subotsky. After a few films aimed at the pop-music market, the real horror output came with his original screenplay for *Dr Terror's House of Horrors* (1964), later novelised by **John Burke**. It was followed by Subotsky's adaptation of **Bloch's** *The Skull* (1965).

Thereafter three or four films followed each year; among the horror scripts by Subotsky were *I, Monster* (1970), based on Jekyll & Hyde, *Tales From the Crypt* (1971) and *The Vault of Horror* (1972). After scripting Burroughs's *At the Earth's Core* (1975), Subotsky left Amicus to form Sword and Sorcery Productions, which is currently filming a Thongor adventure from a novel by Lin Carter.

Eugene Sue (b. Paris, 26 January 1804; d. Savoy, 3 August 1857)
Sue was the French equivalent of such 'penny dreadful' writers as Reynolds and Prest. He initially served as a naval surgeon and used his experiences in his early melodramas that began in 1830. His greatest popularity was reached with the portrayal of the vile and sadistic side of the French capital in *Mysteries of Paris* (1842), which promulgated a host of imitations. *The Wandering Jew* (1844) remains the best-known work about that mythical immortal. In his later books Sue went against the political grain, was condemned as immoral and driven into exile.

Montague Summers (b. nr Bristol, 10 April 1880; d. Richmond, Surrey, 10 August 1948)
Alphonse Joseph-Mary Augustus Montague Summers was ostensibly a Roman Catholic priest, but he delved far more into demonology and arcane lore than one might think decent. His knowledge of the darker side of nature and its literature was profound, and he wrote many books on the subject. These include *The History of Demonology* (1926), *The Vampire, His Kith and Kin* (1928), *The Werewolf* (1933) and *A Popular History of Witchcraft* (1937). His volumes on Gothic fiction, in its widest sense, include the scholarly if stodgy *The Gothic Quest* (1938) and *A Bibliography of the Gothic Novel* (1940).

His greatest contributions to the genre were his anthologies. The first and best was *The Supernatural Omnibus* (1931; 38s: US 1932; 35s) which is still in print (and was recently put in paperback) and includes a brief but thorough history of supernatural fiction. He also edited *Victorian Ghost Stories* (1933; 14s) and *The Grimoire* (1936; 14s), in which his own solitary piece of fiction about a man's discovery of an arcane tome is the title story.

David Sutton (b. Birmingham, Warwicks., 5 October 1947)
For six years David Ambrose Sutton's non-professional magazine *Shadow* was the backbone of macabre literature for British fans. It ran for twenty-one issues from 1968 to 1974 and was crammed with fact and fiction from people like E. C. Bertin, Brian Frost, Richard Davis, Brian Stableford, and most notably two *new* stories by William Hope Hodgson. Another

venture into amateur publishing was a two-volume anthology, *Weird Window* (1970).

Through *Shadow* Sutton was noticed by professional publishers and he was commissioned to compile an anthology of original fiction, *New Writings in Horror and the Supernatural* (1971; 13s). A second *New Writings* (1972; 10s) contained Sutton's own first horror story 'Demoniacal', about the perils of dabbling in the unknown, although he had sold a science fiction story in 1969. With a change in publishers the third volume appeared as *The Satyr's Head* (1975; 10s), but since then he has been concentrating on writing, his short stories appearing in several anthologies. He is currently working on an occult novel, and co-publishing a semi-professional magazine, *Fantasy Tales*, devoted to fiction.

Edmund Gill Swain (b. 1861; d. Peterborough, Northants., 29 January 1938)

E. G. Swain was another who fell under the spell of M. R. James. Swain was chaplain and then proctor at King's College, Cambridge, from 1892 to 1916, during which time he penned his spooky stories published as *The Stoneground Ghost Tales* (1912; 9s), now a very rare book. Swain went on to be the Minor Canon and Librarian at Peterborough Cathedral, but alas published no more ghost stories.

Thomas Burnett Swann (b. Tampa, Fla., 12 October 1928; d. Winter Haven, Fla., 5 May 1976)

Swann's death at 47 of cancer robbed the fantasy world of one of its most enchanting and original talents. An academic who had published several volumes of poetry and critical studies of literary figures like A. A. Milne, Swann taught at Georgia and Florida universities. Although his first fantasy sale was in America, his early recognition came in Britain with his stories in *Science Fantasy*.

Swann concentrated on giving life to early legends, humanely detailing the mythical creatures and heroes as if they were real. It is clear in all his work that he loathes the coming of civilisation, and he strives to capture the freedom of Earth's early days. His first story in this vein was 'Where is the Bird of Fire?' (1962), which recounted the Romulus and Remus legend. This was recently expanded into the novel *The Lady of the Bees* (1976). His first novel, *The Blue Monkeys* (1964; US *The Day of the Minotaur* 1966), told of the passing of the mythical creatures in ancient Crete. The same milieu provided *The Forest of Forever* (1970). *The Weirwoods* (1965) was set in ancient Etruria, *Moondust* (1968) at the Battle of Jericho; *The Goat Without Horns* (1970) has a contemporary Caribbean setting and is narrated by a dolphin. *Green Phoenix* (1972) is set at the fall of Troy, *Wolfwinter* (1973) in the Greece of Sappho. *How Are the*

Mighty Fallen (1974) is based on the story of David and Jonathan, and was written after Swann had undergone several operations for cancer. *The Not-World* (1974) is set in a weird forest near Bristol in the 1700s, *The Minikins of Yam* (1976) in ancient Egypt, *Tournament of Thorns* (1976) is an expansion of his mandrake tale 'The Manor of Roses' (1966), and *The Gods Abide* (1976) takes place in ancient Britain. His last novel, finished in his hospital bed, was *Queen Walks in the Dusk* (1976). Only one collection exists, *Where is the Bird of Fire?* (1970; 3s), but a memorial volume should be mandatory.

Bernard Taylor (b. Swindon, Wilts., 2 October 1936)
Previously an actor, Bernard Irvin Taylor has only recently turned to horror fiction, but with considerable impact. His first story, 'Cera' (1974), tells how a man discovers that the girl he had loved for years was not human, while 'My Very Good Friend' (1974) revels in the nauseous love of a giant praying mantis. His first novel, *The Godsend* (1976), is about a demon-possessed child, and should not be confused with his short story 'The Godsend' (1973) about another vile insect, this time a blood-coloured grasshopper (that story is now titled 'Our First Nanny'). Taylor has completed a second novel, *Sweetheart, Sweetheart.*

Christine Campbell Thomson (b. London, 31 May 1897)
One of the highlights for the horror devotee between the wars was the *Not at Night* anthology series which ran for eleven volumes from *Not at Night* (1925; 15s) to *Nightmare By Daylight* (1936; 15s) (see App. II for full details). C. C. Thomson, the daughter of a Harley Street doctor, is a literary agent who in 1924 married **Oscar Cook** (d. 1952), himself a writer. He had been a government official in British North Borneo and this inspired his fiction, which he based on stories told to him by the natives. He actually knew the original 'Si Urag of the Tail' (1926). Through her agency Miss Thomson sold Cook's stories to *Weird Tales*, plus two of her own, including the evil ghost story 'Out of the Earth' (1927). Although there was no special arrangement with *Weird Tales* close liaison with that magazine's British agent meant that Miss Thomson acquired the stories soon after their publication (in at least one case—see **Keller**—before), and one hundred stories from that magazine will be found in the *Not at Night* series.

Miss Thomson wrote a number of novels, a book about how to write, and her memoirs. She claims her best short story is 'Message for Margie' (*PH5*, 1964). She studied the occult for ten years under **Dion Fortune** and under her present name of Hartley alias has written two non-fiction studies of mysticism and legend—*The Western Mystery Tradition* (1968) and *A Case For Reincarnation* (1972).

Pseudonyms: Dair Alexander (light fiction), Molly Campbell (children's books), Christine Hartley, Flavia Richardson

Johann Ludwig Tieck (b. Berlin, 31 May 1773; d. Berlin, 28 April 1853) Tieck was one of the great romantic German writers and a master of the macabre. After studying theology he turned to delving into literature and legends and started to write. He produced at least two straight horror novels, *Abdallah* (1795) and *The Runenberg* (1804), but more important were his volumes of short fiction, chiefly reworked legends. They range from vampire stories like 'The Bride of the Grave' to fairy tales. An early collection was *Folk Tales* (1797), but the culmination of his work was *Phantasus* (1812–17).

Pseudonym: Peter Leberecht

Rosemary Timperley (b. London, 20 March 1920)
Rosemary Kenyon Timperley is doubtless Britain's leading female writer of horror fiction, with a special bias for ghost stories. She began writing when 25, her stories (not all horror) appearing in many post-war magazines. Her real start came when **Cynthia Asquith** selected 'Christmas Meeting' from *Truth* for *The Second Ghost Book* (1952). Since then her ghost stories have graced many anthologies, periodicals (such as *London Mystery Magazine, Evening News* and *Destiny*), and radio. Besides frequent bizarre contributions to *Morning Story* she had several scripts in the *Just Before Midnight* series (1964), such as 'The Brain', in which a working model comes alive. She also wrote for Capital Radio's *Moment of Terror*. On the whole her ghost stories are gentle and non-horrific.

Books of interest include *The Listening Child* (1956), *The Haunted Garden* (1965), *Walk to San Michele* (1971), *The Long Black Dress* (1972), *Juliet* (1974) and *The Stranger* (1976). All are ghost fantasies, basically gentle except *The Stranger*—which she calls 'nasty!'. Miss Timperley also edited Volumes 5 to 9 of *The Ghost Book* (1969–73).

J. R. R. Tolkien (b. Bloemfontein, 3 January 1892; d. Oxford, 2 September 1973)
John Ronald Reuel Tolkien was born in South Africa but spent his early years in his mother's native city of Birmingham after his father's death in 1895. When his mother died in 1904, Tolkien and his brother were raised by a Catholic priest. His college education was interrupted by the First World War, but he received his M.A. (Oxon) in 1919. Fascinated by languages he became a teacher and Professor of English and later Anglo-Saxon. Early books include *A Middle-English Vocabulary* (1922), and

with E. V. Gordon a critical text on the medieval poem *Sir Gawain and the Green Knight* (1925).

During all this time Tolkien had been inventing his own fantasy world —Middle Earth—and telling little tales to his children. They first took shape as *The Hobbit* (1937), which tells of Bilbo the Hobbit's quest with a band of dwarves and Gandalf the Wizard to recover the dwarves' home and wealth. On route Bilbo acquires a ring from the ancient hobbit Smeagol, which renders the wearer invisible. This ring forms the basis of the later trilogy *Lord of the Rings*. Bilbo bequeaths the ring to Frodo who has the burden of destroying it in the volcano where it was forged, a long and dangerous quest. The trilogy appeared first as *The Fellowship of the Ring* (1954), *The Two Towers* (1955) and *The Return of the King* (1955). No plot summary can do the trilogy justice, for beyond the basic story Tolkien created an entire and wonderful world rich in the cultures, languages and legends of its myriad inhabitants—hobbits, dwarves, wizards, orcs, and ents. It was the US paperback publication of the trilogy in 1965 that began the sudden cult following that made it one of the best-selling books in the world. A 'prequel' to the trilogy has been published in one volume as *The Silmarillion* (1977).

Other works of interest are the simple fairy stories *Farmer Giles of Ham* (1949) and *Smith of Wootton Major* (1967), and Tolkien's essays on fairy tales, *Tree and Leaf* (1964). *The Adventures of Tom Bombadil* (1962) is a slim volume of verse about this enigmatic character from Middle Earth. Of the many books about Tolkien and his works, worthy of recommendation are *Tolkien: A Look Behind the Lord of the Rings* by Lin Carter, and Robert Foster's *A Guide to Middle Earth* (1971), a complete concordance to all the people and places in the books.

Ivan Turgenev (b. Orel, 9 November 1818; d. Paris 3 September 1883) Though born into a noble Russian family, and able to support himself by writing, he became noted for his stand against the Establishment, highlighting the conditions of the peasants. His horror fiction was written in his last years and consists chiefly of fictionalised legends with an original twist, as in 'Klava Milich', about spiritualism, and 'Bubnoff and the Devil', in which we meet the devil's grandmother!

Amos Tutuola (b. Abeokuta, Nigeria, June 1920) When one considers the wealth of fiction by English-language writers about African black magic, it is surprising so few Africans have written about it. Of those who have the most fascinating is Amos Tutuola, who has a vigorous if child-like style that captures the essence of tribal magic and myth. His novels tell essentially of quests, as in *The Palm-Wine*

Drunkard (1952) when a man sets out into the jungle to reclaim his servant from Limbo. Other works are *My Life in the Bush of Ghosts* (1954), *Simbi and the Satyr* (1955), *Feather Woman* (1962) and *Ajaiyi and the Witch Doctor* (1964).

Allen Upward (b. Worcester, Worcs., 1863; d. 12 November 1926)
Upward led an active career, first as a barrister in Ireland, then as Headmaster of Inverness College; and served in the Greco-Turkish War in between. He wrote prodigiously and was noted for his series on the *Secrets of the Courts of Europe* and *International Spies*, both of which ran in *Pearson's* from 1895 to 1905. His contributions to the horror field include the infrequent bizarre story like 'The Man Who Lived Backwards' (1905), and a psychic detective series 'The Ghost Hunters' (1906). *The Discovery of the Dead* (1910) is a weird lost-race novel about the Necromorphs.

Jack Vance (b. San Francisco, 28 August 1916)
Vance is another of those expert sf writers whose output is basically fantasy. His recent profusion of sf adventure novels are simply imaginative fantasy set on other planets. Even his very first sale, 'The World-Thinker' (1945), was fantasy, set on a planet created out of the imagination of its master. But sf aside, Vance has written two exceptional volumes of pure fantasy set on a dim and distant dying Earth occupied by bizarre animals and equally weird people, chiefly magicians vying with each other. First was *The Dying Earth* (1950; 6s). *The Eyes of the Overworld* (1966) is the tale of a quest by Cugel, commanded by the mage Iocuono. The novel's conclusion left it open for a sequel which was not forthcoming, so devotee Michael Shea wrote his own, *A Quest For Simbilis* (1974). Since then Vance has written a few more dying Earth stories, so that novel may yet appear.

Herbert van Thal (b. London, 30 March 1904)
Herbert Maurice van Thal has never written a single horror story, but his name is internationally known as the editor of the annual *Pan Book of Horror Stories*, which began in 1959 and has now reached Volume 18 (see App. II). For most of his life van Thal has been a literary agent, but he has written over fifty books of one form or another since his first in 1927. In 1945 he established his own publishing imprint, Home and van Thal, and for this he edited *Weird Stories* by **Mrs Riddell** and *Twilight Tales* by **Rhoda Broughton**. His first horror anthology was *Told in the Dark* (1950; 11s), followed by *A Book of Strange Stories* (1954; 13s), *Great Ghost Stories* (1960; 10s), *Famous Tales of the Fantastic* (1965; 9s),

Lie Ten Nights Awake (1966; 10s), *Bedside Book of Horror* (1973), and *A Second Bedside Book of Strange Stories* (1976).

G. S. Viereck (b. Munich, 31 December 1884; d. New York, 18 March 1962)

Initially a poet, George Sylvester Viereck established himself as a writer in the US, until he was imprisoned during the Second World War for not declaring his nationality. Thereafter his views caused him to be boycotted. He is most noted in the fantasy field for his Wandering Jew trilogy written with teacher Paul Eldridge (b. 1888). The volumes run *My First Two Thousand Years* (1928), *Salome: the Wandering Jewess* (1930) and *The Invincible Adam* (1932). Forgotten until its recent revival in the US was his first novel *The House of the Vampire* (1907), a powerful psychological chiller of a psychic vampire.

Villiers de L'Isle Adam (b. Saint-Brieuc, 7 November 1838; d. Paris, 19 August 1889)

Jean-Marie Phillipe Auguste Mathias Villiers de L'Isle Adam was a Breton count descended from the last Grand-Master of the Knights of Malta, but the family was impoverished. He lived on the edge of poverty all his life, striving to survive by writing. Though other writers recognised his talent, the public did not, and he died (of cancer) penniless.

Called the first French symbolist writer, Villiers mastered the *conte cruel* as epitomised in his oft-reprinted 'The Torture of Hope', in which a prisoner thinks he has escaped the Inquisition. Two volumes of *Contes Cruels* appeared in 1883 and 1889, and a selection was translated as *Sardonic Tales* (1925; 26s). Villiers was a close friend of **Huysman** and shared his interest in the satanic. His first published story, 'Azraël', was about demonism. Other novels of note were *Axël*, written in 1872, and his satirical sf tale *L'Eve Future*, written in 1876.

E. H. Visiak (b. London, 20 July 1878; d. Hove, Sussex, 30 August 1972)

Edward Harold Visiak was acknowledged as an expert on Milton and his works, but his own fiction was largely ignored. For this reason Visiak devoted himself to poetry and research, a great loss to the fantasy field. His first novel had been *The Haunted Island* (1910) involving piracy, ghosts and a mad magician and set on a seventeenth-century volcanic isle. He returned to the novel form with *Medusa* (1929), a unique and puzzling tale of a voyage into strange and frightening seas. Those aside his only fiction was several short stories he contributed to **Gawsworth's** anthologies in the 1930s, most of which reflect Visiak's interest in the sea and in the borders of sanity. These include his short novel 'The Shadow' in *Crimes, Creeps and Thrills* (1936), never published as a separate book. Just before his death he completed another story to be found in **Hugh Lamb**'s *The Taste of Fear*. A close friend of **David Lindsay**, Visiak contributed an illuminating essay to *The Strange Genius of David Lindsay* (1970).

E. Charles Vivian (b. Norfolk, 1882; d. London, 21 May 1947)

It is strange that a writer as popular as Evelyn Charles Vivian was in the 1920s and 1930s should now be unknown, and details of his life lost in obscurity until recently researched by W. O. G. Lofts.

Apparently a British adventurer and traveller who served in the First World War, Vivian established himself as a writer of fine lost-race adventures with *City of Wonder* (1922) and *Fields of Sleep* (1923; US *The Valley of Silent Men*). Under his Cannell alias he wrote several Oriental fantasies like *The Guardian of the Cup* (1930). Then he gained a new reputation under the name Jack Mann for his series about occult detective Gregory George Gordon Green, known as Gees. After the non-fantastic *Gees' First Case* (1936) came the werewolf adventure *Grey Shapes* (1938), *Nightmare Farm* (1937), *Maker of Shadows* (1938), about an ancient sorcerer's active power, and its sequel *The Glass Too Many* (1940), *The Kleinart Case* (1938), *The Ninth Life* (1939), set against the magic of ancient Egypt, and *Her Ways Are Death* (1939), in which Gees encounters a witch.

Pseudonyms: Charles Cannell, Jack Mann

James Wade (b. Granite City, Ill., 5 January 1930)

American by birth, after Army service in Korea, James Adam Wade settled in Seoul where he now works as a journalist. His main love is music. He began composing his own songs and choral work in 1948 and has since completed several orchestral works and an opera. He is currently working on an opera based on 'A Wicked Voice' by **Vernon Lee**. His main fictional influence is H. P. Lovecraft, whose work he discovered in 1945. His first professional writings appeared in the *Korea Times*, starting with the fantasy 'Temple of the Fox' (1965). 'The Deep Ones' (1969) marked his US debut, in *Tales of the Cthulhu Mythos*. His fiction has appeared in several anthologies including *PH11* and *New Writings in Horror*. Alas he has written little fiction since the tragic death of his wife in 1973.

Karl Edward Wagner (b. Knoxville, Tenn., 12 December 1945)
Wagner burst on the scene in the early 1970s and has rapidly become one
of the major names in the fantasy field. He began work as a practising
psychiatrist, but is now a full-time writer and publisher. His enthusiasm
for collecting old magazines has resulted in a massive, near-complete
library of pulps from which he has been able to select the stories he used
in the three volumes by Wellman, Price and Cave that he edited and
published under the Carcosa imprint (in which he is co-publisher with
David Drake and Jim Groce).

His first novel appeared in 1970, *Darkness Weaves*. It was the first of
a series about the exploits of the Biblical 'Kane', but the publisher so
hacked the manuscript that the book was ruined. The original text finally
saw print in England in 1977. The full series includes *Death Angel's
Shadow* (1973), *Bloodstone* (1975), *Dark Crusade* (1976) and the collection
Night Winds (1977; 6s). He has also continued the Bran Mak Morn series
of Howard in *Legion From the Shadows* (1976), and *Queen of the Night*
(1977). Wagner's first short story, 'In the Pines' (1973), was an effective
ghost tale. His next 'Sticks' (1974), was inspired by a real incident that
happened to artist Lee Coye. The story won the August Derleth Fantasy
Award in 1975. The semi-professional magazine *Midnight Sun* is dedicated to his fiction, and the editor is also publishing Wagner's novel about
occult investigator John Chance, *Sign of the Salamander* (1975–76).
Wagner was recently appointed editor in charge of a partial reissue of
Howard's original Conan stories in paperback.

H. Russell Wakefield (b. Elham, Kent, 9 May 1888; d. London,
2 August 1964)
Of all the great British writers of ghost stories perhaps the most overlooked is Herbert Russell Wakefield. The son of Bishop Wakefield of
Birmingham he was educated at Oxford, and received a degree in history.
From 1920 to 1930 he worked as a publisher, during which time he began
his ghost tales; the first of these was 'The Red Lodge', inspired by a
house in which he had once stayed. His first collection was *They Return
at Evening* (1928; 10s) followed by *Old Man's Beard* (1929; 15s: US *Others
Who Returned*). Wakefield turned to writing full-time in 1930, his output
including mysteries and works on criminology, till in 1951 he became a
civil servant. After a third collection, *Imagine a Man in a Box* (1931; 13s),
two reprint selections appeared with a few new stories, *Ghost Stories*
(1932; 21s) and *A Ghostly Company* (1935; 12s). Two later new collections were *The Clock Strikes Twelve* (1939; 14s: US, 1946; 18s) and
Strayers From Sheol (1961; 14s), the latter still awaiting UK publication.
Wakefield had Derleth to thank for keeping his name alive after the
British market had forsaken him, and his last stories will be found in
Derleth's original anthologies.

John W. Wall
As 'Sarban', Wall is best remembered for his terrifying alternate-world novel *The Sound of His Horn* (1952), set in an England where the Nazis won the war, and the enemy is hunted for sport. He also wrote two fine collections of stories. The title story of *Ringstones* (1951; 5s) is set on the remote Yorkshire moors with a governess and three bizarre children. The lead story of *The Doll Maker* (1953; 3s) tells of a girl who falls under the spell of the enigmatic character known by that name.

Horace Walpole (b. London, 24 September 1717; d. Twickenham, Mddx, 2 March 1797)
No matter what went before, it was Walpole's *The Castle of Otranto* (1764) that began the trend for Gothic horror fiction, and thereby was the direct progenitor of nearly all supernatural horror.

Walpole was the youngest son of the noted Prime Minister, but though he served in Parliament till 1768 he had no interest in politics, and with the inheritance of ample income on his father's death in 1745 he purchased a cottage which he elaborately transformed into his own 'gothic castle' of Strawberry Hill. He wrote some thirty-eight books, but only *Otranto* is really remembered. He initially published it under the alias William Marshall, as the translator of a rare Italian volume written in 1529 by Onuphrio Muralto. Other works of interest are the gruesome tragedy *The Mysterious Mother* (1768), and *Unpublished Tales* (1902), a collection of legends assembled by Spencer Walpole.

Sir Hugh Walpole (b. Auckland, 13 March 1884; d. Keswick, Cumberland, 1 June 1941)
Descended from **Horace Walpole** and the son of Bishop Walpole, then serving in New Zealand, Hugh Seymour Walpole grew up in Cornwall. He became a noted novelist, especially for his stories of cathedral life and his Lakeland saga. He wrote a fair number of ghost stories, and his best known, 'Mrs Lunt' (1927), 'The Snow' (1929), and 'A Little Ghost' (1931), were contributed to **Cynthia Asquith**'s anthologies. They were included in his volume *All Soul's Night* (1933; 16s); an earlier collection was *The Silver Thorn* (1928; 15s). Two novels in the macabre vein were *Portrait of a Man with Red Hair* (1925) and *The Killer and the Slain* (1941). He also edited *A Second Century of Creepy Stories* (1937; 27s).

Elizabeth Walter (b. London)
Miss Walter spent her childhood on the Welsh border, a setting frequently used in her fiction. Her stories range from straight ghost tales to macabre

vignettes in the style of **Dahl** and **Hartley**. Five collections have appeared —*Snowfall* (1965; 5s), *The Sin Eater* (1967; 6s), *Davy Jones's Tale* (1971; 6s), *Come and Get Me* (1973; 7s) and *Dead Woman* (1975; 7s). A collection of her best fiction is being compiled for US publication. Three of her stories, 'Prendergast', 'The Travelling Companion' and 'The Concrete Captain' were adapted for the US television series *Ghost Story*. Miss Walter currently works as a publisher's editor, and is planning a sixth collection.

Evangeline Walton (b. Indianapolis, Ind., 24 November 1907)
One of the true patient craftswomen of fantasy, Miss Walton finally received recognition for her work in 1970, over thirty years after she had started writing. A scholar of Welsh myth, she drew on the *Mabinogion* to produce a charming fantasy, *The Virgin and the Swine* (1936). When it was revived by **Lin Carter** as *The Island of the Mighty* (1970) Miss Walton revealed she had an unpublished sequel, which then appeared as *The Children of Llyr* (1971). This used a separate branch of the *Mabinogion*, and since then she has completed the sequence with *The Song of Rhiannon* (1972) and *The Prince of Annwn* (1974), with an omnibus volume planned. An earlier novel of witchcraft had been *Witch House* (1945), and a historical novel of interest is *The Cross and the Sword* (1956: UK *Son of Darkness* 1957), which tells of the conflict between Saxon and Viking. Her latest project is a trilogy about Theseus.

Donald Wandrei (b. 1908)
Although Wandrei first appeared in *Weird Tales* in 1927 (with the sf story 'The Red Brain') and contributed to that magazine regularly, his name is not immediately linked with the publication. This is probably because early in his career Wandrei made the transition to the major slick magazines like *Esquire*, which published his best-known story 'The Painted Mirror' (1937). Wandrei joined **Derleth** as a partner in establishing the specialist publishing imprint Arkham House in 1939 to perpetuate the name of **Lovecraft**, but his involvement with the firm dwindled after the war. His first book was a volume of poems, *Dark Odyssey* (1931). His stories have been collected as *The Eye and the Finger* (1944; 21s) and *Strange Harvest* (1965; 17s). *The Web of Easter Island* (1948) was a Cthulhu-based novel.

His brother **Howard Wandrei** (1909–56) also wrote many weird and horror stories often under the H. W. Guernsey alias with which he appeared in *Unknown*.

W. T. Webb (b. Coventry, Warwicks., 20 September 1918)
William Thomas Webb has been selling professionally since 1958, but the

bulk of his output was sf. He had a few charming fantasies in *Science Fantasy* such as 'Valley of the Rainbirds' (1961) and 'The Legend' (1962), about a statue that comes to life. Of late more short horror tales have appeared in anthologies and Webb has completed two fantasy novels. *After the Inferno* (1977) is about a stunt-man who finds himself on a quest in a professor's dream-world. *The Eye of Hollerl-Ra* is awaiting publication.

Manly Wade Wellman (b. Kamundongo, Angola, 21 May 1903)
One of the most accomplished writers in the sf, fantasy and mystery fields. Born in Portuguese West Africa, where his father was a medical officer, Wellman learned the native dialect before English. The whole family became writers, the eldest, Paul, being noted for his historical novels. Back in the US, after college, Wellman became a reporter, but began to sell poetry and fiction, an early sale being to *Weird Tales*—'Back to the Beast' (1927) about reversed evolution. He became a mainstay of that magazine during the rest of its lifespan. He also contributed to the sf and detective magazines.

His fantasy sales fall into three clear markets, *Weird Tales*, *Unknown* and *F&SF*. He recalls he learned his trade from **Farnsworth Wright**, 'a tirelessly helpful taskmaster', and *Weird* published many of his best stories. As Field he wrote a series about occult investigator Judge Pursuivant, which began with the werewolf serial *The Hairy Ones Shall Dance* (1938). He later wrote about another psychic sleuth, John Thunstone, who came up against a strange race of creatures, the Shonokins. The series ran from 'The Third Cry to Legba' (1943) to 'The Last Grave of Lill Warren' (1951). His stories for *Unknown* included a Dracula tale, 'The Devil is Not Mocked' (1943), and the noted 'When It Was Moonlight' (1940), detailing a fictional episode in the life of Poe.

Wellman's acquaintance with legends in his local North Carolina provided the basis for his *F&SF* series about John the Minstrel in the 1950s, and these formed his first fantasy collection *Who Fears the Devil?* (1963; 11s). He also wrote a short series about Amerindian life under the alias Levi Crow. An absence of suitable markets made Wellman turn to other areas in the 1950s and he produced some notable historical and biographical works. He has returned to the field in recent years and his stories (some written with his son Wade) have included a series of Sherlock Holmes pastiches. **Karl Wagner** produced an award-winning volume of Wellman's fiction, *Worse Things Waiting* (1973; 29s).

In preparation are a volume of his psychic investigator episodes, *Lonely Vigils*, and a further collection *Don't Look Behind You*.

Pseudonyms: Gabriel Barclay, John Cotton, Levi Crow, Manuel Ferney, Gans T. Field, Juan Perez, Hampton Wells, Wade Wells

H. G. Wells (b. Bromley, Kent, 21 September 1866; d. London, 13 August 1946)
Though he may deservedly rank as the founding father of science fiction, Herbert George Wells wrote a number of fantasies. He dabbled with religious themes in 'The Apple' (1896), about the discovery of the fruit of the tree from which Eve ate, and 'A Dream of Armageddon' (1901) or 'The Story of the Last Trump' (1915). There are dream fantasies like 'The Door in the Wall' (1906) and 'A Moonlight Fable' (1909). 'The Red Room' (1896) is a straight ghost story, whereas 'The Story of the Inexperienced Ghost' (1902) is a humorous one. 'The Cone' (1895) is a gruesome tale of revenge. There are many more, and the best are collected as *The Valley of Spiders* (1964; 13s). Wells was also the first to utilise the horrifying aspect of contact with aliens as portrayed in *The War of the Worlds* (1897-98).

Wallace G. West (b. Kentucky, 1900)
West is better known for his sf than his horror, but he is equally adept at both. Trained as a lawyer, he entered public relations first in the film and then the oil industries. His first sale was a werewolf story, 'Loup-Garou' (1927), and five more followed in *Weird Tales*, ending with the sardonic twist on reincarnation in 'The Laughing Duke' (1932). Two stories rejected as being too gruesome, 'A Thing of Beauty' (1963) and 'Sacrilege' (1965), later appeared in *Magazine of Horror*. A collection of his best stories is in preparation.

Edith Wharton (b. New York, 24 January 1862; d. France, 11 August 1937)
Edith Newbold Wharton was a noted American novelist who went on to win Pulitzer Prizes. She wrote some forty-seven books. She was a friend of Henry James, who encouraged and influenced her, and this is apparent in her supernatural fiction. Best known is 'The Lady's Maid's Bell' where a new maid finds that the ghost of the previous maid is still summoned by the bell. Her earliest collections were *Tales of Men and Ghosts* (1910; 9s) and *Xingu* (1916; 8s); later compilations of new and old material were *Here and Beyond* (1926; 6s) and *Ghosts* (1937; 11s). The last volume, with only one change, was recently reissued as *The Ghost Stories of Edith Wharton* (1973; 11s).

Dennis Wheatley (b. London, 8 January 1897)
One of the most popular novelists working in the field. Born into a family of wine merchants, he entered the business after his education, and became sole owner on his father's death in 1926. He was a Wing

Commander on the Joint Planning Staff of the War Cabinet from 1941 to 1944.

He began writing in the early 1930s, his first novel *The Forbidden Territory* (1933) being very successful. His fiction covers historical, spy, adventure and science fiction, and his weird stories fall into two categories —black magic and lost worlds. The latter include *The Fabulous Valley* (1934), *They Found Atlantis* (1936), *Uncharted Seas* (1938), where he copies Hodgson's seaweed-clogged seas, and *The Man Who Missed the War* (1945), set in an Antarctic paradise. The last three were combined as *Worlds Far From Here* (1952). He is better known for his black magic novels, which began with the classic *The Devil Rides Out* (1935) and its sequel *Strange Conflict* (1941). Later came *The Haunting of Toby Jugg* (1948), *To the Devil a Daughter* (1953), *The Ka of Gifford Hillary* (1956), *The Satanist* (1960) and *They Used Dark Forces* (1964), about Hitler's wartime use of sorcery. His Gregory Sallust novel *The White Witch of the South Seas* (1968) also includes some occult elements. Wheatley demonstrated his knowledge of the powers of darkness in his reference book *The Devil and All His Works* (1971).

He has also edited several anthologies. His massive *A Century of Horror* (1935; 52s) was later reworked as *Quiver of Horror* (1964; 15s) and *Shafts of Fear* (1964; 19s). In 1973 he began the *Dennis Wheatley Library of the Occult* for Sphere Books which now contains over forty volumes, including three *Uncanny Tales* anthologies and *Satanism and Witchcraft* edited by Wheatley. A selection of his own short fiction will be found in *Gunmen, Gallants and Ghosts* (1943; 17s).

Edward Lucas White (b. Bergen, N.J., 18 May 1866; d. Baltimore, Md., 30 March 1934)
A frequently reprinted story in horror anthologies is 'Lukundoo', which tells of an explorer's hideous encounter with African magic. Its author, E. L. White, was a noted US novelist, mostly in the historical field (ancient Greece and Rome). His weird stories came to him in dreams and show a knowledge of other countries' superstitions. The best are collected as *The Song of the Sirens* (1919; 10s) and *Lukundoo* (1927; 10s). White suffered from migraine all his life and eventually gassed himself.

T. H. White (b. India, 29 May 1906; d. at sea, 17 January 1964)
Any fan of Disney cartoons will remember *The Sword in the Stone*. It was based on the novel by Terence Hanbury White which formed the first part of his trilogy about King Arthur. They first appeared as *The Sword in the Stone* (1938), *The Ill-Made Knight* (1940) and *The Witch in the Wood* (1939). He later completely revised them, not always for the best, as *The Once and Future King* (1958), and this version formed the

basis of the musical *Camelot* under which title the book has also appeared. White's father was a policeman in India, and the boy led an unhappy childhood marred by parental quarrels. After qualifying at Cambridge he became a school teacher for six years, but turned to full-time writing in 1936. Among his other novels are the fantasies *Mistress Masham's Repose* (1946), in which a colony of Gulliver's Lilliputians is found living on a huge estate, and *The Elephant and the Kangaroo* (1947), the tale of an English writer who becomes a new Noah commanded to build an ark. White died of heart failure after returning from a successful lecture tour in America.

Henry S. Whitehead (b. Elizabeth, N.J., 5 March 1882; d. Dunedin, Fla., 23 November 1932)

The best basis for writing supernatural or occult fiction is first-hand experience, and this was the inspiration for Dr Henry St Clair Whitehead. Initially a formidable sportsman, he entered the Episcopal Church in 1909 and became a deacon in 1912. From 1921 to 1929 he was Archdeacon to the Virgin Islands in the West Indies, and it was here that he learned much about native superstitions and voodoo. He began writing in 1905, but his emphasis on occult fiction did not begin until he encountered *Weird Tales*. He had twenty-five stories published there, from 'Tea Leaves' (1924) to 'The Chadbourne Episode' (1933). The stories are very well written, with an authenticity which accentuates the feeling of dread expectation. His stories were posthumously collected as *Jumbee* (1944; 14s) and *West India Lights* (1946; 17s).

Not all his fiction has a West Indies locale. 'The Trap' (1932) is a mirror-world fantasy, 'The Moon-Dial' (1932) is set in India, and 'Scar-Tissue' (1946) is a racial memory story of Atlantis.

Oscar Wilde (b. Dublin, 16 October 1854; d. Paris, 30 November 1900)

Although he died in obscurity and poverty after his notorious court case, Wilde is today respected as one of Britain's cleverest wits and playwrights. His works include a few fantasies, such as the humorous ghost story 'The Canterville Ghost' (1887). 'Lord Arthur Savile's Crime' (1887) is about fortune-telling. Wilde wrote to **Heron-Allen** about the subject and the latter applauded the story. At this time he met **Conan Doyle** and each agreed to write a novel for *Lippincott's Monthly*. In Doyle's case he produced his Holmes adventure *The Sign of Four*. For Wilde it was his masterpiece, *The Picture of Dorian Gray* (1890), about the boy who gives his soul so that he remains young while the portrait of him ages. Would that more such literary meetings were as fruitful.

Mary E. Wilkins-Freeman (b. Randolph, Mass., 31 October 1852; d. Metuchen, 13 March 1930)

Some of the best American ghost stories were written by Mary Eleanor Wilkins. She started by writing poetry but became acquainted with novelists while secretary to Oliver Wendell Holmes. She wrote twelve novels, and at least 238 stories, many detective as well as weird. Her two best collections are *Silence* (1898; 6s) and *The Wind in the Rose-Bush* (1903; 6s); a recent compilation is *The Collected Ghost Stories* (1974; 11s).

Charles Williams (b. London, 20 September 1886; d. Oxford, 15 May 1945)

Often linked with C. S. Lewis and **David Lindsay** as Britain's most noted writers of philosophical fantasy, Williams is perhaps the most intriguing. For much of his life he was on the staff of Oxford University Press and was an accomplished lecturer.

Of his works, eight novels are of fantasy interest, and he wrote a fantasy play, *The House of the Octopus* (1945). The first novel was *War in Heaven* (1930), about a fight to the finish between humans and demons. *Many Dimensions* (1931) tells of a special stone which transports a scientist through time. *The Place of the Lion* (1931) is a powerful novel of demonic forces. *The Greater Trumps* (1932) is based on the influence of the tarot cards. *Shadows of Ecstasy* (1933) is a good versus evil thriller, with Christianity—represented by the Holy Grail—fighting primitive African beliefs. *Descent Into Hell* (1937) and *Witchcraft* (1941) are similar thrillers. His last work, *All Hallow's Eve* (1945), is an eerie novel about two women trapped in a life-after-death by the power of a Svengali-like adept. Williams's fantasies might be marred by his philosophical views, but his strength rests in his treatment of the supernatural as commonplace.

Colin Wilson (b. Leicester, Leics., 26 June 1931)

A much respected writer, and an authority on a number of subjects, Wilson has been adopted by horror enthusiasts because of his interest in **H. P. Lovecraft**. Even his first work, 'an inquiry into the nature of the sickness of mankind', was called *The Outsider* (1956)!

Wilson held a number of jobs after leaving school at 16, and worked in a coffee bar while completing his first novel. In 1961 he wrote a study of creative imagination in horror and fantasy fiction, *The Strength to Dream*, and **Derleth** took Wilson to task over his comments about Lovecraft. Indirectly Wilson wrote a fantasy novel in the Lovecraftian vein, *The Mind Parasites* (1967), and subsequently another—*The Philosopher's Stone* (1969). The latter is ostensibly science fiction, and tells of research into immortality that leads to mental time-travelling. Wilson has also written a study of human psi-powers, *The Occult* (1971), and his recent novel *Space Vampires* (1976) combines sf and horror in a plot that dates back to the pulp magazines. He introduced the two BBC television series on psychic phenomena, *Leap in the Dark* (1975 and 1977).

Gahan Wilson (b. Evanston, Ill., 18 February 1935)
Gahan Wilson has a wicked sense of humour which he puts to expert use in a profusion of cartoons in many magazines, most notably *Playboy* and *F&SF* (every issue since April 1965). Many are based on fantasy and the occult—such as one where a priest is squirting an aerosol can with a cross on it at little demons in his church!

Wilson graduated from the Art Institute of Chicago, and after a period in the Air Force settled in New York and established himself as a cartoonist. He has had several volumes of his cartoons collected in book form, the first of which was *Gahan Wilson's Graveside Manner* (1966). He also regularly reviews weird fiction in *F&SF* and has written a few short stories. His earliest were merely extended jokes, and his first serious story was 'The Power of the Mandarin' (1967). He was instrumental in the formation of the first World Fantasy Convention held in 1975, and has edited *The First World Fantasy Awards* (1977).

Donald A. Wollheim (b. New York, 1 October 1914)
As a writer, editor and publisher, Wollheim has considerably enriched the fields of sf and fantasy. As a writer, the bulk of his output has been sf, but he has written a few horror classics such as 'Mimic' (1942), 'The Rag Thing' (1931) and 'Doorslammer' (1963). As editor Wollheim has accomplished much. Among the fantasy magazines he has captained are *Fanciful Tales* and *Avon Fantasy Reader* (see App. III), and he has compiled many excellent anthologies including *The Girl with the Hungry Eyes* (1949; 6s), *Terror in the Modern Vein* (1955; 17s), *The Macabre Reader* (1959; 10s) and *More Macabre* (1961; 8s). *Swordsmen in the Sky* (1964; 5s) is of fantasy interest.

It is as publisher, however, that Wollheim has accomplished most of all. Previously the editor-in-chief at Ace Books, in 1972 he established his own DAW specialist sf/fantasy imprint which has published some of the best fantasy available in recent years. They include works from **Lin Carter, John Jakes, Brian Lumley, Fritz Leiber**, Philip José Farmer, **Andre Norton, Thomas B. Swann**, plus the Dray Prescot series by Alan Burt Akers and the Gor novels of John Norman. He also publishes the three *Year's Best* series of sf, fantasy and horror.

Pseudonyms: David Grinnell (plus many others in sf field)

Everil Worrell (b. Nebraska, 3 November 1893; d. Washington, 27 November 1969)
Everil Worrell had at least nineteen stories in *Weird Tales* between 'The Bird of Space' (1926) and 'Call Not Their Names' (1954). She is best known for her vampire story 'The Canal' (1926); another tale tells of an evil alien visitor to a hospital—'The Grey Killer' (1929).

Pseudonyms: Lireve Monett, (possibly O. M. Cabral)

Farnsworth Wright (b. San Francisco, 1888; d. New York, June 1940)
Weird fiction owes much to Wright, and many writers have acknowledged their debt to him for the painstaking way he nurtured them in professional writing. They include **Robert S. Carr, A. Derleth, H, W. Munn, E. H. Price, Robert Bloch, D. Wandrei** and **M. W. Wellman.**
Wright was a born editor, producing an amateur magazine while at high school. He was in San Francisco when the earthquake hit in 1906, and he promptly left for safer climes. After university he held a variety of jobs and fought in the infantry in the First World War. He assisted Edwin Baird from the first issue of *Weird Tales*, and contributed stories of his own, including 'The Closing Hand' in the first issue. Wright became editor with the November 1924 issue, and remained in control until March 1940. By then the magazine had changed publishers, moving from Chicago to New York. Wright, his health never good, failed rapidly and died soon after, aged only 52. Today the Wright *Weird Tales* is looked upon with nostalgic reverence as the golden period of weird fiction. He also edited the companion magazine *Oriental Stories* (App. III).

Roger Zelazny (b. Cleveland, Ohio, 13 May 1937)
Zelazny exploded on the scene in 1962 and rapidly became one of the major new science fiction talents, scooping up every type of sf award. Yet his works are extremely fantasy-orientated. His first published story had been in a competition in 1954, and thereafter he made no sales until 1962 when he had many bizarre vignettes in *Fantastic*, such as 'On the Road to Splenoba' (1963). He wrote a sword-and-sorcery series about Dilvish the Damned who had returned from Hell. It ran 'Passage to Dilfar', 'The-linde's Song' (both 1965) and 'The Bells of Shoredan' (1966). Of his books, the closest to the fantasy realms are *Creatures of Light and Darkness* (1969) with gods of the Egyptian pantheon transposed to space, and *Jack of Shadows* (1971), set on an Earth that does not rotate and has a civilised light side but a fantasy-haunted night side. He has recently completed a fantasy series about the world of Amber, of which this Earth is but a shadow: *Nine Princes in Amber* (1971), *The Guns of Avalon* (1973), *Sign of the Unicorn* (1975) and *The Hand of Oberon* (1976).

Appendices

The following appendices serve to supplement the body of the *Who's Who* by giving additional information which it was not possible to include elsewhere. They are divided into four sections:

I. A list of specially selected titles of stories and books. This is intended to serve three purposes: to aid readers who know the title of a book and wish to find its author; to supply further information about series and also highlight confusing duplicate titles; and to act as a basic suggested reading list for those who wish to investigate further.

II. A list of anthologies and their important contents. This list is by no means exhaustive, but again acts as a basic suggested reading list. I have selected those anthologies I feel give a varied choice of fiction without a constant repetition of standard stories. I have not listed every content, but merely highlighted those I feel to be the most important.

III. A list of magazines specialising in the genre. Again not exhaustive, it nevertheless provides a thorough coverage of all the important magazines, noting their editors, dates and key stories. There are many hybrid sf and fantasy magazines, but only the major ones are included. Non-fiction magazines are not covered.

IV. A list of World Fantasy and British Fantasy Awards.

An Index to key stories and books

Abyss, The See **Leonid Andreyev** and **David H. Keller**
Adam and Eve and Pinch Me See **A. E. Coppard**
'Akin to Love' A noted story of demon love by **Christianna Brand**
Alabaster Hand, The Story and collection in the M. R. James tradition
  by **A. N. L. Munby**
Alraune See **Hans Heinz Ewers**
Amber Witch, The See **J. W. Meinhold**
American Gothic See **Robert Bloch**
. . . And Now the Screaming Starts! Film adapted by Roger Marshall
  from 'Fengriffen' by **David Case**
Angel of Mons, The See **Arthur Machen**
Anita (1972; 15s) A collection of stories about a delightful teenage witch,
  by Keith Roberts (b. 1935)
Atlan trilogy See **Jane Gaskell**
Atlantis See **John Cowper Powys** (Note also **Cutcliffe Hyne**)

'Back There in the Grass' (1912) A story about the bizarre inhabitant
  of a South Sea island, by Gouverneur Morris (1876–1953)
Beast With Five Fingers, The Story and collection by **W. F. Harvey**.
  Adapted into a notable film by **Curt Siodmak**
'Beckoning Fair One, The' Noted ghost story by **Oliver Onions**
Beetle, The See **Richard Marsh**
'Ben Blower's Story' Also titled 'The Boiler' by American Charles
  F. Hoffman (1806–84), it brilliantly describes Hoffman's own fear,
  claustrophobia
Bewitched This engaging television series, from which a paperback novel
  was adapted by Al Hine, was based on the film *I Married a Witch*
  adapted from *The Passionate Witch* by **Norman Matson**
'Bianca's Hands' See **Theodore Sturgeon**
Birds, The The excellent 1963 film directed by **Alfred Hitchcock** was
  adapted from the story by **Daphne du Maurier**, but a novel on the
  same theme is by **Frank Baker**
Birthgrave, The (1975) An excellent science fantasy by Tanith Lee about
  an accursed girl, the embodiment of the evil of an extinct race
Black Easter (1968) Expansion of serial *Faust Aleph Null* (*If*, 1967). A
  superb black magic novel in which a magician summons every
  demon and literally releases Hell on Earth. The sequel was *The Day
  After Judgement* (1970), both by James Blish (1921–75)
Black Magic See **Marjorie Bowen**

Blue Monkeys, The See **Thomas Burnett Swann**

Boats of the 'Glen Carrig', The See **William Hope Hodgson**

'Body Snatcher, The' See **Robert Louis Stevenson**. In 1945 it was adapted to the screen by Robert Wise with a script by Philip Mac-Donald and Carlos Keith, and starring Boris Karloff and Bela Lugosi

'Bottle Imp, The' See **Baron Fouque** and **R. L. Stevenson**

'Bowmen, The' See **Arthur Machen**

Bride of Frankenstein, The (1935) This film sequel to *Frankenstein*, also directed by James Whale, and starring Boris Karloff, Colin Clive and Elsa Lanchester, was directly responsible for creating the error that Frankenstein was the name of the monster instead of its creator. The screenplay was by John L. Balderston and William Hurlbut, and it was adapted as a novel shortly afterwards in Britain by Michael Egremont (a pen name of Michael Harrison (b. 1907)). A new adaptation was recently novelised by **J. Ramsey Campbell**

Brood of the Witch-Queen, The See **Sax Rohmer**

Burke and Hare Two Irishmen who committed murders in Edinburgh in the 1820s to supply corpses to Dr Robert Knox. Burke was hanged in 1829, but Hare, who turned king's evidence, lived on as a beggar, and blind, in London till the 1860s. The incident was the basis of 'The Body Snatcher' by **R. L. Stevenson**

Burn Witch Burn! This title refers to a novel by **A. Merritt**, and a film, but the two are not the same. Merritt's novel, serialised in *Argosy* in 1932, was later filmed as *The Devil Doll* (1936) produced by Tod Browning from a screenplay by **Garrett Fort, Guy Endore** and Erich von Stroheim. The film, *Burn Witch Burn* (1962), was the US title of the British film *Night of the Eagle* with a script by **Charles Beaumont, Richard Matheson** and George Baxt from *Conjure Wife* by **Fritz Leiber**

Camelot Musical by Lerner and Loewe filmed in 1967. Based on *The Once and Future King* by **T. H. White**

'Camera Obscura' See **Basil Copper**

Can Such Things Be? See **Ambrose Bierce**

'Canal, The' Noted vampire story by **Everil Worrell**

Canterville Ghost, The See **Oscar Wilde**

'Carmilla' Noted vampire story by **J. Sheridan Le Fanu**

Carnacki, the Ghost-Finder See **William Hope Hodgson**

Carrie See **Stephen King**

'Casting the Runes' See **M. R. James**

Castle of Otranto, The See **Horace Walpole**

'Caterpillars' See **E. F. Benson**

Children of the Night See **John F. Blackburn**

Christmas Carol, A See **Charles Dickens**

Circus of Dr Lao, The See **Charles G. Finney**. Also the title story in an anthology by **Ray Bradbury** (see App. II)

'Coat, The' A notable ghost story by A. E. D. Smith

'Cocoon, The' (1946) The tale of a strange and revengeful butterfly, by John B. L. Goodwin

Conan A barbarian warrior who features in a series of stories written initially by **Robert E. Howard**, but later expanded and continued by **L. Sprague de Camp**, Bjorn Nyberg and **Lin Carter**. The series first ran in *Weird Tales* starting with 'The Phoenix on the Sword' (1932). Later de Camp uncovered many unpublished manuscripts, and these were first assembled in hardback by a US specialist publisher. The complete series with the stories assembled in chronological order began to appear in paperback in 1966. The original hardback books ran as follows:

> *Conan the Conqueror* (1950; orig. *The Hour of the Dragon*, WT 1935); *The Sword of Conan* (1952; 4s); *King Conan* (1953; 5s); *The Coming of Conan* (1953; 8s); *Conan the Barbarian* (1955; 5s); *Tales of Conan* (1955; 4s)
>
> *The Return of Conan* (1957) was the work of Björn Nyberg and L. S. de Camp, and was later paperbound as *Conan the Avenger*

The paperback series ran as follows (in reading sequence):

> *Conan* (1967; 7s) by Howard, de Camp and Carter
> *Conan of Cimmeria* (1969; 8s) by Howard, de Camp and Carter
> *Conan the Freebooter* (1968; 5s) by Howard and de Camp
> *Conan the Wanderer* (1968; 4s) by Howard, de Camp and Carter
> *Conan the Adventurer* (1966; 4s) by Howard and de Camp
> *Conan the Buccaneer* (1971) by de Camp and Carter
> *Conan the Warrior* (1967; 3s) by Howard and de Camp
> *Conan the Usurper* (1967; 4s) by Howard and de Camp
> *Conan the Conqueror* (1967) by Howard (see hardback above)
> *Conan the Avenger* (1968) by Nyberg and de Camp (see hardback above)
> *Conan of Aquilonia* (1977; 4s) by de Camp and Carter
> *Conan of the Isles* (1968) by de Camp and Carter

Conjure Wife See **Fritz Leiber**

'Couching at the Door' See **D. K. Broster**

Cthulhu A god-like entity invented by **H. P. Lovecraft** as one of an ancient pantheon of evil beings. It was later developed by other writers into a story cycle, 'the Cthulhu Mythos'. Certain elements appear in early Lovecraft stories like 'The Nameless City' (1921) and 'The Hound' (1925), but it came to the fore in 'The Call of Cthulhu' (1928) and many of his later stories. Other authors who have contributed to the Mythos include: Zealia Bishop, **Robert Bloch**, **Ramsey Campbell**, **Lin Carter**, **Hugh B. Cave**, Henry Hasse,

Hazel Heald, **Robert E. Howard, Henry Kuttner, Frank Belknap Long, Brian Lumley,** Gary Myers, J. Vernon Shea, **Clark Ashton Smith, James Wade, Donald Wandrei, Manly Wade Wellman, Colin Wilson** and above all **August Derleth.** Specific anthologies are *Tales of the Cthulhu Mythos* by Derleth, *The Spawn of Cthulhu* by Carter, *The Disciples of Cthulhu* by E. P. Berglund, and in preparation *New Tales of the Cthulhu Mythos* by Ramsey Campbell

'Dead Smile, The' See **F. Marion Crawford**
'Dead Woman, The' See **David H. Keller** and **Elizabeth Walter**
'Demon Lover, The' Two different stories by **Elizabeth Bowen and Shirley Jackson**
Deryni trilogy See **Katherine Kurtz**
'Devil and Daniel Webster, The' See **Stephen Vincent Benét**
Devil Rides Out, The See **Dennis Wheatley**
Devil's Bride, The See **Seabury Quinn**
Devil's Elixir, The See **E. T. A. Hoffman**
Dian of the Lost Land See **Edison Marshall**
Dr Nikola See **Guy Boothby**
Doctor Satan series See **Paul Ernst**
Door of the Unreal, The See **Gerald Biss**
Down There Trans. of *Là-Bas* by **Joris-Karl Huysman**
Dracula See **Bram Stoker** and **Robert Lory**
Dying Earth, The See **Jack Vance.** Much the same milieu was also used by **Clark Ashton Smith** and **Lin Carter**

Earthsea A setting used for a fantasy trilogy by Ursula K. LeGuin (b. 1929) which traces the life of a wizard. The first volume won the Hornbrook Prize. The series runs: *A Wizard of Earthsea* (1968), *The Tombs of Atuan* (1970) and *The Farthest Shore* (1973)
Elder Gods, The (1939) The only fantasy by John W. Campbell (1910–1971), first published in *Unknown*
Elric See **Michael Moorcock**
'Enoch' (1946) An oft-reprinted story by **Robert Bloch**
Exorcist, The (1973) The novel by William Peter Blatty (b. 1928) that he adapted into the phenomenally successful film. The central theme of a girl possessed by a demon is by no means new and one special earlier example is by **Ray Russell**

Faust The original Dr Georg Faust (1480–1540) was an obscure Swabian who became unpopular among his fellows until he settled in Westphalia and was purported to produce wine by magic and evoke characters from Homer. He obviously made an impact as the myth of his pact with the devil formed the central theme of *Historia von D. Johann Fausten* (1587) by Johann Spies (d. 1607). This chapbook was the basis of Christopher Marlowe's play *The Tragical History of Dr Faustus*, first performed in the 1590s. The legend later formed the basis of a novel by Friedrich M. Klinger, *Fausts Leben* (1791), which also attributed the invention of printing to Faust. The most famous work is *Faust* by **Goethe**. He had initially written a short play on the theme in the 1770s (later published as *Urfaust* 1887). An expansion of the play was published as *Faust* in 1790, and it was only with the encouragement of **Schiller** that Goethe completed the full version. More recently the theme was also used in the philosophical and symbolic novel *Doktor Faustus* (1947) by Thomas Mann (1875–1955). Marlowe's play was filmed as *Doctor Faustus* (1967), starring Richard Burton and Elizabeth Taylor

'Fishhead' (1913) A superb horror story by Irvin S. Cobb (1876–1944) originally written in 1900 but rejected by every magazine as being too horrible

For Fear of Little Men See **John F. Blackburn**

Forgotten Beasts of Eld, The A beautiful fantasy by Patricia A. McKillip telling of a young girl with special powers over animals who has to leave her haven. It won the First World Fantasy Award in 1975 as the Best Novel published in 1974

Frankenstein The original novel was by **Mary Shelley**. The visual appeal of the story was soon proven by the success of a stage play adaptation *Presumption; or the Fate of Frankenstein* (1823) starring T. P. Cooke as the monster. Edison made a film version in 1910, but of course the classic is the James Whale version of 1932 starring Boris Karloff and scripted by **Garrett Fort**

Freaks (1932) A classic horror film directed by Tod Browning and banned for many years because of his too effective use of real freaks. It was based on 'Spurs' by **Tod Robbins**

From Beyond the Grave (1973) A film scripted by Robin Clarke and Raymond Christodoulou from four stories by **R. Chetwynd-Hayes**

Fu-Manchu The inscrutable Oriental doctor created by **Sax Rohmer**. The series ran as follows (UK editions cited first):

> *The Mystery of Dr Fu-Manchu* (1913; US *The Insidious Dr Fu-Manchu*)
> *The Devil Doctor* (1916; US *The Return of Dr Fu-Manchu*)
> *The Si-Fan Mysteries* (1917; US *The Hand of Fu-Manchu*)
> *The Daughter of Fu-Manchu* (1931)
> *The Mask of Fu-Manchu* (1933; US 1932)
> *The Bride of Fu-Manchu* (1933; US *Fu-Manchu's Bride*)
> *The Trail of Fu-Manchu* (1935; US 1934)
> *President Fu-Manchu* (1936)
> *The Drums of Fu-Manchu* (1939)
> *The Island of Fu-Manchu* (1941)

The Shadow of Fu-Manchu (1940; US 1948)
Re-enter Fu-Manchu (1957)
Emperor Fu-Manchu (1959)

'Gentleman from America, The' See **Michael Arlen**
Ghost and Mrs Muir, The Television comedy series based on an original
  novel by R. A. Dick, published in 1945
Ghost Pirates, The See **William Hope Hodgson**
Ghost Ship, The See **Richard Middleton**
Ghost Stories of an Antiquary See **M. R. James**
Glory Road (1963) Fantasy novel of a perilous quest written by Robert
  A. Heinlein (b. 1907)
Golem, The Novel by **Gustav Meyrink**. Made into two effective German
  silent films *The Golem* (1915) and *The Golem and How He Came into
  the World* (1920), both scripted by and starring Paul Wegener
Gor A counter-Earth fantasy world where Tarl Cabot undergoes many
  Burroughs-style adventures, as narrated by John Norman (b. 1931).
  The series runs: *Tarnsman of Gor* (1966), *Outlaw of Gor* (1967),
  Priest-Kings of Gor (1968), *Nomads of Gor* (1969), *Assassins of Gor*
  (1970), *Raiders of Gor* (1971), *Captive of Gor* (1972), *Hunters of Gor*
  (1973), *Marauders of Gor* (1974), *Tribesman of Gor* (1975)
Gormenghast See **Mervyn Peake**
Gray Mouser See **Fritz Leiber**
Great God Pan, The See **Arthur Machen**
Greater Trumps, The See **Charles Williams**
Green Man, The (1969) A remarkable novel by Kingsley Amis (b. 1922)
  which tells how a seventeenth-century magician, Dr Underhill,
  begins to take control over a twentieth-century publican

'Haunters and the Haunted, The' See **Bulwer-Lytton**
Haunting of Hill House, The See **Shirley Jackson**
Hobbit, The See **J. R. R. Tolkien**
'Hollow Land, The' Short novel by **William Morris**
'Horla, The' See **Guy de Maupassant**
Hound of Death, The Story and collection by **Agatha Christie**
Hound of the Baskervilles, The See **Conan Doyle**. It has been made into
  three films, in 1939 starring Basil Rathbone, 1959 starring Peter
  Cushing, and 1972 (made for television) starring Stewart Granger.
Hounds of Tindalos, The Story and collection by **Frank B. Long**
House-Boat on the Styx, A See **John Kendrick Bangs**
House by the Churchyard, The See **Sheridan Le Fanu**
'House By the Crab Apple Tree, The' (1964) A chilling story of lycan-
  thropy by S. S. Johnson (b. 1940)
'House of Sounds, The' See **M. P. Shiel**
House on Half-Moon Street, The (1935; 14s) Story and collection by

Henry Hector Bolitho (1897–1974), better known for his biographies of royalty

House on the Borderland, The See **William Hope Hodgson**

'How Love Came to Professor Guildea' See **Robert S. Hichens**

Hunchback of Notre-Dame, The The title of several films based on the historical novel *Notre Dame de Paris* (1831) by Victor Hugo (1802–1885). The first, filmed in 1923, made the name of Lon Chaney, Sr as Quasimodo. The 1939 version featured Charles Laughton; Anthony Quinn starred in the 1957 remake

I Am Legend See **Richard Matheson**

'In Amundsen's Tent' (1928) A popular story of Antarctic terror by John Martin Leahy (1886–?) from *Weird Tales*

Ingoldsby Legends, The See **Richard H. Barham**

Innocents, The Film based on 'The Turn of the Screw' by **Henry James**

'It' See **Theodore Sturgeon**

Jekyll & Hyde The term has now passed into the English language to describe someone who can be pleasant one moment yet nasty another. It comes from the short novel *The Strange Case of Dr Jekyll and Mr Hyde* by **Robert Louis Stevenson**, but earlier examples of dual personalities will be found in works by E. T. A. Hoffman and James Hogg. Like *Frankenstein*, the visual attraction of the evil Hyde resulted in many stage and film adaptations, the first being in 1887 with actor Richard Mansfield in US. UK playwright J. Comyns Carr (1849–1916) adapted it for the British stage with Henry Irving in 1899. Several short silent films were made from 1908 onwards, the first classic being in 1919 starring Sheldon Lewis. John Barrymore starred in a 1920 version, and in that year a German version was made starring Conrad Veidt and Bela Lugosi. The undoubted classic is Fredric March's 1932 portrayal, for which he won an Oscar. Spencer Tracy underwent his transformation in 1941. Other versions include *The Two Faces of Dr Jekyll* (1961) starring Paul Massie, *I, Monster* (1970) with Christopher Lee and *Dr Jekyll and Sister Hyde* (1972)

John Silence See **Algernon Blackwood**

Jorkens The teller of tales collected by **Lord Dunsany**

Jules de Grandin See **Seabury Quinn**

Jurgen See **James Branch Cabell**

Kai Lung See **Ernest Bramah**

Kane Solomon Kane, the English puritan, is the hero of several stories by **Robert E. Howard**. The Biblical Cain features in several stories by **Karl E. Wagner**

'Kill, The' (1931) Noted werewolf story by Peter Fleming (1907–71), the brother of James Bond creator, Ian Fleming

King in Yellow, The See **Robert W. Chambers**

King Kong The most famous monster film of them all, released in 1933. The idea for the story had come from Merian C. Cooper and he wrote the original novel with Edgar Wallace. The original film screenplay was by James Creelman and Ruth Rose. Merian C. Cooper co-directed it. Dino de Laurentiis updated the film in 1976

King Solomon's Mines See **H. Rider Haggard**

'Lady of the Velvet Collar, The' A story by **Washington Irving** also titled 'The Adventure of the German Student'. Not to be confused with 'The Woman With the Velvet Collar' by **Gaston Leroux**

'Lady or the Tiger? The' (1882) A popular story by Frank R. Stockton (1834–1902) which concluded on a most agonising note leaving the reader guessing as to the fate of the hero. Stockton later wrote a sequel, 'The Discourager of Hesitancy', which was equally infuriating!

'Lady's Maid's Bell, The' See **Edith Wharton**

Lancashire Witches, The See **W. Harrison Ainsworth**

Last Unicorn, The See **Peter S. Beagle**

'Lazarus' See **Leonid Andreyev**

Lilith See **George Macdonald**

Limehouse Nights See **Thomas Burke**

Lodger, The See **Mrs M. B. Lowndes**

Lord of the Flies See **William Golding**

Lord of the Rings See **J. R. R. Tolkien**

Lost Continent, The See **C. J. Cutcliffe Hyne**

Lost Horizon (1933) The famous novel by James Hilton (1900–54) that gave us the name Shangri-La. It was effectively filmed by Frank Capra in 1937, and later was subjected to a musical adaptation in 1973

Lost Stradivarius, The See **J. Meade Falkner**

'Lottery, The' See **Shirley Jackson**

'Loved Dead, The' See **C. M. Eddy**

'Lukundoo' See **Edward Lucas White**

Madhouse (1974) A film directed by James Clark and starring Vincent Price as a veteran horror star whose life is linked with a series of murders. The film includes many clips from early horror films. It was scripted by Greg Morrison from the novel *Devilday* by Angus Hall

Magus, The (1966) A powerful black magic novel by John Fowles (b. 1926) filmed in 1968 starring Michael Caine. Reissued 1977 with a new ending

Maker of Moons, The See **Robert W. Chambers**

Malleus Malificarium (1489) A classic tome on witchcraft compiled by Jakob Sprenger and Henricus Institor, inquisitors under Innocent VIII. It became the standard text used in witch-trials. Recent editions include 1948 with notes by **Montague Summers**, and 1968 edited by Pennethorne Hughes. 'Malleus Malificarum' (1964) is a story by **Charles Birkin**

'Man-Size in Marble' See *E. Nesbit*

'Man With a Thousand Legs, The' See **Frank Belknap Long**

'MS Found in a Bottle' See **Edgar Allan Poe**

'Mark of the Beast, The' See **Rudyard Kipling**

Medusa See **E. H. Visiak**

Melmoth the Wanderer See **Charles Maturin**

Merlin The famous wizard, tutor and mage to King Arthur. No true Arthurian novel can be complete without him, but novels worth recommending that concentrate more on his exploits include *The Sword in the Stone* by **T. H. White**, *Porius* by **John Cowper Powys** and *Merlin's Godson* by **H. Warner Munn**

'Mimic' See **Donald A. Wollheim**

Miss Seaton Bewitched (1971) A weird novel of witchcraft by Heron Carvic, well known for his voice in the part of Gandalf in the BBC Radio serialisation of *The Hobbit* in 1969.

Monk, The See **M. G. Lewis**

'Monkey's Paw, The' See **W. W. Jacobs**

Moonchild See **Aleister Crowley**

'Most Dangerous Game, The' A story by Richard Connell telling of a man shipwrecked on an island and hunted like an animal. James Ashmore Creelman adapted the story for the film *The Hounds of Zaroff* (1932); subsequent versions have been *A Game of Death* (1945) and *Run For the Sun* (1956)

Mulata (1967) This extraordinary fantasy novel by Miguel Angel Asturias (b. 1899) has the highest credentials since it won a Nobel Prize for Literature. The UK edition was called *The Mulatta and Mr Fly*

'Mummy's Foot, The' See **Théophile Gautier**

Münchhausen, Baron The real Baron Freiherr von Münchhausen (1720–97) was a noted army officer and later a mighty hunter. He earned a reputation for telling tall tales about his extraordinary exploits. Several of these saw print in Germany in the early 1780s, but just how much was the work of the Baron is not known. Another German, Rudolf Erich Raspe (1737–94), who had fled to England to avoid criminal charges, collected together these stories, adding others of his own invention as *Baron Münchhausen's Narrative of his Marvellous Travels and Campaigns in Russia* (1785) and this was in turn expanded by Gottfried Bürger in 1786. Münchhausen's name has now become synonymous with extravagant and highly improbable tales

'Murgunstruum' See **Hugh B. Cave**
Mysteries of Udolpho, The See **Ann Radcliffe**
'Mysterious Card, The' (1896) A clever story by Cleveland Moffett
    about a man given a card by a strange woman. He can make no
    sense of the card, but it alienates him from whomever he shows it to.
    Moffett supplied a sequel by popular demand, 'The Mysterious
    Card Unveiled' (1896)

Necromancer, The (1794) A noted black magic novel by German writer
    Lawrence Flammenberg. (See *Northanger Abbey*)
Necromancers, The See **R. H. Benson**
Necronomicon, The This book was originally invented by H. P. Lovecraft
    as part of his Cthulhu Mythos. He related that it contained forbidden
    occult lore set down by the mad Arabian poet Abdul Alhazred in
    730 A.D. His stories contained quotes from the book, and other
    authors added their own. Many readers believed it existed, and there
    were various attempts by fans to produce a copy, and a few rare
    editions exist. Most recently George Hay assembled a complete
    version
'Negotium Perambulans' Story by **E. F. Benson**
'Nemesis of Fire, The' A John Silence story by **Algernon Blackwood**
'Night and Silence' See **Maurice Level**
Night of the Demon (1957) British film version of 'Casting the Runes' by
    M. R. James. The US title was *Curse of the Demon*
Night Side of Nature, The See **Mrs C. Crowe**
Nightmares and Geezenstacks (1961; 47s) A collection of bizarre, humorous
    and weird stories and vignettes by Fredric Brown (1906–72).
Northanger Abbey (1818) A classic novel by Jane Austen (1775–1817)
    which gave the Gothic trend a certain respectability. Within the
    novel Isabella Thorpe recommends seven Gothic novels, viz.:
    Castle of Wolfenbach by Eliza Parsons; *Clermont* by Regina Maria
    Roche (1765–1845); *Mysterious Warnings* by Eliza Parsons; *The
    Necromancer of the Black Forest* (1794) by Lawrence Flammenberg;
    Midnight Bell by **Francis Lathom**; *Orphan of the Rhine* by Eleanor
    Sleath and *Horrid Mysteries* by the Marquis de Grosse
Number Seven, Queer Street See **Margery Lawrence**

'Occurrence at Owl Creek Bridge, An' See **Ambrose Bierce**
'"Oh, Whistle and I'll Come to You, My Lad"' See **M. R. James**
Old English Baron, The See **Clara Reeve**
Omen, The (1976) Film and novel by David Seltzer based on the Devil
    planting an anti-Christ on Earth.
Once and Future King, The See **T. H. White**
'Ooze' See **Anthony M. Rud**
Other Passenger, The See **John Keir Cross**

'Outsider, The' Story by **H. P. Lovecraft**
'Over the River' (1941) A noted vampire story by P. Schuyler Miller (1912–74)

'Pages From a Young Girl's Diary' (UK, Journal) See **Robert Aickman**
'Parasite, The' See **Conan Doyle**
Phantastes See **George Macdonald**
'Phantom Farmhouse, The' See **Seabury Quinn**
Phantom Fighter, The See **Seabury Quinn**
Phantom of the Opera, The The original novel by **Gaston Leroux** has
    long since been dwarfed by the film versions, most notably Lon
    Chaney, Sr's, in 1925. Claude Rains starred in the 1943 remake, and
    Herbert Lom in the 1962 version
'Phantom 'Rickshaw, The' See **Rudyard Kipling**
Phantom Ship, The See **Frederick Marryat**
Phra the Phoenician Novel by **Edward Lester Arnold**. It proved highly
    popular and naturally led to imitations of which the best include
    Valdar the Oft-Born (1895) by George Griffith (1857–1906) and
    Abbs, His Story (1929) by **Cutcliffe Hyne**
'Picture of Dorian Gray' See **Oscar Wilde**
'Pied Piper of Hamelin' The noted legend recounted in a poem by Robert
    Browning (1812–89)
'Pit and the Pendulum, The' See **Edgar Allan Poe**. Vincent Price
    starred in Roger Corman's noted film made in 1961, but a lesser-
    known version made entirely without dialogue and with effective use
    of vision and sound was Edward Abraham's *The Pit* (1960–62)
Prince Zaleski See **M. P. Shiel**
Psycho The novel by **Robert Bloch** was skilfully scripted by Joseph
    Stefano and directed by **Hitchcock** to produce surely the most
    effective shock film

Quatermain, Allan The hero of *King Solomon's Mines* and other adven-
    tures told by **Rider Haggard**
Quatermass See **Nigel Kneale**
'Queen of Spades, The' (1834) The best-known horror story by Alex-
    ander Pushkin (1799–1837)

'Raven, The' A splendid poem by **Edgar Allan Poe**
'Red Lodge, The' See **H. R. Wakefield**
Return, The See **Walter de la Mare**
'Rime of the Ancient Mariner, The' (1798) The famous poem by
    Samuel Taylor Coleridge (1772–1834)
'Ringing the Changes' See **Robert Aickman**
'Rip van Winkle' See **Washington Irving**
'Roads' See **Seabury Quinn**

'Rocking-Horse Winner, The' (1926) Noted ghost story by D. H. Lawrence (1885–1930). Cynthia Asquith had commissioned a story from him for her *Ghost Book* and this story appeared after his first submission 'Glad Ghosts' (1926) proved unsuitable

'Rose For Emily, A' (1930) A famous macabre story by William Faulkner (1897–1962)

Rosemary's Baby (1967) A novel by Ira Levin (b. 1929) about a devil-fathered child. Roman Polanski scripted and directed the film in 1968, starring Mia Farrow

St Leon (1791) A Gothic novel of immortality by William Godwin (1756–1836), the father of Mary Shelley

'Salamander, The' See W. B. Seabrook

Saragossa Manuscript, The See Jan Potocki

'Screaming Skull, The' See F. Marion Crawford

Seven Faces of Dr Lao, The Film by Charles Beaumont from the novel by Charles G. Finney

'Shadow in the Moonlight, The' See Mrs Molesworth

'Shadows on the Wall, The' Story by Mary Wilkins-Freeman

'Shambleau' See C. L. Moore

Shangri-La The lamasery paradise of James Hilton's *Lost Horizon* (see entry)

Shardik (1974) A mammoth fantasy novel by Richard Adams (b. 1920)

Shaving of Shagpat, The (1855) A delightful Oriental fantasy by George Meredith (1828–1909)

She See H. Rider Haggard

'Shining Pyramid, The' See Arthur Machen

Silverlock (1949) An unusual fantasy by John Myers Myers (b. 1906), in which the narrator is shipwrecked on an island that houses all the characters from fiction and myth

'Slime' See Joseph Payne Brennan

'Smoking Leg, The' See John Metcalfe

'Snail Watcher, The' See Patricia Highsmith

Sorcery Club, The See Elliott O'Donnell

'Spectre Bridegroom, The' See Washington Irving

Steppenwolf (1927) A surrealistic novel by Herman Hesse (1877–1962)

'Sticks' See Karl E. Wagner

Strange Case of Miss Annie Spragg, The (1928) A noted reincarnation novel by Louis Bromfield (1896–1956)

Strange Story, A See Bulwer-Lytton

Svengali The hypnotist who exerts strange powers in *Trilby* (1894) by George du Maurier (1834–96)

Sweeney Todd, the Demon Barber See Thomas P. Prest

Sword in the Stone, The See T. H. White

Tales of the Frightened See **Michael Avallone** and **Robert Lory**
Tales of the Genii (1765) Oriental fantasies by the Reverend James Ridley (1736–65)
Tarzan The mighty hero created by **Edgar Rice Burroughs.** First appeared in *Tarzan of the Apes* (1912)
'Terribly Strange Bed, A' See **Wilkie Collins**
'There Shall Be No Darkness' (1950) A noted scientific tale of lycanthropy by James Blish (1921–75)
They Used Dark Forces See **Dennis Wheatley**
Thief of Bagdad, The The popular Arabian fantasy film originally scripted by **Achmed Abdullah** for Douglas Fairbanks in 1924. Other versions starred Sabu and Conrad Veidt in 1940, and Steve Reeves in 1962
'Thing in the Cellar, The' See **David H. Keller**
Thongor The hero of a sword and sorcery series by **Lin Carter**
Three Hearts and Three Lions See **Poul Anderson**
'Three Marked Pennies, The' See **Mary E. Counselman**
'Thurnley Abbey' (1908) A noted ghost story by Perceval Landon (1869–1927), an English barrister
Titus Groan See **Mervyn Peake**
To The Devil a Daughter See **Dennis Wheatley**
Topper See **Thorne Smith**
'Torture of Hope, The' See **Villiers de l'Isle Adam**
'Tractate Middoth' See **M. R. James**
'Travelling Grave, The' See **L. P. Hartley**
Tros See **Talbot Mundy**
'Turn of the Screw, The' See **Henry James**

Uncle Silas See **Sheridan Le Fanu**
Undying Monster, The See **Jessie D. Kerruish**
Uninvited, The See **Dorothy Macardle**
'Upper Berth, The' See **F. Marion Crawford**

'Vacant Lot, The' See **Mary Wilkins-Freeman**
Varney the Vampire See **J. M. Rymer**
Vathek See **William Beckford**
Vice Versa See **F. Anstey**
Victorian Chaise-Longue, The (1953) A noted horror novel of the exchange of lives between a girl of 1954 and one of 1864, written by Marghanita Laski (b. 1915)
Vikram and the Vampire (1869) A collection of various legends compiled by the explorer Sir Richard Burton (1821–96) and his wife. Burton, a master of 35 languages, also prepared an English translation of *The Arabian Nights* (1885–88)
'Voice in the Night, A' See **William Hope Hodgson**
Voyage to Arcturus, A See **David Lindsay**

'Wall Around the World, The' (1953) A charming tale by Theodore R. Cogswell (b. 1918) of a place where magic works

Wandering Jew, The The immortal of legend was one Cartophilus, door-keeper in the service of Pontius Pilate, who struck Jesus, bidding him hurry. Christ replied, 'I am going, but tarry thou until I come again.' Once every hundred years Cartophilus falls into a trance from which he revives as a man of thirty. The legend was first mentioned in *Flores Historiarum* (*c* 1235) by the Benedictine monk of St Alban's, Roger of Wendover. It was expanded by Matthew Paris in *Historia Major* (1259). By the nineteenth century the legends were legion, and it was left to **Eugene Sue** to write the acknowledged classic of his life. The various legends were collected by David Hoffman as *The Chronicles of Cartophilus* (1853–54). Of course the legend inspired many immortality novels such as *St Leon* and above all *Melmoth the Wanderer*. See also **M. P. Shiel** and **G. S. Viereck**

Watership Down (1972) The now classic fantasy of the survival of a rabbit colony, told by Richard Adams (b. 1920)

'Waxwork, The' See **A. M. Burrage**

Well at the World's End, The The noted fantasy novel by **William Morris**, not to be confused with *Well at World's End* by **Neil M. Gunn**

'Wendigo, The' See **Algernon Blackwood**

Were-wolf, The See **Clemence Housman**

Werewolf of Paris, The See **Guy Endore**

'What Was It?' See **Fitz-James O'Brien**

'When it Was Moonlight' See **Manly Wade Wellman**

'Where is the Bird of Fire?' See **Thomas Burnett Swann**

'Where Their Fire is Not Quenched' See **May Sinclair**

'White Wolf of the Hartz Mountains, The' See **Frederick Marryat**

Widdershins See **Oliver Onions**

Wieland See **Charles B. Brown**

'Willows, The' See **Algernon Blackwood**

Wind in the Rose-Bush, The Story and collection by **Mary Wilkins-Freeman**

Winged Pharaoh See **Joan Grant**

Witching Night, The (1952) A black magic novel by C. S. Cody, real name Leslie Waller (b. 1923)

Witchworld Series by **Andre Norton**

Wolf Leader, The See **Alexandre Dumas**

Wolfwinter See **Thomas Burnett Swann**

'Wolves of Darkness' (1932) Notable horror story by Jack Williamson (b. 1908)

Wood Beyond the World, The See **William Morris**

Worm Ouroboros, The See **E. R. Eddison**

'Worms of the Earth' See **Robert E. Howard**
Worse Things Waiting See **Manly Wade Wellman**

Xelucha Story and collection by **M. P. Shiel**

'Yellow Sign, The' See **Robert W. Chambers**
'Yellow Wallpaper, The' A noted macabre story by Charlotte Perkins
   Gilman
'Young Goodman Browne' See **Nathaniel Hawthorne**
'Yours Truly, Jack the Ripper' See **Robert Bloch**

APPENDIX II

Selected weird fiction anthologies
(Note: an asterisk (*) before a title indicates the volume is predominantly (over 50%) new fiction.)

At Close of Eve (1947; 22s) ed. Jeremy Scott UK
Contains all new stories including D. K. Haynes' 'Thou Shalt Not Suffer a Witch', W. Sansom's 'Crabfroth' and Frank Baker's 'Art Thou Languid?' Daniel George provides an informative introduction
Avon Fantasy Reader ed. George Ernsberger US
Two selections (1968; 7s: 1969; 9s) from the magazine of that name featuring chiefly the non-Conan fantasies of R. E. Howard and, of importance, A. Blackwood's 'A Victim of Higher Space', C. L. Moore's 'Shambleau' and D. Wandrei's 'The Painted Mirror'
Berserkers, The (1974; 15s) ed. Roger Elwood US
An all-new selection including D. Gerrold's 'Skinflowers' about a man who wakes to find flowers growing from his skin, and Barry Malzberg's 'Trial of the Blood' about a madman's descent into vampirism. Also fiction from A. Cole, J. Blish, D. Castell, R. A. Lafferty and others
Best Horror Stories UK
A three-volume series edited first by J. K. Cross (1956; 16s: 1965; 15s) and then by Alex Hamilton (1972; 16s). Most stories are readily available elsewhere, although No. 3 includes R. Chetwynd-Hayes' new 'Housebound' and T. F. Powys's all-too seldom seen 'The Hunted Beast'
Beware the Beasts (1970; 10s) ed. Vic Ghidalia & Roger Elwood US
A good selection about terrifying animals including the oft-seen 'The Wendigo' by Blackwood, 'The Mark of the Beast' by Kipling and Poe's 'Metzengerstein', plus the lesser-known 'The Tortoise-shell Cat' by Greye La Spina and 'The House of the Nightmare' by E. L. White. A follow-up volume was *Beware more Beasts* (1975; 7s) which included new fiction by E. D. Hoch, B. N. Malzberg and T. N. Scortia plus a lead novel 'Wolves of Darkness' by J. Williamson, Hodgson's 'Crew of the *Lancing*' and Derleth's 'Beyond the Threshold'
Beware of the Cat (1972; 13s) ed. Michel Parry UK
New and reprinted weird tales about cats including Blackwood's 'Ancient Sorceries' and pieces by R. Campbell, J. S. Le Fanu, T. Sturgeon and B. Pain
Beyond (1963; 9s) ed. Thomas A. Dardis US
A selection of stories from that magazine including Sturgeon's 'Talent', F. Pohl's 'The Ghost Maker' and W. Marks, 'I'd Give a Dollar'. All the stories are highly readable and enjoyable

Black Cap, The (1928; 14s) ed. **Cynthia Asquith**. See *Century of Creepy Stories Book of the Werewolf* (1973; 13s) ed. **Brian J. Frost UK**

Frost provides a thorough survey of the werewolf theme in fiction plus some lesser-known items by **H. W. Munn, S. Quinn, A. Merritt** and **E. O'Donnell** plus **C. Housman's** 'The Were Wolf' complete. Peter Fleming's 'The Kill' has yet another airing

Book of Unknown Tales of Horror (1976; 12s) ed. **Peter Haining UK**

The first of an intended series featuring stories not previously seen in paperback. It highlights **Bram Stoker's** 'The Crystal Cup' which will also be found in *Land of the Unseen* (q.v.) while the other selections are not especially unobtainable. A good buy for the beginner

Century of Creepy Stories, A (1934;70s) **UK**

An anonymous compilation that reprints the contents of *The Black Cap, The Ghost Book, Shudders* and *When Churchyards Yawn* with changes. Includes most of the noted stories by **L. P. Hartley**, plus others by **A. Machen, B. Lowndes, Hu. Walpole, M. R. James, S. Leslie** and **O. Onions**. Hugh Walpole assembled *A Second Century of Creepy Stories* (1937; 27s), a more considered selection including **J. Metcalfe's** 'Mortmain', 'Change' by **A. Machen** and well-known stories by **Le Fanu, Bierce, Blackwood** and **O. Onions**

Century of Horror, A (1935; 52s) ed. **Dennis Wheatley UK**

Includes most of the standard horror stories such as **Blackwood's** 'Ancient Sorceries', **Mrs Oliphant's** 'The Open Door' and **M. R. James's** 'The Treasure of Abbot Thomas', but also a good balance of lesser-known items including 'Lazarus Returns' by **G. Endore**, 'The Canary' by **F. T. Jesse**, 'The Ghoul' by **Sir Hugh Clifford** and 'The House With the Echo' by **T. F. Powys**. Wheatley later made two paperback selections from the volume, *Quiver of Horror* (1964; 15s) and *Shafts of Fear* (1964; 19s) which included several of the lesser-known items, plus new stories by **Charles Birkin**. Wheatley has since made use of further selections for his *Uncanny Tales* series

Circus of Dr Lao and Other Improbable Stories, The (1956; 12s) ed. **Ray Bradbury US**

Besides the title story by **C. G. Finney** this volume presents a good selection of lesser-known fantasies such as 'The Wish' by **R. Dahl**, 'The Summer People' by **S. Jackson** and 'The Man Who Vanished' by **R. M. Coates**

Clans of Darkness, The (1971; 21s) ed. **Peter Haining UK**

A selection of weird stories set in Scotland though not necessarily by Scots writers. Ranges from early thirteenth-century legends through the middle writers like **W. Scott** (here with the revised version of 'Wandering Willie's Tale') and **R. L. Stevenson**, to modern writers like **A. Blackwood** 'The Wolves of God', **J. K. Cross** 'Music When Soft Voices Die', and **A. Hamilton** with a new story 'Dead Men Walk'

Cold Embrace, The (1966; 18s) ed. **Alex Hamilton UK**

Stories by women writers, including title story by M. E. Braddon, 'The Lottery' S. Jackson, 'Akin to Love' C. Brand, 'The Doom of the Griffiths' E. Gaskell, 'John Charrington's Wedding' E. Nesbit, and others

Cold Fear: New Tales of Terror (1977; 15s) ed. Hugh Lamb UK
All new stories including 'Laura' R. Aickman, 'Dinner in a Private Room' C. Birkin, 'Aunty Green' J. Blackburn, 'In the Bag' and 'After the Queen' R. Campbell, 'The Demon in the Stone' A. Cole, 'The House in the Forest' F. Cowles, 'In the Glow Zone' B. Lumley, 'The Man Who Wouldn't Eat' A. Porges, 'The Darkhouse-keeper' R. Timperley

Craft of Terror, The (1966; 15s) ed. Peter Haining UK
Except for Poe's 'Metzengerstein' these are all extracts from Gothic novels such as *The Monk* M. G. Lewis, *The Castle of Otranto* Ho. Walpole, *Vathek* W. Beckford, *Melmoth* C. Maturin and *Varney the Vampire* M. Rymer

Creeps A series edited by Charles Birkin UK
The volumes ran as follows: *Creeps* (1932; 9s), *Shivers* (1932; 9s), *Shudders* (1932; 11s), *Horrors* (1933; 12s), *Nightmares* (1933; 12s), *Quakes* (1933; 13s), *Terrors* (1933; 11s), *Monsters* (1934; 12s), *Panics* (1934; 12s), *Powers of Darkness* (1934; 10s), *Thrills* (1935; 14s), *Tales of Fear* (1935; 12s), *Tales of Dread* (1936; 9s) and *Tales of Death* (1936; 11s). The first three volumes, which were mostly reprint and consisted of stories by H. R. Wakefield, T. Robbins, E. O'Donnell and Birkin, were combined as *The Creeps Omnibus* (1935; 29s) and is excellent value. All the later books were predominantly new fiction and contained worthy pieces by F. Cowles 'The Headless Leper', V. Meik 'The Two Old Women', E. R. Morrough 'The Temple Servant' plus Oswell Blakeston and J. R. Warren

Creeps by Night (1931; 20s) ed. Dashiell Hammett US
An excellent selection for its time, though many of the stories, such as J. Collier's 'Green Thoughts', W. Faulkner's 'A Rose For Emily', P. Fleming's 'The Kill' and H. P. Lovecraft's 'The Music of Erich Zann' are readily available today. Also included are 'The House' A. Maurois, 'The Spider' H. H. Ewers, and I. S. Cobb's 'Faith, Hope and Charity'. The UK 1932 edition was entitled *Modern Tales of Horror*; paperback selections have been *Creeps By Night, The Red Brain* and *Breakdown*

Crimes, Creeps and Thrills (1936; 45s) ed. John Gawsworth UK
New stories of note include 'The Shadow' E. H. Visiak, 'The Uncharted Island' Visiak & Gawsworth, 'The House Opposite' O. Blakeston, 'The Announcement' N. Barker and 'The Shifting Growth' E. Jepson & Gawsworth. Also several by E. H. W. Meyerstein

Dark Mind, Dark Heart (1962; 17s) ed. August Derleth US
New stories include the first by R. Campbell, 'The Church in the High

Street', W. H. Hodgson's 'The Habitants of Middle Islet', J. Metcalfe's 'The Firing Chamber', a revised 'Xélucha' by M. P. Shiel, and others by R. Bloch, J. P. Brennan, R. E. Howard, H. P. Lovecraft and H. R. Wakefield

Dark Things (1971; 24s) ed. **August Derleth** US
Derleth's last anthology with new stories including 'Appointment With Fire' **H. R. Wakefield**, 'The Case of the Double Husband' **M. Lawrence**, 'The Elevator' **J. Wade**, 'The Funny Farm' **R. Bloch**, 'The Knocker at the Portico' **B. Copper**, and 'The Storm-King' **E. Petaja**

Death's Loving Arms (1966; 5s) ed. **John Hanlon** US
Stories selected from the terror pulp *Terror Tales*

Disciples of Cthulhu, The (1976; 9s) ed. **E. Paul Berglund** US
All new stories based on the Cthulhu Mythos with contributions by **B. Lumley, F. Leiber, E. C. Bertin, J. Wade, L. Carter, R. Campbell, J. P. Brennan**

Discoveries in Fantasy (1972; 7s) ed. **Lin Carter** US
A selection of long stories including 'The Vision of Yin' **E. Bramah**, 'The City of Philosophers' **R. Garnett**, 'The Bird With the Golden Beak' **D. Corley** and 'The Miniature' **E. Phillpotts**

Dragons, Elves, and Heroes (1969; 14s) ed. **Lin Carter** US
Extracts from legends, epic poems and ancient sagas such as *Beowulf*, *The Volsunga Saga*, *The Mabinogion*, *The Grettir Saga*, *Morte d'Arthur*, *The Faerie Queen* and *The Shah-Namah*

European Tales of Terror (1968; 11s) ed. **J. J. Strating** UK
One of the more researched of these *Tales* series, including only two oft-printed stories: 'Who Knows?' **G. de Maupassant** and 'Vampires Ltd' **J. Nesvadba**. Other contents by Belcampo, D. Buzzati, J. Cortázar, F. Kafka, A. Schnitzler and others, with notes by the editor

Evil People, The (1968; 13s) ed. **Peter Haining** UK
A balanced selection of stories of witchcraft and voodoo with the best known being 'Secret Worship' **Blackwood** and 'The Snake' **Wheatley**. There is an extract from W. H. Ainsworth's *Lancashire Witches* and noted stories by **W. B. Seabrook, R. Bloch, A. Derleth, B. Copper, A. J. Burks** and **S. Jackson** among others

Fantastic Pulps (1975; 21s) ed. **Peter Haining** UK
Interlinked within a brief history of the pulp magazines is a good selection of stories, both horror and sf, many of which will be familiar to fans of **Sam Moskowitz** who has resurrected several of these on earlier occasions. Of note are J. London's 'A Thousand Deaths', M. Brand's 'John Ovington Returns', 'The Man With the Glass Heart' G. A. England, 'The Wolf Woman' H. Bedford-Jones, 'A Cry From Beyond' V. Rousseau, 'The Tree of Life' C. L. Moore and 'The Sea Shell' R. Bradbury. There is also a brief illustrated section

Fantastic Swordsmen, The (1967; 8s) ed. **L. Sprague de Camp** US
Several of these heroic fantasies are now easily available, such as the

R. E. Howard and H. P. Lovecraft items and Moorcock's 'The Singing Citadel' which first appeared here, but less available are J. Jakes's 'The Girl in the Gem', R. Bloch's 'Black Lotus' and H. Kuttner's 'Dragon Moon'

Far Below and Other Horrors (1974; 11s) ed. Robert Weinberg US
A good selection of lesser-known pieces including the title story by R. B. Johnson, 'Thing of Darkness' G. G. Pendarves, 'The Accursed Isle' M. E. Counselman, 'Out of the Deep' R. E. Howard and 'The Chapel of Mystic Horror' S. Quinn

Fiend in You, The (1962; 16s) ed. Charles Beaumont US
A first-class selection of psychological horror stories, new and reprint, including 'Mute' R. Matheson, 'The Thirteenth Step' F. Leiber, 'Lucy Comes to Stay' R. Bloch, 'The Women' R. Bradbury and 'Fool's Mate' S. Ellin

*Flashing Swords! A sword and sorcery series ed. Lin Carter US
Each volume consists of specially written stories by members of the select group SAGA (The Swordsmen and Sorcerer's Guild of America). No. 1 (1973; 4s), No. 2 (1974; 4s) had stories by L. Carter, P. Anderson, L. S. de Camp, J. Jakes, F. Leiber, M. Moorcock, A. Norton, J. Vance. No. 3 (1976; 5s) titled *Warriors and Wizards* added A. Davidson, and No. 4 (1977; 5s), *Barbarians and Black Magicians*, adds K. Kurtz

Fontana Book of Great Ghost Stories, The UK
An annual series started in 1964. Volumes 1 to 8 ed. Robert Aickman, Volume 9 onwards by R. Chetwynd-Hayes. Aickman's selection was impeccable, and while many of the stories are available elsewhere this series forms an excellent introduction for the newcomer and harbours some good finds as well. The series has deteriorated slightly under Chetwynd-Hayes with a greater variation in quality. Nevertheless they are frequently reprinted and are a useful addition to any collection. Volume 12 appeared in 1976

Fontana Book of Great Horror Stories, The UK
An annual series started in 1966. Volumes 1 to 4 ed. Christine Bernard, Volume 5 onwards by Mary Danby. As with the Ghost series many of these stories are also readily available but they form a cohesive whole in this series and serve as a good introduction to a wide variety of authors. Recent volumes have contained a higher percentage of new fiction and this serves to encourage new writers

*Frighteners ed. Mary Danby UK
A series of all new stories in the *Great Horror* series style. Includes new fiction by S. J. Bounds, R. Chetwynd-Hayes, A. Cole, R. F. Dunkley, B. Fortey, D. K. Haynes, M. Ricketts, B. Taylor and P. Vincent. No. 1 (1974; 17s), No. 2 (1976; 15s)

*Frights (1976; 14s) ed. Kirby McCauley US
A selection of all new stories from R. Aickman, P. Anderson, R. Bloch,

R. Campbell, D. Drake, D. Etchison, D. Grubb, J. Jakes, R. Kirk, B. Lumley, W. F. Nolan, G. Wilson and others
Full Score (1933; 26s) ed. T. I. Fytton Armstrong (J. Gawsworth) UK
Includes of special interest 'The Chemise of Margarita Pareja' L. Hearn, 'A Wonderful Woman' A. Machen, 'Innocence' H. E. Bates, 'A Suet Pudding' T. F. Powys and 'Above the River' J. Gawsworth
Gentlewomen of Evil, The (1967; 13s) ed. Peter Haining UK
A well-balanced selection of fiction by Victorian women. The best known are Mrs Oliphant's 'The Open Door' and A. B. Edwards' 'The Phantom Coach'. Rarer items are 'The Ghost' H. Wood, 'The Lifted Veil' M. A. Evans, 'Sandy the Tinker' Mrs Riddell, 'Eyes of Terror' L. T. Meade and 'At the Dip of the Road' Mrs Molesworth
Ghost Book, The UK
Now a regular series, but initially an occasional selection by Lady C. Asquith (Nos. 1 to 3). Continued by James Turner (No. 4), Rosemary Timperley (Nos. 5 to 9) and Aidan Chambers (No. 10 on). The contents are nearly all new, the first volume (1926; 16s) now recognised for its many classic contents including 'Chemical' A. Blackwood, 'A Recluse' W. de la Mare, 'A Visitor From Down Under' L. P. Hartley, 'The Rocking-Horse Winner' D. H. Lawrence, 'The Duenna' M. B. Lowndes, 'Munitions of War' A. Machen and 'Mrs Lunt' Hu. Walpole. A regular feature of the series until his death was the fiction of L. P. Hartley which will be found in volumes 1 to 9 except No. 4. The modern series commenced with No. 4 (1965; 23s) and since then the leading contributors have been R. Aickman, J. Aiken, D. V. Baker, G. M. Brown, J. Burke, R. Davis, E. Fancett, D. K. Haynes, M. Ross, S. Smith, P. Tabori, R. Timperley, W. Trevor, J. Turner and W. Wilkinson. Volumes 10 and 11 were paperbound as *The Bumper Book of Ghost Stories* (1976; 28s)
Ghostly by Gaslight (1971; 11s) ed. Sam Moskowitz US
A selection of forgotten items from magazines of long-ago, including 'The Story of a Ghost' V. Hunt, 'The Man Who Lived Backwards' A. Upward, 'The Mystery of the Bronze Statue' W. B. Sutton, 'The Enchanted City' H. Murray, and 'The Spider of Guyana' Erckmann-Chatrian. It is interesting to compare this translation of the last story with that included by H. Lamb in *The Taste of Fear*
Ghoul Keepers, The (1961; 9s) ed. Leo Margulies US
Stories selected from *Weird Tales* including 'The Sorcerer's Apprentice' R. Bloch, 'The Lake' R. Bradbury, 'When the Night Wind Howls' de Camp & Pratt, 'The Isle of the Sleeper' E. Hamilton, 'Spawn of Dagon' H. Kuttner, 'Clair de Lune' S. Quinn, and 'The Martian and the Moron' T. Sturgeon
Ghouls, The (1971; 18s) ed. Peter Haining UK
Stories behind the classic horror films, such as 'The Devil and Daniel Webster' S. V. Benét, 'Incident at Owl Creek' A. Bierce, 'The Skull'

R. Bloch, 'Most Dangerous Game' R. Connell, 'The Viy' N. Gogol, 'The Magician' W. S. Maugham, and 'Spurs' T. Robbins. Also readily available stories by R. Bradbury, W. F. Harvey, N. Hawthorne, G. Langelaan, H. P. Lovecraft, R. L. Stevenson and B. Stoker

Golden Cities, Far (1970; 13s) ed. **Lin Carter US**
Extracts from ancient myths, legends and recent imitations. Includes: *Book of Thoth, Arabian Nights, Tales of the Genii, Huon of Bordeaux, Amadis of Gaul, Orlando Furioso*, and fiction by A. France, Voltaire and Mdm. d'Aulnoy

Great British Tales of Terror (1972; 30s) ed. **Peter Haining UK**
Gothic tales from the period 1765–1840. Includes 'Sir Bertrand' A. L. Aikin, 'The Spectre Bride' W. H. Ainsworth, 'The Nymph of the Fountain' W. Beckford, 'The Burial' Byron, 'The Expedition to Hell' J. Hogg, 'The Water Spectre' F. Lathom, 'The Ghost and the Bone-Setter' J. S. Le Fanu, 'The Anaconda' M. G. Lewis, 'Glenallon' Lytton, 'Leixlip Castle' C. Maturin, 'The Vampyre' J. Polidori, 'The Demon of the Hartz' T. P. Prest, 'The Haunted Chamber' A. Radcliffe, 'Maddalena' Ho. Walpole, and many other rare items. An excellent collection with comprehensive notes

Great Short Novels of Adult Fantasy Series ed. **Lin Carter US**
An excellent selection of delightful fantasies
Vol. I (1972; 4s) 'The Maker of Moons' R. W. Chambers, 'Wall of Serpents' de Camp & Pratt, 'The Kingdom of the Dwarves' A. France, 'The Hollow Land' W. Morris
Vol. II (1973; 4s) 'The Transmutation of Ling' E. Bramah, 'The Repairer of Reputations' R. W. Chambers, 'The Woman in the Mirror' G. Macdonald, 'The Lavender Dragon' E. Phillpotts

Great Short Stories of Detection, Mystery and Horror UK
A series edited by **Dorothy L. Sayers** known in US editions as *The Omnibus of Crime*. Each volume had a specific horror section
1st Series (1929; 26s) Subdivided into *Tales of Ghosts and Hauntings*: all well-known stories except for 'Martin's Close' M. R. James; *Tales of Magic & Witchcraft*: Again all well-known stories such as 'Mrs Amworth' E. F. Benson and 'The Monkey's Paw' W. W. Jacobs but also 'The Brute' J. Conrad and 'The Hair' A. J. Alan; *Tales of Nightmare and the Borderland of the Mind*: well-known tales like 'Green Tea' Le Fanu and 'The Seventh Man' Quiller-Couch plus 'The Bad Lands' J. Metcalfe and 'Nobody's House' A. M. Burrage
2nd Series (1931; 42s) Includes several less well-known items like 'No. 17' E. Nesbit, 'The Tree' W. de la Mare, 'The Prayer' V. Hunt, 'The Well' W. W. Jacobs, 'The Resurgent Mysteries' E. Jepson, 'The Double Admiral' J. Metcalfe, 'The Enemy' Hu. Walpole, plus an array of known classics
3rd Series (1934; 35s) A further combination of known classics and

rarer items like 'A Jungle Graduate' **J. F. Dwyer**, 'Double Demon'
W. F. Harvey, 'The Interruption' **W. W. Jacobs**, 'Time-Fuse'
J. Metcalfe, 'The Hill' **R. E. Roberts**, 'The Frontier Guards' **H. R.
Wakefield** and 'The Idol with Hands of Clay' **F. Treves**
While the bulk of the items will be known to devotees, when first issued
these volumes, with the weight of Miss Sayers' name, helped introduce
many people to some of the greatest writing in horror
Great Tales of Terror from Europe and America (1972; 30s) ed. **Peter
Haining** UK
A companion to the *Great British* volume, selecting more Gothic Tales
from the period 1765 to 1840. Most are very scarce items. They include
Germany: 'The New Melusina' **Goethe**, 'The Ghost-Seer' **von
Schiller**, 'The Bride of the Grave' **L. Tieck**, 'The Field of Terror'
La M. Fouque, 'The Cremona Violin' **E. T. A. Hoffman**; *France:*
'The Witch of Eye' **D'Arnaud**, 'The Wandering Jew' extract **E. Sue**;
America: 'Rip van Winkle', 'The German Student' **W. Irving**,
'Carwin the Biloquist' **C. B. Brown**, 'The Christmas Banquet'
N. Hawthorne, 'Hugues, the Wer-Wolf' **S. Menzies**, 'Ben Blower's
Story' **C. F. Hoffman**, 'The Cask of Amontillado' **Poe**
Great Untold Stories of Horror and Fantasy (1969; 11s) US
Credited to both **Alden H. Norton** & **Sam Moskowitz** it is entirely the
work of the latter. Little known items like 'A Study in Destiny' **L. de
Hamong**, 'The Mysterious Card' **C. Moffett**, 'The Black Statue' **H.
Mee** and 'The Seal of Solomon the Great' **W. A. Curtis**, plus 'The
Messenger' **R. W. Chambers**, 'The Monster-Maker' **W. C. Morrow**,
'"Man Overboard!"' **W. Churchill**, and others
Hauntings and Horrors (1969; 10s) ed. **Alden H. Norton** US
Also solely the work of **Sam Moskowitz** it includes 'The Delusion of
Ralph Penwyn' **J. Hawthorne**, 'It Burns Me Up!' **R. Bradbury**,
'Head Man' **R. Bloch**, 'The Albatross' **W. H. Hodgson**, 'The Soul of
Mozart' **W. E. P. French**, and more.
Hell Hath Fury (1963; 7s) ed. George Hay UK
Stories selected from *Unknown* featuring the title novel by Cleve Cartmill,
plus 'The Bleak Shore' **F. Leiber**, 'The Frog' **P. S. Miller**, 'The
Devil's Rescue' **L. R. Hubbard**, 'The Cloak' **R. Bloch** and others
Horror Times Ten (1967; 10s) US
Horrors in Hiding (1973; 10s) US
Horrors Unknown (1971; 11s) US
All these are edited by **Sam Moskowitz** although the first is credited to
Alden Norton and the second co-credited. Again fine selections of
little-known items. The first includes 'The Trunk Lady' **R. Bradbury**,
'Cool Air' **H. P. Lovecraft**, 'That Receding Brow' **M. Brand**, 'His
Unconquerable Enemy' **W. C. Morrow**, and others. The second in-
cludes 'Two Shall Be Born' **S. Quinn**, 'Tell Your Fortune' **R. Bloch**,
'Time to Kill' **H. Kuttner**, 'Alannah' **A. Derleth**, 'Luana the Living'

R. Bradbury, 'The Door of Unrest' O. Henry, 'Thurlow's Ghost Story' J. K. Bangs and others. The third features the round-robin story 'The Challenge From Beyond' written by C. L. Moore, A. Merritt, H. P. Lovecraft, R. E. Howard and F. B. Long. Also included 'From Hand to Mouth' F.-J. O'Brien, both versions of 'The Pendulum' R. Bradbury, 'The Pool of the Stone God' W. Fenimore (believed to be a pen-name of A. Merritt) and many more

Horrors Unseen (1974; 9s) ed. **Sam Moskowitz** US
An important volume as it not only includes the whole of **W. H. Hodgson**'s *The Ghost Pirates* but also its original ending, and 'The Ship that Saw a Ghost' F. Norris, that might have inspired it. Other contents by **R. Bradbury, R. W. Chambers, J. Hilton, L. Housman, C. L. Moore**

Jack the Knife (1975: 10s) ed. **Michel Parry** UK
A fine selection of stories about Jack the Ripper including the original version of M. B. Lowndes' 'The Lodger', 'The Demon Spell' H. Nisbet, 'My Father the Ripper' P. J. Farmer plus new stories by J. F. Pumilia and **R. Campbell**

Land of the Unseen, The (1973; 7s) ed. **George Locke** UK
A limited-edition collection selected from rare Victorian periodicals. Includes 'The Crystal Cup' B. Stoker, 'The Spendid Dead' E. L. Arnold, 'The Pale Lady' A. Dumas, plus others with the title story by E. Favenc

Magic Valley Travellers, The (1974; 23s) ed. **Peter Haining** UK
Welsh tales of fantasy and horror. Contains many early legends and myths with more recent contents 'The Chronic Argonauts' H. G. Wells, 'The Gift of Tongues' A. Machen, 'The Coffin' C. Evans, 'The Sabbath' C. Williams, 'The Dark Isle' R. Bloch and others

Magicians, The (1972; 12s) ed. **Peter Haining** UK
Stories by writers who have been involved personally with the occult. Includes an extract from *Là-Bas* J.-K. Huysmans, 'The Story of the mystical' H. Blavatsky, 'An experiment in Necromancy' A. Crowley, 'Breath of Allah' S. Rohmer, 'With Intent to Steal' A. Blackwood and other items by E. Levi, A. C. Doyle, D. Fortune, L. Spence, G. Gardner and W. B. Yeats

Man who Called Himself Poe, The (1969; 11s) ed. **Sam Moskowitz** US
Stories and articles about Poe, plus pieces by Poe and verse. A clever collection including 'My Adventure with Edgar Allan Poe' J. Hawthorne, 'In Which an Author and His Character Are Well Met' V. Starrett, 'When It Was Moonlight' M. W. Wellman, 'The Man Who Collected Poe' R. Bloch, 'The Man Who Thought He Was Poe' M. Avallone and many other rare items

Mandrake Root (1946; 28s) ed. **Jeremy Scott** UK
A mixture of new and reprint fiction including lesser-known items like 'Everlasting Fire' J. Joyce, 'Changeling' D. K. Haynes, 'The Last Laugh' D. H. Lawrence and 'The Bell of Saint Euschemon' R. Garnett.

A bibliography of other stories is provided

Masterpiece of Thrills (1936; 60s) ed. **John Gawsworth** UK

Another compendium of mostly new stories including 'Death's Door' **N. Barker**, 'Sluice Gates' **O. Blakeston**, 'The Failure' **R. Middleton**, 'In the Mangrove Hall' **E. H. Visiak** and three collaborations between **Gawsworth** and **M. P. Shiel**

Masters of Horror (1968; 9s) ed. **Alden H. Norton** US

Ghost-edited by **Sam Moskowitz** this volume includes 'The Were-Wolf' **C. Housman**, 'Before I Wake' **H. Kuttner**, 'The Candy Skull' **R. Bradbury**, plus better-known items like 'Dracula's Guest' **B. Stoker**, 'The Yellow Sign' **R. W. Chambers**, 'Blind Man's Buff' **H. R. Wakefield** and 'The Women of the Wood' **A. Merritt**, all encompassed by **Moskowitz**'s copious notes

Mayflower Book of Black Magic Stories, The Series ed. **Michel Parry** UK

Volumes include a mixture of new and reprint fiction with the following highlights:

1st (1974; 13s) 'Potential' **R. Campbell**, 'The Vixen' **A. Crowley**, 'The Hand of Glory' **S. Quinn**

2nd (1974; 12s) 'The Sanctuary' **E. F. Benson**, 'The Violinist' **A. Crowley**, 'The Witch-Finder' **F. Cowles**, 'The Necromancers' **M. Bowen**, 'The Children of Ubasti' **S. Quinn**

3rd (1975; 12s) 'Black Magic' **S. Horler**, 'Borgia Pomade' **M. P. Dare**, 'The Cave of Echoes' **H. Blavatsky**, 'Instrument of Darkness' **J. F. Pumilia**, 'The Incense of Abomination' **S. Quinn**

4th (1976; 9s) 'There Shall Be No Darkness' **J. Blish**, 'Blood Debt' **D. Drake**, 'Vigil' **M. W. Wellman**, 'Dolls' **R. Campbell**

5th (1976; 8s) 'The House on the Marsh' **F. Cowles**, 'Hell is Forever' **A. Bester**, 'Lilith's' **R. Campbell**, 'Nellthu' **A. Boucher**

Mighty Barbarians, The (1969; 5s) ed. **Hans Stefan Santesson** US

Mighty Swordsman, The (1970; 6s) ed. **Hans Stefan Santesson** US

Two companion heroic fantasy anthologies. The first includes a new Thongor story, 'Thieves of Zangabal', by **L. Carter**, plus reprints items by **F. Leiber**, **L. S. de Camp**, **H. Kuttner** and **R. E. Howard**. The second features another new Thongor story, 'Keeper of the Emerald Flame', plus a new Conan story 'The People of the Summit' by **B. Nyberg**. Also reprints from **R. Zelazny**, **J. Brunner**, **M. Moorcock** and **R. E. Howard** (another Conan tale)

Mind at Bay (1970; 10s) ed. **Dr Christopher Evans** UK

Mind in Chains (1970; 14s) ed. **Dr Christopher Evans** UK

Two notable anthologies in which Dr Evans applies his formidable knowledge of the inner workings of the mind in selecting stories that explore fear. Apart from a few new stories (by writers like **A. Hamilton**) most of the selections are fairly well-known pieces (such as 'No Ships Pass' **Lady E. Smith**) but all gain a new dimension with the insight of Dr Evans's informative and instructive introductions

My Grimmest Nightmare (1935; 22s) ed. Lady **Cynthia Asquith** UK
Includes 'The Follower' **C. Asquith**, 'By Water' **A. Blackwood**, 'Incubus' **M. Bowen**, 'Serenade for Baboons' **N. Langley**, 'The Blackmailers' **A. Blackwood**
New Tales of Horror (1934; 30s) ed. **John Gawsworth** UK
Includes 17 new stories, and among its most noted contents are 'The Lost Club' **A. Machen**, 'The Amazing Hieroglyphs' **R. Middleton**, 'Medusan Madness' **E. H. Visiak**, 'Scylla and Charybdis' **J. Gawsworth**, 'Murderers' Corner' **C. Duff**, plus **M. P. Shiel, N. Barker, E. H. W. Meyerstein** and others
New Worlds for Old (1971; 15s) ed. Lin Carter US
Not to be confused with A. Derleth's UK science fiction volume, this is a selection of fantasies ranging from 'The Romance of Photogen and Nycteris' **G. Macdonald** to 'The Feast in the House of the Worm' **G. Myers** and encompassing new and lesser known items by **W. Beckford, L. Carter, Dunsany, H. P. Lovecraft, R. E. Howard, C. L. Moore, M. Peake** and more
New Writings in Horror & the Supernatural UK
Series ed. **Dave Sutton**, the third volume of which appeared as *The Satyr's Head*
Vol. 1 (1971; 13s) Includes 'The Time of Waiting' **R. Davis**, 'The Inglorious Rise of the Catsmeat Man' **R. Smyth**, 'Phantasmagoria' **W. T. Webb**, 'Broadcast' **R. Campbell**, 'The Winner' **E. C. Tubb** and more
Vol. 2 (1972; 10s) Includes 'A Bottle of Spirits' **D. Riley**, 'Television Wife' **W. T. Webb**, 'Grooley' **J. Wade**, 'Demoniacal' **D. Sutton**, 'The Ghosts in the Garden' **R. Timperley**, 'Marianne's Boy' **E. Fancett**, 'The Other House' **R. Campbell**
Night Chills (1975; 18s) ed. Kirby McCauley US
A mixture of new and reprint fiction including 'At Midnight, in the Month of June' **R. Bradbury**, 'A: B: O' **W. de la Mare**, 'The Jugular Man' **J. P. Brennan**, 'Alice and the Allergy' **F. Leiber**, 'Yesterday's Witch' **G. Wilson**, 'Call First' **R. Campbell**, 'The Face in the Wind' **C. Jacobi**, 'Sticks', **K. E. Wagner** and more. An excellent selection
Night Side, The (1946; 23s) ed. **August Derleth** US
The UK paperback deleted four stories from the original but retained a good selection of fairly rare items (except **Lovecraft**'s 'The Colour Out of Space') including 'The First Sheaf' **H. R. Wakefield**, 'Mr Minchin's Midsummer' **M. Lawrence**, 'The Three Marked Pennies' **M. E. Counselman**, 'The Night Wire' **H. F. Arnold**, 'The Eerie Mr Murphy' **H. Wandrei** and others
Night's Yawning Peal (1952; 15s) ed. **August Derleth** US
Includes 'Mr George' **S. Grendon (Derleth)**, 'The Loved Dead **C. M. Eddy**, 'The Sign' **Dunsany**, 'The Gorge of the Churels' **H. R**

Wakefield, 'Dhoh' M. W. Wellman, 'Hector' M. West (Derleth), 'Roman Remains' A. Blackwood, 'The Churchyard Yew' J. S. Le Fanu (so attributed but actually written by Derleth) and others. A well-balanced selection, especially for the Derleth fan!

Not at Night UK The title given to a series, ed. Christine Campbell Thomson, featuring both new and reprint items. The highlights are: *Not at Night* (1925; 15s) 'The Tortoise-Shell Cat' G. La Spina, 'Death-Waters' F. B. Long, 'The Third Thumb-Print' M. Levitan *More Not at Night* (1926; 15s) 'Bat's Belfry' A. Derleth, 'The Phantom Drug' A. W. Kapfer, 'The Mystery Under the Sea' D. Keyhoe, 'The Horror on the Links' S. Quinn

You'll Need a Night Light (1927; 15s) 'Si Urag of the Tail' O. Cook, 'The Coffin of Lissa' A. Derleth, 'The Horror at Red Hook' H. P. Lovecraft, 'The Girdle' J. McCord, 'The House of Horror' S. Quinn, 'Out of the Earth' F. Richardson (C. C. Thomson)

Gruesome Cargoes (1928; 15s) 'When Glister Walked' O. Cook, 'The Black Spider' E. Snell, 'When Hell Laughed' C. C. Thomson

By Daylight Only (1929; 20s) 'Bells of Oceana' A. J. Burks, 'Piecemeal' O. Cook, 'The Tenant' A. Derleth, 'The Copper Bowl' G. F. Eliot, 'Pickman's Model' H. P. Lovecraft, 'The Chain' H. W. Munn, 'The Trimmer' D. Newton, 'At Number Eleven' C. C. Thomson

Switch on the Light (1931; 15s) 'Boomerang' O. Cook, 'The Pacer' A. Derleth & M. Schorer, 'The Thought Monster' A. R. Long

At Dead of Night (1931; 15s) 'Four Doomed Men' G. Vace (H. B. Cave), 'His Beautiful Hands' O. Cook, 'Prince Borgia's Mass' A. Derleth, 'The Scourge of Mektoub' P. Ernst, 'The Seeds of Death' D. H. Keller, 'The Wonderful Tune' J. D. Kerruish, 'The Curse of the House of Phipps' S. Quinn, 'The Gray Killer' E. Worrell

Grim Death (1932; 15s) 'The Great White Fear' O. Cook, 'The Black Stone' R. E. Howard, 'Night and Silence' M. Level, 'The Thing in the Cellar' D. H. Keller, 'Helvellyn' R. Muspratt, 'The Inn' G. Preston

Keep on the Light (1933; 15s) 'Cult of the White Ape' H. B. Cave, 'The House of Shadows' M. E. Counselman, 'Golden Lilies' O. Cook, 'The Seven-Locked Room' J. D. Kerruish, 'Tiger dust' B. Morgan, 'Althorpe Abbey' R. Muspratt, 'The Chadbourne Episode' H. S. Whitehead

Terror by Night (1935; 15s) 'The Watcher in the Green Room' H. B. Cave, 'The Accursed Isle' M. E. Counselman, 'The Author's Tale' L. A. Lewis, 'Behind the Yellow Door' C. C. Thomson, 'The Closed Door' H. Ward

*Nightmare by Daylight (1936; 15s) 'The Flute of Seven Stops' D. Fortune, 'The Scream' H. Holland, 'The Dead Woman' D. H. Keller, 'The Gold of Hermodike' J. D. Kerruish

A selection from all these volumes appeared as *Not at Night Omnibus*

(1937; 35s); a US edition, ed. by Herbert Asbury, included selections from the first three volumes and appeared as *Not at Night!* (1928; 25s). Several subsequent paperback selections have been made under variant titles

*Over the Edge (1964; 18s) ed. **August Derleth** US
An all new volume including 'The North Knoll' **J. P. Brennan**, 'The Stone on the Island' **R. Campbell**, 'The Huaco of Señor Peréz' **M. E. Counselman**, 'The Crew of the *Lancing*' **W. H. Hodgson**, 'The Black Gondolier' **F. Leiber**, 'The Renegade' **J. Metcalfe**, and others by **H. R. Wakefield, C. A. Smith** etc.

Pan Book of Horror Stories, The Series ed. **Herbert van Thal** UK
The series began in 1959 (22s) and was initially reprint. A second volume appeared in 1960 (15s) and it became annual from 1962. New stories appeared with the 4th volume (1963; 19s) and became the bulk of the content from the 5th volume (1964; 19s) on. Although the early selections reflected the whole stratum of the horror field, most recent volumes have emphasised, nauseatingly so, the purely physical side of horror, some of the stories showing meagre literary merit. Nevertheless something good crops up in each volume, and it provides a good training ground for new writers. Contents are not listed here but important stories are identified in the body of the *Who's Who* thus *PH2 = Pan Book of Horror Stories* No. 2 (1960)

Perturbed Spirits (1954; 16s) ed. **Randolph C. Bull** UK
Noted reprint volume including 'Wolverden Tower' **G. Allen**, 'The Man With the Nose' **R. Broughton**, 'The Demoiselle D'Ys' **R. W. Chambers**, 'The Dead Valley' **R. A. Cram**, 'The Corpse Light' **D. Donovan**, 'The Invisible Eye' **Erckmann-Chatrian**, 'The Derelict' **W. R. Hodgson**, 'The Devil of the Marsh' **H. B. Marriott-Watson**, 'Mortmain' **J. Metcalfe**, 'The Haunted Station' **H. Nisbet**, 'The Lost Room' **F.-J. O'Brien**, 'Vera' **Villiers de L'Isle Adam**, 'The Fireplace' **H. S. Whitehead**

Playboy Book of Horror and the Supernatural (1967; 28s) US
Assembled by the editors of *Playboy* it includes 'Black Country' and 'Sorcerer's Moon' **C. Beaumont**, 'The Travelling Salesman' and 'Beelzebub' **R. Bloch**, 'Heavy Set' and 'The Life Work of Juan Diaz' **R. Bradbury**, 'Softly Walks the Beetle' **J. Collier**, 'Hey, Look at Me!' **J. Finney**, 'No Such Thing as a Vampire' **R. Matheson**, 'The Party' **W. F. Nolan**, 'Sardonicus' and 'Comet Wine' **R. Russell**, and 'The Sea Was Wet as Wet Could Be' and 'The Manuscript of Dr Arness' **G. Wilson**. A later volume derived from the same source was *Weird Show* (1971; 16s)

Return from the Grave (1976; 20s) ed. **Hugh Lamb** UK
Five new stories by **E. Bertin, R. Campbell, J. Blackburn, R. Haining** and **R. Timperley** plus noted reprints like 'The Tower of Moab' **L. A. Lewis**, 'In the Tomb' **A. Porges**, 'The Slype House'

A. C. Benson, 'The Coffin of Lissa' A. Derleth and 'At Simmel Acres Farm' E. Scott

*Satyr's Head, The (1975; 10s) ed. David Sutton UK
Features the title story by D. A. Riley, plus 'A Pentragram For Cenaide' E. C. Bertin, 'The Business About Fred' J. P. Brennan, 'The Previous Tenant' R. Campbell, 'Aunt Hester' B. Lumley, 'The Nightingale Floors' J. Wade

Seven Masterpieces of Gothic Horror (1963; 7s) ed. Robert D. Spector US
With useful notes this volume features The Castle of Otranto Ho. Walpole and The Old English Baron C. Reeve in entirety plus 'Mistrust' M. G. Lewis, 'The Heir of Mondolfo' M. Shelley, 'The White Old Maid' N. Hawthorne, 'The Fall of the House of Usher' E. A. Poe, 'Carmilla' J. S. Le Fanu

*Shudders (1929; 15s) ed. Lady C. Asquith UK
Noted contents include 'The Playfellow' C. Asquith, 'The Hanging of Alfred Wadham' E. F. Benson, 'The Stranger' A. Blackwood, 'The Travelling Grave' L. P. Hartley, 'Rats' M. R. James, 'The Cosy Room' A. Machen and more

Sorceress in Stained Glass, The (1971; 16s) ed. Richard Dalby UK
Noted for its inclusion of the unreprinted M. R. James story 'A Vignette'. Other reprints include the title story by L. Spence, 'The Other Bed' E. F. Benson, 'A Jug of Syrup' A. Bierce, 'Footprints' A. M. Burrage, 'The Story of the Moor Road' E. & H. Heron, 'The Stone Ship' W. H. Hodgson, 'The House Which was Rent Free' L. B. Reynolds

Spell of Seven, The (1965; 7s) ed. L. Sprague de Camp US
Sword and sorcery volume including 'The Dark Eidolon' C. A. Smith, 'The Hungry Hercynian' L. S. de Camp and now well-known pieces by F. Leiber, Dunsany, M. Moorcock, J. Vance and R. E. Howard

*Splinters (1968; 14s) ed. Alex Hamilton UK
All new stories by M. Baldwin, P. Brent, J. Brunner, A. Burgess, J. Burke, J. A. Cuddon, J. Gaskell, A. Hamilton, W. Trevor and others

Star Book of Horror Series ed. Hugh Lamb UK
A notable series including both new and rare reprinted fiction.
No. 1 (1975; 13s) Includes J. Blackburn's first short story 'Drink to Me Only' and other new stories by J. Burnett, F. Cowles, R. Campbell, R. Haining, plus reprints like 'Waiting For Trains' C. Birkin, 'The Thing in the Hall' E. F. Benson, 'A Christmas Game' A. N. L. Munby and 'Hands' J. K. Cross
No. 2 (1976; 15s) New stories by J. Blackburn, J. Burnett, B. Lumley, A. E. Ellis, R. Campbell plus reprints like 'Into Outer Darkness' H. R. Wakefield, 'One, Two, Buckle My Shoe' N. Barker and 'The Wrong Turning' R. Middleton

*Superhorror (1976; 8s) ed. Ramsey Campbell UK
All new stories by R. Aickman, R. Campbell, D. Castell, D. Drake, R. A. Lafferty, F. Leiber, B. Lumley, J. F. Pumilia

Supernatural Omnibus, The (1931; 38s) ed. **Montague Summers UK**
Still in print today this remains one of the standard horror volumes.
Besides a worthy introduction it contains a host of excellent fiction in-
cluding such lesser-known items as 'Brickett Bottom' **A. Northcote,**
'How the Third Floor Knew the Potteries' **A. B. Edwards,** 'The
Astrologer's Legacy' **R. Pater,** 'The Seeker of Souls' **J. John** and
other items by **R. H. Barham, E. & H. Heron, P. Landon, J. S. Le
Fanu, V. Lee, E. Nesbit** and others
Supernatural Solution, The (1976; 9s) ed. **Michel Parry UK**
Fictional investigations by occult detectives. Includes 'Green Tea' **J. S.
Le Fanu,** 'The Story of Yand Manor House' **E. & H. Heron,** 'The
Gateway of the Monster' **W. H. Hodgson,** 'The Warder of the Door'
L. T. Meade & R. Eustace, 'Blood-Lust' **D. Fortune,** 'The Shining
Pyramid' **A. Machen,** 'The Jest of Warburg Tantavul' **S. Quinn,**
'The Two Graves of Lill Warren' **M. W. Wellman,** 'The Case of the
Red-Headed Women' **D. Wheatley**
Swords and Sorcery (1963; 8s) ed. **L. Sprague de Camp US**
The first such compilation including 'The Valor of Cappen Varra
P. Anderson, 'The Citadel of Darkness' **H. Kuttner,** 'Hellsgarde'
C. L. Moore, and others by **Dunsany, R. E. Howard, F. Leiber,
H. P. Lovecraft, C. A. Smith**
Tales of the Cthulhu Mythos (1969; 19s) ed. **August Derleth US**
New and reprint fiction based on **Lovecraft's** mythos. The new stories
are by **J. V. Shea, R. Campbell, B. Lumley, J. Wade** and **C. Wilson**

Tandem Horror UK

The series was initiated as *The Tandem Book of Horror Stories* (1965; 11s)
ed. **Charles Birkin,** a good selection of reprints. It was continued by
Richard Davis as an all new series
No. 2 (1968; 13s) Stories by J. Birley, **R. Campbell, R. Davis,** E. Fan-
cett, M. Parry, D. E. Piper, R. Smyth, **R. Timperley** and others
No. 3 (1969; 9s) Tales by J. Birley, **J. Burke, R. Campbell,** D. Camp-
ton, **R. Davis,** E. Fancett, D. Piper, **R. Timperley**
*Taste of Fear, The (1976; 13s) ed. **Hugh Lamb UK**
New and reprint fiction. Includes the last stories by **L. T. C. Rolt** and
E. H. Visiak plus other new pieces from **F. Cowles, D. Sutton,**
M. Sims, J. Blackburn, **R. Campbell,** L. Freeman, R. Parkes.
Reprints include 'From the Tideless Sea' **W. H. Hodgson,** 'The
Uttermost Farthing' **A. C. Benson** and a new translation of 'The
Crab Spider' by **Erckmann-Chatrian** (see *Ghostly by Gaslight*)
Terror by Gaslight (1975; 14s) ed. **Hugh Lamb UK**
Victorian reprints such as 'The Beckoning Hand' **G. Allen,** 'Nothing But
the Truth' **R. Broughton,** 'A Dreadful Night' **E. L. Arnold,** 'The
House of Strange Stories' **A. Lang,** 'The Earth Draws' **J. Lie,** 'The

Wondersmith' F.-J. O'Brien, 'The Basilisk' R. M. Gilchrist and others

Terror in the Modern Vein (1955; 17s) ed. Donald A. Wollheim US
A noted reprint volume including 'The Dream Makers' R. Bloch, 'The Republic of the Southern Cross' V. Bryusov, 'Gone Away' A. E. Coppard, 'The Strange Case of Lemuel Jenkins' P. M. Fisher, 'They' R. A. Heinlein, 'Shipshape Home' R. Matheson, and 'Mimic' D. Wollheim

Thrill of Horror, The (1975; 21s) ed. Hugh Lamb UK
Noted for its inclusion of a hitherto unreprinted M. R. James story. Other reprints include 'Only a Dream' H. R. Haggard, 'The Meerschaum Pipe' L. A. Lewis, 'In the Mirror' V. Bryusov, 'A Night of Horror' D. Donovan, 'Eyes for the Blind' F. Cowles, 'Mr Ash's Studio' H. R. Wakefield, 'Pallinghurst Barrow' G. Allen, 'Medusan Madness' E. H. Visiak, 'Out of the Sea' A. C. Benson

*Thrills (c 1934; 20s) ed. John Gawsworth UK
Includes 'The Mysterious Fluid' O. Blakeston, 'The Golden Gong' T. Burke, 'The Haunted Bungalow' C. Duff, 'How it Happened' J. Gawsworth, 'An Accident' E. Jepson, 'The Cutting' E. H. Visiak
Thrills is also a title in the *Creeps* Library (see *Creeps*)

*Thrills, Crimes and Mysteries (c 1935; 63s) ed. John Gawsworth UK
A bumper volume including 'The Invalid' N. Barker, 'The Vivisector Vivisected' Sir R. Ross, 'The Gift of Tongues' A. Machen, 'The Purchester Instrument' M. P. Shiel, 'The Wrong Turning' R. Middleton, 'Rescued' E. H. Visiak, 'The Place of Pain' M. P. Shiel, 'Drake's Drum' A. Machen, 'A Suet Pudding' T. F. Powys, 'There Was a Man Dwelt By a Churchyard' M. R. James, 'The Legacy' E. H. Visiak, and many more

Tide of Terror, A (1972; 17s) ed. Hugh Lamb UK
Introduction by Peter Haining plus reprints like 'The Closed Window' A. C. Benson, 'The Step' E. F. Benson, 'Father Brent's Tale' R. H. Benson, 'Full Circle' A. Blackwood, 'The Tregannet Book of Hours' A. N. L. Munby, 'The Master of Hollow Grange' S. Rohmer, 'The Eyes' T. O. Beachcroft

*Times Anthology of Ghost Stories, The (1975; 13s) UK
Best entries in a competition judged by Kingsley Amis, Patricia Highsmith and Christopher Lee. First prize 'The Doll Named Silvio' M. Kernan, second 'A Scent of Mimosa' F. King, and commendations to 'Marius' F. T. Newman and 'The Locket' Sir L. Grafftey-Smith

*Travellers by Night (1967; 14s) ed. August Derleth US
All new stories from R. Aickman, J. P. Brennan, R. Campbell, M. E. Counselman, D. Drake, W. H. Hodgson, C. Jacobi, M. Lawrence, H. P. Lovecraft, J. Metcalfe, H. R. Wakefield, D. Wandrei and others

*Uncertain Element, The (1950; 14s) ed. Kay Dick UK

New and reprint fiction plus essays and recollections. Fiction includes
'Out of the Deep' W. de la Mare, 'Tyme Tryeth Troth' F. Baker,
'Enoch Soames' M. Beerbohm, 'The Jolly Corner' H. James, 'One
Sunny Afternoon' W. Sansom. Also includes a 'Bibliography of the
Fantastic'

Unexpected, The (1961; 11s) ed. Leo Margulies US
Stories selected from *Weird Tales* including 'The Strange Island of Dr
Nork' R. Bloch, 'The Scrawny One' A. Boucher, 'The Handler'
R. Bradbury, 'The Unwanted' M. E. Counselman, 'The Automatic
Pistol' F. Leiber, 'The Valley was Still' M. W. Wellman

Unknown, The (1963; 11s) ed. Don R. Bensen US
Stories selected from *Unknown*. Includes 'The Misguided Halo' H. Kutt-
ner, 'Yesterday was Monday' T. Sturgeon, 'The Gnarly Man' L. S. de
Camp, 'Trouble With Water' H. L. Gold, 'Mr Jinx' R. Arthur,
'Snulbug' A. Boucher
A second selection was made as *The Unknown 5* (1964; 5s) featuring the
hitherto unpublished 'Author! Author!' I. Asimov, plus reprints 'The
Bargain' C. Cartmill, 'The Hag Seleen' T. Sturgeon, 'Hell is Forever'
A. Bester and 'The Crest of the Wave' J. Rice

Vampires, Werewolves and Other Monsters (1974; 12s) ed. Roger Elwood
US
An all-new selection including 'Diary of a Werewolf' J. P. Brennan,
'Litter' R. Campbell, 'Cry Wolf' B. Copper, 'Problem Child'
B. Lumley, 'Inner Circle' B. N. Malzberg, 'Grimjank' W. T. Webb
and others. (Malzberg has four stories in this volume, two under
pseudonyms)

Victorian Nightmares (1977; 21s) ed. Hugh Lamb UK
Includes such reprints as 'A Bottomless Grave' A. Bierce, 'A Strange
Goldfield' G. Boothby, 'The Tomb' G. de Maupassant, 'The Three
Souls' Erckmann-Chatrian (first translation), 'The Haunted Chair'
R. Marsh, 'The Battle of the Monsters' M. Robertson, and a trio of
humorous ghost stories by J. K. Bangs, G. M. Fenn and J. K.
Snowden

Victorian Tales of Terror (1974; 15s) ed. Hugh Lamb UK
A good reprint selection including 'Xelucha' M. P. Shiel, 'The Black
Lady of Brin Tor' G. Boothby, 'The Mother of Monsters' G. de
Maupassant, 'The Murderer's Violin' Erckmann-Chatrian, 'The
Mask' R. Marsh, 'The Shadow in the Moonlight' Mrs Molesworth,
'The Red Warder of the Reef' J. A. Barry, 'Wolverden Tower'
G. Allen and 'The Cave of Blood' D. Donovan

Walk with the Beast, A (1969; 10s) ed. Charles M. Collins US
A good reprint selection with an informative introduction and such tales
as 'Prince Alberic and the Snake Lady' V. Lee, 'The Headless Miller
of Kobold's Keep' I. Ashkenazy, 'Tiger Cat' D. H. Keller, 'Curious

Adventure of Mr Bond' N. **Barker**, 'The Man and the Snake'
A. **Bierce**
Warlocks and Warriors Two independent heroic fantasy volumes
   ed. L. **Sprague de Camp** (1971; 10s) US
      Reprint selection including 'The Gods of Niom Parma' L. **Carter**,
      'Chu-Bu and Sheemish' **Dunsany**, 'Thunder in the Dawn'
      H. **Kuttner**, 'The Master of the Crabs' C. A. **Smith**, 'The Bells
      of Shoredan' R. **Zelazny**
   ed. Douglas Hill (1971; 6s) UK
      New and reprint including 'The Sleeping Sorceress' M. **Moorcock**,
      'The Ogyr of the Snows' M. **Hillman**, 'The Wager Lost By Winning'
      J. **Brunner**, 'The Wreck of the *Kissing Bitch*' K. **Roberts**
Wave of Fear, A (1973; 17s) ed. Hugh **Lamb** UK
Includes reprints 'The Child' L. A. **Lewis**, 'The Late Occupier' J. D.
   Beresford, 'Basil Netherby' A. C. **Benson**, 'The Wishing Well'
   E. F. **Benson**, 'The Traveller' R. H. **Benson**, 'Marjorie's on Starlight'
   C. **Birkin**, 'Clairvoyance' D. K. **Broster**, 'Terrible Mrs Green'
   F. **Cowles**, 'A Honeymoon in Hate' V. **Meik**, 'Hawley Bank Foundry'
   L. T. C. **Rolt**, 'Huguenin's Wife' M. P. **Shiel**
Way of the Werewolf (1966; 8s) ed. Douglas Hill UK
New and reprinted fiction including 'Wolves Don't Cry' B. **Elliott**, 'Canis
   Lupus Sapiens' A. **Hamilton**, 'The Phantom Farmhouse' S. **Quinn**,
   'The Gâloup' C. **Seignolle**
Weird Legacies (1977; 9s) ed. Mike **Ashley** UK
Stories selected from *Weird Tales* including 'The Ducker' R. **Bradbury**,
   'The Three Marked Pennies' M. E. **Counselman**, 'The Distortion
   Out of Space' F. **Flagg**, 'He That Hath Wings' E. **Hamilton**, 'Skulls in
   the Stars' R. E. **Howard**, 'The Utmost Abomination' C. A. **Smith** &
   L. **Carter**
Weird Tales Volumes selected from *Weird Tales*
   ed. Peter **Haining** (1976; 22s) Produced with facsimile contents
      including art, letters, verse and fillers. Selection includes 'Black
      Hound of Death' R. E. **Howard**, 'Frozen Beauty' S. **Quinn**, 'The
      Garden of Adompha' C. A. **Smith**, 'Beyond the Phoenix' H. **Kutt-
      ner**, 'The Black Monk' G. G. **Pendarves**, 'The Passing of a God'
      H. S. **Whitehead**, 'Heart of Atlantan' N. **Dyalhis**, 'The Phantom
      Slayer' F. **Leiber**, 'Roman Remains' A. **Blackwood**, 'The Shot-
      Tower Ghost' M. E. **Counselman**, 'Ooze' A. M. **Rud**
   ed. Leo **Margulies** (1964; 8s) Ghost-edited by Sam **Moskowitz** it
      includes 'A Question of Etiquette' R. **Bloch**, 'The Sea Witch'
      N. **Dyalhis**, 'Pigeons from Hell' R. E. **Howard**, 'Spider Mansion'
      F. **Leiber**
   A follow-up volume was *Worlds of Weird* (1965; 7s) including 'The
      Sapphire Goddess' N. **Dyalhis**, 'Roads' S. **Quinn**, 'Mother of
      Toads' C. A. **Smith**

When Churchyards Yawn (1931; 15s) ed. **Lady C. Asquith** UK
Includes 'A Threefold Cord' **A. Blackwood,** 'The Cotillon' **L. P.
Hartley,** 'Beauty and the Beast' **C. H. B. Kitchin,** 'A Little Ghost'
Hu. Walpole
Wild Night Company, The (1970; 22s) ed. **Peter Haining** UK
Irish Tales of Terror ranging from traditional tales through items by
D. Defoe, C. R. Maturin, J. S. Le Fanu to more recent fiction like
'The Man from Kilsheelan' **A. E. Coppard,** 'The Dead Smile' **F. M.
Crawford,** 'Hell Fire' **J. Joyce,** 'Witch Wood' **Dunsany,** 'The
Haunted Spinney' **E. O'Donnell,** 'The Moon Bog' **H. P. Lovecraft,**
'A Wild Night in Galway' **R. Bradbury**
Year's Best Fantasy Stories, The Series ed. **Lin Carter** US
No. 1 (1975; 11s) Includes 'The Sword Dyrnwyn' **L. Alexander,** 'Jewel
Quest' **H. Bok,** 'The Jewel of Arwen' **M. Z. Bradley,** 'The Emperor's
Fan' **L. S. de Camp,** 'The Temple of Abomination' **R. E. Howard,**
'The Double Tower' **C. A. Smith,** 'The Seventeen Virgins' **J. Vance**
No. 2 (1976; 12s) Includes new and reprint stories, 'Milord Sir Smith,
the English Wizard' **A. Davidson,** 'The Lamp From Atlantis' **L. S.
de Camp,** 'The Demoness' **T. Lee,** 'The Night of the Unicorn'
T. B. Swann
Year's Best Horror Stories, The Series ed. initially by **Richard Davis**
in UK. US editions differ and series now continued by **Gerald Page,**
while Davis's volumes appear as *The Orbit Book of Horror Stories*
No. 1 (1971; 14s) UK & US same. Includes 'I Wonder What He Wanted'
E. Bertin, 'The Scar' **R. Campbell,** 'When Morning Comes' **E. Fan-
cett,** 'The Sister City' **B. Lumley,** 'Prey' **R. Matheson,** 'Winter'
K. Reed, 'Lucifer' **E. C. Tubb**
No. 2 (1972; 10s) UK edition includes 'The Animal Fair' **R. Bloch,**
'Napier Court' **R. Campbell,** 'The Knocker at the Portico' **B. Copper,**
'David's Worm' **B. Lumley,** 'Thirst' **G. Page,** 'The Woman With
the Mauve Face' **R. Timperley**
No. 3 (1973; 9s) UK edition includes 'Pages From a Young Girl's
Journal' **R. Aickman,** 'Like Two White Spiders' **E. Bertin,** 'The Old
Horns' **R. Campbell,** 'Events at Poroth Farm' **T. E. D. Klein,**
'Haggopian' **B. Lumley**
US No. 2 (1974; 11s) Selects from UK Nos. 2 & 3
US No. 3 (1975; 13s) UK edition *The First Orbit Book of Horror Stories.*
Includes new and reprint fiction, 'The Taste of Your Love' **E. Bertin,**
'The Man in the Underpass' **R. Campbell,** 'The Whimper of
Whipped Dogs' **H. Ellison,** 'The House of Cthulhu' **B. Lumley,**
'Judas Story' **B. M. Stableford,** 'Forget-Me-Not' **B. Taylor**
US No. 4 (1976; 14s) ed. **G. Page.** Includes reprint fiction such as
'Christmas Present' **R. Campbell,** 'And Don't Forget the One Red
Rose' **A. Davidson,** 'Something Had to Be Done' **D. Drake,** 'The
Glove' **F. Leiber,** 'The Black Captain' **H. W. Munn;** plus new

fiction from Hal Clement and G. N. Gabbard and an article by
E. H. Price

Young Magicians, The (1969; 18s + verse) ed. **Lin Carter** US
Heroic fantasy including 'The Way of Ecben' **J. B. Cabell**, 'The Whelm-
ing of Oom' **L. Carter**, 'Ka the Appalling' **L. S. de Camp**, 'Cursed
Be the City' **H. Kuttner**, 'Through the Dragon Glass' **A. Merritt**,
'Turjan of Miir' **J. Vance**

Weird and horror fiction magazines

(Note: Title of magazine followed by the dates of the first and last issues, and the number of issues)

Ace Mystery (May–September 1936; 3) US
Editor: Harry Widmer
A terror pulp with the emphasis on sadism. Lead novels by Frederick
  C. Davis. Other chief writers: **Hugh B. Cave, G. T. Fleming-Roberts,
  Paul Ernst.** Most important story: 'Coyote Woman' by Charles
  Marquis Warren (July '36) about a desert vampire
Adventures in Horror (October 1970–October 1971; 7) US
Editor: Theodore S. Hecht
Became *Horror Stories* from third issue (February '71). Sensationalistic
  magazine with emphasis on sex. Little notable fiction
Alien Worlds (Summer 1966; 1) UK
Editors: Charles Partington & Harry Nadler
An attempt at a professional magazine by the editors of the fanzine *Alien*.
  Poor sales ended its life after a promising first issue with full-colour
  illustrations, and fiction by Kenneth Bulmer, **Ramsey Campbell** and
  Harry Harrison. Sf and horror
Arkham Collector, The (Summer 1967–Summer 1971; 10) US
Editor: **August Derleth**
A regular pamphlet issued to provide news and information about the
  publishers Arkham House and its authors. Included fiction and verse
  by **Lin Carter, Ramsey Campbell, Brian Lumley, James Wade**
  and others
Arkham Sampler, The (Winter 1948–Autumn 1949; 8) US
Editor: **August Derleth**
The forerunner of *Arkham Collector* was noted more for its news and
  informative articles. It carried fiction both new and reprint chiefly by
  Derleth (4), **Ray Bradbury** (3), **H. R. Wakefield** (3) and **John
  Wyndham** (2)
Avon Fantasy Reader (February 1947–Winter 1952; 18) US
Editor: **Donald A. Wollheim**
Essentially a regular paperback anthology, reprinting most notable
  stories of sf, fantasy and horror interest. Occasionally included new
  stories. Authors include **W. H. Hodgson, R. E. Howard, D. H.
  Keller, H. P. Lovecraft, A. Merritt, C. L. Moore, F. Owen,
  S. Rohmer, H. S. Whitehead.** Two paperback selections from the

magazine were edited by George Ernsberger as *The Avon Fantasy Reader* (1968; 7s) and *The 2nd Avon Fantasy Reader* (1969; 9s)

Beyond (July 1953–Spring 1955; 10) US
Editor H. L. Gold
Fantasy companion to *Galaxy*, full title was *Beyond Fantasy Fiction*. Dealt in amusing, serious and way-out fantasy stories with the emphasis on quality. Chief authors Theodore Cogswell (4) most noted for 'The Wall Around the World' (September '53), Jerome Bixby (3), and **Theodore Sturgeon** (2) noted for 'Talent' (September '53). A paperback selection was published as *Beyond* (1963; 9s), edited by Thomas Dardis

Bizarre Fantasy Tales (Fall 1970–March 1971; 2) US
Editor: **Robert A. W. Lowndes**
A reprint digest emphasising supernatural fiction. Carried lead long stories each issue by **H. S. Whitehead** and **A. Blackwood**

Bizarre Mystery Magazine (October 1965–January 1966; 3) US
Editor: John Poe
Sub-headed 'Murder—Black Magic—Suspense—Horror', contained a reprint lead novel every issue plus new short stories. Authors include R. E. Alter, **A. Derleth**, T. M. Disch, **J. Jakes**, A. Porges

Black Cat (Winter 1970; 1) Can
Editor: ?
Canadian reprint magazine that selected from turn-of-the-century magazines. Not to be confused with the legendary *Black Cat* (1895–1923) that carried new fiction of all kinds including horror and fantasy

Book of Terror, The (December 1949; 1) US
Editor: ?
Low-grade magazine with only high-spot a story by **E. H. Price**

Book of Weird Tales, A (Summer 1960; 1) UK
Editor: Cliff Lawton
Reprint magazine with good selection but killed by poor distribution. Lead story 'The Curse of Amen-Ra' by **V. Rousseau**

Brief Fantastic Tales (early 1950s; 1) Can
Editor: ?
Extremely rare small-size magazine edited from Toronto. Contained four stories of average quality

Coven 13 (September 1969–March 1970; 4) US
Editor: Arthur H. Landis
A handsome digest magazine containing all new fiction with the emphasis on witchcraft and magic. Carried serial *Let There Be Magick* by James R. Keaveny (Arthur Landis). Authors include A. Caillou, J. W. Cirrito, H. Ellison, **R. E. Howard**. Magazine later changed publishers and was retitled *Witchcraft & Sorcery* (see entry)

Dime Mystery (December 1932–November 1950; 159) US
Editor-in-charge: Rogers Terrill (many sub-editors)

The first of the many terror pulps it began as a straight detective magazine and later returned to mysteries. The main terror period ran from October '33 to September '38 (60 issues) during which time the sub-editor was Henry Treat Sperry and the leading writers were W. Blassingame (39), **Paul Ernst** (35), Arthur Leo Zagat (27), Wayne Rogers (24), John H. Knox (21) and **H. B. Cave** (19)

Dream World (February–August 1957; 3) US
Editor: Paul Fairman
A magazine inspired by the special 'dream' issue of *Fantastic*, it emphasised mildly sexy fantasies. The fiction was not memorable however apart from a few reprints (e.g. **Thorne Smith**). Authors include Milton Lesser (3), Randall Garrett (2), D. J. Granger (2), H. Ellison (2)

Dr Death (February–April 1935; 3) US
Editor: probably Arthur Ward
A terror magazine based on a lead novel about an occult scientist intent on taking over the world. Novels written by Harold Ward

Eerie Mysteries (August 1938–April 1939; 4) US
Editor: Harry Widmer
Essentially a mystery magazine with an emphasis on terror, but with little notable fiction written by authors whose identity has long since been lost under the house pseudonym anonymity

Eerie Stories (August 1937; 1) US
Editor: Harry Widmer
Forerunner of the above with more emphasis on terror

Eerie Tales (July 1941; 1) Can
Editor: possibly Thomas P. Kelley
A bona fide fantasy magazine that alas vanished into oblivion. Readers are still awaiting the end of Thomas P. Kelley's serial *The Weird Queen*

Famous Fantastic Mysteries (September 1939–June 1953; 81) US
Editor: Mary Gnaedinger
One of the best-loved of all pulp magazines it was essentially a reprint publication, the publishers drawing upon the wealthy stock of the Munsey magazines such as *All-Story*, *Argosy* and *Cavalier*. It featured early sf and fantastic romances. Later issues reprinted notable books long unavailable in the US. Initially relied heavily on **A. Merritt**, George Allen England and **J. U. Giesy**, but later reprinted **H. R. Haggard, W. H. Hodgson, E. C. Vivian, Sax Rohmer, Edison Marshall** and John Taine

Famous Monsters of Filmland (January 1958–current; 130) US
Editor: Forrest J. Ackerman
Although outside the scope of this book this magazine is included because it was the first (and still the best) of the film monster magazines and it started a trend that reached a crest in the early 1960s. It occasionally included fiction but the emphasis was on articles about horror films and numerous stills

Fanciful Tales (Fall 1936; 1) US
Editor: **Donald A. Wollheim**
A semi-professional magazine with the emphasis on fantasy. Stories by
H. P. Lovecraft, D. Wollheim, D. H. Keller and **A. Derleth**
among others
Fantastic (Summer 1952–current; 193) US
Editors: Howard Browne (Summer '52–August '56 (25)); Paul Fairman
(October '56–November '58 (24)); Cele Goldsmith Lalli (December
'58–June '65 (79)); Joseph Ross (September '65–November '67 (14));
Harry Harrison (January–October '68 (5)); Barry N. Malzberg
(December '68–April '69 (3)); Ted White (June '69–current)
Currently one of the few fantasy magazines. It was born as a posh digest
companion to *Amazing Stories* and later superseded *Fantastic Adven-
tures* (*q.v.*). The first issue contained excellent fiction but it later
rapidly deteriorated as the publisher's budget was curtailed. Under
Fairman's editorship the magazine was totally dull, but under Cele
Goldsmith it recovered admirably. She coaxed many new writers to its
pages, uppermost Piers Anthony, Thomas M. Disch, Ursula K. Le
Guin, **Roger Zelazny** and David Bunch. The issues from 1962–65 are
bursting with first-class fiction especially in the sword and sorcery sub-
genre where it featured the Grey Mouser stories by **Leiber**, the Brak
adventures by **Jakes**, **Zelazny**'s Dilvish stories. It also ran a classic
reprint department conducted by **Sam Moskowitz** which resurrected
many fine but overlooked stories by **R. S. Carr, M. D. Armstrong,
P. Ernst, R. Bloch**, and N. Schachner among others. It dropped in
quality when it changed publishers in 1965 with a new policy of almost
entirely reprinted contents and only recently increased in quality with
a returned emphasis on sword and sorcery and featuring **Lin Carter,
L. S. de Camp, F. Leiber, R. E. Howard** and **Karl Wagner**. It also
runs regular articles by de Camp on fantasy writers, and is noted for its
superb covers by Stephen Fabian.
Fantastic Adventures (May 1939–March 1953; 129) US
Editors: Ray Palmer (May '39–July '46 (56)); William Hamling (September '46–February '51 (48)); Howard Browne
The original sister magazine to *Amazing Stories*, it frequently featured
science fiction, and its fantasy content was chiefly left to **Robert Bloch**,
who wrote a madcap series of stories about Lefty Feep, David Wright
O'Brien and Leroy Yerxa. The quality was variable but among the
weeds exist veritable orchids. These include 'Enchanted Bookself' by
W. P. McGivern (March '43), 'The Court of Kublai Khan' by D. V.
Reed (March '48), 'You're All Alone' by **Fritz Leiber** (July '50), 'The
Eye of Tandyla' by **L. S. de Camp** (May '51), 'Medusa Was a Lady'
by W. Tenn (October '51) and several stories by T. Sturgeon notably
The Dreaming Jewels (February '50) and 'Excalibur and the Atom'
(August '51). It later merged with *Fantastic*

Fantastic Novels (July 1940–April 1941/March 1948–June 1951; 25) US
Editor: Mary Gnaedinger
Companion to *Famous Fantastic Mysteries* also featuring reprints mostly
    by A. Merritt, Ray Cummings and C. B. Stilson
Fantasy & Science Fiction, The Magazine of (Fall 1949–current; 315+ US
Editors: Anthony Boucher & J. F. McComas (Fall '49–August '54 (39));
    Boucher alone (September '54–August '58 (48)); R. P. Mills (Septem-
    ber '58–March '62 (43)); Avram Davidson (April '62–November '64
    (32)); Joseph Ferman (December '64–December '65 (13)), Ed Ferman
    (January '66–current)
The leading fantasy magazine for quality fiction. It has always featured
a satisfying blend of sf, horror and fantasy, both in new and reprinted
stories. Paramount among its early contributors were T. Sturgeon,
A. Porges, R. Bretnor, P. Anderson, M. W. Wellman and
R. Matheson. During the late 1950s and early '60s the emphasis was
more on sf, but under Ed Ferman's editorship it has frequently
featured superb fantasies, especially the work of T. B. Swann,
R. Zelazny, J. Vance, H. Ellison, R. Aickman, L. S. de Camp,
K. Roberts, B. Lumley and Karl Wagner. Gahan Wilson's cartoons
have featured since the April '65 issue. Occasional issues have been
devoted to various writers: T. Sturgeon (September '62), R. Brad-
bury (May '63), I Asimov (October '66)—he also provides a regular
science column—F. Leiber (July '69), P. Anderson (April '71),
J. Blish (April '72), F. Pohl (September '73), R. Silverberg (April '74),
D. Knight (November '76)
Fantasy & Terror (1973–current; 6) US
Editor: Jessie Amos Salmonson, now Jessica Amanda Salmonson
A semi-professional magazine featuring competent fiction by new writers
    including A. Samalman, E. C. Bertin, D. Schweitzer and A. Weiss.
    Special emphasis on verse
Fantasy Fiction (May–November 1950; 2) US
Editor: Curtis Mitchell
The second issue was titled *Fantasy Stories*. It predominantly relied on
    reprints retitled to give the impression of true stories such as Theodore
    Roscoe's 'On Account of a Woman' becoming 'She Said "Take Me if
    You Dare"'. Beneath the sensational titles were some good stories
    including I. S. Cobb's 'Fishhead' and Max Brand's 'John Ovington
    Returns'.
Fantasy Fiction Magazine (March–November 1953; 4) US
Editor: Lester del Rey
A high quality magazine now much sought after. A Hannes Bok cover
    graced every issue which featured first-class fiction by Robert Sheckley,
    P. Anderson, F. Pratt, plus two new Conan stories of Howard
    reworked by de Camp. Lead novel of the last issue was 'Web of the
    Worlds' by H. Harrison & K. MacLean

Fear! (May-July 1960; 2) US
Editor: Joseph L. Marx
An above average magazine featuring mostly new fiction though reprinting a story each by W. **Collins** and **R. S. Hichens**. Writers included **John Jakes** and **Arthur Porges**
Fireside Ghost Stories (1937; 1) UK
Editor: ? (One of the *Master Thriller* series)
A special Christmas magazine featuring reprinted material by **C. Dickens**, Hector Bolitho and **R. Thurston Hopkins**
Forgotten Fantasy (October 1970–June 1971; 5) US
Editor: Douglas Menville
A beautiful magazine consisting entirely of reprints from long ago. The first four issues serialised the novel of a world inside the Earth, *The Goddess of Atvatabar* by William Bradshaw; other notable resurrections were 'The Parasite' A. **C. Doyle**, 'The Birthmark' N. **Hawthorne**, 'The Hollow Land' W. **Morris**
Gamma (Summer 1963–September 1965; 5) US
Editors: Charles E. Fritch and Jack Matcha
Overlooked by many fantasy enthusiasts as a science fiction magazine, *Gamma* featured many fine horror stories, not least **P. Highsmith**'s 'The Snail Watcher'. Other writers include **R. Matheson**, **R. Bloch**, **C. Beaumont**, **R. Bradbury**, **W. Faulkner**, and **D. Etchison** with both new and reprinted fiction
Ghosts and Goblins (1938; 1) UK
Editor: ? (One of the *Master Thriller* series)
A special one-shot including fiction by **R. T. Hopkins**, H. Rawle and G. Radcliffe
Ghost Stories (July 1926–January 1932; 64) US
Editors: W. Adolphe Roberts (July '26–?August '29 (38)); George Bond, D. E. Wheeler (unspecified period); Harold Hersey (April '30–January '32 (19))
A much overlooked magazine that attempted to present its fiction as true stories, enhanced by posed trick photographs. Featured many articles and experiences. It also reprinted many famous stories with revised titles, such as 'The Woman's Ghost Story' by **Blackwood** becoming 'The Specter That Asked for a Kiss'. Leading writers: Harold S. Corbin (29), Edwin Goewey (20), **V. Rousseau** (14) and W. A. Roberts (11). Also single stories by **R. E. Howard**, **C. Jacobi**, **F. B. Long**, **N. Dyalhis**
Ghoul (Winter 1976; 1) UK
Editor: Penny Grant
A poor attempt at combining a film and fiction magazine. The highspot was a study of E. A. Poe by Walter Gillings. Included reprinted fiction by **Charles Birkin** and **R. Chetwynd-Hayes** (who also wrote several humorous features)

Haunt of Horror (June–August 1973; 2) US
Editor: Gerard Conway
A prose magazine from the Marvel Comics publishers presented good quality fiction enhanced by beautiful covers and interior art. Reprinted **Fritz Leiber's** *Conjure Wife* as a serial, plus new fiction by **R. Campbell**, H. Ellison, R. A. Lafferty, John K. Diomede and others. Poor circulation brought an immediate axe

Horror Stories (January 1935–April 1941; 41) US
Editor: Steve Farrelly under Rogers Terrill
Companion to *Dime Mystery* and *Terror Tales* as one of the main terror pulps emphasising sadistic and physical horror rather than supernatural. Leading writers: Ray Cummings (24), Wayne Rogers (21), Francis James (18), A. J. Burks (17), Paul Ernst (16)

Impulse (March 1966–February 1967; 12) UK
Editor: Ostensibly Keith Roberts
A continuation of *Science Fantasy* it featured both sf and fantasy, most notably Roberts's *Pavane* series

Macabre (June 1957–current; 23) US
Editor: **Joseph Payne Brennan**
A semi-professional magazine issued irregularly as a vehicle for **Brennan's** verse and fiction, but also including contributions by other writers

Magazine of Horror (August 1963–April 1971; 36) US
Editor: **Robert A. W. Lowndes**
A predominantly reprint magazine very personally edited showing a responsible selection of classic stories plus forgotten gems from *Weird Tales* and *Strange Tales*. R. E. Howard, C. A. Smith, A. J. Burks, A. Eadie, E. Worrell, H. P. Lovecraft and F. B. Long featured heavily among the reprints; the most notable new writer was **Steffan B. Aletti**

Marvellous Magazine (May 1, 1802–April 2, 1804) UK
Editor: ?
Almost certainly the first horror magazine, consisting of unauthorised abridgements of Gothic novels and stories, most notably the work of **Mrs Radcliffe**: *Mysteries of Udolpho* being cut by one-tenth as 'The Veiled Picture'. Many imitations followed, not least *Tell-Tale* and *The Ghost*

A. Merritt's Fantasy Magazine (December 1949–October 1950; 5) US
Editor: Mary Gnaedinger
Companion to *Famous Fantastic Mysteries* and *Fantastic Novels*, also relied on reprints. **Merritt** aside, it featured novels by **E. C. Vivian**, F. Faust and G. A. England

Mind Magic (June–December 1931; 6) US
Editors: **August Derleth** (1–4); G. R. Bay (5–6)
Became *Myself* for the last two issues. An occult magazine featuring fiction by writers like V. **Rousseau**, R. M. Farley and Joe Skidmore

Mysterious Traveller, The (November 1951–October 1952; 5) US
Editor: **Robert Arthur**
Inspired by the radio programme of the same name it relied on reprinted
    material in the mystery and macabre vein, calling on the works of
    Agatha Christie, R. Arthur, Ray Bradbury, J. D. Carr, Richard
    Sale, **A. Derleth, W. H. Hodgson** and John Creasey. Good quality
Mystery Tales (March 1938–May 1940; 9) US
Editor: Robert O. Erisman
A later terror pulp with special emphasis on sex and sadism. Mediocre
    fiction written under house names but also including work by **Wyatt
    Blassingame, H. Kuttner,** Wayne Rogers, Bruno Fischer (as
    Russell Gray), Ray Cummings and **A. J. Burks**
Mystic (November 1953–July 1956; 16) US
Editor: Ray Palmer
With an emphasis on the occult, early issues included much fiction, but
    the articles later took pride of place, and with a title change to *Search*
    in October '56, it went entirely non-fiction. Writers included **J. P.
    Brennan** and **R. B. Johnson**
New Witchcraft (Summer–September 1975; 4) US
Editor: Brian Netschen
Poor distribution killed this equally poor magazine that relied mostly on
    articles and reprinted fiction, including work by **S. Quinn**
Occult Shorts (June–August 1945; 2) UK
Editor: ? (A Gerald G. Swan publication)
With a title that implies some kind of psychic garment, this wartime
    publication featured short stories by little known writers such as W. P.
    Cockcroft, H. Rawle and A. C. Bailey
Oriental Stories (October 1930–January 1934; 14) US
Editor: **Farnsworth Wright**
Retitled *Magic Carpet* from January '33. Companion to *Weird Tales* with
    contents clearly indicated by the title. Not all fantasy, but featured
    stories by **Frank Owen** (8), **E. H. Price** (6), **O. A. Kline** (7), James
    W. Bennett (5), S. B. H. Hurst (8) and Warren H. Miller (9)
Out of this World (Winter '54–Spring '55; 2) UK
Editor: John S. Manning (pseud. for Michael Nahum & Sol de Salle)
A companion to *Supernatural Stories* which later used the title on a few
    issues. The entire contents were published under house names, except
    for A. J. Merak. Best story 'The Nightmare Road' by Ray Cosmic!
    Second issue later reprinted in part in *Supernatural* 36
Phantom (April 1957–July 1958; 16) UK
Editor: Leslie Syddall
A good quality magazine featuring both new fiction and reprints, often
    from *Weird Tales*. New stories by Martin Thomas, **R. L. Fanthorpe,**
    Peter Dale and others—possibly pseudonymous
Prize Ghost Stories (1963; 1) US

Editor: ?

A magazine that reprinted fiction from *Ghost Stories* and other Mac-Fadden publications. 17 stories including **H. G. Wells** and **V. Rousseau**

Science Fantasy (Summer 1950–February 1966; 81) UK

Editors: Walter Gillings (Summer–Winter 1950) (2)); E. J. Carnell (Winter 51–April '64 (62)); Kyril Bonfiglioli

While early issues were predominantly science fiction, under Carnell it took a definite swing to fantasy, initially with various lead novels by Kenneth Bulmer and John Brunner. No. 44 (December '60) was a special weird issue, and the magazine was then featuring the delightful fantasies of **T. B. Swann** and later the Elric stories by **Moorcock**. Under Bonfiglioli the magazine reverted to a sf emphasis, but is remembered for K. Roberts's stories about a juvenile witch, Anita

Screen Chills and Macabre Stories (1957; 1) UK

Editor: ?

An abortive early attempt at a film magazine presenting fictionalised versions of 'The Dead That Walk' and 'I was a Teenage Werewolf' plus 'Them Ones' by **R. Bloch**

Shock (May–September 1960; 3) US

Editor: ?

A competent magazine using both new and reprinted fiction notably by **R. Bloch, R. Bradbury, H. Kuttner** and **T. Sturgeon**. Poor sales however caused it to cease, but it was revived in 1962 as *Shock Mystery Tales* in digest and then large-size format and lasted for several issues featuring terror stories emphasising sex and sadism

Sinister Stories (February–May 1941; 3) US

Editor: Costa Carousso

A terror pulp of little merit with stories by **H. B. Cave**, Russell Gray, Ray Cummings and Francis James among others

Spicy Mystery Stories (July 1934–December 1942; 70+) US

Editor: Lawrence Cadman

As the title suggests this pulp placed special emphasis on sex, with gruesome consequences. An exceedingly below average magazine it remains an example of some of the more titillating style of terror fiction. Many leading writers contributed however as it meant a quick sale, and here may be found the work of **E. H. Price, W. Blassingame, H. B. Cave, R. E. Howard,** Howard Wandrei, R. L. Bellem and others

Startling Mystery Magazine (February–April 1940; 2) US

Editor: Costa Carousso

Another terror pulp of little consequence. See *Sinister Stories*

Startling Mystery Stories (Summer 1966–March 1971; 18) US

Editor: **Robert A. W. Lowndes**

A companion to *Magazine of Horror* it concentrated, as the title implies, on horrifying mysteries—not always supernatural. Predominantly

reprint, it featured almost every issue a Jules de Grandin adventure by
S. Quinn, as well as reprinting Paul Ernst's Dr Satan series, and
many of Edward Hoch's Simon Ark. The editor brought the same
atmosphere to this as to all his very personal magazines. It printed the
first two stories by Stephen King

Strange Detective Mysteries (October 1937–1942; ? 29) US
Editors: Willard Crosby, Ejler Jacobson, John Bender (at unspecified
times)
A borderline magazine featuring cases solved by unusual detectives. The
emphasis was on more gruesome murders. Stories often under house
names but also writers like W. Blassingame, P. Ernst and W. Rogers

Strange Detective Stories (? August 1932–February 1934; 19?) US
Editor: ?
An early example of bizarre fictional detectives such as E. H. Price's
Pierre d'Artois. Included stories by R. E. Howard, A. J. Burks and
others

Strange Fantasy (Spring 1969–Fall 1970; 6) US
Editor: ?
A reprint magazine from the publishers of *Fantastic* that used material
from that magazine, notably by F. Leiber, J. Jakes, U. K. Le Guin,
R. Zelazny and H. Ellison. Collectors should not be confused by the
numbering system which starts at No. 8!

Strange Stories (February 1939–February 1941; 13) US
Editor-in-charge: Leo Margulies
A much overlooked magazine that included some first-class material as
well as much of average quality. Included work by August Derleth
(18), Robert Bloch (12), Henry Kuttner (11) notably with his two
heroic fantasies about Prince Raynor, and M. W. Wellman (5)

Strange Tales (September 1931–January 1933; 7) US
Editor: Harry Bates
An early rival to *Weird Tales* that often ran fiction of superior quality by
the same writers. These included H. B. Cave (4), H. S. Whitehead
(6), V. Rousseau (3), and C. A. Smith (5). Most of its fiction was
reprinted in *Magazine of Horror* and *Startling Mystery Stories*

Strange Tales (February–March 1946; 2) UK
Editor: Walter Gillings
A reprint magazine selecting from *Weird Tales*, *Strange Tales* and *Strange
Stories* with fiction by R. Bloch, R. Bradbury, C. A. Smith, H. P.
Lovecraft and others

Strangest Stories Ever Told, The (Summer 70; 1) US
Editor: ?
Another reprint magazine using the archives of *Amazing Stories* and
Fantastic Adventures. Featured 'The Sword of Ra' by G. St Reynard

Supernatural Magazine, The (June–September 1809; 4) UK
Editor: ?

May have had more issues. Emanating from Dublin it does not appear to have included any original fiction, but featured reprints of weird Gothic tales

Supernatural Stories (Spring 1954–Summer 1966; 70) UK
Editors: Michael Nahum and Sol de Salle
Initially a digest magazine, it later became a pocket book series, the magazine being issued with a companion novel. For this reason the numbering of the series reaches 109, but only 70 issues relate to short story volumes. The bulk of the contents were written by **R. L. Fanthorpe** under a host of pen names, plus A. J. Merak

Suspense (Spring 1951–April 1952; 4) US
Editor: Theodore Irwin
Inspired by the radio and television programme *Suspense* this magazine presented new and reprint material in the weird, fantasy, sf and crime fields but failed to appeal. It was however of above average quality and even included a **F. Leiber** Grey Mouser adventure

Tales of Ghosts and Haunted Houses (December 1939; 1) UK
Editor: ? (One of the *Master Thriller* series)
A special Christmas one-shot featuring ten stories by little-known writers and with intriguing titles like 'The Curator Chats' and 'The Corpse Sat Up'

Tales of Magic & Mystery (December 1927–April 1928; 5) US
Editor: Walter B. Gibson
Besides featuring articles on the occult and stage and home 'magic' (including a serialised article on bullet-catching), this magazine included much fiction both new and reprint by noted writers like **Frank Owen**, Miriam Allen de Ford, Archie Binns, and its most noted content, **H. P. Lovecraft**'s 'Cool Air'

Tales of Terror (1937; 1) UK
Editor: ? (One of the *Master Thriller* series)
Six stories, new and reprint, by H. H. Bolitho, J. Creasey, E. Snell, C. V. Tench and others

Tales of Terror from the Beyond (Summer 1964; 1) US
Editor: Patrick Masulli
A second issue was advertised but might not have appeared. Chiefly reprint fiction with most of the stories by Stanton Coblentz from *Weird Tales*

Tales of the Frightened (Spring–August 1957; 2) US
Editor: **Michael Avallone**
Issued after the success of the radio programme of that name it included only average stories by many well-known writers such as John Wyndham, A. B. Chandler and P. Anderson. Boris Karloff provided 'The Frightened' in each issue; the best story was **Avallone**'s own 'The Man Who Thought He was Poe'

Tales of the Uncanny (1937–38; 3) UK

Editor: ? (One of the *Master Thriller* series)

One of the better of the series with new and reprint fiction by Douglas Newton, J. Russell Warren, H. H. Bolitho, **O. Onions, S. Horler,** and **R. Thurston Hopkins** among others—all worth reading

Terror Tales (September 1934–March 1941; 51) US

Editor: Steve Farrelly and Loring Dowst under Rogers Terrill

The third of the pulp magazines that spearheaded the vogue for sadistic horror during the 1930s. Leading contributors: Wayne Rogers (26), **W. Blassingame** (25), Ray Cummings (22), **Paul Ernst** (19), Arthur Leo Zagat (18) and **A. J. Burks** (17)

Thrill Book, The (1 March–15 October 1919; 16) US

Editors: Harold Hersey (8), Ronald Oliphant (8)

Originally intended to be a fantasy magazine it became a general adventure pulp but did feature a fair quantity of good weird stories by **Greye La Spina,** Perley Poore Sheehan, **S. Quinn,** M. Leinster, **Tod Robbins** and **J. U. Giesy**

Thriller (February–July 1962; 3) US

Editor: Harry Schreiner

A large-size magazine that failed to make an impact though it was of a readable quality

Thrilling Mystery (October 1935–Fall 1944; 61) US

Editor-in-charge: Leo Margulies

A more moderate terror pulp with greater emphasis on evil characterization. Again few supernatural stories, but often more bizarre natural solutions. Leading writers: G. T. Fleming-Roberts (38), Ray Cummings (33), **H. Kuttner** (28), John H. Knox (25) and **A. J. Burks** (16). Later issues were more straight detective fiction

True Twilight Tales (Fall 1963–Spring 1964; 2) US

Editor: Helen Gardiner

A third issue may have appeared. Reprinted fiction from *Ghost Stories* and *True Strange.* The 'true' should be ignored

Uncanny Tales (Oct 1938–May 1940; 7) US

Editor: Robert O. Erisman

Not to be confused with the Canadian sf/fantasy *Uncanny Tales,* this was one of the sex-emphasising terror pulps. Mostly fiction under house names; recognised writers include A. **J. Burks,** Mindret Lord, Russell Gray, Ray Cummings and R. L. Bellem

Unknown (March 1939–October 1943; 39) US

Editor: John W. Campbell

Became *Unknown Worlds* from October '41. If any magazine rivalled *Weird Tales* for supremacy it was *Unknown,* which certainly contained the more literary and original fiction. Pure delightful fantasies, both humorous and serious, often in the vein of 'anything goes'. Nearly every story is worth reviving. Among its most noted contents were the early Grey Mouser stories by **F. Leiber,** the Harold Shea tales by

Pratt and **de Camp**, novels like *Fear* and *The Ultimate Adventure* by **L. Ron Hubbard**, Jack Williamson's *Darker Than You Think* and *The Reign of Wizardry* and T. Sturgeon's 'It'. Leading authors were **T. Sturgeon** (17), **L. Ron Hubbard** (13), **L. S. de Camp** (15), **Malcolm Jameson** (11), Cleve Cartmill (10) and F. B. Long (10). A later magazine compilation from the series was *From Unknown Worlds* (1948; 14s); anthologies derived from the contents are George Hay's *Hell Hath Fury* and Don Bensen's *The Unknown* and *The Unknown Five*

Web Terror Stories (October 1958–June 1965?; ?) US
Editor: Robert C. Sproul
The magazine began as *Saturn Web Detective*, changing from a science fiction magazine. The emphasis rapidly shifted to terror in the vein of the old pulps *Web Detective*, becoming *Web Terror* in August '62. Most stories mediocre, by writers like Bill Ryder and Al James, with frequent use of house names. Occasional appearances by **John Jakes** and Marion Z. Bradley

Weird and Occult Library (Spring–Autumn 1960; 3) UK
Editor: ? (a Gerald G. Swan magazine)
Including new and reprint material this magazine often published stories bought in the 1940s but only now given a lease of life. Writers included H. Rawle, J. R. Fearn, K. Hammond and others

Weirdbook (1968–current; 10) US
Editor: W. Paul Ganley
A semi-professional magazine that features new fiction often by big-name authors, notably **R. E. Howard, H. W. Munn, J. P. Brennan** and newcomers **Gerald Page, Eddy Bertin,** Janet Fox and Darrell Schweitzer. Emphasis given to weird verse. First series (10 issues) large-size format, currently undergoing a change

Weird Mystery (Fall 1970–Summer 1971; 4) US
Editor: ?
Another reprint magazine utilising the fiction from *Fantastic* and *Fantastic Adventures* featuring **R. Bloch,** U. K. Le Guin, **Arthur Porges** and others

Weird Pocket Library (1943; 1) UK
Weird Shorts (1944; 1) UK
Weird Story Magazine (1940 and *c* 1946; 2) UK
Editors: ? (all Gerald G. Swann magazines)
These three were magazines along the line of *Occult Shorts* and *Weird and Occult Library* with brief tales by little known British writers

Weird Tales (March 1923– September 1954; 279. Summer 1973–Summer 1974; 4) US
Editors: Edwin Baird (March '23–April '24 (12)); **Otis A. Kline** (May '24 (1)); Farnsworth Wright (November '24–March '40 (179)); **Dorothy McIlwraith** (May '40–September '54 (87)); **Sam Moskowitz**

235

This legendary magazine is the home of the American weird fiction of the twentieth century. Few US writers in the field who were active during its thirty-year life can have written without one eye on that market. Derided by some as a cheap pulp its pages nevertheless contained some of the greatest tales of the supernatural and bizarre ever written. It has been constantly mined by anthologists starting with the British *Not at Night* series edited by C. C. Thomson, and more specifically of late by Leo Margulies and Peter Haining. It is impossible to highlight all the important stories. Today the magazine is most remembered for its stories by H. P. Lovecraft, its Conan adventures by R. E. Howard and its verbal pyrotechnics by C. A. Smith. And yet during its lifetime by far the most popular author was S. Quinn, chiefly through his long-running Jules de Grandin series. Those aside, the most internationally acclaimed authors from its pages are R. Bradbury, R. Bloch and A. Derleth. Despite these names, *Weird Tales* carried numerous stories by little known authors and this often proved exceedingly popular—good stories were 'The Night Wire' by H. F. Arnold (September '26), 'The Copper Bowl' by G. F. Eliot (December '28) and the contributions by Kirk Mashburn and Nictzin Dyalhis. An early piece, 'The Loved Dead' by C. M. Eddy, caused such an uproar that issues were withdrawn from sale, but it is believed to have helped the magazine financially; much the same rumour clings to O. A. Kline's *Tam, Son of the Tiger* (1931). The magazine is noted for its purchase of Tennessee Williams's first story 'The Vengeance of Nitocris' (August '28) plus several stories by Robert S. Carr, notably 'Spider-bite' (June '26). Its fiction varied in content to cover every form of weird story, ranging from the gruesome terror of many of Paul Ernst's Dr Satan series to the delightful Oriental fantasies of Frank Owen. Under Wright the magazine frequently featured reprints both from known classics and from earlier issues of the magazine. A complete set of *Weird Tales* is both a thorough library of all that is good (and some that is bad) in weird fiction, as well as a good investment. Such a set would be worth well over £1,000. Revived under Sam Moskowitz the magazine suffered from poor distribution, failing to reach a break-even point in sales. These last four issues were notable for Moskowitz's invaluable study of W. H. Hodgson and reprints of his lesser-known stories. The leading writers for the magazine were as follows: S. Quinn (145), A. Derleth (137), Edmond Hamilton (80), R. Bloch (71), C. A. Smith (62), R. E. Howard (55), H. P. Lovecraft (54), M. W. Wellman (46), P. Ernst (38), A. V. Harding (36), F. Owen (34), A. J. Burks (32), M. E. Counselman (31), F. B. Long (30), H. Lawlor (29), E. H. Price (28), R. Bradbury (25), A. Eadie (25), H. S. Whitehead (25), H. Kuttner (24), D. H. Keller (22), G. G. Pendarves (19), G. La Spina (18), E. Worrell (18), C. Jacobi (18), O. A. Kline (17) and C. L. Moore (16)

Weird Terror Tales (Winter 1969–Fall 1970; 3) US
Editor: **Robert A. W. Lowndes**
A reprint magazine treated with the same personal attention as all of
Lowndes's periodicals. Contents include **H. W. Munn**'s 'The Wheel',
H. S. Whitehead's 'The Trap', **H. B. Cave**'s 'Stragella' and stories by
Derleth, Bertin, Lovecraft, Poe and **Aletti**
Weird World (Autumn 1955–Spring 1956; 2) UK
Editor: ?
Issued from Birkenhead this magazine contained mostly new fiction, some
quite readable, from unknown writers. Best story 'The Man Who
Loved Cats' by Konstanton Faber
Whispers (July 1973–current; 9) US
Editor: **Stuart David Schiff**
A semi-professional periodical which appears irregularly, but is always
well worth the wait. The editor, a US Army dentist, provides a vast
amount of publishing news and manages to acquire first-class fiction,
verse and articles from many big names. Noted fiction has been
'House of Cthulhu' **B. Lumley**, 'The Song of the Bone' **D. Drake**,
'Sticks' **K. E. Wagner**, 'The Soft Wall' **D. Etchison**, 'Take Me, For
Instance' **H. B. Cave**, 'The Glove' **F. Leiber** and 'The Barrow Troll'
D. Drake. Issues 6 and 7 (June 1975) were combined as a special
Weird Tales issue
Witchcraft & Sorcery (January 1971–74; 6) US
Editor: **Gerald W. Page**
A continuation of *Coven 13* with new editor and publisher, but retained
the numbering. May still be current but no issue seen since No. 10. A
large-size magazine with poor distribution it nevertheless presents new
fiction attractively illustrated. Has included fiction by **R. E. Howard,
A. E. van Vogt, B. Lumley, A. Derleth, E. Petaja, M. W. Wellman**
and **E. H. Price** (who also provides a regular column of fascinating
reminiscences)
Witch's Tales (November–December 1936; 2) US
Editor: **Tom Chadburn**
Inspired by the radio programme of the same name, it included lead
novels written by that programme's mainstay, Alonzo Dean Cole. The
remainder was mostly reprinted fiction from turn-of-the-century UK
magazines, plus an assortment of 'true' experiences
Worlds Beyond (December 1950–February 1951; 3) US
Editor: **Damon Knight**
Essentially a sf magazine, Knight selected many bona fide fantasies to fill
out the contents. Several were reprints and in all included good material
by **J. Vance, W. F. Temple, P. Wylie** and **C. M. Kornbluth**
Worlds of Fantasy (September 1968–Spring 1971; 4) US
Editor: **Lester del Rey**
This should not be confused with the UK juvenile sf magazine of the

same name that should be avoided at all costs. This publication featured many good stories by all the leading names in fantasy, all with new contributions. Lead novels were 'The Mirror of Wizardry' a Brak adventure by J. Jakes, 'Long Live Lord Kor!' by A. Norton, *The Tombs of Atuan*, the second Earthsea novel by U. K. Le Guin, and *Reality Doll* (*Destiny Doll* in book form) by C. D. Simak. The last three issues were spoiled by bad covers and poor printing

APPENDIX IV

Awards

August Derleth Fantasy Award

Awarded by the British Fantasy Society. Inaugurated in 1971 at the
suggestion of **Ramsey Campbell**. First presented in 1972 for novel
only, then from 1973 to 1976 for novel, short stories, film and comic.
From 1977 ADFA restricted to Best Novel, with the British Fantasy
Award introduced for the other categories, with the addition of artist

1972   *The Knight of the Swords* by Michael Moorcock
1973   Novel: *The King of the Swords* by Michael Moorcock
       Story: 'The Fallible Fiend' by L. Sprague de Camp
       Film: *Tales From the Crypt*
       Comic: *Conan* (Marvel)
1974   Novel: *Hrolf Kraki's Saga* by Poul Anderson
       Story: 'The Jade Man's Eyes' by Michael Moorcock
       Film: *The Legend of Hell House*
       Comic: *Conan*
1975   Novel: *The Sword and the Stallion* by Michael Moorcock
       Story: 'Sticks' by Karl Edward Wagner
       Film: *The Exorcist*
       Comic: *Savage Sword of Conan*
1976   Novel: *The Hollow Lands* by Michael Moorcock
       Story: *The 2nd Book of Fritz Leiber* (collection)
       Film: *Monty Python and the Holy Grail*
       Comic: *Savage Sword of Conan*
1977   Novel: *The Dragon and the George* by Gordon R. Dickson (ADFA)
       Story: 'Two Suns Setting' by Karl Edward Wagner (BFA)
       Film: *The Omen* (BFA)
       Artist: Mike Kaluta (BFA)

World Fantasy Award

Awarded at the annual World Fantasy Convention first held in Providence, Rhode Island in October 1975. The initial organisation was by
Gahan Wilson. The Awards are chosen from nominations by a selected
panel

1975   Novel: *The Forgotten Beasts of Eld* by Patricia A. McKillip
       Story: 'Pages From a Young Girl's Diary' by Robert Aickman
       Collection: *Worse Things Waiting* by Manly Wade Wellman
       Artist: Lee Brown Coye
       Life Award (for services to the genre): Robert Bloch
1976   Novel: *Bid Time Return* by Richard Matheson
       Story: 'Belsen Express' by Fritz Leiber
       Artist: Frank Frazetta
       Life Award: Fritz Leiber

BIBLIOGRAPHY

During the course of preparing this *Who's Who* I had occasion to use a considerable number of general reference works, such as *Who Was Who*, *Contemporary Authors* or the *Dictionary of National Biography*. It was made very plain to me just how few books did specialise in horror and fantasy fiction or even accord it more than scant coverage. I therefore recommend for further reading the following works which I consulted in full or in part. I must also acknowledge the anthologists too numerous to mention (but especially Peter Haining, August Derleth, Hugh Lamb, Sam Moskowitz and Michel Parry) who painstakingly provide informative and invaluable introductions and notes to their anthologies.

Carter, Lin, *Imaginary Worlds* (Ballantine Books, New York, 1973)

Carter, Lin, *Tolkien: A Look Behind the Lord of the Rings* (Ballantine Books, New York, 1969)

Cockcroft, T. G. L., *Index to the Weird Fiction Magazines* (published privately, New Zealand, 1962 and 1964)

de Camp, L. Sprague, *Lovecraft: A Biography* (Doubleday, New York, 1975)

de Camp, L. Sprague, *Literary Swordsmen* (Arkham House, Wisconsin, 1977)

Douglas, Drake, *Horrors* (John Baker, London, 1967)

James, Louis, *Fiction For the Working Man 1830–1850* (Oxford, 1963)

Jones, Robert K., *The Shudder Pulps* (Fax Collectors, Oregon, 1975)

Jones, Robert K., *Index to the Weird Menace Pulps* (Opar Press, 1972)

Locke, George, *Ferret Fantasy's Christmas Annuals* for 1972 and 1973 (published privately, 1972 and 1974)

Locke, George, *Search & Research* (2 issues, November 1973 and June 1974)

Lupoff, Richard A., *Edgar Rice Burroughs: Master of Adventure* (Ace Books, New York, 1968 (revised edition))

Moskowitz, Sam, *Explorers of the Infinite* (World Publishing Co., Ohio, 1963)

Moskowitz, Sam, *Science Fiction by Gaslight* (World Pub. Co., Ohio, 1968)

Moskowitz, Sam, *Under the Moons of Mars* (Holt, Rinehart and Winston, New York, 1970)

Owings, Mark & Chalker, Jack L., *The Revised H. P. Lovecraft Bibliography* (Mirage Press, Maryland, 1973)

Sieger, James R., *Ghost Stories Index* (Opar Press, Colorado, 1973)

Sirius Press, *An Index to Unknown and Unknown Worlds* (Wisconsin, 1955)

Summers, Montague, *The Gothic Quest* (Fortune Press, London, 1969 edn)

Tuck, Donald H., *The Encyclopedia of Science Fiction and Fantasy, Vol. 1* (Advent, Chicago, 1974); *Vol. 2* (private, Tasmania, 1959)

Turner, E. S., *Boys Will Be Boys* (Penguin Books edition, London, 1976)

Weinberg, Robert (editor), *WT50* (privately published, Illinois, 1974)

Wolff, Robert Lee, *Strange Stories* (Gambit Inc., Boston, 1971)